Heterogeneous Computing
with OpenCL 2.0

Heterogeneous Computing with OpenCL 2.0
Third Edition

David Kaeli

Perhaad Mistry

Dana Schaa

Dong Ping Zhang

AMSTERDAM • BOSTON • HEIDELBERG • LONDON
NEW YORK • OXFORD • PARIS • SAN DIEGO
SAN FRANCISCO • SINGAPORE • SYDNEY • TOKYO

Morgan Kaufmann is an imprint of Elsevier

Acquiring Editor: Todd Green
Editorial Project Manager: Charlie Kent
Project Manager: Priya Kumaraguruparan
Cover Designer: Matthew Limbert

Morgan Kaufmann is an imprint of Elsevier
225 Wyman Street, Waltham, MA 02451, USA

ISBN: 978-0-12-801414-1

British Library Cataloguing in Publication Data
A catalogue record for this book is available from the British Library

Library of Congress Cataloging-in-Publication Data
A catalog record for this book is available from the Library of Congress

For information on all MK publications
visit our website at www.mkp.com

Working together
to grow libraries in
developing countries

www.elsevier.com • www.bookaid.org

Contents

List of Figures xi
List of Tables xvii
Foreword xix
Acknowledgments xxi

CHAPTER 1   Introduction 1
  1.1 Introduction to Heterogeneous Computing......................... 1
  1.2 The Goals of This Book 2
  1.3 Thinking Parallel 2
  1.4 Concurrency and Parallel Programming Models.................. 7
  1.5 Threads and Shared Memory 8
  1.6 Message-Passing Communication 9
  1.7 Different Grains of Parallelism 10
     1.7.1 Data Sharing and Synchronization....................... 11
     1.7.2 Shared Virtual Memory 11
  1.8 Heterogeneous Computing with OpenCL 12
  1.9 Book Structure 13
  References 14

CHAPTER 2   Device Architectures 15
  2.1 Introduction 15
  2.2 Hardware Trade-offs... 15
     2.2.1 Performance Increase with Frequency,
          and its Limitations 17
     2.2.2 Superscalar Execution 18
     2.2.3 Very Long Instruction Word............................. 19
     2.2.4 SIMD and Vector Processing............................ 21
     2.2.5 Hardware Multithreading................................ 22
     2.2.6 Multicore Architectures 25
     2.2.7 Integration: Systems-on-Chip and the APU 26
     2.2.8 Cache Hierarchies and Memory Systems.................. 28
  2.3 The Architectural Design Space 29
     2.3.1 CPU Designs... 29
     2.3.2 GPU Architectures....................................... 33
     2.3.3 APU and APU-like Designs............................... 37
  2.4 Summary 38
  References 39

CHAPTER 3   Introduction to OpenCL.......................................41
   3.1 Introduction 41
       3.1.1 The OpenCL Standard.......................................41
       3.1.2 The OpenCL Specification 42
   3.2 The OpenCL Platform Model.....................................43
       3.2.1 Platforms and Devices.....................................44
   3.3 The OpenCL Execution Model 45
       3.3.1 Contexts 45
       3.3.2 Command-Queues 47
       3.3.3 Events 48
       3.3.4 Device-Side Enqueuing 49
   3.4 Kernels and the OpenCL Programming Model 50
       3.4.1 Compilation and Argument Handling 53
       3.4.2 Starting Kernel Execution on a Device 55
   3.5 OpenCL Memory Model 56
       3.5.1 Memory Objects 56
       3.5.2 Data Transfer Commands 59
       3.5.3 Memory Regions 60
       3.5.4 Generic Address Space 62
   3.6 The OpenCL Runtime with an Example 62
       3.6.1 Complete Vector Addition Listing 66
   3.7 Vector Addition Using an OpenCL C++ Wrapper 69
   3.8 OpenCL for CUDA Programmers 71
   3.9 Summary 73
       Reference 73

CHAPTER 4   Examples..75
   4.1 OpenCL Examples...75
   4.2 Histogram 75
   4.3 Image Rotation...83
   4.4 Image Convolution 91
   4.5 Producer-Consumer 99
   4.6 Utility Functions 107
       4.6.1 Reporting Compilation Errors............................107
       4.6.2 Creating a Program String...............................108
   4.7 Summary 109

CHAPTER 5   OpenCL Runtime and Concurrency Model 111
   5.1 Commands and the Queuing Model 111
       5.1.1 Blocking Memory Operations............................111

5.1.2 Events 112

5.1.3 Command Barriers and Markers 113

5.1.4 Event Callbacks.. 114

5.1.5 Profiling Using Events.................................... 114

5.1.6 User Events 115

5.1.7 Out-of-Order Command-Queues......................... 116

5.2 Multiple Command-Queues..................................... 118

5.3 The Kernel Execution Domain: Work-Items,
       Work-Groups, and NDRanges 121

5.3.1 Synchronization.. 124

5.3.2 Work-Group Barriers 125

5.3.3 Built-In Work-Group Functions.......................... 128

5.3.4 Predicate Evaluation Functions 128

5.3.5 Broadcast Functions 129

5.3.6 Parallel Primitive Functions 129

5.4 Native and Built-In Kernels 130

5.4.1 Native kernels 130

5.4.2 Built-In kernels 132

5.5 Device-Side Queuing.. 132

5.5.1 Creating a Device-Side Queue 135

5.5.2 Enqueuing Device-Side Kernels 136

5.6 Summary 142

Reference 142

CHAPTER 6   OpenCL Host-Side Memory Model **143**

6.1 Memory Objects 144

6.1.1 Buffers... 144

6.1.2 Images... 145

6.1.3 Pipes... 147

6.2 Memory Management 148

6.2.1 Managing Default Memory Objects 149

6.2.2 Managing Memory Objects with Allocation Options.... 155

6.3 Shared Virtual Memory 159

6.4 Summary 161

CHAPTER 7   OpenCL Device-Side Memory Model **163**

7.1 Synchronization and Communication 164

7.1.1 Barriers.. 165

7.1.2 Atomics 166

7.2 Global Memory 168

7.2.1 Buffers... 168

7.2.2 Images 169
7.2.3 Pipes 173
7.3 Constant Memory 175
7.4 Local Memory 175
7.5 Private Memory 178
7.6 Generic Address Space 178
7.7 Memory Ordering 180
7.7.1 Atomics Revisited 183
7.7.2 Fences 185
7.8 Summary 186

CHAPTER 8   Dissecting OpenCL on a Heterogeneous System **187**
8.1 OpenCL on an AMD FX-8350 CPU 187
8.1.1 Runtime Implementation 188
8.1.2 Vectorizing Within a Work-Item 191
8.1.3 Local Memory 191
8.2 OpenCL on the AMD Radeon R9 290X GPU 192
8.2.1 Threading and the Memory System...................... 194
8.2.2 Instruction Set Architecture and Execution Units 196
8.2.3 Resource Allocation 200
8.3 Memory Performance Considerations in OpenCL 201
8.3.1 Global Memory 201
8.3.2 Local Memory as a Software-Managed Cache 205
8.4 Summary 211
References 211

CHAPTER 9   Case study: Image clustering **213**
9.1 Introduction 213
9.2 The Feature Histogram on the CPU 215
9.2.1 Sequential Implementation 215
9.2.2 OpenMP parallelization 216
9.3 OpenCL Implementation 217
9.3.1 Naive GPU Implementation: GPU1 217
9.3.2 Coalesced Memory Accesses: GPU2 218
9.3.3 Vectorizing Computation: GPU3 221
9.3.4 Move SURF Features to Local Memory: GPU4 223
9.3.5 Move Cluster Centroids to Constant Memory:
       GPU5 225
9.4 Performance Analysis 227
9.4.1 GPU Performance 227

9.5 Conclusion 228
References 228

CHAPTER 10   OpenCL Profiling and Debugging **229**
10.1 Introduction 229
10.2 Profiling OpenCL Code Using Events 229
10.3 AMD CodeXL 231
10.4 Profiling Using CodeXL 232
  10.4.1   Collecting OpenCL Application Traces 233
  10.4.2   Host API Trace View 235
  10.4.3   Summary Pages View 236
  10.4.4   Collecting GPU Kernel Performance
            Counters 236
  10.4.5   CPU Performance Profiling Using CodeXL 237
10.5 Analyzing Kernels Using CodeXL 238
  10.5.1   KernelAnalyzer Statistics and ISA Views 239
  10.5.2   KernelAnalyzer Analysis View 242
10.6 Debugging OpenCL Kernels Using CodeXL 243
  10.6.1   API-Level Debugging 244
  10.6.2   Kernel Debugging 245
10.7 Debugging Using `printf` 246
10.8 Summary 247

**CHAPTER 11   Mapping High-Level Programming Languages
                to OpenCL 2.0** **249**
11.1 Introduction 249
11.2 A Brief Introduction to C++ AMP 250
  11.2.1   C++ AMP array_view 251
  11.2.2   C++ AMP *parallel_for_each*, or Kernel
            Invocation 252
11.3 OpenCL 2.0 as a Compiler Target 254
11.4 Mapping Key C++ AMP Constructs to OpenCL 254
11.5 C++ AMP Compilation Flow 259
11.6 Compiled C++ AMP Code 260
11.7 How Shared Virtual Memory in OpenCL 2.0 Fits in 261
11.8 Compiler Support for Tiling in C++ AMP 263
  11.8.1   Dividing the Compute Domain 263
  11.8.2   Specifying the Address Space and Barriers 264
11.9 Address Space Deduction 265

11.10 Data Movement Optimization 267
    11.10.1 discard_data() 267
    11.10.2 array_view<const T, N> 268
11.11 Binomial Options: A Full Example 268
11.12 Preliminary Results 270
11.13 Conclusion 271
Reference 272

CHAPTER 12   **WebCL: Enabling OpenCL Acceleration of Web Applications** 273
12.1 Introduction 273
12.2 Programming with WebCL................................... 273
12.3 Synchronization 281
12.4 Interoperability with WebGL............................... 282
12.5 Example Application 282
12.6 Security Enhancement 285
12.7 WebCL on the Server... 286
12.8 Status and Future of WebCL 288
References 288
Works Cited.. 288

CHAPTER 13   **Foreign lands**.. 291
13.1 Introduction 291
13.2 Beyond C and C++ 291
13.3 Haskell OpenCL 293
    13.3.1 Module Structure 294
    13.3.2 Environments 295
    13.3.3 Reference Counting............................... 295
    13.3.4 Platform and Devices 296
    13.3.5 The Execution Environment...................... 296
13.4 Summary 299
References 299

Index 301

List of Figures

Fig. 1.1   (a) Simple sorting: a divide-and-conquer implementation, breaking the list into shorter lists, sorting them, and then merging the shorter sorted lists. (b) Vector-scalar multiply: scattering the multiplies and then gathering the results to be summed up in a series of steps.   3

Fig. 1.2   Multiplying elements in arrays A and B, and storing the result in an array C.   4

Fig. 1.3   Task parallelism present in fast Fourier transform (FFT) application. Different input images are processed independently in the three independent tasks.   5

Fig. 1.4   Task-level parallelism, where multiple words can be compared concurrently. Also shown is finer-grained character-by-character parallelism present when characters within the words are compared with the search string.   6

Fig. 1.5   After all string comparisons in Figure 1.4 have been completed, we can sum up the number of matches in a combining network.   6

Fig. 1.6   The relationship between parallel and concurrent programs. Parallel and concurrent programs are subsets of all programs.   8

Fig. 2.1   Out-of-order execution of an instruction stream of simple assembly-like instructions. Note that in this syntax, the destination register is listed first. For example, add a,b,c is a = b+c.   18

Fig. 2.2   VLIW execution based on the out-of-order diagram in Figure 2.1.   20

Fig. 2.3   SIMD execution where a single instruction is scheduled in order, but executes over multiple ALUs at the same time.   21

Fig. 2.4   The out-of-order schedule seen in Figure 2.1 combined with a second thread and executed simultaneously.   23

Fig. 2.5   Two threads scheduled in a time-slice fashion.   24

Fig. 2.6   Taking temporal multithreading to an extreme as is done in throughput computing: a large number of threads interleave execution to keep the device busy, whereas each individual thread takes longer to execute than the theoretical minimum.   25

Fig. 2.7   The AMD Puma (left) and Steamroller (right) high-level designs (not shown to any shared scale). Puma is a low-power design that follows a traditional approach to mapping functional units to cores. Steamroller combines two cores within a module, sharing its floating-point (FP) units.   26

Fig. 2.8   The AMD Radeon HD 6970 GPU architecture. The device is divided into two halves, where instruction control (scheduling and dispatch) is performed by the wave scheduler for each half. The 24 16-lane SIMD cores execute four-way VLIW instructions on each SIMD lane and contain private level 1 (L1) caches and local data shares (scratchpad memory).   27

Fig. 2.9   The Niagara 2 CPU from Sun/Oracle. The design intends to make a high level of threading efficient. Note its relative similarity to the GPU design seen in Figure 2.8. Given enough threads, we can cover all memory access time with useful compute, without extracting instruction-level parallelism (ILP) through complicated hardware techniques.   32

Fig. 2.10   The AMD Radeon R9 290X architecture. The device has 44 cores in 11 clusters. Each core consists of a scalar execution unit that handles branches and basic integer operations, and four 16-lane SIMD ALUs. The clusters share instruction and scalar caches.   35

Fig. 2.11   The NVIDIA GeForce GTX 780 architecture. The device has 12 large cores that NVIDIA refers to as "streaming multiprocessors" (SMX). Each SMX has 12 SIMD units (with specialized double-precision and special function units), a single L1 cache, and a read-only data cache.   36

Fig. 2.12   The A10-7850K APU consists of two Steamroller-based CPU cores and eight Radeon R9 GPU cores (32 16-lane SIMD units in total). The APU includes a fast bus from the GPU to DDR3 memory, and a shared path that is optionally coherent with CPU caches.   37

Fig. 2.13   An Intel i7 processor with HD Graphics 4000 graphics. Although not termed "APU" by Intel, the concept is the same as for the devices in that category from AMD. Intel combines four Haswell x86 cores with its graphics processors, connected to a shared last-level cache (LLC) via a ring bus.   38

Fig. 3.1   An OpenCL platform with multiple compute devices. Each compute device contains one or more compute units. A compute unit is composed of one or more processing elements (PEs). A system could have multiple platforms present at the same time. For example, a system could have an AMD platform and an Intel platform present at the same time.   43

Fig. 3.2   Some of the Output from the CLInfo program showing the characteristics of an OpenCL platform and devices. We see that the AMD platform has two devices (a CPU and a GPU). The output shown here can be queried using functions from the platform API.   46

Fig. 3.3   Vector addition algorithm showing how each element can be added independently.   50

Fig. 3.4   The hierarchical model used for creating an NDRange of work-items, grouped into work-groups.   52

Fig. 3.5   The OpenCL runtime shown denotes an OpenCL context with two compute devices (a CPU device and a GPU device). Each compute device has its own command-queues. Host-side and device-side command-queues are shown. The device-side queues are visible only from kernels executing on the compute device. The memory objects have been defined within the memory model.   54

Fig. 3.6   Memory regions and their scope in the OpenCL memory model.   61

Fig. 3.7   Mapping the OpenCL memory model to an AMD Radeon HD 7970 GPU.   62

Fig. 4.1   A histogram generated from a 256-bit image. Each bin corresponds to
           the frequency of the corresponding pixel value.   76
Fig. 4.2   An image rotated by 45°. Pixels that correspond to an out-of-bounds
           location in the input image are returned as black.   83
Fig. 4.3   Applying a convolution filter to a source image.   91
Fig. 4.4   The effect of different convolution filters applied to the same source
           image: (a) the original image; (b) blurring filter; and (c) embossing filter. 92
Fig. 4.5   The producer kernel will generate filtered pixels and send them via a
           pipe to the consumer kernel, which will then generate the histogram:
           (a) original image; (b) filtered image; and (c) histogram of filtered image. 99
Fig. 5.1   Multiple command-queues created for different devices declared
           within the same context. Two devices are shown, where one
           command-queue has been created for each device.   118
Fig. 5.2   Multiple devices working in a pipelined manner on the same data. The
           CPU queue will wait until the GPU kernel has finished.   119
Fig. 5.3   Multiple devices working in a parallel manner. In this scenario, both
           GPUs do not use the same buffers and will execute independently.
           The CPU queue will wait until both GPU devices have finished.   120
Fig. 5.4   Executing the simple kernel shown in Listing 5.5. The different
           work-items in the NDRange are shown.   121
Fig. 5.5   Within a single kernel dispatch, synchronization regarding execution
           order is supported only within work-groups using barriers. Global
           synchronization is maintained by completion of the kernel, and the
           guarantee that on a completion event all work is complete and memory
           content is as expected.   126
Fig. 5.6   Example showing OpenCL memory objects mapping to arguments for
           `clEnqueueNativeKernel()` in Listing 5.8.   131
Fig. 5.7   A single-level fork-join execution paradigm compared with nested
           parallelism thread execution.   133
Fig. 6.1   An example showing a scenario where a buffer is created and
           initialized on the host, used for computation on the device, and
           transferred back to the host. Note that the runtime could have also
           created and initialized the buffer directly on the device. (a) Creation
           and initialization of a buffer in host memory. (b) Implicit data transfer
           from the host to the device prior to kernel execution. (c) Explicit
           copying of data back from the device to the host pointer.   150
Fig. 6.2   Data movement using explicit read-write commands. (a) Creation of an
           uninitialized buffer in device memory. (b) Explicit data transfer from
           the host to the device prior to execution. (c) Explicit data transfer from
           the device to the host following execution.   151
Fig. 6.3   Data movement using map/unmap. (a) Creation of an uninitialized
           buffer in device memory. (b) The buffer is mapped into the host's
           address space. (c) The buffer is unmapped from the host's
           address space.   158
Fig. 7.1   The memory spaces available to an OpenCL device.   164

Fig. 7.2   Data race when incrementing a shared variable. The value stored depends on the ordering of operations between the threads.   166

Fig. 7.3   Applying Z-order mapping to a two-dimensional memory space.   172

Fig. 7.4   The pattern of data flow for the example shown in the `localAccess` kernel.   177

Fig. 8.1   High-level design of AMD's Piledriver-based FX-8350 CPU.   188

Fig. 8.2   OpenCL mapped onto an FX-8350 CPU. The FX-8350 CPU is both the OpenCL host and the device in this scenario.   189

Fig. 8.3   Implementation of work-group execution on an x86 architecture.   190

Fig. 8.4   Mapping the memory spaces for a work-group (work-group 0) onto a Piledriver CPU cache.   192

Fig. 8.5   High-level Radeon R9 290X diagram labeled with OpenCL execution and memory model terms.   193

Fig. 8.6   Memory bandwidths in the discrete system.   195

Fig. 8.7   Radeon R9 290X compute unit microarchitecture.   197

Fig. 8.8   Mapping OpenCL's memory model onto a Radeon R9 290X GPU.   201

Fig. 8.9   Using vector reads provides a better opportunity to return data efficiently through the memory system. When work-items access consecutive elements, GPU hardware can achieve the same result through coalescing.   203

Fig. 8.10   Accesses to nonconsecutive elements return smaller pieces of data less efficiently.   203

Fig. 8.11   Mapping the Radeon R9 290X address space onto memory channels and DRAM banks.   204

Fig. 8.12   Radeon R9 290X memory subsystem.   205

Fig. 8.13   The accumulation pass of the prefix sum shown in Listing 8.2 over a 16-element array in local memory using 8 work-items.   208

Fig. 8.14   Step 1 in Figure 8.13 showing the behavior of an LDS with eight banks.   209

Fig. 8.15   Step 1 in Figure 8.14 with padding added to the original data set to remove bank conflicts in the LDS.   210

Fig. 9.1   An image classification pipeline. An algorithm such as SURF is used to generate features. A clustering algorithm such as *k*-means then generates a set of centroid features that can serve as a set of visual words for the image. The generated features are assigned to each centroid by the histogram builder.   214

Fig. 9.2   Feature generation using the SURF algorithm. The SURF algorithm accepts an image as an input and generates an array of features. Each feature includes position information and a set of 64 values known as a `descriptor`.   214

Fig. 9.3   The data transformation kernel used to enable memory coalescing is the same as a matrix transpose kernel.   219

Fig. 9.4   A transpose illustrated on a one-dimensional array.   220

Fig. 10.1   The session explorer for CodeXL in profile mode. Two application timeline sessions and one GPU performance counter session are shown.   233

Fig. 10.2   The Timeline View of CodeXL in profile mode for the Nbody
             application. We see the time spent in data transfer and kernel execution. 234
Fig. 10.3   The API Trace View of CodeXL in profile mode for the Nbody application. 235
Fig. 10.4   CodeXL Profiler showing the different GPU kernel performance
             counters for the Nbody kernel.   237
Fig. 10.5   AMD CodeXL explorer in analysis mode. The NBody OpenCL kernel
             has been compiled and analyzed for a number of different graphics
             architectures.   240
Fig. 10.6   The ISA view of KernelAnalyzer. The NBody OpenCL kernel has been
             compiled for multiple graphics architectures. For each architecture,
             the AMD IL and the GPU ISA can be evaluated.   241
Fig. 10.7   The Statistics view for the Nbody kernel shown by KernelAnalyzer. We
             see that the number of concurrent wavefronts that can be scheduled is
             limited by the number of vector registers.   241
Fig. 10.8   The Analysis view of the Nbody kernel is shown. The execution
             duration calculated by emulation is shown for different graphics
             architectures.   242
Fig. 10.9   A high-level overview of how CodeXL interacts with an OpenCL
             application.   243
Fig. 10.10   CodeXL API trace showing the history of the OpenCL functions called.   244
Fig. 10.11   A kernel breakpoint set on the Nbody kernel.   246
Fig. 10.12   The Multi-Watch window showing the values of a global memory buffer
             in the Nbody example. The values can also be visualized as an image.   247
Fig. 11.1   C++ AMP code example—vector addition.   250
Fig. 11.2   Vector addition, conceptual view.   251
Fig. 11.3   Functor version for C++AMP vector addition (conceptual code).   256
Fig. 11.4   Further expanded version for C++AMP vector addition (conceptual
             code).   257
Fig. 11.5   Host code implementation of *parallel_ for_each* (conceptual code).   259
Fig. 11.6   C++ AMP Lambda—vector addition.   260
Fig. 11.7   Compiled OpenCL SPIR code—vector addition kernel.   261
Fig. 12.1   WebCL objects.   275
Fig. 12.2   Using multiple command-queues for overlapped data transfer.   280
Fig. 12.3   Typical runtime involving WebCL and WebCL.   283
Fig. 12.4   Two triangles in WebGL to draw a WebCL-generated image.   284

List of Tables

Table 4.1   The OpenCL Features Covered by Each Example   76
Table 6.1   Summary of Options for SVM   159
Table 9.1   The Time Taken for the Transpose Kernel   227
Table 9.2   Kernel Running Time (ms) for Different GPU Implementations   228
Table 10.1   The Command States that can be Used to Obtain Timestamps from
              OpenCL Events   230
Table 11.1   Mapping Key C++ AMP Constructs to OpenCL   255
Table 11.2   Conceptual Mapping of Data Members on the Host Side and on the
              Device Side   258
Table 11.3   Data Sharing Behavior and Implications of OpenCL 2.0 SVM Support 262
Table 12.1   Relationships Between C Types Used in Kernels and *setArg()*'s
              webcl.type   277

Foreword

In the last few years computing has entered the heterogeneous computing era, which aims to bring together in a single device the best of both central processing units (CPUs) and graphics processing units (GPUs). Designers are creating an increasingly wide range of heterogeneous machines, and hardware vendors are making them broadly available. This change in hardware offers great platforms for exciting new applications. But, because the designs are different, classical programming models do not work very well, and it is important to learn about new models such as those in OpenCL.

When the design of OpenCL started, the designers noticed that for a class of algorithms that were latency focused (spreadsheets), developers wrote code in C or C++ and ran it on a CPU, but for a second class of algorithms that where throughput focused (e.g. matrix multiply), developers often wrote in CUDA and used a GPU: two related approaches, but each worked on only one kind of processor—C++ did not run on a GPU, CUDA did not run on a CPU. Developers had to specialize in one and ignore the other. But the real power of a heterogeneous device is that it can efficiently run applications that mix both classes of algorithms. The question was how do you program such machines?

One solution is to add new features to the existing platforms; both C++ and CUDA are actively evolving to meet the challenge of new hardware. Another solution was to create a new set of programming abstractions specifically targeted at heterogeneous computing. Apple came up with an initial proposal for such a new paradigm. This proposal was refined by technical teams from many companies, and became OpenCL. When the design started, I was privileged to be part of one of those teams. We had a lot of goals for the kernel language: (1) let developers write kernels in a single source language; (2) allow those kernels to be functionally portable over CPUs, GPUs, field-programmable gate arrays, and other sorts of devices; (3) be low level so that developers could tease out all the performance of each device; (4) keep the model abstract enough, so that the same code would work correctly on machines being built by lots of companies. And, of course, as with any computer project, we wanted to do this fast. To speed up implementations, we chose to base the language on C99. In less than 6 months we produced the specification for OpenCL 1.0, and within 1 year the first implementations appeared. And then, time passed and OpenCL met real developers . . .

So what happened? First, C developers pointed out all the great C++ features (a real memory model, atomics, etc.) that made them more productive, and CUDA developers pointed out all the new features that NVIDIA added to CUDA (e.g. nested parallelism) that make programs both simpler and faster. Second, as hardware architects explored heterogeneous computing, they figured out how to remove the early restrictions requiring CPUs and GPUs to have separate memories. One great hardware change was the development of integrated devices, which provide both a

GPU and a CPU on one die (NVIDIA's Tegra and AMD's APUS are examples). And third, even though the specification was written with great care and there was a conformance suite, implementers of the compilers did not always read the specification in the same way—sometimes the same program could get a different answer on a different device.

All this led to a revised and more mature specification—OpenCL 2.0.

The new specification is a significant evolution which lets developers take advantage of the new integrated GPU/CPU processors.

The big changes include the following:

- Shared virtual memory—so that host and device code can share complex pointer-based structures such as trees and linked lists, getting rid of the costly data transfers between the host and devices.
- Dynamic parallelism—so that device kernels can launch work to the same device without host interaction, getting rid of significant bottlenecks.
- Generic address spaces—so that single functions can operate on either GPU or CPU data, making programming easier.
- C++-style atomics—so that work-items can share data over work-groups and devices, enabling a wider class of algorithms be realized in Open CL.

This book provides a good introduction to OpenCL, either for a class on OpenCL programming, or as part of a class on parallel programming. It will also be valuable to developers who want to learn OpenCL on their own.

The authors have been working on high performance mixing GPUs and CPUs for quite some time. I highly respect their work. Previous versions of the book covering previous versions of OpenCL were well received, and this addition expands that work to cover all the new OpenCL 2.0 features.

I encourage potential readers to go through the book, learn OpenCL, and build the exciting applications of the future.

Norm Rubin
Research Scientist, NVIDIA
Visiting Scholar, Northeastern University
January 2015

Acknowledgments

We thank Todd Green, Charlotte Kent, Priya Kumaraguruparan, and Kaitlin Herbert from Morgan Kaufmann/Elsevier, and Bob Whitecotton, Phil Rogers, and Manju Hegde from AMD for their support of and effort on this project.

We also thank Jack Chung, Wen-Mei Hwu, Yun-Wei Lee, and Ray Sung from Multicoreware, and Lifan Xu, Mikaël Bourges-Sévenier, and Rémi Arnaud, for their significant contributions to individual chapters.

We acknowledge Lee Howes for his thorough and thoughtful editing and reviewing of early drafts of this text, and we thank both Lee and Ben Gaster for their contributions to previous editions of the book.

Introduction

1.1 INTRODUCTION TO HETEROGENEOUS COMPUTING

Heterogeneous computing includes both serial and parallel processing. With heterogeneous computing, tasks that comprise an application are mapped to the best processing device available on the system. The presence of multiple devices on a system presents an opportunity for programs to utilize concurrency and parallelism, and improve performance and power. Open Computing Language (OpenCL) is a programming language developed specifically to support heterogeneous computing environments. To help the reader understand many of the exciting features provided in OpenCL 2.0, we begin with an introduction to heterogeneous and parallel computing. We will then be better positioned to discuss heterogeneous programming in the context of OpenCL.

Today's heterogeneous computing environments are becoming more multifaceted, exploiting the capabilities of a range of multicore microprocessors, central processing units (CPUs), digital signal processors, reconfigurable hardware (field-programmable gate arrays), and graphics processing units (GPUs). Presented with so much heterogeneity, the process of mapping the software task to such a wide array of architectures poses a number of challenges to the programming community.

Heterogeneous applications commonly include a mix of workload behaviors, ranging from control intensive (e.g. searching, sorting, and parsing) to data intensive (e.g. image processing, simulation and modeling, and data mining). Some tasks can also be characterized as compute intensive (e.g. iterative methods, numerical methods, and financial modeling), where the overall throughput of the task is heavily dependent on the computational efficiency of the underlying hardware device. Each of these workload classes typically executes most efficiently on a specific style of hardware architecture. No single device is best for running all classes of workloads. For instance, control-intensive applications tend to run faster on superscalar CPUs, where significant die real estate has been devoted to branch prediction mechanisms, whereas data-intensive applications tend to run faster on vector architectures, where the same operation is applied to multiple data items, and multiple operations are executed in parallel.

1

1.2 THE GOALS OF THIS BOOK

The first edition of this book was the first of its kind to present OpenCL programming in a fashion appropriate for the classroom. In the second edition, we updated the contents for the OpenCL 1.2 standard. In this version, we consider the major changes in the OpenCL 2.0 standard, and we also consider a broader class of applications. The book is organized to address the need for teaching parallel programming on current system architectures using OpenCL as the target language. It includes examples for CPUs, GPUs, and their integration in the accelerated processing unit (APU). Another major goal of this book is to provide a guide to programmers to develop well-designed programs in OpenCL targeting parallel systems. The book leads the programmer through the various abstractions and features provided by the OpenCL programming environment. The examples offer the reader a simple introduction, and then proceed to increasingly more challenging applications and their associated optimization techniques. This book also discusses tools for aiding the development process in terms of profiling and debugging such that the reader need not feel lost in the development process. The book is accompanied by a set of instructor slides and programming examples, which support its use by an OpenCL instructor. Please visit http://store.elsevier.com/9780128014141 for additional information.

1.3 THINKING PARALLEL

Most applications are first programmed to run on a single processor. In the field of high-performance computing, different approaches have been used to accelerate computation when provided with multiple computing resources. Standard approaches include "divide-and-conquer" and "scatter-gather" problem decomposition methods, providing the programmer with a set of strategies to effectively exploit the parallel resources available in high-performance systems. Divide-and-conquer methods iteratively break a problem into smaller subproblems until the subproblems fit well on the computational resources provided. Scatter-gather methods send a subset of the input data set to each parallel resource, and then collect the results of the computation and combine them into a result data set. As before, the partitioning takes account of the size of the subsets on the basis of the capabilities of the parallel resources. Figure 1.1 shows how popular applications such as sorting and a vector-scalar multiply can be effectively mapped to parallel resources to accelerate processing.

Programming has become increasingly challenging when faced with the growing parallelism and heterogeneity present in contemporary computing systems. Given the power and thermal limits of complementary metal-oxide semiconductor (CMOS) technology, microprocessor vendors find it difficult to scale the frequency of these devices to derive more performance, and have instead decided to place multiple processors, sometimes specialized, on a single chip. In their doing so, the problem of extracting parallelism from a application is left to the programmer, who must decompose the underlying tasks and associated algorithms in the application and map them efficiently to a diverse variety of target hardware platforms.

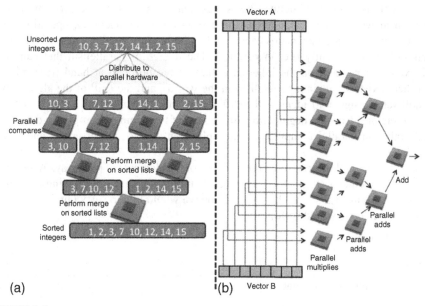

FIGURE 1.1

(a) Simple sorting: a divide-and-conquer implementation, breaking the list into shorter lists, sorting them, and then merging the shorter sorted lists. (b) Vector-scalar multiply: scattering the multiplies and then gathering the results to be summed up in a series of steps.

In the past 10 years, parallel computing devices have been increasing in number and processing capabilities. During this period, GPUs appeared on the computing scene, and are today providing new levels of processing capability at very low cost. Driven by the demands of real-time three-dimensional graphics rendering (a highly data-parallel problem), GPUs have evolved rapidly as very powerful, fully programmable, task- and data-parallel architectures. Hardware manufacturers are now combining CPU cores and GPU cores on a single die, ushering in a new generation of heterogeneous computing. Compute-intensive and data-intensive portions of a given application, called *kernels*, may be offloaded to the GPU, providing significant performance per watt and raw performance gains, while the host CPU continues to execute non-kernel tasks.

Many systems and phenomena in both the natural world and the man-made world present us with different classes of parallelism and concurrency:

- Molecular dynamics—every molecule interacting with every other molecule.
- Weather and ocean patterns—millions of waves and thousands of currents.
- Multimedia systems—graphics and sound, thousands of pixels and thousands of wavelengths.
- Automobile assembly lines—hundreds of cars being assembled, each in a different phase of assembly, with multiple identical assembly lines.

Parallel computing, as defined by Almasi and Gottlieb [1], is a form of computation in which many calculations are carried out simultaneously, operating on the principle that large problems can often be divided into smaller ones, which are then solved concurrently (i.e. in parallel). The degree of parallelism that can be achieved is dependent on the inherent nature of the problem at hand (remember that there exists significant parallelism in the world), and the skill of the algorithm or software designer to identify the different forms of parallelism present in the underlying problem. We begin with a discussion of two simple examples to demonstrate inherent parallel computation: multiplication of two integer arrays and text searching.

Our first example carries out multiplication of the elements of two arrays A and B, each with N elements storing the result of each multiply in the corresponding element of array C. Figure 1.2 shows the computation we would like to carry out. The serial C++ program code would be follows:

```
1    for  ( i =0;  i <N;  i++)
2        C[ i ]  =  A[ i ]  *  B[ i ];
```
LISTING 1.1

Multiplying elements of an array.

This code possesses significant parallelism, though a very low compute intensity. Low compute intensity in this context refers to the fact that the ratio of arithmetic operations to memory operations is small. The multiplication of each element in A

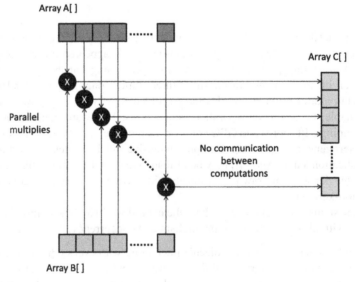

FIGURE 1.2

Multiplying elements in arrays A and B, and storing the result in an array C.

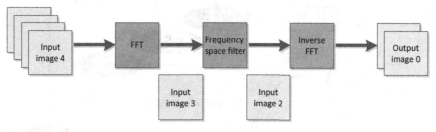

FIGURE 1.3

Task parallelism present in fast Fourier transform (FFT) application. Different input images are processed independently in the three independent tasks.

and B is independent of every other element. If we were to parallelize this code, we could choose to generate a separate execution instance to perform the computation of each element of C. This code possesses significant data-level parallelism because the same operation is applied across all of A and B to produce C.

We could also view this breakdown as a simple form of task-level parallelism. A task is a piece of work to be done or undertaken, sometimes used instead of the operating system term *process*. In our discussion here, a task operates on a subset of the input data. However, task parallelism generalizes further to execution on pipelines of data or even more sophisticated parallel interactions. Figure 1.3 shows an example of task parallelism in a pipeline to support filtering of images in frequency space using a fast Fourier transform.

Let us consider a second example. The computation we are trying to carry out is to find the number of occurrences of a string of characters in a body of text (see Figure 1.4). Assume that the body of text has already been appropriately parsed into a set of N words. We could choose to divide the task of comparing the string against the N potential matches into N comparisons (i.e. tasks). In each task a string of characters is matched against the text string. This approach, although rather naïve in terms of search efficiency, is highly parallel. The process of the input text string being compared against each of the set of potential words presents N parallel tasks. Each parallel task is carrying out the same set of operations. There is even further parallelism within a single comparison task, where the matching on a character-by-character basis presents a finer-grained degree of parallelism. This example exhibits both data-level parallelism (we are going to be performing the same operation on multiple data items) and task-level parallelism (we can compare the input string against multiple different words concurrently).

Once the number of matches has been determined, we need to accumulate them to compute the total number of occurrences. Again, this summing can exploit parallelism. In this step, we introduce the concept of "reduction," where we can utilize parallel resources to combine partial sums in a very efficient manner. Figure 1.5 shows the reduction tree, which illustrates this summation process performed in $\log N$ steps.

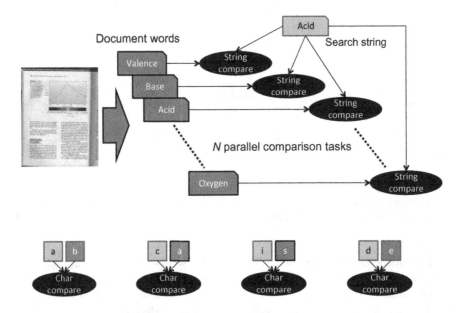

Finer-grained character-by-character parallelism

FIGURE 1.4

Task-level parallelism, where multiple words can be compared concurrently. Also shown is finer-grained character-by-character parallelism present when characters within the words are compared with the search string.

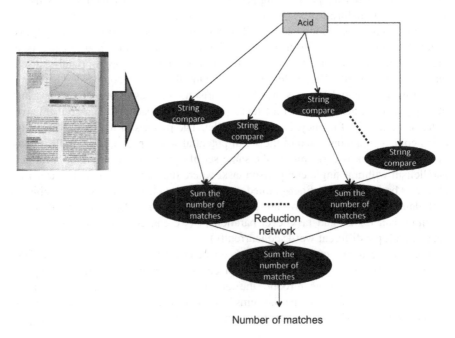

Number of matches

FIGURE 1.5

After all string comparisons in Figure 1.4 have been completed, we can sum up the number of matches in a combining network.

1.4 CONCURRENCY AND PARALLEL PROGRAMMING MODELS

Next, we discuss concurrency and parallel processing models so that when attempting to map an application developed in OpenCL to a parallel platform, we can select the right model to pursue. Although all of the following models can be supported in OpenCL, the underlying hardware may restrict which model will be practical to use.

Concurrency is concerned with two or more activities happening at the same time. We find concurrency in the real world all the time—for example, carrying a child in one arm while crossing a road or, more generally, thinking about something while doing something else with one's hands. When talking about concurrency in terms of computer programming, we mean a single system performing multiple tasks independently. Although it is possible that concurrent tasks may be executed at the same time (i.e. in parallel), this is not a requirement. For example, consider a simple drawing application, which is either receiving input from the user via the mouse and keyboard or updating the display with the current image. Conceptually, receiving input and processing input are operations (i.e. tasks) different from updating the display. These tasks can be expressed in terms of concurrency, but they do not need to be performed in parallel. In fact, in the case in which they are executing on a single core of a CPU, they cannot be performed in parallel. In this case, the application or the operating system should switch between the tasks, allowing both some time to run on the core.

Parallelism is concerned with running two or more activities in parallel with the explicit goal of increasing overall performance. For example, consider the following assignments:

```
1   Step  1:  A = B + C
2   Step  2:  D = E + G
3   Step  3:  R = A + D
```

LISTING 1.2

Three steps in a computation.

The assignments of A and D in steps 1 and 2 (respectively) are said to be independent of each other because there is no data flow between these two steps. The variables E and G on the right side of step 2 do not appear on the left side of step 1. Vice versa, the variables B and C on the right sides of step 1 do not appear on the left side of step 2.). Also the variable on the left side of step 1 (A) is not the same as the variable on the left side of step 2 (D). This means that steps 1 and 2 can be executed in parallel (i.e. at the same time). Step 3 is dependent on both steps 1 and 2, so cannot be executed in parallel with either step 1 or step 2.

Parallel programs must be concurrent, but concurrent programs need not be parallel. Although many concurrent programs can be executed in parallel, interdependencies between concurrent tasks may preclude this. For example, an interleaved execution would still satisfy the definition of concurrency while not executing in parallel. As a result, only a subset of concurrent programs are parallel, and the set

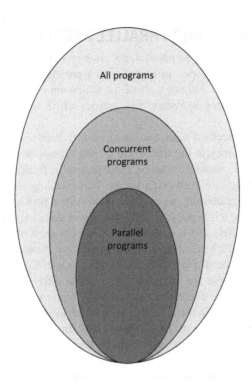

FIGURE 1.6

The relationship between parallel and concurrent programs. Parallel and concurrent programs are subsets of all programs.

of all concurrent programs is itself a subset of all programs. Figure 1.6 shows this relationship.

In the remainder of this section some well-known approaches to programming heterogeneous, concurrent and parallel systems are introduced with the aim of providing a foundation before we introduce OpenCL in Chapters 2 and 3.

1.5 THREADS AND SHARED MEMORY

A running program (called a process) may consist of multiple subprograms that each maintains its own independent control flow, and which as a group are allowed to run concurrently. These subprograms are called threads. All of the threads executing within a process share some resources (e.g., memory, open-files, global variables), but also have independent local storage (e.g., stack, automatic variables). Threads communicate with each other using variables allocated in the globally shared address space. Communication requires synchronization constructs to ensure that multiple threads are not updating the same memory location at the same time.

In shared memory systems, all processors have the ability to view the same address space (i.e., they view the same global memory). A key feature of the shared memory model is the fact that the programmer is not responsible for managing data movement. For these types of systems, it is especially important that the programmer and hardware have a well-defined agreement concerning updates to global data shared between threads. This agreement is called a memory consistency model. Memory consistency models are often supported in programming languages using higher-level constructs such as mutexes and semaphores, or acquire/release semantics as in the case of Java, C/C++11, and OpenCL. By having the programmer explicitly inform the hardware when certain types of synchronization must be performed, the hardware is able to execute concurrent programs with much greater efficiency.

As the number of processor cores increase, there is a significant cost to supporting shared memory in hardware. The length of wires (latency, power), number of interfaces between hardware structures, and number of shared bus clients quickly become limiting factors. The extra hardware required typically grows exponentially in terms of its complexity as we attempt to add additional processors. This has slowed the introduction of multicore and multiprocessor systems at the low end, and it has limited the number of cores working together in a consistent shared memory system to relatively low numbers because shared buses and coherence protocol overheads become bottlenecks. More relaxed shared memory systems scale better, although in all cases, scaling the number of cores in a shared memory system comes at the cost of complicated and expensive interconnects. Most multicore CPU platforms support shared memory in one form or another. OpenCL supports execution on shared memory devices.

1.6 MESSAGE-PASSING COMMUNICATION

An alternative to shared memory is to use a message-passing model. This model uses explicit intercommunication between a set of concurrent tasks that need to share data during computation. Multiple tasks can reside on the same physical device and/or across an arbitrary number of devices. Tasks exchange data through communications by sending and receiving explicit messages. Data transfer usually requires complementary operations to be performed by each process. For example, a send operation must have a matching receive operation.

From a programming perspective, message-passing implementations commonly comprise a library of hardware-independent routines for sending and receiving messages. The programmer is responsible for explicitly managing communication between tasks. Historically, a variety of message-passing libraries have been available since the 1980s. The Message Passing Interface (MPI) library is currently the most popular message-passing middleware [2]. Different implementations of the MPI library differ substantially from each other, making it difficult for programmers to develop performance-portable applications.

1.7 DIFFERENT GRAINS OF PARALLELISM

Whether we are using shared memory with threads, or explicit message passing, we can also vary the size (i.e. the grain) of the parallel unit of execution. The parallel unit of execution simply refers to the amount of independent work done by each executing thread. In discussion of parallel computing, granularity is a measure of the ratio of computation to communication.

The grain of parallelism is constrained by the inherent characteristics of the algorithms constituting the application. It is important that the parallel programmer select the right granularity to reap the full benefits of the underlying platform, because choosing the right grain size can help to expose additional degrees of parallelism. Sometimes the selection of granularity is referred to as *chunking*, determining the amount of data to assign to each task. Selecting the right chunk size can help provide further acceleration on parallel hardware. The following is a list of the trade-offs that factor into this key parallel programming attribute:

Chunking using fine-grained parallelism with a large number of independent tasks needs to consider the following:

- Compute intensity needs to be moderate so that each independent unit of parallelism has sufficient work to do.
- The cost of communication needs to be low so that each independent unit of parallelism can execute independently.
- Workload scheduling is important in fine-grained parallelism owing to the large number of independent tasks that can execute in parallel. The flexibility provided by an effective workload scheduler can and achieve load balance when a large number of tasks are being executed.

Chunking using coarse-grained parallelism needs to consider the following:

- Compute intensity needs to be higher than in the fine-grained case since there are fewer tasks that will execute independently.
- Coarse-grained parallelism would require the developer to identify complete portions of an application that can serve as a task.

Given these trade-offs, which granularity will lead to the best implementation? The most efficient granularity is dependent on the algorithm and the hardware environment in which it is run. In most cases, if the overhead associated with communication and synchronization is high relative to the amount of the computation in the task at hand, it will generally be advantageous to work at a coarser granularity as this will limit the overhead of communication and scheduling. Fine-grained parallelism can help reduce overhead due to load imbalance and memory delays (this is particularly true on a GPU, which depends on zero-overhead fine-grained thread switching to hide memory latencies).

If we have a computation that involves performing the same set of operations over a large amount of data, we can treat the data as a vector, and perform the same operation over multiple data inputs, generating multiple data outputs in a single vector operation. This grain of processing allows us to utilize a single instruction, multiple data (SIMD) style of operation, and typically leverages parallel hardware to perform the operation on different input data, in parallel. This grain of parallelism uses the size of the vector or the width of the SIMD unit to obtain execution speedup.

In the attempt to find the best computing grain, why not just issue copies of the same program to the available processing elements or nodes, relaxing the ordering between the execution of these copies so that they can run efficiently on a shared system with many processors? While an SIMD model has similarities to a single program, multiple data (SPMD) model, an SPMD model does not limit synchronization to instruction boundaries as does an SIMD model, and instead allows copies of the task or kernel to be run concurrently.

1.7.1 DATA SHARING AND SYNCHRONIZATION

A key factor to consider when developing heterogeneous software is the amount of data sharing that is inherent in a single task or across multiple tasks. Consider the case in which two tasks run that do not share any data. As long as the runtime system or operating system has access to adequate execution resources, the two tasks can be run concurrently or even in parallel. If halfway through the execution of the first task, the first task generates a result that was subsequently required by the second task, then we would have to introduce some form of synchronization into the system, and parallel execution—at least across the synchronization point—becomes more challenging.

When one is writing concurrent software, data sharing and synchronization play a critical role. Examples of data sharing in concurrent programs include the following:

- The input of a task is dependent on the result of another task—for example, in a producer-consumer or pipeline execution model.
- When intermediate results are combined together (e.g. as part of a reduction, as in our word search example shown in Figure 1.5).

Ideally, we would attempt to parallelize only portions of an application that are void of data dependencies, but that may not always be the case. Explicit synchronization primitives such as barriers and locks may be used to support synchronization when necessary. Although we only raise this issue here, later chapters revisit this question in OpenCL, providing a mechanism to support communication between host and device programs or when synchronization between tasks is required.

1.7.2 SHARED VIRTUAL MEMORY

In many heterogeneous systems, execution is split between different devices, and explicit synchronization and communication is used to communicate data values between the tasks running on each device. Shared virtual memory is a contract between the hardware and the software that allows devices to share a common view of memory, easing the task of programming and eliminating the need for explicit communication. OpenCL 2.0 introduces support for shared virtual memory, reducing expensive communication messages during execution, and removing the need to maintain multiple copies of a memory address on each device. We will discuss shared virtual memory in the context of OpenCL in detail in later chapters.

OpenCL 2.0 provides three different types of sharing:

- coarse-grained buffer sharing,
- fine-grained buffer sharing,
- fine-grained system sharing.

Using any flavor of shared virtual memory requires OpenCL implementations to make addresses meaningful between the host and devices in the system. This enables pointer-based data structures (such as linked lists) that could not previously be supported in OpenCL. Coarse-grained buffer sharing supports updates at the granularity of entire buffers and is achieved through API calls. Fine-grained buffer and system sharing support updates at the granularity of individual bytes within a buffer or anywhere in host memory, respectively. Fine-grained sharing support is achieved using synchronization points with ordering defined by the memory consistency model. These topics are covered in greater depth in Chapters 6 and 7.

1.8 HETEROGENEOUS COMPUTING WITH OPENCL

Now that the reader has more background on heterogeneous and parallel programming concepts, we will identify features that are supported in OpenCL. We begin with a brief history and overview of the language.

OpenCL is a heterogeneous programming framework that is managed by the nonprofit technology consortium the Khronos Group [3]. OpenCL is a framework for developing applications that execute across a range of device types made by different vendors. The first version of OpenCL, version 1.0, was released in 2008, and appeared in Apple's Mac OSX Snow Leopard. AMD announced support for OpenCL in the same timeframe, and in 2009 IBM announced support for OpenCL in its XL compilers for the Power architecture. In 2010, the Khronos Group released version 1.1 of the OpenCL specification, and in 2011 released version 1.2. The first edition of this book covered many of the features introduced in OpenCL 1.2. In 2013, the Khronos Group released OpenCL 2.0, which includes the following features:

- Nested parallelism
- Shared virtual memory
- Pipe memory objects
- C11 atomics
- Improved images
- Additional features

OpenCL supports multiple levels of parallelism and efficiently maps to homogeneous or heterogeneous, single- or multiple-device systems consisting of CPUs,

GPUs, and other types of devices limited only by the imagination of vendors. OpenCL defines both a device-side language and a host management layer for the devices in a system. The device-side language is designed to efficiently map to a wide range of memory systems and execution models. The host language aims to support efficient plumbing for complicated concurrent programs with low overhead. Together, these provide the developer with a path to efficiently move from algorithm design to implementation.

OpenCL provides parallel computing using task-based and data-based parallelism. OpenCL kernels employ a SPMD-like model, where units of parallelism (called work-items) execute instances of the kernel in a way that maps effectively to both scalar and vector hardware. Support for OpenCL is rapidly expanding as a wide range of platform vendors have adopted OpenCL for their hardware. These vendors represent broad market segments, from mobile and embedded (ARM, Imagination, MediaTek, Texas Instruments) to desktop and high-performance computing (AMD, Apple, Intel, NVIDIA, and IBM). The architectures supported include multicore CPUs (including x86, ARM, and Power), throughput and vector processors such as GPUs, and fine-grained parallel devices such as field-programmable gate arrays (Altera, Xilinx). Most importantly, OpenCL's cross-platform, industry-wide support makes it an excellent programming model for developers to learn and use, with the confidence that it will continue to be widely available for years to come with ever-increasing scope and applicability.

OpenCL 2.0 provides support for shared virtual memory, a topic we will treat in depth later in this book. Shared virtual memory is an important feature to ease programmer burden, especially when one is working with APU devices that share a common physical memory system. OpenCL 2.0 also introduces new memory consistency support, providing acquire/release semantics to relieve the programmer from fiddling with error-prone explicit locking. Support for shared memory communication, pipes, and other features of OpenCL 2.0 will be described in more detail in later chapters.

1.9 BOOK STRUCTURE

This book is organized as follows:

- Chapter 1 (this chapter) introduces many concepts related to the development of parallel algorithms and software. The chapter covers concurrency, threads, and different grains of parallelism: many of the fundamentals of parallel software development.
- Chapter 2 presents some of the architectures that support OpenCL, including CPUs, GPUs, and APUs. Different styles of architectures, including SIMD and very long instruction word, are discussed. This chapter also covers the concepts of multicore and throughput-oriented systems, as well as advances in heterogeneous architectures.

- Chapter 3 presents an introduction to OpenCL, including the host API and the OpenCL C language. The chapter includes a look into programming your first OpenCL application.
- Chapter 4 dives into OpenCL programming examples, including histogram, image rotation, and convolution, and demonstrates some of the OpenCL 2.0 features, such as pipe memory objects. An example in this chapter also utilizes OpenCL's C++ wrapper.
- Chapter 5 discusses concurrency and execution in the OpenCL programming model. In this chapter we discuss kernels, work-items, and the OpenCL execution and memory hierarchies. We also show how queuing and synchronization work in OpenCL such that the reader gains an understanding of how to write OpenCL programs that interact with memory correctly.
- Chapter 6 covers the OpenCL host-side memory model, including resource and memory management.
- Chapter 7 continues with OpenCL's device-side memory model. The device-side memory model deals with how units of execution access data in the various memory spaces. This chapter also includes updates to OpenCL's consistency model, including memory ordering and scope.
- Chapter 8 dissects OpenCL on three very different heterogeneous platforms: (1) the AMD FX-8350 GPU, (2) the AMD Radeon R9 290X GPU, and (3) the AMD A10-7850K APU. This chapter also considers memory optimizations.
- Chapter 9 provides a case study, looking at imaging clustering and search.
- Chapter 10 considers OpenCL profiling and debugging using AMD CodeXL.
- Chapter 11 covers C++AMP, a version of C++ that allows the user to leverage the availability of parallel hardware.
- Chapter 12 discusses WebCL, enabling Web-based applications to harness the power of an OpenCL device from within a browser.
- Chapter 13 discusses how OpenCL can be accessed from within other languages such as Java, Python and Haskell.

REFERENCES

[1] G. S. Almasi, A. Gottlieb, Highly Parallel Computing, Benjamin-Cummings Publishing Co., Inc., Redwood City, CA, USA, 1989.
[2] W. Gropp, E. Lusk, A. Skjellum, Using MPI: Portable Parallel Programming with the Message-passing Interface, second ed., MIT Press, 1999.
[3] Khronos Group, OpenCL, 2014. https://www.khronos.org/opencl/.

Device architectures

2.1 INTRODUCTION

OpenCL has been developed by a wide range of industry groups to satisfy the need to standardize programming models that can achieve high performance across the range of devices available on the market. Each of these companies has specific goals in mind for OpenCL and targets for what features OpenCL should have to be able to run correctly on a specific architecture. To this end, OpenCL has a range of features that attempt to allow detection of unique hardware capabilities (e.g. the clGetDeviceInfo application programming interface (API) call).

Although OpenCL is designed to be a platform-independent API, at the algorithm level and consequently at the level of kernel implementation, true platform independence in terms of performance is still a goal (versus a reality). While version 2.0 of the OpenCL standard has made some large strides in this area, as developers we still need to understand the potential advantages of different hardware features, the key runtime characteristics of these devices, and where these devices fit into the different classes of computer architectures. Once the reader is equipped with this deeper understanding of the targeted hardware, he or she can make informed choices when designing parallel algorithms and software. This understanding should also provide the reader with insight into the philosophy behind OpenCL's design in terms of programming, memory, and runtime models.

OpenCL's parallelism model is intended to run efficiently on serial, symmetric multiprocessing, multithreaded, and single instruction, multiple data (SIMD) or vector devices. In this chapter, we discuss some of these devices and the overall design space in which they sit.

2.2 HARDWARE TRADE-OFFS

Given the history of OpenCL and its early use for graphics APIs and pixel shaders, it is easy to understand how OpenCL has developed as a leading language targeted for graphics processing unit (GPU) programming. As a result, OpenCL has become a popular programming API for the high-performance computing market. However, as the number of platforms supporting OpenCL grows (particularly in the embedded systems space), the overall impact of OpenCL should increase substantially.

What is not necessarily clear from this discussion is what a GPU really is and how it differs from these "other devices." When we develop general-purpose code for a GPU, is the device still a graphics processor, or is it a more generic entity? If it is a graphics processor, is that due to the device carrying some amount of graphics-specific logic, or is it the architectural style overall?

More questions arise when we try to think about this question in any detail. How many cores does a GPU have? To answer that question, we have to decide on a definition for "core." What is a "many-core" device, and is it significantly different from a "multicore" device? In general, different architectures choose different approaches to increase performance for a given power/transistor budget. Rather than there simply being a raw compute power/electrical power/area trade-off, hardware developers have always also had to consider programming effort. The trade-off between these factors has created a wide divergence in designs.

Multicore central processing units (CPUs) allow us to maintain clock frequencies and hardware complexity that are comparable to those of single-core CPUs, while adding more cores as transistor sizes reduce. With careful design, power consumption can be kept within reasonable limits. SIMD and very long instruction word (VLIW) architectures attempt to further increase the amount of useful work being performed by improving the ratio of arithmetic operations to control logic. In such cases, it can be difficult to generate workloads to keep the arithmetic logic units (ALUs) satisfied. Multithreading approaches this from a different angle. Rather than increasing the ratio of computation to control logic, it increases the amount of useful work available to occupy computation logic during periods in which indirectly useful work is occupying noncompute logic such as memory pipelines. Thereby multithreading increases the utilization of the device we already have. Threading can be seen from the software side, in which case it can apply to multicore chips as much as to single-core designs, but it can also be viewed in terms of single cores managing multiple software threads. Caches and memory system trade-offs allow different architectures to target different data access patterns while trading off transistors for different uses.

In all these cases, we can apply the trade-offs to an individual core or a set of cores, depending on our definition of a core. However, we do not need to apply the same trade-off across an entire device. Heterogeneity can enable hardware optimizations for multiple types of algorithms running simultaneously, offering better performance on both and hence overall. The traditional, and at the present time common, example of this at the system level is the GPU plus CPU combination we see in modern PCs (along with other lower-performance processors scattered throughout the system). The latest generations of high-performance processors combine these two aspects into a single device, which AMD calls the accelerated processing unit (APU) [1].

In reality, we see combinations of these factors in different designs with different target markets, applications, and price points. In this section, we examine some of these architectural features and discuss to what degree various common architectures apply them.

2.2.1 PERFORMANCE INCREASE WITH FREQUENCY, AND ITS LIMITATIONS

The easiest way, as a developer, to think about code we are writing is to create software that executes linearly: perform one task, complete that task, perform another task. It is considerably more difficult for a developer to write parallel code; this is true even for limited SIMD or vector parallelism as is common in graphics. Multicomponent pixels make this relatively simple as the logical entity maps well to the programming concept. In other applications, where the logical concepts do not map as effectively to programming vectors, extracting SIMD operations can be substantially more difficult. For this reason, architectures have historically aimed to increase the performance of a single, narrow, thread of execution before moving to parallelism, with extreme, multithreaded parallelism relegated to high-performance specialist machines in particular markets.

Shrinking of complementary metal-oxide semiconductor (CMOS) circuitry has allowed distances between transistors to scale fairly consistently for an extended period of time. The shrinking of distances and reduction in size of the capacitors allowed hardware architects to clock circuits at a higher rate. In turn, this led to Gordon Moore's famous self-fulfilling prophecy about transistor density and its misinterpretations in the realm of execution frequency and overall performance. Certainly, increasing the frequency allowed the performance of nonparallel code to increase consistently during that time, such that it became an expectation for software developers until the early twenty-first century.

During the past decade, it has become obvious that continued scaling of clock frequencies of CPUs is not practical, largely due to power and heat dissipation constraints. The reason for this is that power consumption is dependent on frequency in a nonlinear manner. CMOS dynamic power consumption is approximated by the combination of dynamic and static power:

$$P = ACV^2F + VI_{\text{leak}},$$

where A is the activity factor, or fraction of the number of transistors in the circuit that are switching, C is the capacitance of the circuit, V is the voltage applied across the circuit, F is the switching frequency, and I_{leak} is an estimate of the current due to leakage of transistors.

It appears from this equation that power is linear with frequency. In reality, to increase the frequency, one has to increase the rate of flow of charge into and out of the capacitors in the circuit. This requires a comparable increase in voltage, which both scales the dynamic term and increases the latter, static, term in the equation. For a long time, voltages could reduce with each process generation such that frequency scaling would not increase the power consumption uncontrollably. However, as process technology has reached the small sizes we see today, we can no longer scale the voltage down without increasing the error rate of transistor switching, and hence frequency scaling requires voltage increases. The increase in power consumption and heat dissipation from any increase in frequency is then substantial.

As a second problem, increasing the clock frequency on-chip requires either an increase of off-chip memory bandwidth to provide data fast enough to not stall the workload running through the processor or an increase of the amount of caching in the system.

If we are unable to continue increasing the frequency with the goal of obtaining higher performance, we require other solutions. The heart of any of these solutions is to increase the number of operations performed in a given clock cycle.

2.2.2 SUPERSCALAR EXECUTION

Superscalar and, by extension, out-of-order execution is one solution that has been included on CPUs for a long time; it has been included on x86 designs since the beginning of the Pentium era. In these designs, the CPU maintains dependence information between instructions in the instruction stream and schedules work onto unused functional units when possible. An example of this is shown in Figure 2.1.

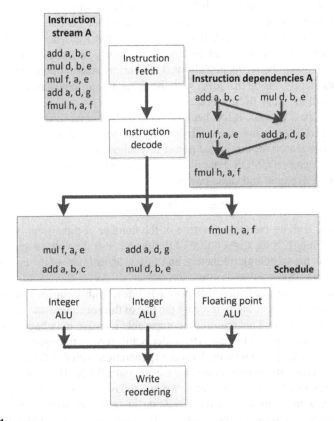

FIGURE 2.1

Out-of-order execution of an instruction stream of simple assembly-like instructions. Note that in this syntax, the destination register is listed first. For example, add a,b,c is a = b+c.

The major beneficiary of out-of-order logic is the software developer. By extracting parallelism from the programmer's code automatically within the hardware, serial code performs faster without any extra developer effort. Indeed, superscalar designs predate frequency scaling limitations by a decade or more, even in popular mass-produced devices, as a way to increase overall performance superlinearly. However, these designs are not without their disadvantages.

Out-of-order scheduling logic requires a substantial investment in transistors and hence CPU die area to maintain queues of in-flight instructions and maintain information on interinstruction dependencies to deal with dynamic schedules throughout the device. In addition, speculative instruction execution quickly becomes necessary to expand the window of out-of-order instructions to execute in parallel. Such speculative execution results in throwaway work and hence wasted energy. As a result, out-of-order execution in a CPU has shown diminishing returns; the industry has taken other approaches to increase performance as transistor size has decreased, even on the high-performance devices in which superscalar logic was formerly feasible. On embedded and special-purpose devices, extraction of parallelism from serial code has never been as much of a goal, and such designs have historically been less common in these areas.

Good examples of superscalar processors are numerous, from Seymour Cray's CDC 6600 to numerous RISC designs in the 1990s. Currently, high-end CPUs are mostly superscalar. Many GPUs also have superscalar capabilities.

2.2.3 VERY LONG INSTRUCTION WORD

VLIW execution is a heavily compiler-dependent method for increasing instruction-level parallelism in a processor. Rather than depending entirely on complex out-of-order control logic that maintains dependencies in hardware, as we saw when discussing superscalar execution, VLIW execution moves this dependence analysis work into the compiler. Instead of a scalar instruction stream being provided, each issued instruction in a VLIW processor is a long instruction word comprising multiple instructions intended to be issued in parallel. This instruction will be mapped directly to the execution pipelines of the processor.

An example of VLIW execution is shown in Figure 2.2. This is the same set of instructions as we saw in Figure 2.1, but rather than being fetched serially, they are fetched in three horizontally arranged packets of up to three instructions. We now see that the dependence structure of this instruction stream is linear, and the hardware will treat it that way rather than extracting and tracking a more complicated dependence graph. The VLIW instruction packets are decoded, and each individual part of the instruction stream maps to a given computation unit in the processor for execution. In some VLIW designs, as in this example, the computation units are heterogeneous, and hence some instructions will only ever be scheduled into a given lane of the VLIW packet stream. Other architectures present more homogeneous hardware such that any instruction can be issued in any location, and only dependence information limits the possibilities.

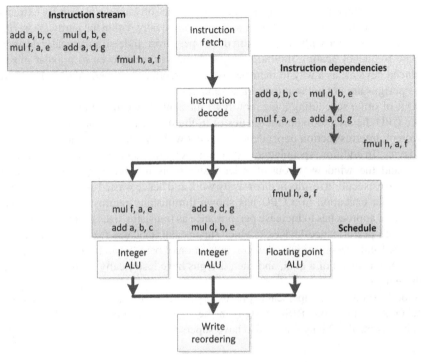

FIGURE 2.2

VLIW execution based on the out-of-order diagram in Figure 2.1.

In the example in Figure 2.2, we see that the instruction schedule has gaps: the first two VLIW packets are missing a third entry, and the third VLIW packet is missing its first and second entries. Obviously, the example is very simple, with few instructions to pack, but it is a common problem with VLIW architectures that efficiency can be lost owing to the compiler's inability to fully fill packets. This may be due to limitations in the compiler or may be due simply to an inherent lack of parallelism in the instruction stream. In the latter case, the situation will be no worse than for out-of-order execution but will be more efficient as the scheduling hardware is reduced in complexity. The former case would end up as a trade-off between efficiency losses from unfilled execution slots and gains from reduced hardware control overhead. In addition, there is an extra cost in compiler development to take into account when performing a cost-benefit analysis for VLIW execution over hardware schedule superscalar execution.

VLIW designs commonly appear in digital signal processor chips. High-end consumer devices currently include the Intel Itanium line of CPUs (known as explicitly parallel instruction computing, EPIC) and AMD's HD6000 series GPUs.

2.2.4 SIMD AND VECTOR PROCESSING

SIMD and its generalization in vector parallelism aim for improved efficiency from a slightly different angle compared with the previously discussed concepts. Whereas VLIW and hardware-managed superscalar execution both address extraction of independent instruction parallelism from unrelated instructions in an instruction stream, SIMD and vector parallelism directly allow the hardware instructions to target data-parallel execution.

A single SIMD instruction encapsulates a request that the same operation be performed on multiple data elements in parallel. Contrast this with the scalar operation performed by each instruction in the other approaches to parallelism. Vector computation generalizes this approach and usually works over long sequences of data elements, often pipelining computations over the data rather than executing on all elements simultaneously, and more generally supports gathered read and scattered write operations to and from memory.

If we again look at a variation on the running example as seen in Figure 2.3, we can see that the instruction stream is now issued linearly rather than out of order. However, each of these instructions now executes over a vector of four ALUs at the same time. The integer instructions issue one by one through the four-way integer vector ALU on the left, and the floating-point instructions issue similarly through the

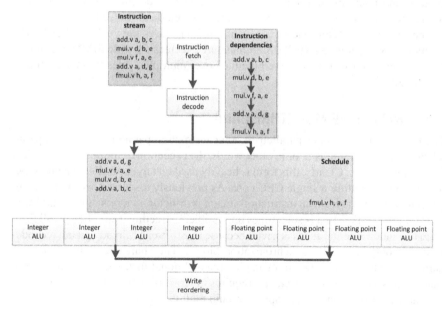

FIGURE 2.3

SIMD execution where a single instruction is scheduled in order, but executes over multiple ALUs at the same time.

four-way floating-point ALU on the right. Note that although in this example we are issuing the instructions linearly, there is no reason to assume that we cannot perform these operations within a superscalar or VLIW pipeline, and we will see architectures that do just that in our later discussion.

The advantage of SIMD execution is that relative to ALU work, the amount of scheduling and the amount of instruction decode logic can both be decreased. We are now performing four operations with a single instruction and a single point in the dependence schedule.

Of course, as with the previous proposals, there are trade-offs. A significant amount of code is not data parallel, and hence it is not possible to find vector instructions to issue. In other cases, it is simply too difficult for the compiler to extract data parallelism from code. For example, vectorization of loops is an ongoing challenge, with little success in anything but the simplest cases. In these cases, we end up with unutilized ALUs, and thus transistor wastage.

Vector processors originated in the supercomputer market, but SIMD designs are common in many market segments. CPUs often include SIMD pipelines with explicit SIMD instructions in a scalar instruction stream, including the various forms of Streaming SIMD Extensions (SSE) and Advanced Vector Extensions (AVX) on x86 chips, the AltiVec extensions for PowerPC, and ARM's NEON extensions. GPU architectures historically included explicit SIMD operations to support pixel vectors, and many modern GPUs also execute over wide implicit SIMD vectors, where the scalar instruction stream describes a single lane. Indeed, such machines can be considered vector machines because in many cases the vector is logical. For example, AMD's Radeon R9 290X architecture executes 64-wide SIMD operations. These wide vector instructions are pipelined over multiple cycles through a 16-lane SIMD unit.

2.2.5 HARDWARE MULTITHREADING

The third common form of parallelism, after instruction parallelism and data parallelism, is thread parallelism, or in other words, the execution of multiple independent instruction streams. Clearly, this form is heavily used on large, parallel machines, but it is also useful within a single CPU core. As previously discussed, extracting independent instructions from an instruction stream is difficult, in terms of both hardware and compiler work, and it is sometimes impossible. Extracting instruction parallelism from two independent threads is trivial because those threads already guarantee independence outside explicit synchronization blocks. The challenge of implementing hardware multithreading lies in managing the additional instruction stream and the state that a second instruction stream requires in terms of registers and cache.

There are two main ways to apply on-chip multithreading:

1. Simultaneous multithreading (SMT)
2. Temporal multithreading

SMT is visualized in Figure 2.4. In this approach, instructions from multiple threads are interleaved on the execution resources by an extension to the superscalar scheduling logic that tracks both instruction dependencies and source threads.

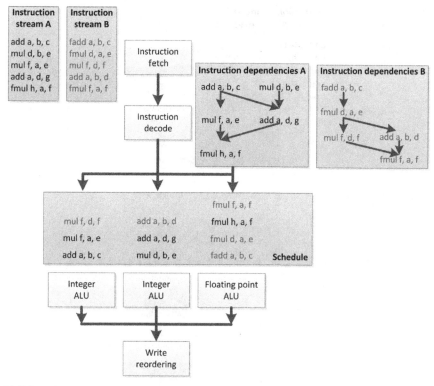

FIGURE 2.4

The out-of-order schedule seen in Figure 2.1 combined with a second thread and executed simultaneously.

The goal is for the execution resources to be more effectively utilized, and in Figure 2.4 that is the case. A higher proportion of execution slots are occupied with useful work. The cost of this approach is that state storage must be increased, and the instruction dependence and scheduling logic become more complicated as they now manage two distinct sets of dependencies, resources, and execution queues.

Figure 2.5 shows the simpler time-sliced version of chip multithreading. In this case, each thread is executed in consecutive execution slots in round-robin fashion. For the purposes of simplification, the diagram shows a single shared ALU.

The following are advantages of this approach:

- The logic to handle the scheduling is simple.
- Pipeline latency can be covered by scheduling more threads, reducing the amount of forwarding logic.
- Stalls of a single thread due to a cache miss, waiting for a branch to be computed, or similar events can be covered by changing the order of thread execution and running more threads than necessary to cover pipeline latency.

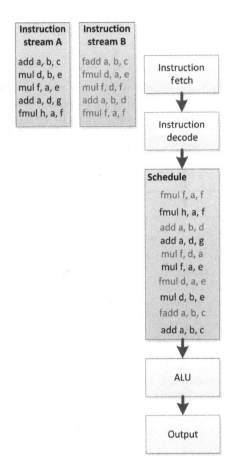

FIGURE 2.5

Two threads scheduled in a time-slice fashion.

This last case is the most useful in scaling to complicated problems. Many architectures are able to run more threads than necessary. When a thread reaches some sort of stall, it can be removed from the ready queue such that only threads in the ready queue are scheduled for execution. Once the stall ends, the thread can be placed back in the ready queue. In this manner, although a single thread might execute more slowly than on an out-of-order machine, the total throughput of the machine is kept high, and utilization of compute resources can be maintained without overcomplicating the control logic. Taken to an extreme, this sort of heavy multithreading can be viewed as throughput computing: maximizing throughput at the possible expense of latency. The principle is shown in Figure 2.6.

Both forms of chip multithreading are common. The MTA design from Tera is a classic time-sliced multithreading supercomputer. The MTA design suffered from manufacturing difficulties; however, Cray's subsequent implementation, the MTA-2

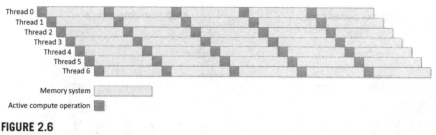

FIGURE 2.6

Taking temporal multithreading to an extreme as is done in throughput computing: a large number of threads interleave execution to keep the device busy, whereas each individual thread takes longer to execute than the theoretical minimum.

design, utilized 128 register sets per CPU using fast thread switching between threads within this state and skipping stalled threads. The XMT design extends this further to fit multithreaded processors in standard AMD Opteron-based Cray systems. Sun's Niagara series of chips implements a multicore multithreaded design (eight per core) to achieve low power and high throughput on data-center workloads. Intel's Pentium 4 and then later Nehalem and successor designs implement a form of SMT known as hyperthreading. Modern GPU designs run numerous threads in a temporal fashion on each core, where the number is generally resource limited: on the current generation of AMD GPUs, this is usually 8–16 threads per core to cover latency and stalls.

2.2.6 MULTICORE ARCHITECTURES

Conceptually at least, the obvious approach to increasing the amount of work performed per clock cycle is simply to clone a single CPU core multiple times on the chip. In the simplest case, each of these cores executes largely independently, sharing data through the memory system, usually through a cache coherency protocol. This design is a scaled-down version of traditional multisocket server symmetric multiprocessing systems that have been used to increase performance for decades, in some cases to extreme degrees.

However, multicore systems come in different guises, and it can be very difficult to define a core. For example, a mainstream CPU, at the high end, generally includes a wide range of functional blocks such that it is independent of other cores on the chip, barring interfacing logic, memory controllers, and so on, that would be unlikely to count as cores. However the line can be blurred. For example, AMD's Steamroller (high-power core) design, shown alongside the simpler Puma (low-power core) design in Figure 2.7, shares functional units between pairs of cores in a replicable unit termed a module. A single thread will run on each core in a traditional fashion while the hardware interleaves floating-point instructions onto the shared floating-point pipelines. The aim of such a design is to raise efficiency by improving occupancy of functional units.

In a similar manner, GPU designs have a different definition for "core." Modern GPUs have tens of cores—at the current high end there are between 32 and 64, with levels of complexity that depend on the specific architecture. Many GPU designs,

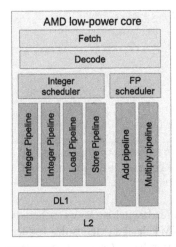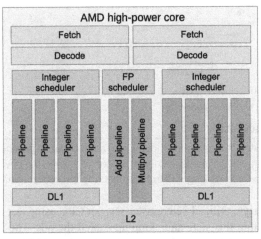

FIGURE 2.7

The AMD Puma (left) and Steamroller (right) high-level designs (not shown to any shared scale). Puma is a low-power design that follows a traditional approach to mapping functional units to cores. Steamroller combines two cores within a module, sharing its floating-point (FP) units.

such as the Graphics Core Next-based [2] designs from AMD and the Fermi and Kepler derivatives from NVIDIA [3], follow a relatively CPU-like design. However, some designs diverge substantially. For example, if we look at the AMD Radeon HD 6970 high-level diagram in Figure 2.8, we see a similar approach to Bulldozer taken to an extreme. Although the device has 24 SIMD cores, by looking at the execution units in the fairest way to compare them with traditional CPUs, we see those SIMD cores execute only ALU operations—both floating point and integer. Instruction scheduling, decode, and dispatch are executed by the wave scheduler units. The wave schedulers are so named because the unit of scheduling is a wide SIMD thread context known as a wavefront. Indeed, on the AMD Radeon HD 6970, there are two wave schedulers to prevent overly high complexity, whereas lower-capability parts in the series use only one wave scheduler and scale the number of SIMD cores.

2.2.7 INTEGRATION: SYSTEMS-ON-CHIP AND THE APU

In the embedded space, a more heterogeneous approach to multicore design is common. To achieve low power, embedded developers have constructed complicated systems-on-chip (SoCs) combining various components into a compact and cost-effective design. Combining specialized components in this way allows devices to be optimized for a particular use case and power envelope, which is particularly important in markets such as the design of cell phones.

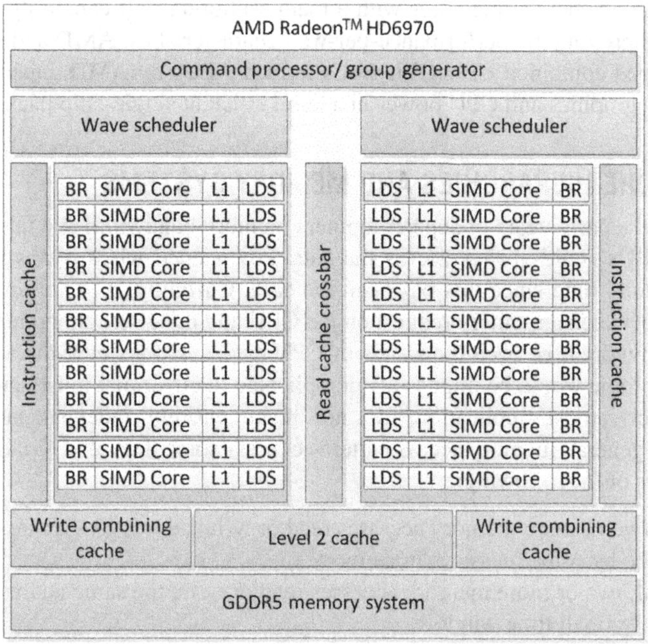

FIGURE 2.8

The AMD Radeon HD 6970 GPU architecture. The device is divided into two halves, where instruction control (scheduling and dispatch) is performed by the wave scheduler for each half. The 24 16-lane SIMD cores execute four-way VLIW instructions on each SIMD lane and contain private level 1 (L1) caches and local data shares (scratchpad memory).

Benefits from SoCs include the following:

- Combining multiple elements into a single device allows there to be a single manufacturing process and a single product to deal with, allowing lower manufacturing costs.
- The smaller number of packages takes up less space in a final device, allowing lower device cost and a smaller form factor, which are vital in markets such as mobile telephony.
- Smaller distances mean less power is used during communication and easier sharing of data through a single memory system.
- Lower communication latencies can lead to improved turnaround times for workloads dispatched to coprocessors.

Good examples of this approach in the cell phone space are the Snapdragon SoC from Qualcomm and the OMAP series from Texas Instruments. Designs such as these combine an implementation of the ARM instruction set architecture (ISA), a mobile GPU, memory controllers, and various wireless and media processing components. At the higher-performance end of the market, Sony, Toshiba, and IBM developed the Cell Broadband Engine processor, which combines a number of small, high-performance but simple cores with a main traditional full-capability core with the aim of improving the performance-per-watt characteristics. AMD and Intel have both developed combined CPU-GPU SoCs termed APUs by AMD, enabling high-performance graphics and CPU power in a more efficient single-chip package.

2.2.8 CACHE HIERARCHIES AND MEMORY SYSTEMS

Whereas in the early years of supercomputers memory bandwidth and latency were such that CPUs could always access the data they needed when it was needed, it has been a long time since this has been the case. Currently, it is not unusual that the latency between a memory request on the CPU and the data being returned from memory is hundreds or even thousands of CPU cycles. On a single-threaded CPU, out-of-order logic would be impossibly complicated to cover that much latency.

Fortunately, most applications do not make entirely independent memory accesses. In general, memory access patterns express some degree of locality, which will be either of the following:

• Spatial: two or more memory accesses read or write addresses that are near each other, by some measure, in memory.
• Temporal: two or more memory accesses read or write the same address within a relatively small time window.

These two forms of locality lead to the conclusion that if we can store a value read from memory and its neighbors, later reads will be able to reuse that data. As a result, CPU designers have added complicated layers of intermediate memory caches to support this optimization.

Caches come in various designs, but they can be divided into two general categories that are applied depending on the workload. CPU caches tend to be designed to minimize latency. To achieve this, caches are large with complicated hierarchies to move as much of the data as close to the CPU core as possible. Out-of-order logic can cover only a limited amount of latency, so the fewer cycles to access data, the better. In addition, keeping data close to the execution units minimizes power consumption: long-distance data movement is a significant component of CPU power usage.

Throughput processors are more latency tolerant, using threading to cover the cycles between request and data return. In these designs, the goal of caching is less to minimize latency, so the large multilevel hierarchy is less common, and more to reduce traffic across the limited memory buses. Smaller caches that allow neighboring accesses to be caught but are concerned less with very long periods of reuse are often seen in these situations, acting more as spatial filters. Wide SIMD units and programming models aim for efficient coalesced memory access to increase the size of memory transaction issues. The result is that dedicating logic to arithmetic units becomes a better use of transistors. In addition, higher-latency, higher-bandwidth memory interconnects allow this design to work more efficiently. One extension of this bias toward spatial locality that we often see in GPU design is to lay memory out such that two-dimensional accesses are efficiently cached.

Some designs including GPUs and the Cell processor include software-managed scratchpad memory spaces as well as or in place of cache hierarchies. These buffers enable higher performance at a given power and area budget, but they require more complicated programming.

The reality of any given design is that it balances caching levels and features on the basis of the expected workloads for the processor. Unfortunately, there is no right answer for all processor design-workload combinations.

2.3 THE ARCHITECTURAL DESIGN SPACE

In the real world, we do not see many architectures that fit cleanly into just one of the previously mentioned categories. The reality is that computer architecture is a huge design space with enormous variation in all directions. Common current architectures sit in that design space at various points.

This is most important in helping us realize that some of the publicly held viewpoints of today's architectures can be overly simplistic. For example, in the domain of GPUs, we often encounter statements such as the following:

- CPUs are serial, GPUs are parallel.
- CPUs have a small number of cores, GPUs have hundreds.
- GPUs run thousands of threads, CPUs run one (or two).

The reality of any design is far more complicated than that, with wide variation in internal buffers, the number of pipelines, the type of pipelines, and so on. The theme of this chapter is to show that the difference between GPUs and CPUs, or indeed most modern architectures, is not fundamental. Most of the visible architectural differences we commonly see today are simply points on a sliding scale, a set of parameterization knobs applied to basic designs. These are the differences the average programmer needs to understand: only the expert need be concerned with ratios between buffer sizes and arranging instructions for hardware co-issue.

In this section, we discuss several real architectures and where they fit in the design space, trading off some of the features we discussed previously. It is hoped that this will help to give a more nuanced feel for architectural trade-offs and help to develop views on what algorithms may or may not work well on real architectures. The goal is to show that the wide SIMD and state storage design of GPUs is a long way along a spectrum from simple CPUs in terms of use of area, and that maximum performance and ease of achieving good performance depend on these design choices.

2.3.1 CPU DESIGNS

The devices that most people are used to developing on can be loosely described as "CPUs." Even within this space, there is considerable variation in how different forms of parallelism are utilized.

Low-power CPUs

At the very lowest end of the power spectrum, CPU cores are very simple, in-order cores. At this level, power consumption is the most important factor in design, with performance a secondary consideration. Such designs often do not support floating-point operations and have no need for parallelism.

Currently, the most widespread low-power CPU ISA is the ARM ISA developed in intellectual property (IP) form by ARM Holdings. The ARM architecture originated in the Acorn RISC machine concept from Acorn Computers as a desktop architecture, but recently the simplicity of the architecture has made it dominant in the mobile and embedded markets, with a foray into Acorn's own desktop projects from 1996 to 1998 as the DEC-manufactured StrongARM. ARM designs come in a wide variety of forms because the ISA IP is licensed to manufacturers who are at liberty to design their own cores. Usually, ARM cores are combined within SoCs with other units such as cellular modems, embedded graphics processors, video accelerators, and similar devices.

Most variants on the ARM ISA have been in-order cores with three to seven pipeline stages. The Cortex-A8, Cortex-A9, and Cortex-A15 cores, based on the ARMv7 ISA, are superscalar and multicore with up to four symmetric cores. The ARMv7-based cores optionally support the NEON SIMD instructions, giving 64- and 128-bit SIMD operations in each core.

ARMv8-A cores add a 64-bit instruction set, and updated NEON extensions with more 128-bit registers, double-precision support, and cryptography instructions. The high-end Cortex-A57, based on the ARMv8-A architecture, targets mid-range performance, has eight-wide instruction issue, and trading performance for power, an out-of-order pipeline. The smaller Cortex-A53 retains the in-order pipeline, although it supports dual instruction issue.

The Puma microarchitecture (shown in Figure 2.7) is the low-power core in AMD's current CPU lineup, designed for a power range of 2–25 W. To achieve the low-power figures, Puma cores are clocked more slowly than the high-end parts, and are carefully designed to reduce overhead in the data-path—at the cost of lower peak performance. Puma is a 64-bit design, supports two-way out-of-order issue, and also has two 128-bit SIMD units that can combine to execute AVX operations.

Intel's Atom designs have historically taken a slightly different approach to performance compared with AMD's Puma. Before the Silvermont microarchitecture, Atom did not support out-of-order execution, and used SMT to make up for lack of single-thread performance. Starting with Silvermont, the designs from Intel and AMD use similar techniques for trading off power and performance.

In general, low-power CPUs can be characterized by in-order or narrow out-of-order execution with relatively narrow SIMD units. Variation in the number of cores can be used for scaling to various power-performance points in multithreaded situations. In all cases, features are kept simple and frequencies are kept low compared with those in desktop CPUs as a method for reducing power consumption.

Mainstream desktop CPUs

Mainstream desktop CPUs from AMD and Intel do not look much different from the Puma design. In each case, they slightly increase the complexity of each element.

The Haswell microarchitecture is the current mainstream desktop CPU core from Intel. Previous generations, such as Sandy Bridge [4] and Ivy Bridge (Sandy Bridge die shrink), supported 128-bit SSE operations and 256-bit AVX operations. Haswell [5] added support for AVX2—an update to AVX providing support for a greater number of integer instructions. The Haswell pipeline issues up to eight operations of mixed types in parallel, with the possible mix of operations determined by the functional units connected to its eight scheduling "ports." The out-of-order engine can handle up to 192 operations in flight at a time.

Intel added hardware multithreading support to Nehalem, Sandy Bridge's predecessor, and maintained this in Sandy Bridge and Haswell. In this case, it is true SMT: each core can mix operations from a pair of threads in the execution units. This increase in scheduling complexity is traded against the increased utilization of the functional units.

AMD's Steamroller core, seen in Figure 2.7, increases parallel thread execution by taking a middle ground between increasing core count and increasing the number of threads per core. The approach used in Steamroller is to create a second independent integer core with its own set of private ALUs, state and scheduler. However, the fetch unit, floating-point ALUs, and the level 2 (L2) cache are shared between pairs of cores. AMD refers to this shared, two-core design as a "module." The goal of the module is to share only functional units that are not likely to be heavily contended in real workloads. In the previous Bulldozer and Piledriver microarchitectures, the decode unit was also shared between cores in a module. However, in Steamroller, decode has been replicated in both cores.

Each core supports out-of-order execution through four ALU pipelines. The shared floating-point ALU is a pair of 128-bit (SSE) SIMD units that can combine to execute AVX instructions. To provide power savings within mobile devices, the Steamroller microarchitecture also introduced a dynamically resizable L2 cache—portions of which can be powered down depending on the workload characteristics.

With mainstream CPUs, then, we see wide multi-issue, out-of-order hardware, high clock speeds, and large caches—all features intended to maintain high single-threaded performance with reasonably high power draw. In-core multithreading is kept minimal or is nonexistent, and SIMD units are set at a width that does not waste too much area when they are not in use.

Server CPUs

Intel's Itanium architecture and its more successful successors (the latest being the Itanium 9500), represent an interesting attempt to make a mainstream server processor based on VLIW techniques [6]. The Itanium architecture includes a large number of registers (128 integer and 128 floating point registers). It uses a VLIW approach known as EPIC, in which instructions are stored in 128-bit, three-instruction bundles. The CPU fetches four instruction bundles per cycle from its L1 cache and can hence executes 12 instructions per clock cycle. The processor is designed to be efficiently combined into multicore and multisocket servers.

The goal of EPIC is to move the problem of exploiting parallelism from runtime to compile time. It does this by feeding back information from execution traces into the compiler. It is the task of the compiler to package instructions into the VLIW/EPIC packets, and as a result, performance on the architecture is highly dependent on compiler capability. To assist with this, numerous execution masks, dependence flags between bundles, prefetch instructions, speculative loads, and rotating register files are built into the architecture. To improve the throughput of the processor, the latest Itanium microarchitectures have included SMT, with the Itanium 9500 supporting independent front-end and back-end pipeline execution.

The SPARC T-series family (Figure 2.9), originally from Sun and under continuing development at Oracle, takes a throughput computing multithreaded approach

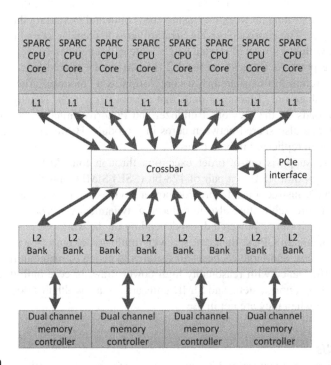

FIGURE 2.9

The Niagara 2 CPU from Sun/Oracle. The design intends to make a high level of threading efficient. Note its relative similarity to the GPU design seen in Figure 2.8. Given enough threads, we can cover all memory access time with useful compute, without extracting instruction-level parallelism (ILP) through complicated hardware techniques.

to server workloads [7]. Workloads on many servers, particularly transactional and Web workloads, are often heavily multithreaded, with a large number of lightweight integer threads using the memory system. The UltraSPARC Tx and later SPARC Tx CPUs are designed to efficiently execute a large number of threads to maximize overall work throughput with minimal power consumption. Each of the cores is designed to be simple and efficient, with no out-of-order execution logic, until the SPARC T4. Within a core, the focus on thread-level parallelism is immediately apparent, as it can interleave operations from eight threads with only a dual issue pipeline. This design shows a clear preference for latency hiding and simplicity of logic compared with the mainstream x86 designs. The simpler design of the SPARC cores allows up to 16 cores per processor in the SPARC T5.

To support many active threads, the SPARC architecture requires multiple sets of registers, but as a trade-off requires less speculative register storage than a superscalar design. In addition, coprocessors allow acceleration of cryptographic operations, and an on-chip Ethernet controller improves network throughput.

As mentioned previously, the latest generations, the SPARC T4 and T5, back off slightly from the earlier multithreading design. Each CPU core supports out-of-order execution and can switch to a single-thread mode where a single thread can use all of the resources that previously had to be dedicated to multiple threads. In this sense, these SPARC architectures are becoming closer to other modern SMT designs such as those from Intel.

Server chips, in general, try to maximize parallelism at the cost of some single-threaded performance. As opposed to desktop chips, more area is devoted to supporting quick transitions between thread contexts. When wide-issue logic is present, as in the Itanium processors, it relies on help from the compiler to recognize instruction-level parallelism.

2.3.2 GPU ARCHITECTURES

Like CPUs, GPU architectures come in a wide variety of options. Here, we briefly discuss several before going into more depth about OpenCL programming for a high-end GPU in Chapter 8. GPUs tend to be heavily multithreaded with sophisticated hardware task management because the graphics workloads they are designed to process consist of complex vertex, geometry, and pixel processing task graphs. These tasks and the pixels they process are highly parallel, which gives a substantial amount of independent work to process for devices with multiple cores and highly latency-tolerant multithreading. It is important to understand that barring sophisticated mechanisms to manage task queues, or to hide SIMD execution behind hardware management systems, GPUs are simply multithreaded processors with their parameterization aimed at processing large numbers of pixels very efficiently.

Handheld GPUs
Handheld GPUs have gained general-purpose capabilities, with ARM, Imagination Technologies, MediaTek, and Qualcomm now offering fully OpenCL-compliant

IP. At this scale, GPUs consist of a small number of shader cores, where each executes a large number of individual threads on a small-pixel-size SIMD unit not entirely dissimilar to an SSE vector pipeline. ARM's Mali-T760 architecture uses three types of computation pipelines in each of up to 16 shader cores. Intercore task management supports managing workloads across the cores: GPU threading, in general, is hardware controlled rather than exposed to the operating system. An embedded design such as the Mali-T760 can share the same global memory with embedded CPUs, reducing the need to copy data across memory spaces; in the ARM design, this data is fully cached.

At the high end: AMD Radeon R9 290X and NVIDIA GeForce GTX 780

High-end desktop GPUs and their derivatives for the high-performance computing and workstation segments aim more for performance than maximal power efficiency. To achieve high memory bandwidth, a large number of pins are dedicated to memory traffic, and high-bandwidth-per-pin (possibly lower-latency) memory protocols may be used, such as GDDR5. These devices use a mixture of features to improve compute throughput, including wide SIMD arrays to maximize arithmetic throughput for a given number of issued instructions.

The AMD Radeon R9 290X architecture seen in Figure 2.10 has 16 SIMD lanes in hardware and uses vector pipelining to execute a 64-element vector over four cycles. The NVIDIA GeForce GTX 780 architecture (Figure 2.11) also uses a 16-wide SIMD unit, and executes a 32-element vector over two cycles. Both devices are multithreaded, supporting numerous wide SIMD threads on each core. On the AMD architecture, for example, each core possesses one scalar core and four SIMD units associated with a banked register file: each of those four SIMD units can have up to 10 vector threads (AMD refers to these as "wavefronts") in flight, one of which can be chosen on each issue cycle for that SIMD unit. That gives a total of up to 40 vector threads per core, and hence 1760 active vector threads across the entire device (or 112,640 individual work-items!). The NVIDIA design offers similarly high numbers: however, in both cases the actual concurrency is limited by the amount of state each thread uses, and the realistic number is likely to be lower.

In the AMD and NVIDIA architectures, the intermediate language that programs the device is a lanewise SIMD model such that the instruction stream represents a single lane of the SIMD unit, an approach that NVIDIA calls "single instruction, multiple thread.". It has also been called "single program, multiple data on SIMD". The ISA that this compiles down to may or may not be lanewise, and in the AMD case it is an explicit scalar plus vector ISA where program counters are managed explicitly on a per-wavefront basis and divergent branches are managed using explicit mask registers. We will discuss this in more detail in Chapter 8.

Instruction-level parallelism is achieved in various ways. The AMD Radeon R9 290X design issues multiple instructions per cycle, each from a different active program counter, where one vector instruction will be issued on each cycle to a different vector unit. The NVIDIA GeForce GTX 780 can co-issue two threads at once over four execution pipelines. Older AMD designs such as the Radeon HD 6970 used VLIW instruction issue. In fact, the Radeon HD 6970 and Radeon R9 290X are

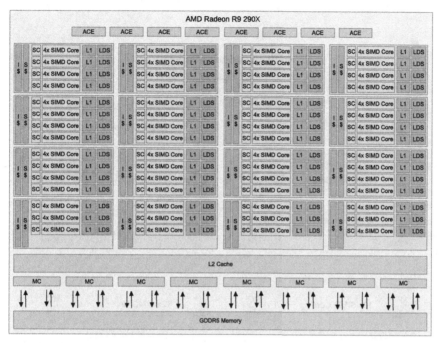

FIGURE 2.10

The AMD Radeon R9 290X architecture. The device has 44 cores in 11 clusters. Each core consists of a scalar execution unit that handles branches and basic integer operations, and four 16-lane SIMD ALUs. The clusters share instruction and scalar caches.

very similar in their execution unit design, the difference lies largely in the instruction issue, such that one issues in a compiler-structured fashion from one thread and the other issues at runtime from four threads. All of these designs are superscalar in that execution resources can issue memory access, arithmetic, and other operations from threads running on the same core, but not necessarily the same thread, and in this sense they are throughput architectures optimizing the throughput of a set of threads over the latency of a single thread.

Like the mobile GPUs on the market, the high-end AMD and NVIDIA models comprise multiple cores. If we define a core as the closest reasonable mapping to the equivalent in a CPU, the Radeon R9 290X has 44 cores (each with four vector units) and the NVIDIA design has 12 (though each substantially larger, with 12 vector units). Each core has a scratchpad memory buffer known as local memory in OpenCL which is allocated on a per-work-group basis.

It should be clear that the high-end GPU design is heavily weighted toward thread state, allowing fast switching between multiple program instances and high throughput. As opposed to high-end CPUs, GPUs do not rely on complex out-of-order or multi-issue pipelines for single-thread performance. Instead, GPU designs are throughput oriented, and rely very heavily on thread-level parallelism to utilize their large numbers of vector processing units.

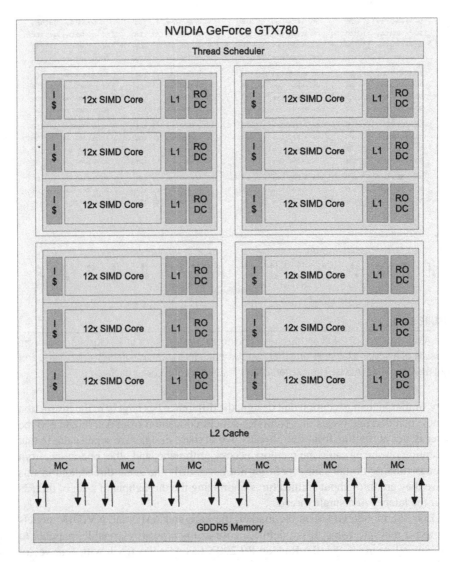

FIGURE 2.11

The NVIDIA GeForce GTX 780 architecture. The device has 12 large cores that NVIDIA refers to as "streaming multiprocessors" (SMX). Each SMX has 12 SIMD units (with specialized double-precision and special function units), a single L1 cache, and a read-only data cache.

2.3.3 APU AND APU-LIKE DESIGNS

SoCs have been common in embedded markets for a long time. Currently, there is a move toward SoCs being used for much higher performance systems and applications. Such fused processors, most obviously combining CPU and GPU designs, in addition to the less strongly marketed video decoders, random number generators, and encryption circuits, have become prevalent in the netbook, notebook, and low-end desktop spaces. As transistors have continued to shrink and less performance benefit can be gained from adding additional CPU cores, these SoCs have also permeated high-end desktops. In this space we see the power saving capabilities of integration combined with the substantial compute capability of a discrete GPU that needs only be enabled when higher performance is needed, thus offering power savings overall. Currently, the major architectures in this market are AMD's Puma-based and Steamroller-based products and Intel's Haswell products.

The AMD designs targeted at low-power and low-end mainstream products with a 4.5-15-W power budget are known as Beema and Mullins, and are based on the low-power Puma CPU core combined with a low-end Radeon R9 GPU. These components are produced together on a single silicon die in a 28-nm process. AMD's higher-performance APU, Kaveri, is based on the Steamroller core and a significantly higher performance GPU. A simplified Kaveri A10-7850K diagram is shown in Figure 2.12.

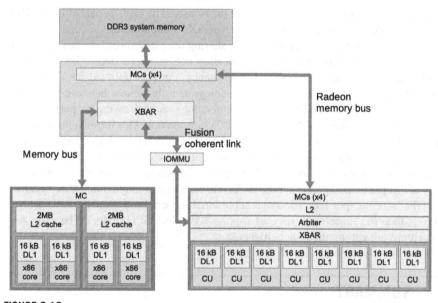

FIGURE 2.12

The A10-7850K APU consists of two Steamroller-based CPU cores and eight Radeon R9 GPU cores (32 16-lane SIMD units in total). The APU includes a fast bus from the GPU to DDR3 memory, and a shared path that is optionally coherent with CPU caches.

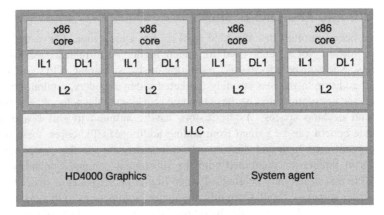

FIGURE 2.13

An Intel i7 processor with HD Graphics 4000 graphics. Although not termed "APU" by Intel, the concept is the same as for the devices in that category from AMD. Intel combines four Haswell x86 cores with its graphics processors, connected to a shared last-level cache (LLC) via a ring bus.

Intel's high-end Core i7 APU design (Figure 2.13) is based on four cores of the Haswell microarchitecture core discussed previously. The GPU is part of Intel's HD series GPU design with full OpenCL and DirectX 11 capabilities.

The APU architectures offer scope for sharing data structures between GPU and CPU cores such that the major communication bottleneck of many GPU compute workloads is alleviated. This means that latency can be improved for workloads dispatched to the GPU, and more tightly integrated algorithms between GPU and CPU cores can be created that are currently not practical owing to performance constraints arising from the latency of the PCI Express bus. This improvement comes at the cost of CPU-style memory bandwidth shared between both devices, losing the very high bandwidth exotic memory interfaces of discrete GPUs. It is likely that this trade-off is advantageous in the wide range of algorithms that are inefficient when they are implemented purely on the GPU. This advantage may come either because the GPU's throughput-based design is suboptimal for serial code, and the APU design may reduce the turnaround time of mixing CPU and GPU code, or because the algorithms are communication bottlenecked.

2.4 SUMMARY

In this chapter, we discussed the types of architecture that OpenCL might run on and the trade-offs in the architectural design space that these architectures embody. After examining OpenCL more closely, in Chapter 8, we discuss how the OpenCL model maps to a specific architecture in the form of a combination of a Piledriver-based AMD FX-8350 CPU and a Radeon R9 290X GPU.

The content of this chapter will benefit from further reading; however, for many of the specific devices, concise references can be difficult to find. The fourth edition of *Computer Organization and Design* [8] discusses many architectural issues in depth and various other processor designs. It also contains a section on NVIDIA's GPU architecture. The fifth edition of *Computer Architecture* [9] extends these concepts.

REFERENCES

[1] Advanced Micro Devices, Incorporated, AMD Fusion Family of APUs: Enabling a Superior, Immersive PC Experience, Advanced Micro Devices, Incorporated, Sunnyvale, CA, 2011.

[2] Advanced Micro Devices, Incorporated, White paper: AMD Graphics Core Next (GCN) Architecture, Advanced Micro Devices, Incorporated, Sunnyvale, CA, 2012.

[3] NVIDIA Corporation, NVIDIA Kepler Compute Architecture, NVIDIA Corporation, Santa Clara, CA, 2014.

[4] Sandy Bridge Arch; http://www.intel.com/content/dam/doc/manual/64-ia-32-architec tures-optimization-manual.pdf

[5] Haswell Arch; http://www.intel.com/content/dam/www/public/us/en/documents/manuals /64-ia-32-architectures-optimization-manual.pdf

[6] Intel Corporation, Intel Itanium 2 Processor: Hardware Developer's Manual, Intel Corporation, Santa Clara, CA, 2002.

[7] G. Grohoski, Niagara-2: A highly threaded server-on-a-chip, in: 18th Hot Chips Symposium, August, 2006.

[8] D.A. Patterson, J.L. Hennessy, Computer Organization and Design, 4th ed., Morgan Kaufmann, Burlington, MA, 2008.

[9] J.L. Hennessy, D.A. Patterson, Computer Architecture: A Quantitative Approach, 5th ed., Morgan Kaufmann, Burlington, MA, 2011.

Introduction to OpenCL

3.1 INTRODUCTION

This chapter introduces OpenCL, the programming fabric that will allow us to weave our application to execute concurrently. Programmers familiar with C and C++ should have little trouble understanding the OpenCL syntax. We begin by reviewing the OpenCL standard.

3.1.1 THE OpenCL STANDARD

OpenCL was refined into an initial proposal by Apple in collaboration with technical teams at AMD, IBM, Qualcomm, Intel, and NVIDIA, and was submitted to the Khronos Group. The initial 1.0 specification was released by the Khronos Group in 2008. OpenCL 1.0 defined the host application programming interface (API) and the OpenCL C kernel language used for executing data-parallel programs on different heterogeneous devices. Follow-up releases of OpenCL 1.1 and OpenCL 1.2 enhanced the OpenCL standard with features such as OpenGL interoperability, additional image formats, synchronization events, and device partitioning. In November 2013, the Khronos Group announced the ratification and public release of the finalized OpenCL 2.0 specification. A number of additional features were added to the OpenCL standard, such as shared virtual memory, nested parallelism, and generic address spaces. These advanced features have the potential to simplify parallel application development, and improve the performance portability of OpenCL applications.

Open programming standards designers are tasked with a very challenging objective: arrive at a common set of programming standards that are acceptable to a range of competing needs and requirements. The Khronos Group, which manages the OpenCL standard, has done a good job addressing these requirements. It has developed an API that is general enough to run on significantly different architectures while being adaptable enough that each hardware platform can still achieve high performance. Using the core language and correctly following the specification, any program designed for one vendor can execute on another vendor's hardware. The model set forth by OpenCL creates portable, vendor- and device-independent programs that are capable of being accelerated on many different hardware platforms.

The code that executes on an OpenCL device, which in general is not the same device as the host central processing unit (CPU), is written in the OpenCL C language. OpenCL C is a restricted version of the C99 language with extensions appropriate for executing data-parallel code on a variety of heterogeneous devices. The OpenCL C programming language also implements a subset of the C11 atomics and synchronization operations. While the OpenCL API itself is a C API, there are third-party bindings for many languages, including Java, C++, Python, and .NET. Additionally, a number of popular libraries in domains such as linear algebra and computer vision have integrated OpenCL to leverage heterogeneous platforms and gain substantial performance improvements.

3.1.2 THE OpenCL SPECIFICATION

The OpenCL specification is defined in four parts, which it refers to as *models*. The models are summarized here, and are explained in detail in the following sections.

1. **Platform model:** Specifies that there is one *host* processor coordinating execution, and one or more *device* processors whose job it is to execute OpenCL C *kernels*. It also defines an abstract hardware model for devices.
2. **Execution model**: Defines how the OpenCL environment is configured by the host, and how the host may direct the devices to perform work. This includes defining an environment for execution on the host, mechanisms for host-device interaction, and a concurrency model used when configuring kernels. The concurrency model defines how an algorithm is decomposed into OpenCL work-items and work-groups.
3. **Kernel programming model:** Defines how the concurrency model is mapped to physical hardware.
4. **Memory model:** Defines memory object types, and the abstract memory hierarchy that kernels use regardless of the actual underlying memory architecture. It also contains requirements for memory ordering and optional shared virtual memory between the host and devices.

In a typical scenario, we might observe an OpenCL implementation executing on a platform consisting of a host x86 CPU using a graphics processing unit (GPU) device as an accelerator. The host sets up a kernel for the GPU to run and sends a command to the GPU to execute the kernel with some specified degree of parallelism. This is the execution model. The memory for the data used by the kernel is allocated by the programmer to specific parts of an abstract memory hierarchy specified by the memory model. The runtime and driver will map these abstract memory regions to the physical hierarchy. Finally, the GPU creates hardware threads to execute the kernel, and maps them to its hardware units. This is done using the programming model. Throughout this chapter, these ideas are discussed in further detail.

This chapter begins by introducing the OpenCL models, including the OpenCL API related to each model. Once the OpenCL host API has been described, it is demonstrated using a vector addition program. The full listing of the vector addition program is given at the end of the chapter in Section 3.6. The same vector addition program is then used to illustrate the OpenCL C++ API, and a comparison of an OpenCL program with a CUDA program.

3.2 THE OpenCL PLATFORM MODEL

An OpenCL platform consists of a host connected to one or more OpenCL devices. The platform model defines the roles of the host and the devices, and provides an abstract hardware model for devices. A device is divided into one or more *compute units*, which are further divided into one or more *processing elements*. A diagram of these concepts is provided in Figure 3.1.

The platform model is key to application development for portability between OpenCL-capable systems. Even within a single capable system, there could be a number of different OpenCL platforms which could be targeted by any given application. The platform model's API allows an OpenCL application to adapt and choose the desired platform and compute device for executing its computation.

In the API, a platform can be thought of as a common interface a vendor-specific OpenCL runtime. The devices that a platform can target are thus limited to those with which a vendor knows how to interact. For example, if company A's platform is chosen, it likely will not be able to communicate with company B's GPU. However, platforms are not necessarily vendor exclusive. For example, implementations from AMD and Intel should be able to create platforms that target each other's x86 CPUs as devices.

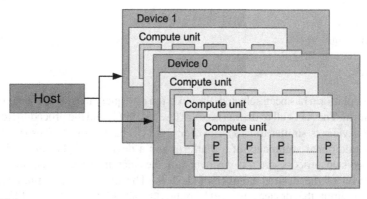

FIGURE 3.1

An OpenCL platform with multiple compute devices. Each compute device contains one or more compute units. A compute unit is composed of one or more processing elements (PEs). A system could have multiple platforms present at the same time. For example, a system could have an AMD platform and an Intel platform present at the same time.

The platform model also presents an abstract device architecture that programmers target when writing OpenCL C code. Vendors map this abstract architecture to the physical hardware. The platform model defines a device as a group of multiple compute units, where each compute unit is functionally independent. Compute units are further divided into processing elements. Figure 3.1 illustrates this hierarchical model. As an example, the AMD Radeon R9 290X graphics card (device) comprises 44 vector processors (compute units). Each compute unit has four 16-lane SIMD engines, for a total of 64 lanes (processing elements). Each SIMD lane on the Radeon R9 290X executes a scalar instruction. This allows the GPU device to execute a total of $44 \times 16 \times 4 = 2816$ instructions at a time.

3.2.1 PLATFORMS AND DEVICES

The API call `clGetPlatformIDs()` is used to discover the set of available OpenCL platforms for a given system. The most robust code will call `clGetPlatformIDs()` twice when querying the system for OpenCL platforms. The first call to `clGetPlatformIDs()` passes an unsigned integer pointer as the `num_platforms` argument and `NULL` for the platforms argument. The pointer is populated with the available number of platforms. The programmer can then allocate space (pointed to by `platforms`) to hold the platform objects (of type `cl_platform_id`). For the second call to `clGetPlatformIDs()`, the `platforms` pointer is passed to the implementation with enough space allocated for the desired number (`num_entries`) of platforms. After platforms have been discovered, the `clGetPlatformInfo()` API call can be used to determine which implementation (vendor) the platform was defined by. This API call, and all further API functions discussed in this chapter, are illustrated in the vector addition source code listing in Section 3.6.

```
cl_int
clGetPlatformIDs(
    cl_uint num_entries,
    cl_platform_id *platforms,
    cl_uint *num_platforms)
```

Once a platform has been selected, the next step is to query the devices available to that platform. The API call to do this is `clGetDeviceIDs()`, and the procedure for discovering devices is similar to `clGetPlatformIDs()`. The call to `clGetDeviceIDs()` takes the additional arguments of a platform and a device type, but otherwise the same three-step process occurs: discovery of the quantity of devices, allocation, and retrieval of the desired number of devices. The `device_type` argument can be used to limit the devices to GPUs only (`CL_DEVICE_TYPE_GPU`), CPUs only (`CL_DEVICE_TYPE_CPU`), all devices (`CL_DEVICE_TYPE_ALL`), as well as other options. The same option should be used for both calls to `clGetDeviceIDs()`. As with platforms, the `clGetDeviceInfo()` API call is used to retrieve information such as name, type, and vendor from each device.

```
cl_int
clGetDeviceIDs(
    cl_platform_id platform,
    cl_device_type device_type,
    cl_uint num_entries,
    cl_device_id *devices,
    cl_uint *num_devices)
```

The CLInfo program in the AMD accelerated parallel processing (APP) software development kit (SDK) uses `clGetPlatformInfo()` and `clGetDeviceInfo()` to print detailed information about the OpenCL-supported platforms and devices in a system. Hardware details such as memory sizes and bus widths are available using these commands, and the rest of the properties should become clear after completion of this chapter. A snippet of the output from CLInfo is shown in Figure 3.2.

3.3 THE OpenCL EXECUTION MODEL

The OpenCL platform model allows us to build a topology of a system with a coordinating host processor, and one or more devices that will be targeted to execute our OpenCL kernels. In order for the host to request that a kernel be executed on a device, a *context* must be configured that enables the host to pass commands and data to the device.

3.3.1 CONTEXTS

In OpenCL, a *context* is an abstract environment within which coordination and memory management for kernel execution is valid and well defined. A context coordinates the mechanisms for host-device interaction, manages the memory objects available to the devices, and keeps track of the programs and kernels that are created for each device. The API function to create a context is `clCreateContext()`.

```
cl_context
clCreateContext (
    const cl_context_properties *properties,
    cl_uint num_devices,
    const cl_device_id *devices,
    void (CL_CALLBACK *pfn_notify)(
        const char *errinfo,
        const void *private_info,
        size_t cb,
        void *user_data),
    void *user_data,
    cl_int *errcode_ret)
```

Number of platforms:	1
Platform Profile:	FULL_PROFILE
Platform Version:	OpenCL 2.0 AMD-APP (1642.5)
Platform Name:	AMD Accelerated Parallel Processing
Platform Vendor:	Advanced Micro Devices, Inc.
Platform Extensions:	cl_khr_icd cl_amd_event_callback cl_amd_offline_devices
Platform Name:	AMD Accelerated Parallel Processing
Number of devices:	2
Device Type:	CL_DEVICE_TYPE_GPU
Vendor ID:	1002h
Board name:	AMD Radeon R9 200 Series
Device Topology:	PCI[B#1, D#0, F#0]
Max compute units:	40
Max work group size:	256
Native vector width int:	1
Max clock frequency:	1000Mhz
Max memory allocation:	2505572352
Image support:	Yes
Max image 3D width:	2048
Cache line size:	64
Global memory size:	3901751296
Platform ID:	0x7f54fb22cfd0
Name:	Hawaii
Vendor:	Advanced Micro Devices, Inc.
Device OpenCL C version:	OpenCL C 2.0
Driver version:	1642.5 (VM)
Profile:	FULL_PROFILE
Version:	OpenCL 2.0 AMD-APP (1642.5)
Extensions:	cl_khr_fp64 cl_amd_fp64 cl_khr_global_int32_base_atomics

cl_khr_global_int32_extended_atomics cl_khr_local_int32_base_atomics

Device Type:	CL_DEVICE_TYPE_CPU
Vendor ID:	1002h
Board name:	
Max compute units:	8
Max work items dimensions:	3
Max work items[0]:	1024
Max work items[1]:	1024
Name:	AMD FX(tm)-8120 Eight-Core Processor
Vendor:	AuthenticAMD
Device OpenCL C version:	OpenCL C 1.2
Driver version:	1642.5 (sse2,avx,fma4)
Profile:	FULL_PROFILE

FIGURE 3.2

Some of the Output from the CLInfo program showing the characteristics of an OpenCL platform and devices. We see that the AMD platform has two devices (a CPU and a GPU). The output shown here can be queried using functions from the platform API.

The `properties` argument is used to restrict the scope of the context. It may provide a specific platform, enable graphics interoperability, or enable other parameters in the future. Limiting the scope of a context to a given platform allows the programmer to provide contexts for multiple platforms and fully utilize a system comprising resources from a mixture of vendors. Next, the devices that the programmer wants to use with the context must be supplied. A user callback can also be provided when a programmer is creating a context, and can be used to report additional error information that might be generated throughout its lifetime.

OpenCL also provides a different API call for creating a context that alleviates the need to build a list of devices. The call `clCreateContextFromType()` allows a programmer to create a context that automatically includes all devices of the specified type (e.g. CPUs, GPUs, and all devices). After creation of a context, the function `clGetContextInfo()` can be used to query information such as the number of devices present and the device objects. In OpenCL, the process of discovering platforms and devices and setting up a context can be tedious. However, after the code to perform these steps has been written, it can be reused for almost any project.

3.3.2 COMMAND-QUEUES

The execution model specifies that devices perform tasks based on *commands* which are sent from the host to the device. Actions specified by commands include executing kernels, performing data transfers, and performing synchronization. It is also possible for a device to send certain commands to itself, which is discussed later in the chapter.

A *command-queue* is the communication mechanism that the host uses to request action by a device. Once the host has decided which devices to work with and a context has been created, one command-queue needs to be created per device. Each command-queue is associated with only one device—this is required because the host needs to be able to submit commands to a specific device when multiple devices are present in the context. Whenever the host needs an action to be performed by a device, it will submit commands to the proper command-queue. The API call `clCreateCommandQueueWithProperties()` is used to create a command-queue and associate it with a device.

```
cl_command_queue
clCreateCommandQueueWithProperties(
    cl_context context,
    cl_device_id device,
    cl_command_queue_properties properties,
    cl_int* errcode_ret)
```

The `properties` parameter of `clCreateCommandQueueWithProperties()` is a bit field that is used to enable profiling of commands (`CL_QUEUE_PROFILING_ENABLE`) and/or to allow out-of-order execution of commands (`CL_QUEUE_OUT_OF_ORDER_EXEC_MODE_ENABLE`). Both are discussed in Chapter 5.

For in-order command-queues (the default), commands are pulled from the queue in the order they are received. Out-of-order command-queues allow the OpenCL implementation to search for commands that can be rearranged to execute more efficiently. If out-of-order command-queues are used, it is up to the user to specify dependencies that enforce a correct execution order.

Any API call that submits a command to a command-queue will begin with *clEnqueue* and require a command-queue as a parameter. For example, the clEnqueueReadBuffer() call requests that the device send data to the host, and clEnqueueNDRangeKernel() requests that a kernel is executed on the device. These calls will be discussed in detail later in this chapter.

In addition to API calls that submit commands to command-queues, OpenCL includes barrier operations that can be used to synchronize execution of command-queues. The API calls clFlush() and clFinish() are barrier operations for a command-queue. The clFinish() call blocks execution of the host thread until all of the commands in a command-queue have completed execution; it's functionality is synonymous with a synchronization barrier. The clFlush() call blocks execution until all of the commands in a command-queue have been removed from the queue. This means that the commands will definitely be submitted to the device, but will not necessarily have completed execution. Each API call requires only the desired command-queue as an argument.

```
cl_int clFlush(cl_command_queue command_queue);
cl_int clFinish(cl_command_queue command_queue);
```

3.3.3 EVENTS

In the OpenCL API, objects called *events* are used to specify dependencies between commands. As we discuss the various *clEnqueue* API calls, you will notice that all of them have three parameters in common: a pointer to a list of events that specify dependencies for the current command, the number of events in the wait list, and a pointer to an event that will represent the execution of the current command. The returned event can in turn be used to specify a dependency for future events. The array of events used to specify dependencies for a command is referred to as a *wait list*. Specifying dependencies with events is detailed in Chapter 5.

In addition to providing dependencies, events enable the execution status of a command to be queried at any time. As the event makes its way through the execution process, its status is updated by the implementation. The command will have one of six possible states:

- Queued: The command has been placed into a command-queue.
- Submitted: The command has been removed from the command-queue and has been submitted for execution on the device.
- Ready: The command is ready for execution on the device.
- Running: Execution of the command has started on the device.
- Ended: Execution of the command has finished on the device.
- Complete: The command and all of its child commands have finished.

The concept of child commands is related to device-side enqueuing, and is discussed in the next section. Successful completion is indicated when the event status associated with a command is set to CL_COMPLETE. Unsuccessful completion results in abnormal termination of the command, which is indicated by setting the event status to a negative value. In this case, the command-queue associated with the abnormally terminated command and all other command-queues in the same context may no longer be available. Querying an event's status is done using the API call clGetEventInfo().

In addition to supplying dependencies between commands as they are enqueued, the API also includes the function clWaitForEvents(), which causes the host to wait for all events specified in the wait list to complete execution.

```
cl_int
clWaitForEvents (
    cl_uint num_events,
    const cl_event *event_list)
```

3.3.4 DEVICE-SIDE ENQUEUING

Until now, we have described the execution model in terms of a master-worker paradigm where the host (master) sends commands to the device (worker). This execution model provides a simple paradigm for coordinating execution between the host and the device. However, in many cases the amount of work that has to be dispatched cannot be determined statically—especially in algorithms where each stage is dependent on the previous one. For example, in a combinatorial optimization application, the size of the search region may define the number of work-groups required. However the size of the region may only be known from the previous iteration. In previous versions of OpenCL, this situation would require communication from the device to the host in order to appropriately set up the dimensions of the next kernel. To remove this requirement and potentially improve performance, OpenCL 2.0 provides a new feature in the execution model known as *device-side enqueuing*.

A kernel executing on a device now has the ability to enqueue another kernel into a device-side command-queue (shown in Figure 3.5). In this scenario, the kernel currently executing on a device is referred to as the *parent kernel*, and the kernel that is enqueued is known as the *child kernel*. Parent and child kernels execute asynchronously, although a parent kernel is not registered as complete until all its child kernels have completed. We can check that a parent kernel has completed execution when its event object is set to CL_COMPLETE. The device-side command-queue is an out-of-order command-queue, and follows the same behavior as the out-of-order command-queues exposed to the host. Commands enqueued to a device-side command-queue generate and use events to enforce dependencies just as the command-queue on the host. These events, however, are visible only to the parent kernel running on the device. Device-side enqueuing is discussed in more detail in Chapter 5.

3.4 KERNELS AND THE OpenCL PROGRAMMING MODEL

The execution model API enables an application to manage the execution of OpenCL commands. The OpenCL commands describe the movement of data and the execution of kernels that process this data to perform some meaningful task. OpenCL kernels are the parts of an OpenCL application that actually execute on a device. Like many CPU concurrency models, an OpenCL kernel is syntactically similar to a standard C function; the key differences are a set of additional keywords and the concurrency model that OpenCL kernels implement. When developing concurrent programs for a CPU using operating system threading APIs or OpenMP, for example, the programmer considers the physical resources available (e.g. CPU cores) and the overhead of creating and switching between threads when their number substantially exceeds the resource availability. With OpenCL, the goal is often to represent parallelism programmatically at the finest granularity possible. The generalization of the OpenCL interface and the low-level kernel language allows efficient mapping to a wide range of hardware. The following discussion presents three versions of a function that performs an element-wise vector addition: a serial C implementation, a threaded C implementation, and an OpenCL C implementation. The code for a serial C implementation of the vector addition is shown in Listing 3.1 and executes a loop with as many iterations as there are elements to compute. Each loop iteration adds the corresponding locations in the input arrays together and stores the result into the output array. A diagram of the vector addition algorithm is shown in Figure 3.3.

```
1   // Perform an element-wise addition of A and B and store in C.
2   // There are N elements per array.
3   void vecadd(int *C, int* A, int *B, int N)
4   {
5       for(int i = 0; i < N; ++i)
6       {
7           C[i] = A[i] + B[i];
8       }
9   }
```

LISTING 3.1

Serial vector addition.

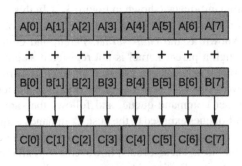

FIGURE 3.3

Vector addition algorithm showing how each element can be added independently.

For a simple multicore device, we could either use a low-level coarse-grained threading API, such as Win32 or POSIX threads, or a data-parallel model such as OpenMP. Writing a coarse-grained multithreaded version of the same function would require dividing the work (i.e. loop iterations) between the threads. Because there may be a large number of loop iterations and the work per iteration is small, we would need to chunk the loop iterations into a larger granularity, a technique called strip mining [1]. The code for the multithreaded version may be as in Listing 3.2.

```
1   // Perform an element-wise addition of A and B and store in C.
2   // There are N elements per array and NP CPU cores.
3   void vecadd(int *C, int* A, int *B, int N, int NP, int tid)
4   {
5       int ept = N/NP; // elements per thread
6       for(int i = tid*ept; i < (tid+1)*ept; ++i)
7       {
8           C[i] = A[i] + B[i];
9       }
10
11  }
```

LISTING 3.2

Vector addition chunked for coarse-grained parallelism (e.g., POSIX threads on a CPU). The input vector is partitioned among the available cores.

The unit of concurrent execution in OpenCL C is a *work-item*. Each work-item executes the kernel function body. Instead of manually strip mining the loop, we will map a single iteration of the loop to a work-item. We tell the OpenCL runtime to generate as many work-items as elements in the input and output arrays and allow the runtime to map those work-items to the underlying hardware, and hence CPU or GPU cores, in whatever way it deems appropriate. Conceptually, this is very similar to the parallelism inherent in a functional "map" operation (cf., mapReduce) or a data-parallel `for` loop in OpenMP. When an OpenCL device begins executing a kernel, it provides intrinsic functions that allow a work-item to identify itself. In the following code, the call to `get_global_id(0)` allows the programmer to make use of the position of the current work-item to access a unique element in the array. The parameter "0" to the `get_global_id()` function assumes that we have specified a one-dimensional configuration of work-items, and therefore only need its ID in the first dimension.

```
1   // Perform an element-wise addition of A and B and store in C
2   // N work-items will be created to execute this kernel.
3   __kernel
4   void vecadd(__global int *C, __global int* A, __global int *B)
5   {
6       int tid = get_global_id(0); // OpenCL intrinsic function
7       C[tid] = A[tid] + B[tid];
8   }
```

LISTING 3.3

OpenCL vector addition kernel.

Given that OpenCL describes execution in fine-grained work-items and can dispatch vast numbers of work-items on architectures with hardware support for fine-grained threading, it is easy to have concerns about scalability. The hierarchical concurrency model implemented by OpenCL ensures that scalable execution can be achieved even while supporting a large number of work-items. When a kernel is executed, the programmer specifies the number of work-items that should be created as an n-dimensional range (NDRange). An NDRange is a one-, two-, or three-dimensional index space of work-items that will often map to the dimensions of either the input or the output data. The dimensions of the NDRange are specified as an N-element array of type `size_t`, where N represents the number of dimensions used to describe the work-items being created.

In the vector addition example, our data will be one-dimensional and, assuming that there are 1024 elements, the size can be specified by an array of one, two, or three values. The host code to specify a one-dimensional NDRange for 1024 elements may look like the following:

```
size_t indexSpace[3] = {1024, 1, 1};
```

Achieving scalability comes from dividing the work-items of an NDRange into smaller, equally sized *work-groups* (Figure 3.4). An index space with N dimensions requires work-groups to be specified using the same N dimensions; thus, a three-dimensional index space requires three-dimensional work-groups. Work-items within a work-group have a special relationship with one another: they can perform barrier operations to synchronize and they have access to a shared memory address space. A work-group's size is fixed per dispatch, and so communication costs between work-items do not increase for a larger dispatch. The fact that the communication cost between work-items is not dependent on the size of the dispatch allows OpenCL implementations to maintain scalability for larger dispatches.

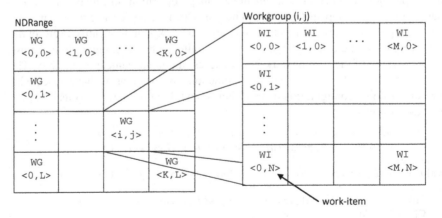

FIGURE 3.4

The hierarchical model used for creating an NDRange of work-items, grouped into work-groups.

For the vector addition example, the work-group size might be specified as

```
size_t workgroupSize[3] = {64, 1, 1};
```

If the total number of work-items per array is 1024, this results in the creation of 16 work-groups (1024 work-items/(64 work-items per work-group) = 16 work-groups). For hardware efficiency, the work-group size is usually fixed to a favorable size. In previous versions of the OpenCL specification, the index space dimensions would have to be rounded up to be a multiple of the work-group dimensions. In the kernel code, we would then have to specify that extra work-items in each dimension simply return immediately without outputting any data. However, the OpenCL 2.0 specification allows each dimension of the index space that is not evenly divisible by the work-group size to be divided into two regions: one region where the number of work-items per work-group is as specified by the programmer, and another region of *remainder work-groups* which have fewer work-items. Since work-group sizes can be nonuniform in multiple dimensions, there are up to four different sizes possible for a two-dimensional NDRange, and up to eight different sizes for a three-dimensional NDRange.

For programs such as vector addition in which work-items behave independently (even within a work-group), OpenCL allows the work-group size to be ignored by the programmer altogether and to be generated automatically by the implementation; in this case, the developer can pass NULL when defining the work-group size.

3.4.1 COMPILATION AND ARGUMENT HANDLING

An OpenCL *program* is a collection of OpenCL C kernels, functions called by the kernel, and constant data. For example, an algebraic solver application could contain a vector addition kernel, a matrix multiplication kernel, and a matrix transpose kernel within the same OpenCL program. OpenCL source code is compiled at runtime through a series of API calls. Runtime compilation gives the system an opportunity to optimize OpenCL kernels for a specific compute device. Runtime compilation also enables OpenCL kernel source code to run on a previously unknown OpenCL-compatible compute device. There is no need for an OpenCL application to have been prebuilt against the AMD, NVIDIA, or Intel runtimes, for example, if it is to run on compute devices produced by all of these vendors. OpenCL software links only to a common runtime layer called the installable client driver (ICD). All platform-specific activity is delegated to the respective vendor runtime through a dynamic library interface.

The process of creating a kernel from source code is as follows:

1. The OpenCL C source code is stored in a character array. If the source code is stored in a file on a disk, it must be read into memory and stored as a character array.
2. The source code is turned into a program object, `cl_program`, by calling `clCreateProgramWithSource()`.

3. The program object is then compiled, for one or more OpenCL devices, with `clBuildProgram()`. If there are compile errors, they will be reported here.
4. A kernel object, `cl_kernel`, is then created by calling `clCreateKernel` and specifying the program object and kernel name.

The final step of obtaining a `cl_kernel` object is similar to obtaining an exported function from a dynamic library. The name of the kernel that the program exports is used to request it from the compiled program object. The name of the kernel is passed to `clCreateKernel()`, along with the program object, and the kernel object will be returned if the program object was valid and the particular kernel is found. The relationship between an OpenCL program and OpenCL kernels is shown in Figure 3.5, where multiple kernels can be extracted from an OpenCL program. Each context can have multiple OpenCL programs that have been generated from OpenCL source code.

```
cl_kernel
clCreateKernel (
    cl_program program,
    const char *kernel_name,
    cl_int *errcode_ret)
```

The precise binary representation of an OpenCL kernel object is vendor specific. In the AMD runtime, there are two main classes of devices: x86 CPUs and GPUs. For x86 CPUs, `clBuildProgram()` generates x86 instructions that can be directly executed on the device. For the GPUs, it will create AMD's GPU intermediate language, a high-level intermediate language that will be just-in-time compiled for a specific GPU's architecture later, generating what is often known as instruction set

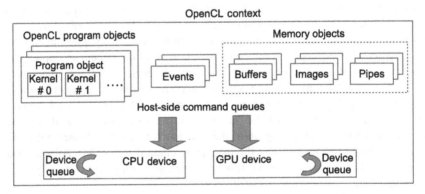

FIGURE 3.5

The OpenCL runtime shown denotes an OpenCL context with two compute devices (a CPU device and a GPU device). Each compute device has its own command-queues. Host-side and device-side command-queues are shown. The device-side queues are visible only from kernels executing on the compute device. The memory objects have been defined within the memory model.

architecture (ISA) code. NVIDIA uses a similar approach, calling its intermediate representation parallel thread execution (PTX). The advantage of using such an intermediate language is to allow the GPU ISA to change from one device or generation to another in what is still a very rapidly developing architectural space.

An additional feature of the build process is the ability to generate both the final binary format and various intermediate representations and serialize them (e.g. write them out to disk). As with most objects, OpenCL provides a function to return information about program objects, `clGetProgramInfo()`. One of the flags to this function is `CL_PROGRAM_BINARIES`, which returns a vendor-specific set of binary objects generated by `clBuildProgram()`. In addition to `clCreateProgramWithSource()`, OpenCL provides `clCreateProgramWithBinary()`, which takes a list of binaries that matches its device list. The binaries are previously created using `clGetProgramInfo()`. Using a binary representation of OpenCL kernels allows OpenCL programs to be distributed without exposing kernel source code as plain text.

Unlike invoking functions in C programs, we cannot simply call a kernel with a list of arguments. Executing a kernel requires dispatching it through an enqueue function. Owing to the syntax of C and the fact that kernel arguments are persistent (and hence we need not repeatedly set them to construct the argument list for such a dispatch), we must specify each kernel argument individually using `clSetKernelArg()`. This function takes a kernel object, an index specifying the argument number, the size of the argument, and a pointer to the argument. The type information in the kernel parameter list is then used by the runtime to unbox (similar to casting) the data to its appropriate type.

```
cl_int
clSetKernelArg (
    cl_kernel kernel,
    cl_uint arg_index,
    size_t arg_size,
    const void *arg_value)
```

3.4.2 STARTING KERNEL EXECUTION ON A DEVICE

Enqueuing a command to a device to begin kernel execution is done with a call to `clEnqueueNDRangeKernel()`. A command-queue must be specified so the target device is known. The kernel object identifies the code to be executed. Four fields are then related to work-item creation. The `work_dim` parameter specifies the number of dimensions (one, two, or three) in which work-items will be created. The `global_work_size` parameter specifies the number of work-items in each dimension of the NDRange, and `local_work_size` specifies the number of work-items in each dimension of the work-groups. The parameter `global_work_offset` can be used to provide an offset so that the global IDs of the work-items do not start at zero.

```
cl_int
clEnqueueNDRangeKernel(
    cl_command_queue command_queue,
    cl_kernel kernel,
    cl_uint work_dim,
    const size_t *global_work_offset,
    const size_t *global_work_size,
    const size_t *local_work_size,
    cl_uint num_events_in_wait_list,
    const cl_event *event_wait_list,
    cl_event *event)
```

As with all *clEnqueue* API calls, an event_wait_list is provided, and for non-NULL values the runtime will guarantee that all corresponding events will have completed before the kernel begins execution. Similarly, clEnqueueNDRangeKernel() is asynchronous: it will return immediately after the command is enqueued in the command-queue and likely before the kernel has even started execution. An API call such as clWaitForEvents() or clFinish() can be used to block host execution on the host until the kernel completes execution.

3.5 OpenCL MEMORY MODEL

Memory subsystems differ greatly between computing platforms. To support code portability, OpenCL's approach is to define an abstract memory model that programmers can target when writing code and vendors can map to their actual memory hardware. The OpenCL memory model describes the structure of the memory system exposed by an OpenCL platform to the OpenCL program. The memory model must define how the values in memory are seen from each of these units of execution. The memory model allows a programmer to reason about the correctness of OpenCL programs.

The OpenCL memory model tells programmers what they can expect from an OpenCL implementation: which memory operations are guaranteed to happen in which order and which memory values each read operation will return. The memory consistency model in OpenCL is based on the memory model from the ISO C11 programming language. Chapters 6 and 7 are dedicated to the OpenCL memory model, including details on the memory consistency model and shared virtual memory. Here we provide information on types of memory objects that are defined by OpenCL, and the memory regions that make up the abstract memory model. With this information, we will be able to execute our first OpenCL program.

3.5.1 MEMORY OBJECTS

OpenCL kernels usually require some sort of input data (e.g. arrays or multidimensional matrices) and generate some sort of output data. Before execution can begin, the input data needs to be accessible by the device. In order for data to be transferred to a device, it must first be encapsulated as a memory object. In order for output data to be generated, space must also be allocated and encapsulated as a memory object. OpenCL defines three types of memory objects: *buffers*, *images*, and *pipes*.

Buffers

Buffers are equivalent to arrays in C created using `malloc()`, where data elements are stored contiguously in memory. Conceptually, it may help to visualize an OpenCL buffer object as a pointer that is valid on a device. The API function `clCreateBuffer()` allocates space for the buffer and returns a memory object.

```
cl_mem
clCreateBuffer(
    cl_context context,
    cl_mem_flags flags,
    size_t size,
    void *host_ptr,
    cl_int *errcode_ret)
```

The `clCreateBuffer()` API call is similar to `malloc` in C, or C++'s new operator. Creating a buffer requires supplying the size of the buffer and a context in which the buffer will be allocated; it is visible for all devices associated with the context. Optionally, the caller can supply flags that specify that the data is read only, write only, or read-write. Other flags also exist that specify additional options for creating and initializing a buffer. One simple option is to supply a host pointer with data used to initialize the buffer. We see from the signature that an OpenCL buffer is linked to a context, not a device, so it is the runtime that determines the precise time the data is moved. Buffer movement to and from specific devices is managed by the OpenCL runtime to satisfy data dependencies.

Images

Images are OpenCL memory objects that abstract the storage of physical data to allow device-specific optimizations. Unlike buffers, images cannot be directly referenced as if they were arrays. Further, adjacent data elements are not guaranteed to be stored contiguously in memory. The purpose of using images is to allow the hardware to take advantage of spatial locality and to utilize the hardware acceleration available on many devices.

```
cl_mem
clCreateImage(
    cl_context context,
    cl_mem_flags flags,
    const cl_image_format *image_format,
    const cl_image_desc *image_desc,
    void *host_ptr,
    cl_int *errcode_ret)
```

Unlike buffers, which do not have a data type or dimensions, an image is created using descriptors that provide specific details to the hardware about the data. The elements of an image are represented by a format descriptor (`cl_image_format`). The format descriptor specifies how the image elements are stored in memory using the concept of channels. The *channel order* specifies the number of elements that make up an image element (up to four elements, based on the traditional use of RGBA pixels), and the *channel type* specifies the size of each element. These elements can be sized anywhere from one to four bytes and in various different formats (e.g. integer or floating point). Other metadata are provided by an image descriptor (`cl_image_desc`), which includes the type of the image and the dimensions. An example using images is provided in Chapter 4, and the architectural design and trade-offs for images are discussed in detail in Chapters 6 and 7.

To support the abstraction provided by images, OpenCL C provides dedicated function calls for reading from and writing to images. The dedicated functions for reading and writing images allow a vendor to optimize image access routines independently from each other and possibly utilize hardware acceleration. Compared with buffers, the image read and write functions take additional parameters and are specific to the image's data type. For example, the function `read_imagef()` is used for reading floating-point values and `read_imageui()` is used for reading unsigned integers. While there are many variations on these function signatures, read accesses usually require at least the coordinates to access and a *sampler* object. A sampler specifies how out-of-bounds image accesses are handled, whether interpolation should be used, and if coordinates are normalized. Writing to an image requires manual conversion to the proper storage data format (i.e. storing in the proper channel and with the proper size), as well as the destination coordinates.

In previous versions of the OpenCL standard, a kernel was not allowed to both read from and write to a single image. However, OpenCL 2.0 has relaxed this restriction by providing synchronization operations that let programmers safely read and write a single image within a kernel.

Pipes

A pipe memory object is an ordered sequence of data items (referred to as *packets*) that are stored on the basis of a first in, first out (FIFO) method. A pipe has a write endpoint into which data items are inserted, and a read endpoint from which data items are removed. When creating a pipe using the OpenCL API call `clCreatePipe()`, one must supply the packet size along with the number of entries in the pipe (i.e. the maximum number of packets that can fit into the pipe at once). The function `clGetPipeInfo()` can return information about the size of the pipe and the maximum number of packets that can reside in the pipe. The properties argument is reserved for future use, and should be `NULL` in OpenCL 2.0.

```
cl_mem
clCreatePipe (
    cl_context context,
    cl_mem_flags flags,
```

```
cl_uint pipe_packet_size,
cl_uint pipe_max_packets,
const cl_pipe_properties *properties,
cl_int *errcode_ret)
```

At any time, only one kernel may write into a pipe, and only one kernel may read from a pipe. To support the producer-consumer design pattern, one kernel connects to the write endpoint (the producer), while another kernel connects to the read endpoint (the consumer). The same kernel may not be both the writer and the reader for a pipe.

As with images, pipes are opaque data structures that can be accessed only via intrinsic function calls provided by OpenCL C (e.g. `read_pipe()` and `write_pipe()`). OpenCL C also provides functions for reserving sections of a pipe to read from and to write to. The intrinsic functions allow pipes to be accessed on a work-group granularity, without otherwise having individual work-items access the pipe and then perform synchronization. Pipes are described in more detail in Chapter 6.

3.5.2 DATA TRANSFER COMMANDS

Before a kernel is executed, it is usually necessary to copy data from a host array into an allocated area of memory that is encapsulated as a memory object. Initializing buffers and images is possible within their respective *clCreate* calls. The host pointer arguments within the *clCreate* calls can be used to initialize memory objects with data from host memory. This allows us to initialize a memory object without the need to consider data movement any further. After the memory object is initialized, the runtime is responsible for ensuring that data is moved between devices as required by dependencies.

Despite the runtime's management of data movement, we will often desire to initiate data transfers manually for performance reasons (described in Chapter 6). Explicit data transfers are also required to retrieve data back to host memory. Therefore, in general, we will often use the explicit data transfer commands to write the data to a device before the first time a memory object is used, and to read the data from a device after the last time it is used. Assuming that our memory object is a buffer, data in host memory is transferred to and from a buffer using calls to `clEnqueueWriteBuffer()` and `clEnqueueReadBuffer()`, respectively. If a kernel using a buffer is executed on a device with a discrete memory such as a GPU, the buffer may be transferred to the device when this command executes (e.g. across the PCI Express bus). The API calls for reading from and writing to buffers are very similar. The signature for `clEnqueueWriteBuffer()` is as follows:

```
cl_int
clEnqueueWriteBuffer (
    cl_command_queue command_queue,
    cl_mem buffer,
    cl_bool blocking_write,
```

```
size_t offset,
size_t cb,
const void *ptr,
cl_uint num_events_in_wait_list,
const cl_event *event_wait_list,
cl_event *event)
```

In addition to the command-queue, the `clEnqueueWriteBuffer` function requires the buffer memory object, the number of bytes to transfer, and an offset within the buffer. The combination of offset and number of bytes allows a subset of the buffer data to be written. The `blocking_write` option should be set to `CL_TRUE` if the programmer wants the transfer to complete before the function returns—effectively turning the otherwise asynchronous API call into a blocking call. Alternatively, setting `blocking_write` to `CL_FALSE` will cause `clEnqueueWriteBuffer()` to return immediately (likely well before the write operation has completed). Writing to and reading from buffers is shown in the vector addition at the end of the chapter.

3.5.3 MEMORY REGIONS

OpenCL classifies memory as either *host memory* or *device memory*. Host memory is directly available to the host, and is defined outside OpenCL. Data moves between the host and devices using functions within the OpenCL API or through a shared virtual memory interface. Alternatively, device memory is memory which is available to executing kernels.

OpenCL divides device memory into four named *memory regions* as shown in Figure 3.6. These memory regions are relevant within OpenCL kernels. Within a kernel, keywords are associated with each region, and are used to specify where a variable should be created or where the data that it points to resides. Memory regions are logically disjoint, and data movement between different memory regions is controlled by the kernel developer. Each memory region has its own performance characteristics. Owing to these characteristics, accessing data for computation from the right memory region can greatly affect performance.

The following provides a short description of each memory region.

- Global memory is visible to all work-items executing a kernel (similarly to the main memory on a CPU-based host system). Whenever data is transferred from the host to the device, the data will reside in global memory. Any data that is to be transferred back from the device to the host must also reside in global memory. The keyword `global` or `__global` is added to a pointer declaration to specify that data referenced by the pointer resides in global memory. For example, in the OpenCL C code at the end of the chapter, `global int* A` denotes that the data pointed to by A resides in global memory (although we will see that A actually resides in private memory).

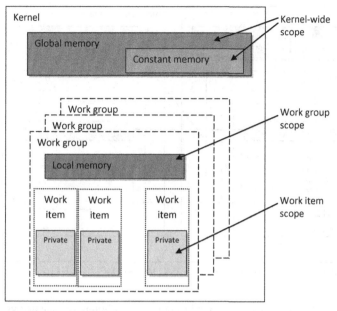

FIGURE 3.6

Memory regions and their scope in the OpenCL memory model.

- Constant memory is not specifically designed for every type of read-only data, but rather is specifically designed for data where each element is accessed simultaneously by all work-items. Variables whose values never change (e.g. a data variable holding the value of π) also fall into this category. Constant memory is modeled as a part of global memory, so memory objects that are transferred to global memory can be specified as constant. Data is mapped to constant memory by using either the keyword `constant` or `__constant`.
- Local memory is a memory that is shared between work-items within a work-group. It is common for local memory to be mapped to on-chip memory, such as software-managed scratchpad memory. As such, accesses may have much shorter latency and much higher bandwidth than global memory. Calling `clSetKernelArg()` with a size, but no argument, allows local memory to be allocated at runtime. Within an OpenCL C kernel, a kernel parameter that corresponds to local memory is defined as a `local` or `__local` pointer (e.g. `local int* sharedData`). Alternatively, arrays can be statically declared in local memory by appending the keyword `local` (e.g. `local int[64] sharedData`), although this requires specifying the array size at compile time.
- Private memory is memory that is unique to an individual work-item. Local variables and nonpointer kernel arguments are private by default. In practice,

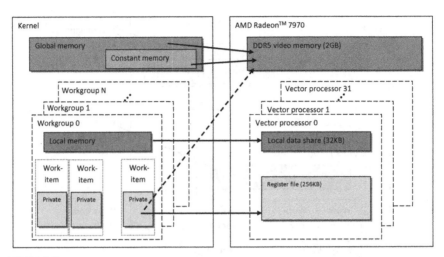

FIGURE 3.7

Mapping the OpenCL memory model to an AMD Radeon HD 7970 GPU.

these variables are usually mapped to registers, although private arrays and any spilled registers are usually mapped to an off-chip (i.e. long-latency) memory.

Figure 3.7 details the relationship between OpenCL memory regions and those found on an AMD Radeon HD 7970 GPU.

3.5.4 GENERIC ADDRESS SPACE

In earlier versions of the OpenCL specification, named address spaces sometimes required the creation of multiple versions of callable functions simply to manipulate data from different address spaces. To save programmer effort, a single generic address space was added to OpenCL 2.0, which is closely modeled after the concept of a generic address space used in the embedded C standard (ISO/IEC 9899:1999). The generic address space supports conversion of pointers to and from private, local, and global address spaces, and hence lets a programmer write a single function that at compile time can take arguments from any of the three named address spaces. The generic address space is discussed further in Chapter 7.

3.6 THE OpenCL RUNTIME WITH AN EXAMPLE

OpenCL's four models discussed in the previous sections are exposed to application developers by their runtime APIs. The platform model is used to enable a host and one or more devices to participate in executing an OpenCL application. The application developer implements their core computation using OpenCL kernels whose execution is defined by the programming model. The computation that a kernel performs manipulates data in a way defined by the memory model. The developer leverages the execution model to submit commands to devices to perform data movement and execute kernels. This section puts all of these ideas together with our first complete OpenCL application.

The main steps to execute a simple OpenCL application are summarized below:

1. Discovering the platform and devices
2. Creating a context
3. Creating a command-queue per device
4. Creating memory objects (buffers) to hold data
5. Copying the input data onto the device
6. Creating and compiling a program from the OpenCL C source code
7. Extracting the kernel from the program
8. Executing the kernel
9. Copying output data back to the host
10. Releasing the OpenCL resources

The following code implements each of the summarized steps. Much of the setup to execute an OpenCL application is generic code that is required to allow implementations to span hardware platforms containing multiple styles of architectures from multiple vendors. Therefore, much of this code can be reused directly on many applications, and potentially abstracted into user-defined functions. The C++ API, shown later, is also less verbose than the C API.

We now discuss each step enumerated above. After this section, a full program listing is provided.

1. **Discovering the platform and devices:** Before a host can request that a kernel be executed on a device, a platform and a device or devices must be discovered.

```
cl_int status;  // Used for error checking

// Retrieve the number of platforms
cl_uint numPlatforms = 0;
status = clGetPlatformIDs(0, NULL, &numPlatforms);

// Allocate enough space for each platform
cl_platform_id *platforms = NULL;
platforms = (cl_platform_id*)malloc(numPlatforms*sizeof
    (cl_platform_id));

// Fill in the platforms
status = clGetPlatformIDs(numPlatforms, platforms, NULL);

// Retrieve the number of devices
cl_uint numDevices = 0;
```

```
status = clGetDeviceIDs(platforms[0], CL_DEVICE_TYPE_ALL,
    0, NULL, &numDevices);

// Allocate enough space for each device
cl_device_id *devices;
devices = (cl_device_id*)malloc(numDevices*sizeof(cl_device_id));

// Fill in the devices
status = clGetDeviceIDs(platforms[0], CL_DEVICE_TYPE_ALL,
    numDevices, devices, NULL);
```

In the complete program listing that follows, we will assume that we are using the first platform and device that are found, which will allow us to reduce the number of function calls required. This will help provide clarity and brevity when viewing the source code.

2. **Creating a context:** Once the device or devices have been discovered, the context can be configured on the host.

```
// Create a context that includes all devices
cl_context context = clCreateContext(NULL, numDevices,
    devices, NULL, NULL, &status);
```

3. **Creating a command-queue per device:** Once the host has decided which devices to work with and a context has been created, one command-queue needs to be created per device (i.e. each command-queue is associated with only one device). The host will ask the device to perform work by submitting commands to the command-queue.

```
// Only create a command-queue for the first device
cl_command_queue cmdQueue = clCreateCommandQueueWithProperties
    (context, devices[0], 0, &status);
```

4. **Creating buffers to hold data:** Creating a buffer requires supplying the size of the buffer and a context in which the buffer will be allocated; it is visible to all devices associated with the context. Optionally, the caller can supply flags that specify that the data is read only, write only, or read-write. By passing NULL as the fourth argument, we are not initializing the buffer at this step.

```
// Allocate 2 input and one output buffer for the three vectors in
//    the vector addition
cl_mem bufA = clCreateBuffer(context, CL_MEM_READ_ONLY, datasize,
    NULL, &status);
cl_mem bufB = clCreateBuffer(context, CL_MEM_READ_ONLY, datasize,
    NULL, &status);
cl_mem bufC = clCreateBuffer(context, CL_MEM_WRITE_ONLY, datasize,
    NULL, &status);
```

5. **Copying the input data onto the device:** The next step is to copy data from a host pointer to a buffer. The API call takes a command-queue argument, so data will likely be copied directly to the device. By setting the third argument to CL_TRUE, we can ensure that data is copied before the API call returns.

```
// Write data from the input arrays to the buffers
status = clEnqueueWriteBuffer(cmdQueue, bufA, CL_TRUE, 0,
    datasize, A, 0, NULL, NULL);
status = clEnqueueWriteBuffer(cmdQueue, bufB, CL_TRUE, 0,
    datasize, B, 0, NULL, NULL);
```

6. **Creating and compiling a program from the OpenCL C source code:** The vector addition kernel shown in Listing 3.3 is stored in a character array, programSource, and is used to create a program object which is then compiled. When we compile a program, we also supply the information for each device that the program may target.

```
// Create a program with source code
cl_program program = clCreateProgramWithSource(context, 1,
    (const char**)&programSource, NULL, &status);

// Build (compile) the program for the device
status = clBuildProgram(program, numDevices, devices, NULL,
    NULL, NULL);
```

7. **Extracting the kernel from the program:** The kernel is created by selecting the desired function from within the program.

```
// Create the vector addition kernel
cl_kernel kernel = clCreateKernel(program, "vecadd", &status);
```

8. **Executing the kernel:** Once the kernel has been created and data has been initialized, the buffers are set as arguments to the kernel. A command to execute the kernel can now be enqueued into the command-queue. Along with the kernel, the command requires specification of the NDRange configuration.

```
// Set the kernel arguments
status = clSetKernelArg(kernel, 0, sizeof(cl_mem), &bufA);
status = clSetKernelArg(kernel, 1, sizeof(cl_mem), &bufB);
status = clSetKernelArg(kernel, 2, sizeof(cl_mem), &bufC);

// Define an index space of work-items for execution.
// A work-group size is not required, but can be used.
size_t indexSpaceSize[1], workGroupSize[1];

indexSpaceSize[0] = datasize/sizeof(int);
workGroupSize[0] = 256;
```

```
// Execute the kernel for execution
status = clEnqueueNDRangeKernel(cmdQueue, kernel, 1, NULL,
    indexSpaceSize, workGroupSize, 0, NULL, NULL);
```

9. **Copying output data back to the host:** This step reads data back to a pointer on the host.

```
// Read the device output buffer to the host output array
status = clEnqueueReadBuffer(cmdQueue, bufC, CL_TRUE, 0,
    datasize, C, 0, NULL, NULL);
```

10. **Releasing resources:** Once the kernel has completed execution and the resulting output has been retrieved from the device, the OpenCL resources that were allocated can be freed. This is similar to any C or C++ program where memory allocations, file handles, and other resources are explicitly released by the developer. As shown below, each OpenCL object has its own API calls to release its resources. The OpenCL context should be released last since all OpenCL objects such as buffers and command-queues are bound to a context. This is similar to deleting objects in C++, where member arrays must be freed before the object itself is freed.

```
clReleaseKernel(kernel);
clReleaseProgram(program);
clReleaseCommandQueue(cmdQueue);
clReleaseMemObject(bufA);
clReleaseMemObject(bufB);
clReleaseMemObject(bufC);
clReleaseContext(context);
```

3.6.1 COMPLETE VECTOR ADDITION LISTING

The following is the complete listing for the vector addition example. It follows the same steps from the previous section, but uses the first platform and device for simplicity.

```
1  // This program implements a vector addition using OpenCL
2
3  // System includes
4  #include <stdio.h>
5  #include <stdlib.h>
6  // OpenCL includes
7  #include <CL/cl.h>
8
9  // OpenCL kernel to perform an element-wise addition
10 const char* programSource =
11 "__kernel \n"
12 "void vecadd(__global int *A,            \n"
13 "            __global int *B,            \n"
14 "            __global int *C)             \n"
```

```
15  "{                                                \n"
16  "                                                 \n"
17  "   // Get the work-item's unique ID              \n"
18  "   int idx = get_global_id(0);                   \n"
19  "                                                 \n"
20  "   // Add the corresponding locations of         \n"
21  "   // 'A' and 'B', and store the result in 'C'.  \n"
22  "   C[idx] = A[idx] + B[idx];                     \n"
23  "}                                                \n"
24  ;
25
26  int main() {
27      // This code executes on the OpenCL host
28
29      // Elements in each array
30      const int elements = 2048;
31
32      // Compute the size of the data
33      size_t datasize = sizeof(int)*elements;
34
35      // Allocate space for input/output host data
36      int *A = (int*)malloc(datasize); // Input array
37      int *B = (int*)malloc(datasize); // Input array
38      int *C = (int*)malloc(datasize); // Output array
39
40      // Initialize the input data
41      int i;
42      for(i = 0; i < elements; i++) {
43          A[i] = i;
44          B[i] = i;
45      }
46
47      // Use this to check the output of each API call
48      cl_int status;
49
50      // Get the first platform
51      cl_platform_id platform;
52      status = clGetPlatformIDs(1, &platform, NULL);
53
54      // Get the first device
55      cl_device_id device;
56      status = clGetDeviceIDs(platform, CL_DEVICE_TYPE_ALL, 1, &device,
              NULL);
57
58      // Create a context and associate it with the device
59      cl_context context = clCreateContext(NULL, 1, &device, NULL, NULL,
              &status);
60
61      // Create a command-queue and associate it with the device
62      cl_command_queue cmdQueue = clCreateCommandQueueWithProperties
              (context, device, 0, &status);
63
```

```
64    // Allocate two input buffers and one output buffer for the three
         vectors in the vector addition
65    cl_mem bufA = clCreateBuffer(context, CL_MEM_READ_ONLY, datasize,
         NULL, &status);
66    cl_mem bufB = clCreateBuffer(context, CL_MEM_READ_ONLY, datasize,
         NULL, &status);
67    cl_mem bufC = clCreateBuffer(context, CL_MEM_WRITE_ONLY,
         datasize, NULL, &status);
68
69    // // Write data from the input arrays to the buffers
70    status = clEnqueueWriteBuffer(cmdQueue, bufA, CL_FALSE, 0,
         datasize, A, 0, NULL, NULL);
71    status = clEnqueueWriteBuffer(cmdQueue, bufB, CL_FALSE, 0,
         datasize, B, 0, NULL, NULL);
72
73    // Create a program with source code
74    cl_program program = clCreateProgramWithSource(context, 1,
         (const char**)&programSource, NULL, &status);
75
76    // Build (compile) the program for the device
77    status = clBuildProgram(program, 1, &device, NULL, NULL, NULL);
78
79    // Create the vector addition kernel
80    cl_kernel kernel = clCreateKernel(program, "vecadd", &status);
81
82    // Set the kernel arguments
83    status = clSetKernelArg(kernel, 0, sizeof(cl_mem), &bufA);
84    status = clSetKernelArg(kernel, 1, sizeof(cl_mem), &bufB);
85    status = clSetKernelArg(kernel, 2, sizeof(cl_mem), &bufC);
86
87    // Define an index space of work-items for execution.
88    // A work-group size is not required, but can be used.
89    size_t indexSpaceSize[1], workGroupSize[1];
90
91    // There are 'elements' work-items
92    indexSpaceSize[0] = elements;
93    workGroupSize[0] = 256;
94
95    // Execute the kernel
96    status = clEnqueueNDRangeKernel(cmdQueue, kernel, 1, NULL,
         indexSpaceSize, workGroupSize, 0, NULL, NULL);
97
98    // Read the device output buffer to the host output array
99    status = clEnqueueReadBuffer(cmdQueue, bufC, CL_TRUE, 0,
         datasize, C, 0, NULL, NULL);
100
101   // Free OpenCL resources
102   clReleaseKernel(kernel);
103   clReleaseProgram(program);
104   clReleaseCommandQueue(cmdQueue);
105   clReleaseMemObject(bufA);
106   clReleaseMemObject(bufB);
```

```
107        clReleaseMemObject(bufC);
108        clReleaseContext(context);
109
110        // Free host resources
111        free(A);
112        free(B);
113        free(C);
114
115        return 0;
116    }
```

LISTING 3.4

OpenCL vector addition using the C API.

3.7 VECTOR ADDITION USING AN OpenCL C++ WRAPPER

The Khronos Group has defined a C++ wrapper API to go with the OpenCL standard. The C++ API corresponds closely to the C API (e.g. cl::Memory maps to cl_mem), but offers the benefits of a high-level language such as classes and exception handling. The following source listing provides a vector addition example that corresponds to the C version in Listing 3.4.

```
1   #define __CL_ENABLE_EXCEPTIONS
2
3   #include <CL/cl.hpp>
4   #include <iostream>
5   #include <fstream>
6   #include <string>
7   #include <vector>
8
9   int main() {
10      const int elements = 2048;
11      size_t datasize = sizeof(int)*elements;
12
13      int *A = new int[elements];
14      int *B = new int[elements];
15      int *C = new int[elements];
16
17      for(int i = 0; i < elements; i++) {
18          A[i] = i;
19          B[i] = i;
20      }
21
22      try {
23      // Query for platforms
24      std::vector <cl::Platform> platforms;
25      cl::Platform::get(&platforms);
26
27      // Get a list of devices on this platform
28      std::vector <cl::Device> devices;
```

```
29      platforms [0]. getDevices (CL_DEVICE_TYPE_ALL, &devices);
30
31      // Create a context for the devices
32      cl :: Context context (devices);
33
34      // Create a command-queue for the first device
35      cl :: CommandQueue queue = cl :: CommandQueue (context, devices [0]);
36
37      // Create the memory buffers
38      cl :: Buffer bufferA = cl :: Buffer (context, CL_MEM_READ_ONLY,
            datasize);
39      cl :: Buffer bufferB = cl :: Buffer (context, CL_MEM_READ_ONLY,
            datasize);
40      cl :: Buffer bufferC = cl :: Buffer (context, CL_MEM_WRITE_ONLY,
            datasize);
41
42      // Copy the input data to the input buffers using the
43      // command-queue for the first device
44      queue. enqueueWriteBuffer (bufferA, CL_TRUE, 0, datasize, A);
45      queue. enqueueWriteBuffer (bufferB, CL_TRUE, 0, datasize, B);
46
47      // Read the program source
48      std :: ifstream sourceFile ("vector_add_kernel.cl");
49      std :: string sourceCode (std :: istreambuf_iterator < char > (
            sourceFile),
50          (std :: istreambuf_iterator < char > ()));
51      cl :: Program :: Sources source (1, std :: make_pair (sourceCode. c_str (),
            sourceCode. length () + 1));
52
53      // Create the program from the source code
54      cl :: Program program = cl :: Program (context, source);
55
56      // Build the program for the devices
57      program. build (devices);
58
59      // Create the kernel
60      cl :: Kernel vecadd_kernel (program, "vecadd");
61
62      // Set the kernel arguments
63      vecadd_kernel. setArg (0, bufferA);
64      vecadd_kernel. setArg (1, bufferB);
65      vecadd_kernel. setArg (2, bufferC);
66
67      // Execute the kernel
68      cl :: NDRange global (elements);
69      cl :: NDRange local (256);
70      queue. enqueueNDRangeKernel (vecadd_kernel, cl :: NullRange, global,
            local);
71
72      // Copy the output data back to the host
73      queue. enqueueReadBuffer (bufferC, CL_TRUE, 0, datasize, C);
74  }
```

```
75      catch( cl :: Error error )
76      {
77          std :: cout << error.what() << "(" << error.err() << ")" << std
                :: endl ;
78      }
79      return 0;
80  }
```

LISTING 3.5

OpenCL vector addition with the C++ API.

3.8 OpenCL FOR CUDA PROGRAMMERS

NVIDIA's CUDA C is an API similar to OpenCL. A comparison of OpenCL and CUDA versions of the vector addition example is shown in Listing 3.6. Listing 3.6 shows that OpenCL and CUDA follow a one-to-one mapping for most of their commands. The reason for the additional API calls and function parameters in OpenCL is the fact that platform discovery and program compilation at runtime are required in OpenCL. Since CUDA C targets only NVIDIA's GPUs, there is only a single platform that can be discovered automatically, and the program compilation step to PTX can be done when the host binary is compiled.

With OpenCL, platforms are discovered at runtime, and the program can choose a target device at runtime as well. Program compilation cannot be done prior to runtime because the intermediate language (IL)/ISA of the device that will execute a kernel is unknown. For example, with OpenCL it is perfectly reasonable that a kernel may have been developed and tested on an AMD GPU. However, it would also need to run on an OpenCL-compatible GPU from Intel that has a different ISA. The platform discovery and the runtime compilation of the program makes this possible.

The other major difference between OpenCL and the CUDA C API is that CUDA C provides special operators for kernel launching, with the requirement that code may only be compiled using a toolchain that includes an NVIDIA-supplied preprocessor. The code that the preprocessor generates will end up looking very much like OpenCL code.

```
1   #include <stdio.h>
2   #include <stdlib.h>
3   #include <math.h>
4
5   // CUDA kernel. Each thread computes one element of C
6   __global__ void vecAdd(int *A, int *B, int *C, int elements)
7   {
8       // Compute the global thread ID using CUDA intrinsics
9       int id = blockIdx.x*blockDim.x+threadIdx.x;
10
11      // Must check that the thread is not out of bounds
```

```
12          if (id < elements)
13              C[id] = A[id] + B[id];
14  }
15
16  int main( int argc, char* argv[] )
17  {
18      // Elements in each array
19      const int elements = 2048;
20
21      // Compute the size of the data
22      size_t datasize = sizeof(int)*elements;
23
24      // Allocate space for input/output host data
25      int *A = (int*)malloc(datasize); // Input array
26      int *B = (int*)malloc(datasize); // Input array
27      int *C = (int*)malloc(datasize); // Output array
28
29      // Device input vectors
30      int *bufA;
31      int *bufB;
32      //Device output vector
33      int *bufC;
34
35      // Allocate memory for each vector on GPU
36      cudaMalloc(&bufA, datasize);
37      cudaMalloc(&bufB, datasize);
38      cudaMalloc(&bufC, datasize);
39
40      int i;
41      // Initialize vectors on host
42      for( i = 0; i < elements; i++ ) {
43          A[i] = i;
44          B[i] = i;
45      }
46
47      // Copy host vectors to device
48      cudaMemcpy(bufA, A, datasize, cudaMemcpyHostToDevice);
49      cudaMemcpy(bufB, B, datasize, cudaMemcpyHostToDevice);
50
51      int blockSize, gridSize;
52
53      // Number of threads in each thread block
54      blockSize = 256;
55
56      // Number of thread blocks in grid
57      gridSize = elements/blockSize;
58
59      // Execute the kernel
60      vecAdd<<<gridSize, blockSize>>>(bufA, bufB, bufC, elements);
61
62      // Copy array back to host
63      cudaMemcpy(C, bufC, datasize, cudaMemcpyDeviceToHost);
```

```
64
65        // Release device memory
66        cudaFree(bufA);
67        cudaFree(bufB);
68        cudaFree(bufC);
69
70        // Release host memory
71        free(A);
72        free(B);
73        free(C);
74
75        return 0;
76   }
```

LISTING 3.6

Vector addition using the CUDA C API.

3.9 SUMMARY

In this chapter, we provided an introduction to the basics of using the OpenCL standard when developing parallel programs. We have described the different abstraction models defined in the standard and also presented a basic example of an OpenCL program to place some of the abstraction in context.

REFERENCE

[1] K. Cooper, L. Torczon, Engineering a Compiler, Morgan Kaufmann, Burlington, MA, 2011.

Examples

4.1 OpenCL EXAMPLES

This chapter discusses some basic OpenCL examples, which allow us to summarize our understanding of the specification discussed in Chapter 3. These examples demonstrate the programming steps needed to write complete OpenCL applications. We also include an example using the C++ wrapper application programming interface (API) for developers who have a preference for C++. The examples discussed here will serve as a baseline to compare more optimized code, which can be written after later chapters have been studied.

Table 4.1 summarizes the OpenCL features used by each example discussed in further sections. The reader can use this information to focus on examples of interest.

Full listings of each program are provided at the end of each respective section. Additionally, listings of utility functions used within the examples are provided at the end of the chapter. The utility functions include code to check and report OpenCL errors, to read OpenCL programs in from a file to a string (required for program creation), and to report program compilation errors.

4.2 HISTOGRAM

A histogram is used to count or visualize the frequency of data (i.e. the number of occurrences) over units of discrete intervals, called bins. Histograms have many applications within data and image processing. In this example, we will create a histogram of the frequency of pixel values within a 256-bit image. Figure 4.1 shows a pixel histogram generated for the adjacent input image. This example will illustrate the use of local memory, and local and global atomic operations within an OpenCL kernel.

Conceptually, the histogram algorithm itself is very simple. In the case where each value corresponds to a bin, a histogram could be computed as follows:

Table 4.1 The OpenCL Features Covered by Each Example

Example	Features
Histogram	Local memory, local atomics, global atomics, barriers, memory fences
Image rotation	Images, samplers
Image convolution	C++ API, constant memory, images, samplers
Producer-consumer	Pipes, multiple devices

 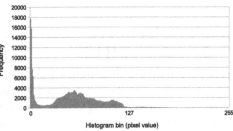

FIGURE 4.1

A histogram generated from a 256-bit image. Each bin corresponds to the frequency of the corresponding pixel value.

```
int histogram[HIST_BINS]

main( ) {
   for (each input value) {
      histogram[value]++
   }
}
```

Unlike the vector addition example in Chapter 3, computing a histogram is not embarrassingly parallel, as the increment operation could lead to a race condition with a multithreaded program. A simple, albeit inefficient, way to parallelize the algorithm would be to use an atomic operation each time a histogram bin is incremented. Consider the pseudocode function below, which could be used to run a multithreaded version of a histogram computation.

```
int histogram[HIST_BINS]

createHistogram( ) {
   for (each of my values) {
      atomic_add(histogram[value], 1)
   }
}
```

```
main( ) {
    for (number of threads) {
        spawn_thread(createHistogram)
    }
}
```

This implementation is inefficient because each update requires an atomic operation. A higher-performance alternative would be to have each thread create a separate local histogram, containing only its values. Once a thread has completed its histogram, the data can be added atomically to the global histogram.

```
int histogram[HIST_BINS]

createHistogram( ) {

    int localHistogram[HIST_BINS]

    for (each of my values) {
        localHistogram[value]++
    }

    for (each bin) {
        atomic_add(histogram[bin], localHistogram[bin])
    }
}

main( ) {
    for (number of threads) {
        spawn_thread(createHistogram)
    }
}
```

In many cases, parallelizing an algorithm for OpenCL is very similar to parallelizing an algorithm for a multithreaded CPU—although the granularity of decomposition may differ. As with the first multithreaded CPU algorithm, it would be inefficient for the OpenCL algorithm to have work-items reading values and incrementing bins from a shared histogram in global memory. As we will discuss in Chapter 8, global memory accesses on GPUs are very inefficient compared with register or local memory accesses. As with the multithreaded CPU implementation, the large number of atomic operations on the same location would further degrade performance.

However, we also would not want to create a local copy of the histogram per work-item. GPUs store their private work-item data in registers, and when registers run out, spilling occurs to global memory and is very detrimental to performance.

The best approach is then to create a local version of the histogram per work-group. Work-items within a work-group have shared access to local memory, which on GPU architectures is mapped to fast on-chip memory. As with the second version of the multithreaded CPU algorithm, after the work-group has finished creating its local copy of the histogram, it can perform a single pass of atomic writes to the shared global memory histogram. However, implementing a per-work-group histogram comes with one additional wrinkle: we now have race conditions within local memory. This is where some architectural knowledge of the target device is required. For many GPUs, atomic accesses to local memory are fairly efficient. On AMD Radeon GPUs, atomic units are built into on-chip scratchpad storage. Therefore, atomic operations on local memory are much less costly than atomic accesses to global memory. Therefore, in the following example we will use local atomic operations when generating local histograms.

An OpenCL kernel for this implementation of a histogram algorithm might be follows:

```
1
2   #define HIST_BINS 256
3
4   __kernel
5   void histogram(__global int *data,
6                              int  numData,
7                       __global int *histogram)
8   {
9       __local int localHistogram[HIST_BINS];
10      int lid = get_local_id(0);
11      int gid = get_global_id(0);
12
13      /* Initialize local histogram to zero */
14      for (int i = lid;
15          i < HIST_BINS;
16          i += get_local_size(0))
17      {
18          localHistogram[i] = 0;
19      }
20
21      /* Wait until all work-items within
22       * the work-group have completed their stores */
23      barrier(CLK_LOCAL_MEM_FENCE);
24
25      /* Compute local histogram */
26      for (int i = gid;
27          i < numData;
28          i += get_global_size(0))
29      {
30          atomic_add(&localHistogram[data[i]], 1);
31      }
32
33      /* Wait until all work-items within
34       * the work-group have completed their stores */
35      barrier(CLK_LOCAL_MEM_FENCE);
36
```

```
37        /* Write the local histogram out to
38         * the global histogram */
39        for (int i = lid;
40              i < HIST_BINS;
41              i += get_local_size(0))
42        {
43            atomic_add(&histogram[i], localHistogram[i]);
44        }
45   }
```

LISTING 4.1

Histogram kernel in OpenCL.

The implementation of the histogram algorithm as shown in Listing 4.1 comprises five steps:

1. Initialize the local histogram bins to zero (Line 14).
2. Synchronize to ensure that all updates have completed (Line 23).
3. Compute the local histogram (Line 26).
4. Synchronize again to ensure that all updates have completed (Line 35).
5. Write the local histogram out to global memory (Line 39).

Steps 1, 3, and 5 illustrate a common OpenCL technique for reading data from, or writing data to a shared location (global or local memory). When we need each location to be accessed by only a single work-item, we can begin with a work-item's unique ID and stride by the size of the total number of work-items (i.e. the work-group size when accessing local memory, or the NDRange size when accessing global memory). In step 1, we stride by the work-group size to initialize each value in the local histogram to zero. This allows our code to change work-group sizes, potentially as a performance optimization, and still remain functionally correct. Step 3 uses the same technique to read from global memory, and step 5 again uses the technique to write out of local memory.

Steps 2 and 4 use a barrier to synchronize between steps, and specify a memory fence to ensure that all work-items in the work-group have the same view of memory before proceeding. Barriers and memory fences will be discussed in detail in Chapter 7. For now it is sufficient to understand that all work-items in the work-group must reach the barrier before any of them can proceed past it, and the local memory fence ensures that all updates to local memory are visible to the entire work-group when the barrier completes.

For the updates to the global histogram to generate correct results, we also need to initialize the global histogram's values to zero. The most straightforward way to initialize the buffer is to use the host API call clEnqueueFillBuffer() after the buffer has been created. The signature for clEnqueueFillBuffer() is as follows:

```
cl_int
clEnqueueFillBuffer(
    cl_command_queue command_queue,
    cl_mem buffer,
```

```
const void *pattern,
size_t pattern_size,
size_t offset,
size_t size,
cl_uint num_events_in_wait_list,
const cl_event *event_wait_list,
cl_event *event)
```

A call to `clEnqueueFillBuffer()` is similar to the C `memset()` function. The parameter `buffer` is the memory object that will be initialized with the data specified by `pattern`. Unlike `memset()`, the pattern for `clEnqueueFillBuffer()` can be specified in any scalar or vector integer or floating point data type supported by OpenCL. The parameter `pattern_size` specifies the size of the type holding the pattern. The parameter `size` is used to specify the number of bytes to initialize, and must be a multiple of `pattern_size`. Providing an `offset` begins initialization at an offset within the buffer.

Aside from initializing the histogram buffer, the host-side program is very similar to the host program in the vector addition example in Chapter 3. Listing 4.2 provides the complete source code for the histogram host program. The kernel source in Listing 4.1 would need to be stored in a file named `histogram.cl` to be read in by Listing 4.2. Note that the code utilizes a few helper functions provided in Section 4.6. The functions to read and write BMP files are provided with the full code package online (http://booksite.elsevier.com/9780128014141).

```
1   /* System includes */
2   #include <stdio.h>
3   #include <stdlib.h>
4   #include <string.h>
5
6   /* OpenCL includes */
7   #include <CL/cl.h>
8
9   /* Utility functions */
10  #include "utils.h"
11  #include "bmp-utils.h"
12
13  static const int HIST_BINS = 256;
14
15  int main(int argc, char **argv)
16  {
17      /* Host data */
18      int *hInputImage = NULL;
19      int *hOutputHistogram = NULL;
20
21      /* Allocate space for the input image and read the
22       * data from disk */
23      int imageRows;
24      int imageCols;
```

```
25      hInputImage = readBmp(".././Images/cat.bmp", &imageRows, &
            imageCols);
26      const int imageElements = imageRows*imageCols;
27      const size_t imageSize = imageElements*sizeof(int);
28
29      /* Allocate space for the histogram on the host */
30      const int histogramSize = HIST_BINS*sizeof(int);
31      hOutputHistogram = (int*)malloc(histogramSize);
32      if (!hOutputHistogram) { exit(-1); }
33
34      /* Use this to check the output of each API call */
35      cl_int status;
36
37      /* Get the first platform */
38      cl_platform_id platform;
39      status = clGetPlatformIDs(1, &platform, NULL);
40      check(status);
41
42      /* Get the first device */
43      cl_device_id device;
44      status = clGetDeviceIDs(platform, CL_DEVICE_TYPE_GPU, 1, &device,
            NULL);
45      check(status);
46
47      /* Create a context and associate it with the device */
48      cl_context context;
49      context = clCreateContext(NULL, 1, &device, NULL, NULL, &status);
50      check(status);
51
52      /* Create a command-queue and associate it with the device */
53      cl_command_queue cmdQueue;
54      cmdQueue = clCreateCommandQueue(context, device, 0, &status);
55      check(status);
56
57      /* Create a buffer object for the input image */
58      cl_mem bufInputImage;
59      bufInputImage = clCreateBuffer(context, CL_MEM_READ_ONLY,
            imageSize, NULL,
60              &status);
61      check(status);
62
63      /* Create a buffer object for the output histogram */
64      cl_mem bufOutputHistogram;
65      bufOutputHistogram = clCreateBuffer(context, CL_MEM_WRITE_ONLY,
66          histogramSize, NULL, &status);
67      check(status);
68
69      /* Write the input image to the device */
70      status = clEnqueueWriteBuffer(cmdQueue, bufInputImage, CL_TRUE,
71          0, imageSize,
72              hInputImage, 0, NULL, NULL);
73      check(status);
```

```
74
75    /* Initialize the output histogram with zeros */
76    int zero = 0;
77    status = clEnqueueFillBuffer(cmdQueue, bufOutputHistogram, &zero,
78         sizeof(int), 0, histogramSize, 0, NULL, NULL);
79    check(status);
80
81    /* Create a program with source code */
82    char *programSource = readFile("histogram.cl");
83    size_t programSourceLen = strlen(programSource);
84    cl_program program = clCreateProgramWithSource(context, 1,
85       (const char**)&programSource, &programSourceLen, &status);
86    check(status);
87
88    /* Build (compile) the program for the device */
89    status = clBuildProgram(program, 1, &device, NULL, NULL, NULL);
90    if (status != CL_SUCCESS) {
91        printCompilerError(program, device);
92        exit(-1);
93    }
94
95    /* Create the kernel */
96    cl_kernel kernel;
97    kernel = clCreateKernel(program, "histogram", &status);
98    check(status);
99
100   /* Set the kernel arguments */
101   status  = clSetKernelArg(kernel, 0, sizeof(cl_mem), &
102       bufInputImage);
103   status |= clSetKernelArg(kernel, 1, sizeof(int), &imageElements);
104   status |= clSetKernelArg(kernel, 2, sizeof(cl_mem), &
          bufOutputHistogram);
105   check(status);
106
107   /* Define the index space and work-group size */
108   size_t globalWorkSize[1];
109   globalWorkSize[0] = 1024;
110
111   size_t localWorkSize[1];
112   localWorkSize[0] = 64;
113
114   /* Enqueue the kernel for execution */
115   status = clEnqueueNDRangeKernel(cmdQueue, kernel, 1, NULL,
116       globalWorkSize, localWorkSize, 0, NULL, NULL);
117   check(status);
118
119   /* Read the output histogram buffer to the host */
120   status = clEnqueueReadBuffer(cmdQueue, bufOutputHistogram,
121        CL_TRUE, 0,
122          histogramSize, hOutputHistogram, 0, NULL, NULL);
123   check(status);
124
```

```
125      /* Free OpenCL resources */
126      clReleaseKernel(kernel);
127      clReleaseProgram(program);
128      clReleaseCommandQueue(cmdQueue);
129      clReleaseMemObject(bufInputImage);
130      clReleaseMemObject(bufOutputHistogram);
131      clReleaseContext(context);
132
133      /* Free host resources */
134      free(hInputImage);
135      free(hOutputHistogram);
136      free(programSource);
137
138      return 0;
139  }
```

LISTING 4.2

Full source code for the histogram host program. Note that `check(cl_int status)` is a utility function that compares the command status to `CL_SUCCESS`.

4.3 IMAGE ROTATION

Rotation is a common image processing routine with applications in matching, alignment, and other image-based algorithms. The input to an image rotation routine is an image, the rotation angle θ, and a point about which rotation is done, with an example result shown in Figure 4.2.

The coordinates of a point (x, y) when rotated by an angle θ around (x_0, y_0) become (x', y'), as shown by the following equations:

Original image

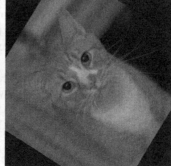
After rotation of 45°

FIGURE 4.2

An image rotated by 45°. Pixels that correspond to an out-of-bounds location in the input image are returned as black.

$$x' = \cos\theta(x - x_0) + \sin\theta(y - y_0),$$
$$y' = -\sin\theta(x - x_0) + \cos\theta(y - y_0).$$

From the equations, it is clear that the pixel that will be stored in each output location (x', y') can be computed independently. Note that for each output location, the input location will likely not be an integer value. Therefore, we will take advantage of OpenCL's built-in support for floating-point coordinates and linear interpolation to provide a higher-quality result when producing the output image.

By having each work-item correspond to an output location, we can intuitively map each work-item's global ID to (x', y') in the previous equations. We can also determine (x_0, y_0), which corresponds to the center of the image, as soon as we load the image from disk. We therefore have two equations and two unknowns, which allows us to compute the location read by each work-item when computing the rotation:

$$x = x'\cos\theta - y'\sin\theta + x_0,$$
$$y = x'\sin\theta + y'\cos\theta + y_0.$$

This corresponds to the following OpenCL C pseudocode:

```
gidx = get_global_id(0)
gidy = get_global_id(1)
x0   = width/2
y0   = height/2
x    = gidx*cos(theta) - gidy*sin(theta) + x0
y    = gidx*sin(theta) + gidy*cos(theta) + y0
```

Listing 4.3 shows the implementation of an OpenCL kernel that performs image rotation. As discussed in Chapter 3, images are opaque objects and must be accessed using functions based on the data type. In this kernel, we use read_imagef() (Line 38), since we are working with floating-point data. As with all functions used to access an image, read_imagef() returns a 4-wide vector data type. Since we are working with a single-channel image (described next), we are interested only in the first component, which we can access by appending .x to the end of the function call (Line 38). The call to write to an image also takes a 4-wide vector regardless of the actual data type, but will be handled appropriately by the hardware. Therefore, on the call to write_imagef(), we must cast the result to a float4 vector (Line 41).

```
1   __constant sampler_t sampler =
2       CLK_NORMALIZED_COORDS_FALSE |
3       CLK_FILTER_LINEAR            |
4       CLK_ADDRESS_CLAMP;
5
6   __kernel
7   void rotation(
8       __read_only image2d_t inputImage,
9       __write_only image2d_t outputImage,
```

```
10                            int imageWidth,
11                            int imageHeight,
12                            float theta)
13    {
14        /* Get global ID for output coordinates */
15        int x = get_global_id(0);
16        int y = get_global_id(1);
17
18        /* Compute image center */
19        float x0 = imageWidth/2.0f;
20        float y0 = imageHeight/2.0f;
21
22        /* Compute the work-item's location relative
23         * to the image center */
24        int xprime = x-x0;
25        int yprime = y-y0;
26
27        /* Compute sine and cosine */
28        float sinTheta = sin(theta);
29        float cosTheta = cos(theta);
30
31        /* Compute the input location */
32        float2 readCoord;
33        readCoord.x = xprime*cosTheta - yprime*sinTheta + x0;
34        readCoord.y = xprime*sinTheta + yprime*cosTheta + y0;
35
36        /* Read the input image */
37        float value;
38        value = read_imagef(inputImage, sampler, readCoord).x;
39
40        /* Write the output image */
41        write_imagef(outputImage, (int2)(x, y), (float4)(value, 0.f, 0.f,
              0.f));
42    }
```

LISTING 4.3

Image rotation kernel.

The image sampler (`sampler_t sampler`) in Listing 4.3 is used to describe how to access an image. Samplers specify the type of coordinate system used when accessing the image, what to do when out-of-bounds accesses occur, and whether or not to interpolate if an access lies between multiple indices.

The coordinate system can either be normalized (i.e. range from 0 to 1) or use pixel-based integer addresses. Providing `CLK_NORMALIZED_COORDS_FALSE` specifies that we will be using pixel-based addressing. OpenCL also allows a number of addressing modes to be used for handling out-of-bounds accesses. For this example, we use `CL_ADDRESS_CLAMP`, specifying that the value produced by an out-of-bounds access is 0 for channels `RG` and `B`, and it returns either 0 or 1 for channel `A` (on the basis of the image format). The result is that out-of-bounds pixels are returned as black. Finally, the sampler allows us to specify a filtering mode. The filtering mode determines how a value is obtained from the coordinates provided by the image access. The option CLK_FILTER_NEAREST simply returns the image element that is nearest to the coordinate provided. Alternatively, CLK_FILTER_LINEAR provides a linear interpolation of the surrounding pixels. For this image rotation example, we will use linear interpolation to provide a higher-quality rotated image.

In previous versions of OpenCL, the size of the global work-item configuration for the NDRange had to be a multiple of the work-group size in each dimension. This would often lead to cases where the NDRange size was larger than the data to which it was being mapped. When this occurred, programmers would have to pass metadata to the kernel to identify which work-items were valid—for example, the image width and height would be needed for the kernel in this example. Out-of-bounds work-items would have to be excluded from computation, sometimes leading to strange or inefficient code. In OpenCL 2.0, devices are required to support NDRanges whose work-groups can be a variable size at the boundaries. These are referred to as *remainder work-groups* and are discussed in Chapter 5. This new feature of OpenCL allows the kernel in Listing 4.3 to be concise and efficient.

As with the previous example, the setup for this program is similar to that for the vector addition program. The creation of the images used in the kernel is the distinguishing feature of this example. After reading in the input image from a file in the host code, we will convert the elements to single-precision floating-point data, and use this to seed our OpenCL image object.

Allocating image objects to hold the input and output images is done using the clCreateImage() API call. When the image is being created, the number of dimensions (e.g. one, two, or three) and the size of the image are specified by an image descriptor (type cl_image_desc). The pixel type and channel layout within the image are specified using an image format (type cl_image_format). Recall from Chapter 3 that every element of an image stores data in up to four channels, with the channels enumerated as R, G, B, and A. Thus, an image that will hold a four-element vector type should use CL_RGBA for the channel order within the image format. Alternatively, in an image where each pixel is represented as a single value (e.g. a pixel from a grayscale image or an element of a matrix), the data can be specified to use only a single channel by specifying CL_R for the channel order. This example assumes grayscale data and so only uses a single channel. When specifying the data type within the image format, one specifies integer types by a combination of signedness and size. For example, CL_SIGNED_INT32 is a 32-bit signed integer, and CL_UNSIGNED_INT8 is the equivalent of an unsigned character in C. Single-precision floating-point data is specified by CL_FLOAT, and is the type of data used in the example.

Listing 4.4 shows the host code used to create the input and output images for this example. After the image has been created, we use the API call clEnqueueWriteImage() to transfer the input data from the host into the image object.

```
1  /* The image descriptor describes how the data will be stored
2   * in memory. This descriptor initializes a 2D image with no pitch */
3  cl_image_desc desc;
4  desc.image_type = CL_MEM_OBJECT_IMAGE2D;
5  desc.image_width = width;
6  desc.image_height = height;
7  desc.image_depth = 0;
8  desc.image_array_size = 0;
9  desc.image_row_pitch = 0;
10 desc.image_slice_pitch = 0;
11 desc.num_mip_levels = 0;
12 desc.num_samples = 0;
13 desc.buffer = NULL;
14
15 /* The image format describes the properties of each pixel */
16 cl_image_format format;
17 format.image_channel_order = CL_R; // single channel
18 format.image_channel_data_type = CL_FLOAT;
19
20 /* Create the input image and initialize it using a
21  * pointer to the image data on the host. */
22 cl_mem inputImage = clCreateImage(context, CL_MEM_READ_ONLY,
23    &format, &desc, NULL, NULL);
24
25 /* Create the output image */
26 cl_mem outputImage = clCreateImage(context, CL_MEM_WRITE_ONLY,
27    &format, &desc, NULL, NULL);
28
29 /* Copy the host image data to the device */
30 size_t origin[3] = {0, 0, 0}; // Offset within the image to copy from
31 size_t region[3] = {width, height, 1}; // Elements to per dimension
32 clEnqueueWriteImage(queue, inputImage, CL_TRUE,
33    origin, region, 0 /* row-pitch */, 0 /* slice-pitch */,
34    hostInputImage, 0, NULL, NULL);
```

LISTING 4.4

Creation of image objects for the rotation example.

The complete source code for the image rotation host program is provided in Listing 4.5.

```
1  /* System includes */
2  #include <stdio.h>
3  #include <stdlib.h>
4  #include <string.h>
5
6  /* OpenCL includes */
7  #include <CL/cl.h>
8
9  /* Utility functions */
10 #include "utils.h"
11 #include "bmp-utils.h"
```

```
12
13   int main(int argc, char **argv)
14   {
15      /* Host data */
16      float *hInputImage = NULL;
17      float *hOutputImage = NULL;
18
19      /* Angle for rotation (degrees) */
20      const float theta = 45.0f;
21
22      /* Allocate space for the input image and read the
23       * data from disk */
24      int imageRows;
25      int imageCols;
26      hInputImage = readBmpFloat("cat.bmp", &imageRows, &imageCols);
27      const int imageElements = imageRows*imageCols;
28      const size_t imageSize = imageElements*sizeof(float);
29
30      /* Allocate space for the output image */
31      hOutputImage = (float*)malloc(imageSize);
32      if (!hOutputImage) { exit(-1); }
33
34      /* Use this to check the output of each API call */
35      cl_int status;
36
37      /* Get the first platform */
38      cl_platform_id platform;
39      status = clGetPlatformIDs(1, &platform, NULL);
40      check(status);
41
42      /* Get the first device */
43      cl_device_id device;
44      status = clGetDeviceIDs(platform, CL_DEVICE_TYPE_GPU, 1, &device,
             NULL);
45      check(status);
46
47      /* Create a context and associate it with the device */
48      cl_context context;
49      context = clCreateContext(NULL, 1, &device, NULL, NULL, &status);
50      check(status);
51
52      /* Create a command-queue and associate it with the device */
53      cl_command_queue cmdQueue;
54      cmdQueue = clCreateCommandQueue(context, device, 0, &status);
55      check(status);
56
57      /* The image descriptor describes how the data will be stored
58       * in memory. This descriptor initializes a 2D image with no
             pitch */
59      cl_image_desc desc;
60      desc.image_type = CL_MEM_OBJECT_IMAGE2D;
61      desc.image_width = imageCols;
```

```
62    desc.image_height = imageRows;
63    desc.image_depth = 0;
64    desc.image_array_size = 0;
65    desc.image_row_pitch = 0;
66    desc.image_slice_pitch = 0;
67    desc.num_mip_levels = 0;
68    desc.num_samples = 0;
69    desc.buffer = NULL;
70
71    /* The image format describes the properties of each pixel */
72    cl_image_format format;
73    format.image_channel_order = CL_R; // single channel
74    format.image_channel_data_type = CL_FLOAT;
75
76    /* Create the input image and initialize it using a
77     * pointer to the image data on the host. */
78    cl_mem inputImage = clCreateImage(context, CL_MEM_READ_ONLY,
79        &format, &desc, NULL, NULL);
80
81    /* Create the output image */
82    cl_mem outputImage = clCreateImage(context, CL_MEM_WRITE_ONLY,
83        &format, &desc, NULL, NULL);
84
85    /* Copy the host image data to the device */
86    size_t origin[3] = {0, 0, 0}; // Offset within the image to copy
                                     from
87    size_t region[3] = {imageCols, imageRows, 1}; // Elements to per
                                     dimension
88    clEnqueueWriteImage(cmdQueue, inputImage, CL_TRUE,
89        origin, region, 0 /* row-pitch */, 0 /* slice-pitch */,
90        hInputImage, 0, NULL, NULL);
91
92    /* Create a program with source code */
93    char *programSource = readFile("image-rotation.cl");
94    size_t programSourceLen = strlen(programSource);
95    cl_program program = clCreateProgramWithSource(context, 1,
96        (const char**)&programSource, &programSourceLen, &status);
97    check(status);
98
99    /* Build (compile) the program for the device */
100   status = clBuildProgram(program, 1, &device, NULL, NULL, NULL);
101   if (status != CL_SUCCESS) {
102       printCompilerError(program, device);
103       exit(-1);
104   }
105
106   /* Create the kernel */
107   cl_kernel kernel;
108   kernel = clCreateKernel(program, "rotation", &status);
109   check(status);
110
111   /* Set the kernel arguments */
```

```
112      status  = clSetKernelArg(kernel , 0, sizeof(cl_mem), &inputImage);
113      status |= clSetKernelArg(kernel , 1, sizeof(cl_mem), &outputImage);
114      status |= clSetKernelArg(kernel , 2, sizeof(int), &imageCols);
115      status |= clSetKernelArg(kernel , 3, sizeof(int), &imageRows);
116      status |= clSetKernelArg(kernel , 4, sizeof(float), &theta);
117      check(status);
118
119      /* Define the index space and work−group size */
120      size_t globalWorkSize[2];
121      globalWorkSize[0] = imageCols;
122      globalWorkSize[1] = imageRows;
123
124      size_t localWorkSize[2];
125      localWorkSize[0] = 8;
126      localWorkSize[1] = 8;
127
128      /* Enqueue the kernel for execution */
129      status = clEnqueueNDRangeKernel(cmdQueue, kernel , 2, NULL,
130          globalWorkSize, localWorkSize , 0, NULL, NULL);
131      check(status);
132
133      /* Read the output image buffer to the host */
134      status = clEnqueueReadImage(cmdQueue, outputImage , CL_TRUE,
135          origin , region , 0 /* row−pitch */, 0 /* slice−pitch */,
136          hOutputImage, 0, NULL, NULL);
137      check(status);
138
139      /* Write the output image to file */
140      writeBmpFloat(hOutputImage, "rotated−cat.bmp", imageRows,
             imageCols, "cat.bmp");
141
142      /* Free OpenCL resources */
143      clReleaseKernel(kernel);
144      clReleaseProgram(program);
145      clReleaseCommandQueue(cmdQueue);
146      clReleaseMemObject(inputImage);
147      clReleaseMemObject(outputImage);
148      clReleaseContext(context);
149
150
151      /* Free host resources */
152      free(hInputImage);
153      free(hOutputImage);
154      free(programSource);
155
156      return 0;
157  }
```

LISTING 4.5

Full source code for the image rotation host program.

4.4 IMAGE CONVOLUTION

In image processing, convolution is a commonly used algorithm that modifies the value of each pixel in an image by using information from neighboring pixels. A convolution kernel, or *filter*, describes how each pixel will be influenced by its neighbors. For example, a blurring filter will take the weighted average of neighboring pixels so that large differences between pixel values are reduced. By using the same source image and changing only the filter, one can produce effects such as sharpening, blurring, edge enhancing, and embossing.

Convolution algorithms works by iterating over each pixel in the source image. For each source pixel, the filter is centered over the pixel, and the values of the filter multiply the pixel values that they overlay. A sum of the products is then taken to produce a new pixel value. Figure 4.3 provides a visual representation for this algorithm. Figure 4.4b shows the effect of a blurring filter and Figure 4.4c shows the effect of an embossing filter on the same source image seen in Figure 4.4a.

The code shown in Listing 4.6 performs a serial convolution in C/C++. The two outer loops iterate over pixels in the source image, selecting the next source pixel. At each source pixel, the filter is applied to the neighboring pixels. Notice that the filter can try to access pixels that are out-of-bounds. To handle this situation, we provide four explicit checks within the innermost loop to set the out-of-bounds coordinate to the nearest border pixel.

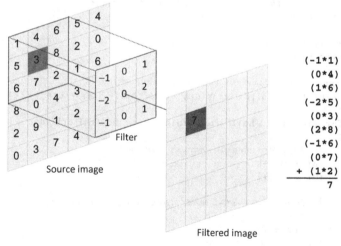

FIGURE 4.3

Applying a convolution filter to a source image.

(a)   (b)   (c)

FIGURE 4.4

The effect of different convolution filters applied to the same source image: (a) the original image; (b) blurring filter; and (c) embossing filter.

```
1    /* Iterate over the rows of the source image */
2    for (int i = 0; i < rows; i++)
3    {
4        /* Iterate over the columns of the source image */
5        for (int j = 0; j < cols; j++)
6        {
7            /* Reset sum for new source pixel */
8            int sum = 0;
9
10           /* Apply the filter to the neighborhood */
11           for (int k = -halfFilterWidth; k <= halfFilterWidth; k++)
12           {
13               for (int l = -halfFilterWidth; l <= halfFilterWidth; l++)
14               {
15                   /* Indices used to access the image */
16                   int r = i+k;
17                   int c = j+l;
18
19                   /* Handle out-of-bounds locations by clamping to
20                    * the border pixel */
21                   r = (r < 0) ? 0 : r;
22                   c = (c < 0) ? 0 : c;
23                   r = (r >= rows) ? rows-1 : r;
24                   c = (c >= cols) ? cols-1 : c;
25
26                   sum += Image[r][c] *
27                           Filter[k+halfFilterWidth][l+halfFilterWidth];
```

```
28                }
29            }
30
31            /* Write the new pixel value */
32            outputImage[i][j] = sum;
33        }
34    }
```

LISTING 4.6

Serial implementation of image convolution.

In OpenCL, using image memory objects to implement a convolution has a few advantages over an implementation using buffers. Image sampling comes with options to automatically handle out-of-bounds accesses (as we saw in the image rotation example), and also provides optimized caching of two-dimensional data (covered in Chapter 7).

The OpenCL implementation of the convolution kernel is fairly straightforward, and is written similarly to the C version. In the OpenCL version, we create one work-item per output pixel, using parallelism to remove the two outer loops from Listing 4.6. The task of each work-item is to execute the two innermost loops, which perform the filtering operation. As in the previous example, reads from the source image must be performed using an OpenCL construct that is specific to the data type. For this example, read_imagef() is used again. The full OpenCL kernel is shown in Listing 4.7.

Accesses to an image always return a four-element vector (one per channel). In the previous example, we appended .x to the image access function to return the first component. In this example, we will declare both pixel (the value returned by the image access) and sum (resultant data that is copied to the output image) as type float4. We then use the x-component when accumulating the filtered pixel value (Line 45).

The convolution filter is a perfect candidate for constant memory in this example because all work-items access the same element each iteration. Simply adding the keyword __constant in the signature of the function (Line 7) places the filter in constant memory.

```
1    __kernel
2    void convolution(
3                __read_only image2d_t inputImage,
4                __write_only image2d_t outputImage,
5                            int rows,
6                            int cols,
7                __constant float* filter,
8                            int filterWidth,
9                        sampler_t sampler)
10   {
11       /* Store each work-item's unique row and column */
12       int column = get_global_id(0);
13       int row = get_global_id(1);
```

```
14
15      /* Half the width of the filter is needed for indexing
16       * memory later */
17      int halfWidth = (int)(filterWidth/2);
18
19      /* All accesses to images return data as four-element vectors
20       * (i.e., float4), although only the      x      component will contain
21       * meaningful data in this code */
22      float4 sum = {0.0f, 0.0f, 0.0f, 0.0f};
23
24      /* Iterator for the filter */
25      int filterIdx = 0;
26
27      /* Each work-item iterates around its local area on the basis of
         the
28       * size of the filter */
29      int2 coords; // Coordinates for accessing the image
30
31      /* Iterate the filter rows */
32      for(int i = -halfWidth; i <= halfWidth; i++)
33      {
34          coords.y = row + i;
35          /* Iterate over the filter columns */
36          for(int j = -halfWidth; j <= halfWidth; j++)
37          {
38              coords.x = column + j;
39
40              /* Read a pixel from the image. A single-channel image
41               * stores the pixel in the      x      coordinate of the returned
42               * vector. */
43                  float4 pixel;
44              pixel = read_imagef(inputImage, sampler, coords);
45              sum.x += pixel.x * filter[filterIdx++];
46          }
47      }
48
49      /* Copy the data to the output image */
50      coords.x = column;
51      coords.y = row;
52      write_imagef(outputImage, coords, sum);
53  }
```

LISTING 4.7

Image convolution kernel using OpenCL images.

In the previous example, we created the sampler directly from within the kernel. In this example, we create a sampler using the host API and pass it as a kernel argument. For this example, we will be using the C++ API (the C++ sampler constructor has identical parameters).

The host API signature to create a sampler in C is as follows:

```
cl_sampler clCreateSampler(
    cl_context context,
    cl_bool normalized_coords,
    cl_addressing_mode addressing_mode,
    cl_filter_mode filter_mode,
    cl_int *errcode_ret)
```

With use of the C++ API, the signature is as follows:

```
cl::Sampler::Sampler(
    const Context& context,
    cl_bool normalized_coords,
    cl_addressing_mode addressing_mode,
    cl_filter_mode filter_mode,
    cl_int * err = NULL)
```

The sampler utilized by our kernel could therefore be created as follows:

```
cl::Sampler sampler = new cl::Sampler(context, CL_FALSE,
    CLK_ADDRESS_CLAMP_TO_EDGE, CLK_FILTER_NEAREST);
```

As in the rotation example, this sampler uses unnormalized coordinates. However, here we show two different options for the remaining sampler parameters: the filtering mode returns the nearest pixel without interpolation (CLK_FILTER_NEAREST), and the addressing mode for out-of-bounds accesses returns the nearest border pixel (CL_ADDRESS_CLAMP_TO_EDGE).

With the C++ API, a two-dimensional image is created using the Image2D class, which requires an ImageFormat object as an argument. Unlike with the C API, an image descriptor is not required.

The signatures for the Image2D and ImageFormat constructors are as follows:

```
cl::Image2D::Image2D(
    Context& context,
    cl_mem_flags flags,
    ImageFormat format,
    ::size_t width,
    ::size_t height,
    ::size_t row_pitch = 0,
    void * host_ptr = NULL,
    cl_int * err = NULL)

cl::ImageFormat::ImageFormat(
    cl_channel_order order,
    cl_channel_type type)
```

We can therefore create the input and output images used for the convolution using calls such as

```
cl::ImageFormat imageFormat = cl::ImageFormat(CL_R, CL_FLOAT);
cl::Image2D inputImage = cl::Image2D(context, CL_MEM_READ_ONLY,
    imageFormat, imageCols, imageRows);
cl::Image2D outputImage = cl::Image2D(context, CL_MEM_WRITE_ONLY,
    imageFormat, imageCols, imageRows);
```

The full source code listing for the image convolution host program using the C++ API is provided in Listing 4.8. In the host program, a 5 × 5 Gaussian blurring filter is used for the convolution.

```
1  #define __CL_ENABLE_EXCEPTIONS
2
3  #include <CL/cl.hpp>
4  #include <fstream>
5  #include <iostream>
6  #include <vector>
7
8  #include "utils.h"
9  #include "bmp-utils.h"
10
11 static const char* inputImagePath = "../../Images/cat.bmp";
12
13 static float gaussianBlurFilter[25] = {
14     1.0f/273.0f,  4.0f/273.0f,  7.0f/273.0f,  4.0f/273.0f,  1.0f/273.0f,
15     4.0f/273.0f, 16.0f/273.0f, 26.0f/273.0f, 16.0f/273.0f,  4.0f/273.0f,
16     7.0f/273.0f, 26.0f/273.0f, 41.0f/273.0f, 26.0f/273.0f,  7.0f/273.0f,
17     4.0f/273.0f, 16.0f/273.0f, 26.0f/273.0f, 16.0f/273.0f,  4.0f/273.0f,
18     1.0f/273.0f,  4.0f/273.0f,  7.0f/273.0f,  4.0f/273.0f,  1.0f/273.0f
           };
19 static const int gaussianBlurFilterWidth = 5;
20
21 int main()
22 {
23     float *hInputImage;
24     float *hOutputImage;
25
26     int imageRows;
27     int imageCols;
28
29     /* Set the filter here */
30     int filterWidth = gaussianBlurFilterWidth;
31     float *filter = gaussianBlurFilter;
32
33     /* Read in the BMP image */
34     hInputImage = readBmpFloat(inputImagePath, &imageRows, &imageCols);
35
36     /* Allocate space for the output image */
37     hOutputImage = new float [imageRows*imageCols];
38
39     try
40     {
41         /* Query for platforms */
```

```
42        std :: vector <cl :: Platform > platforms ;
43        cl :: Platform :: get(& platforms );
44
45        /* Get a list of devices on this platform */
46        std :: vector <cl :: Device > devices ;
47        platforms [0]. getDevices (CL_DEVICE_TYPE_GPU, &devices );
48
49        /* Create a context for the devices */
50        cl :: Context context ( devices );
51
52        /* Create a command−queue for the first device */
53        cl :: CommandQueue queue = cl :: CommandQueue ( context , devices [0]);
54
55        /* Create the images */
56        cl :: ImageFormat imageFormat = cl :: ImageFormat(CL_R, CL_FLOAT);
57        cl :: Image2D inputImage = cl :: Image2D ( context , CL_MEM_READ_ONLY,
58            imageFormat , imageCols , imageRows );
59        cl :: Image2D outputImage = cl :: Image2D ( context ,
60            CL_MEM_WRITE_ONLY,
61            imageFormat , imageCols , imageRows );
62
63        /* Create a buffer for the filter */
64        cl :: Buffer filterBuffer = cl :: Buffer ( context , CL_MEM_READ_ONLY,
65            filterWidth ∗ filterWidth ∗ sizeof ( float ));
66
67        /* Copy the input data to the input image */
68        cl :: size_t <3> origin ;
69        origin [0] = 0;
70        origin [1] = 0;
71        origin [2] = 0;
72        cl :: size_t <3> region ;
73        region [0] = imageCols ;
74        region [1] = imageRows ;
75        region [2] = 1;
76        queue . enqueueWriteImage ( inputImage , CL_TRUE, origin , region ,
77            0, 0,
78            hInputImage );
79
80        /* Copy the filter to the buffer */
81        queue . enqueueWriteBuffer ( filterBuffer , CL_TRUE, 0,
82            filterWidth ∗ filterWidth ∗ sizeof ( float ), filter );
83
84
85        /* Create the sampler */
86        cl :: Sampler sampler = cl :: Sampler ( context , CL_FALSE,
87            CL_ADDRESS_CLAMP_TO_EDGE, CL_FILTER_NEAREST );
88
89        /* Read the program source */
90        std :: ifstream sourceFile ("image−convolution . cl");
91        std :: string sourceCode (
92            std :: istreambuf_iterator <char >( sourceFile ),
93            ( std :: istreambuf_iterator <char >()));
```

```
94          cl :: Program :: Sources source (1,
95             std :: make_pair ( sourceCode . c_str () ,
96             sourceCode . length () + 1));
97
98          /* Make program from the source code */
99          cl :: Program program = cl :: Program ( context , source );
100
101         /* Build the program for the devices */
102         program . build ( devices );
103
104         /* Create the kernel */
105         cl :: Kernel kernel ( program , "convolution");
106
107         /* Set the kernel arguments */
108         kernel . setArg (0 , inputImage );
109         kernel . setArg (1 , outputImage );
110         kernel . setArg (2 , filterBuffer );
111         kernel . setArg (3 , filterWidth );
112         kernel . setArg (4 , sampler );
113
114         /* Execute the kernel */
115         cl :: NDRange global ( imageCols , imageRows );
116         cl :: NDRange local (8 , 8);
117         queue . enqueueNDRangeKernel ( kernel , cl :: NullRange , global ,
118             local );
119         /* Copy the output data back to the host */
120         queue . enqueueReadImage ( outputImage , CL_TRUE , origin , region ,
121             0 , 0 ,
122             hOutputImage );
123
124         /* Save the output BMP image */
125         writeBmpFloat ( hOutputImage , "cat−filtered .bmp", imageRows ,
126             imageCols ,
127             inputImagePath );
128     }
129     catch ( cl :: Error error )
130     {
131         std :: cout << error . what () << "(" << error . err () << ")" << std ::
                endl ;
132     }
133
134     free ( hInputImage );
135     delete hOutputImage ;
136     return 0;
137 }
```

LISTING 4.8

Full source code for the image convolution host program.

4.5 PRODUCER-CONSUMER

In many OpenCL applications, output from one kernel will be used as input to a second kernel. In other words, the first kernel *produces* some data that will be *consumed* by the second kernel. For some applications, the producer and consumer can operate concurrently, with the consumer processing data as it is generated by the producer. OpenCL 2.0 has introduced pipe memory objects to facilitate producer-consumer applications. Pipes have the potential to offer utility regardless of whether or not the producer-consumer kernels execute serially or concurrently.

In this example, we will use pipes to create a producer-consumer application using kernels from two of the examples already discussed in this chapter: convolution and histogram. The convolution kernel will first process an image, then as output pixels are generated they will be passed to the histogram kernel using a pipe (shown in Figure 4.5). To illustrate additional functionality, and to show a potential use case for an accelerated processing unit, we will implement this example using multiple devices. The convolution kernel will execute on the device's GPU, and the histogram kernel will execute on the device's CPU. Executing the kernels on multiple devices will also enable concurrent execution of the two kernels, with the pipe used to pass data as it is generated. A detailed description of pipe objects is provided in Chapter 6. For now, we will describe only the basics required to understand this example.

Pipes are memory objects that contain data (called `packets`) organized a first in, first out (FIFO) structure. Memory allocated for a pipe exists in global memory, and is simultaneously accessible by multiple kernels. The data stored within a pipe is not accessible from the host.

For a given kernel, pipes may be read only (`__read_only`) or write only (`__write_only`), but cannot be read-write. If a pipe is not specified as read only or write only, the compiler will default to read only. A pipe is declared as a kernel parameter by specifying the keyword `pipe`, an access type, and a data type of the packets. For example, `pipe __read_only float *input` would create a read-only pipe that contains single-precision floating-point data.

(a)   (b)   (c)

FIGURE 4.5

The producer kernel will generate filtered pixels and send them via a pipe to the consumer kernel, which will then generate the histogram: (a) original image; (b) filtered image; and (c) histogram of filtered image.

To access a pipe, OpenCL C provides intrinsic functions read_pipe() and write_pipe() with the following signatures:

```
int read_pipe (pipe gentype p, gentype *ptr)

int write_pipe (pipe gentype p, const gentype *ptr)
```

When a work-item calls read_pipe() (Listing 4.10, Line 16), a packet is read from pipe p into ptr. The function returns 0 if a packet is read from the pipe, or a negative value if the pipe is empty. Similarly, a call to write_pipe() (Listing 4.9, Line 50) writes a packet from ptr to pipe p. The function returns 0 if the value was written to the pipe, or a negative value if the pipe is full.

Listings 4.9 and 4.10 show the kernel implementations for our application. Since we are specifically targeting the consumer kernel for a CPU, it is written to utilize only a single work-item when creating the histogram. Also, since we are explicitly targeting a CPU, we will place the histogram directly in global memory (Chapter 8 discusses these trade-offs in detail).

```
1   __constant sampler_t sampler =
2       CLK_NORMALIZED_COORDS_FALSE |
3       CLK_FILTER_NEAREST          |
4       CLK_ADDRESS_CLAMP_TO_EDGE ;
5
6   __kernel
7   void producerKernel (
8       image2d_t __read_only inputImage ,
9       pipe __write_only float *outputPipe ,
10      __constant float* filter ,
11      int filterWidth )
12  {
13      /* Store each work-item's unique row and column */
14      int column = get_global_id(0);
15      int row = get_global_id(1);
16
17      /* Half the width of the filter is needed for indexing
18       * memory later */
19      int halfWidth = (int)(filterWidth/2);
20
21      /* Used to hold the value of the output pixel */
22      float sum = 0.0f;
23
24      /* Iterator for the filter */
25      int filterIdx = 0;
26
27      /* Each work-item iterates around its local area on the basis of
              the
28       * size of the filter */
29      int2 coords; // Coordinates for accessing the image
30
31      /* Iterate the filter rows */
32      for(int i = -halfWidth; i <= halfWidth; i++)
33      {
```

```
34          coords.y = row + i;
35          /* Iterate over the filter columns */
36          for(int j = -halfWidth; j <= halfWidth; j++)
37          {
38              coords.x = column + j;
39
40              /* Read a pixel from the image. A single channel image
41               * stores the pixel in the    x    coordinate of the returned
42               * vector. */
43              float4 pixel;
44              pixel = read_imagef(inputImage, sampler, coords);
45              sum += pixel.x * filter[filterIdx++];
46          }
47      }
48
49      /* Write the output pixel to the pipe */
50      write_pipe(outputPipe, &sum);
51 }
```

LISTING 4.9

Convolution kernel (producer).

```
1
2  __kernel
3  void consumerKernel(
4      pipe __read_only float *inputPipe,
5      int totalPixels,
6      __global int *histogram)
7  {
8      int pixelCnt;
9      float pixel;
10
11     /* Loop to process all pixels from the producer kernel */
12     for (pixelCnt = 0; pixelCnt < totalPixels; pixelCnt++)
13     {
14         /* Keep trying to read a pixel from the pipe
15          * until one becomes available */
16         while(read_pipe(inputPipe, &pixel));
17
18         /* Add the pixel value to the histogram */
19         histogram[(int)pixel]++;
20     }
21 }
```

LISTING 4.10

Convolution kernel (producer).

Although data stored within the pipe is not accessible from the host, the host API is still required to create the pipe object (as described in Chapter 3). The API call to create a pipe is as follows:

```
cl_pipe clCreatePipe(
    cl_context context,
```

```
cl_mem_flags flags,
cl_uint pipe_packet_size,
cl_uint pipe_max_packets,
const cl_pipe_properties *properties,
cl_int *errcode_ret)
```

In this scenario, we will not assume that the two kernels are guaranteed to run concurrently; therefore, we will create a pipe object with a size large enough to contain the entire image:

```
cl_mem pipe = clCreatePipe(context, 0, sizeof(float),
    imageRows*imageCols, NULL, &status);
```

Utilizing multiple devices with this application requires a few additional steps in the host setup compared with the examples we have seen so far. When creating a context, one must supply two devices (one CPU device, and one GPU device), and each device requires its own command-queue. Additionally, the program object will now be used to generate two kernels. Launching the kernels is done by enqueuing them onto their respective command-queues: the producer (convolution) kernel will be enqueued onto the GPU command-queue, and the consumer (histogram) kernel will be enqueued onto the CPU command-queue. All of these steps are illustrated in the host program source code provided in Listing 4.11.

```
1   /* System includes */
2   #include <stdio.h>
3   #include <stdlib.h>
4   #include <string.h>
5
6   /* OpenCL includes */
7   #include <CL/cl.h>
8
9   /* Utility functions */
10  #include "utils.h"
11  #include "bmp-utils.h"
12
13  /* Filter for the convolution */
14  static float gaussianBlurFilter[25] = {
15      1.0f/273.0f,   4.0f/273.0f,   7.0f/273.0f,   4.0f/273.0f,  1.0f/273.0f,
16      4.0f/273.0f,  16.0f/273.0f,  26.0f/273.0f,  16.0f/273.0f,  4.0f/273.0f,
17      7.0f/273.0f,  26.0f/273.0f,  41.0f/273.0f,  26.0f/273.0f,  7.0f/273.0f,
18      4.0f/273.0f,  16.0f/273.0f,  26.0f/273.0f,  16.0f/273.0f,  4.0f/273.0f,
19      1.0f/273.0f,   4.0f/273.0f,   7.0f/273.0f,   4.0f/273.0f,  1.0f/273.0f
            };
20  static const int filterWidth = 5;
21  static const int filterSize = 25*sizeof(float);
22
23  /* Number of histogram bins */
24  static const int HIST_BINS = 256;
25
26  int main(int argc, char **argv)
27  {
```

```
28    /* Host data */
29    float *hInputImage = NULL;
30    int *hOutputHistogram = NULL;
31
32    /* Allocate space for the input image and read the
33     * data from disk */
34    int imageRows;
35    int imageCols;
36    hInputImage = readBmpFloat(".././Images/cat.bmp", &imageRows, &
             imageCols);
37    const int imageElements = imageRows*imageCols;
38    const size_t imageSize = imageElements*sizeof(float);
39
40    /* Allocate space for the histogram on the host */
41    const int histogramSize = HIST_BINS*sizeof(int);
42    hOutputHistogram = (int*)malloc(histogramSize);
43    if (!hOutputHistogram) { exit(-1); }
44
45    /* Use this to check the output of each API call */
46    cl_int status;
47
48    /* Get the first platform */
49    cl_platform_id platform;
50    status = clGetPlatformIDs(1, &platform, NULL);
51    check(status);
52
53    /* Get the devices */
54    cl_device_id devices[2];
55    cl_device_id gpuDevice;
56    cl_device_id cpuDevice;
57    status = clGetDeviceIDs(platform, CL_DEVICE_TYPE_GPU, 1, &gpuDevice
             , NULL);
58    check(status);
59    status = clGetDeviceIDs(platform, CL_DEVICE_TYPE_CPU, 1, &cpuDevice
             , NULL);
60    check(status);
61    devices[0] = gpuDevice;
62    devices[1] = cpuDevice;
63
64    /* Create a context and associate it with the devices */
65    cl_context context;
66    context = clCreateContext(NULL, 2, devices, NULL, NULL, &status);
67    check(status);
68
69    /* Create the command-queues */
70    cl_command_queue gpuQueue;
71    cl_command_queue cpuQueue;
72    gpuQueue = clCreateCommandQueue(context, gpuDevice, 0, &status);
73    check(status);
74    cpuQueue = clCreateCommandQueue(context, cpuDevice, 0, &status);
75    check(status);
76
```

```
77      /* The image descriptor describes how the data will be stored
78       * in memory. This descriptor initializes a 2D image with no
                pitch */
79      cl_image_desc desc;
80      desc.image_type = CL_MEM_OBJECT_IMAGE2D;
81      desc.image_width = imageCols;
82      desc.image_height = imageRows;
83      desc.image_depth = 0;
84      desc.image_array_size = 0;
85      desc.image_row_pitch = 0;
86      desc.image_slice_pitch = 0;
87      desc.num_mip_levels = 0;
88      desc.num_samples = 0;
89      desc.buffer = NULL;
90
91      /* The image format describes the properties of each pixel */
92      cl_image_format format;
93      format.image_channel_order = CL_R; // single channel
94      format.image_channel_data_type = CL_FLOAT;
95
96      /* Create the input image and initialize it using a
97       * pointer to the image data on the host. */
98      cl_mem inputImage;
99      inputImage = clCreateImage(context, CL_MEM_READ_ONLY,
100         &format, &desc, NULL, NULL);
101
102     /* Create a buffer object for the output histogram */
103     cl_mem outputHistogram;
104     outputHistogram = clCreateBuffer(context, CL_MEM_WRITE_ONLY,
105         histogramSize, NULL, &status);
106     check(status);
107
108      /* Create a buffer for the filter */
109     cl_mem filter;
110     filter = clCreateBuffer(context, CL_MEM_READ_ONLY, filterSize,
111         NULL, &status);
112     check(status);
113
114     cl_mem pipe;
115     pipe = clCreatePipe(context, 0, sizeof(float),
116         imageRows*imageCols, NULL, &status);
117
118     /* Copy the host image data to the GPU */
119     size_t origin[3] = {0, 0, 0}; // Offset within the image to copy
                from
120     size_t region[3] = {imageCols, imageRows, 1}; // Elements to per
                dimension
121     status = clEnqueueWriteImage(gpuQueue, inputImage, CL_TRUE,
122         origin, region, 0 /* row-pitch */, 0 /* slice-pitch */,
123         hInputImage, 0, NULL, NULL);
124     check(status);
125
```

```
126      /* Write the filter to the GPU */
127      status = clEnqueueWriteBuffer(gpuQueue, filter, CL_TRUE, 0,
128          filterSize, gaussianBlurFilter, 0, NULL, NULL);
129      check(status);
130
131      /* Initialize the output histogram with zeros */
132      int zero = 0;
133      status = clEnqueueFillBuffer(cpuQueue, outputHistogram, &zero,
134          sizeof(int), 0, histogramSize, 0, NULL, NULL);
135      check(status);
136
137      /* Create a program with source code */
138      char *programSource = readFile("producer-consumer.cl");
139      size_t programSourceLen = strlen(programSource);
140      cl_program program = clCreateProgramWithSource(context, 1,
141          (const char**)&programSource, &programSourceLen, &status);
142      check(status);
143
144      /* Build (compile) the program for the devices */
145      status = clBuildProgram(program, 2, devices, NULL, NULL, NULL);
146      if (status != CL_SUCCESS) {
147          printCompilerError(program, gpuDevice);
148          exit(-1);
149      }
150
151      /* Create the kernels */
152      cl_kernel producerKernel;
153      cl_kernel consumerKernel;
154      producerKernel = clCreateKernel(program, "producerKernel",
155          &status);
156      check(status);
157      consumerKernel = clCreateKernel(program, "consumerKernel",
158          &status);
159      check(status);
160
161      /* Set the kernel arguments */
162      status  = clSetKernelArg(producerKernel, 0, sizeof(cl_mem),
163          &inputImage);
164      status |= clSetKernelArg(producerKernel, 1, sizeof(cl_mem), &pipe);
165      status |= clSetKernelArg(producerKernel, 2, sizeof(cl_mem),
166          &filter);
167      status |= clSetKernelArg(producerKernel, 3, sizeof(int),
                 &filterWidth);
168      check(status);
169
170      status  = clSetKernelArg(consumerKernel, 0, sizeof(cl_mem), &pipe);
171      status |= clSetKernelArg(consumerKernel, 1, sizeof(int),
172          &imageElements);
172      status |= clSetKernelArg(consumerKernel, 2, sizeof(cl_mem),
                 &outputHistogram);
173      check(status);
174
```

```
175    /* Define the index space and work-group size */
176    size_t producerGlobalSize[2];
177    producerGlobalSize[0] = imageCols;
178    producerGlobalSize[1] = imageRows;
179
180    size_t producerLocalSize[2];
181    producerLocalSize[0] = 8;
182    producerLocalSize[1] = 8;
183
184    size_t consumerGlobalSize[1];
185    consumerGlobalSize[0] = 1;
186
187    size_t consumerLocalSize[1];
188    consumerLocalSize[0] = 1;
189
190    /* Enqueue the kernels for execution */
191    status = clEnqueueNDRangeKernel(gpuQueue, producerKernel, 2, NULL,
192        producerGlobalSize, producerLocalSize, 0, NULL, NULL);
193    check(status);
194
195    status = clEnqueueNDRangeKernel(cpuQueue, consumerKernel, 1, NULL,
196        consumerGlobalSize, consumerLocalSize, 0, NULL, NULL);
197    check(status);
198
199    /* Read the output histogram buffer to the host */
200    status = clEnqueueReadBuffer(cpuQueue, outputHistogram, CL_TRUE, 0,
201        histogramSize, hOutputHistogram, 0, NULL, NULL);
202    check(status);
203
204    /* Free OpenCL resources */
205    clReleaseKernel(producerKernel);
206    clReleaseKernel(consumerKernel);
207    clReleaseProgram(program);
208    clReleaseCommandQueue(gpuQueue);
209    clReleaseCommandQueue(cpuQueue);
210    clReleaseMemObject(inputImage);
211    clReleaseMemObject(outputHistogram);
212    clReleaseMemObject(filter);
213    clReleaseMemObject(pipe);
214    clReleaseContext(context);
215
216    /* Free host resources */
217    free(hInputImage);
218    free(hOutputHistogram);
219    free(programSource);
220
221    return 0;
222 }
```

LISTING 4.11

Full source code for a producer-consumer host program.

4.6 UTILITY FUNCTIONS

Because OpenCL is meant to be system agnostic, a few common tasks cannot be done as automatically as we are used to when writing regular C/C++ programs. The good news is that once implemented, they can be reused for all future OpenCL applications.

4.6.1 REPORTING COMPILATION ERRORS

When we attempt to compile and link our OpenCL program object (with clBuildProgram(), or clCompileProgram() and clLinkProgram()), it may happen that there are errors in the OpenCL C source that prevent a successful build. In this case the host application does not automatically print the compiler error message and quit. Instead, the OpenCL API call fails with the appropriate return value, and it is up to the programmer to retrieve the compiler output.

When an OpenCL program object fails to build, a build log is generated and kept with the program object. The log can be retrieved from the API call clGetProgramBuildInfo() by passing the argument CL_PROGRAM_BUILD_LOG to the parameter param_name. Similarly to other API calls that we have seen, clProgramBuildInfo() should be called twice: first to figure out the size of the data being returned, and second to actually retrieve the data after allocation of sufficient space.

In the source code listings provided in this chapter, we use a custom function called printCompilerError() whenever we detect a build error. The source code for our implementation of printCompilerError() is provided in Listing 4.12.

```
1   void printCompilerError(cl_program program, cl_device_id device) {
2       cl_int status;
3
4       size_t logSize;
5       char *log;
6
7       /* Get the log size */
8       status = clGetProgramBuildInfo(program, device,
            CL_PROGRAM_BUILD_LOG,
9                   0, NULL, &logSize);
10      check(status);
11
12      /* Allocate space for the log */
13      log = (char*)malloc(logSize);
14      if (!log) {
15          exit(-1);
16      }
17
18      /* Read the log */
19      status = clGetProgramBuildInfo(program, device,
            CL_PROGRAM_BUILD_LOG,
20                  logSize, log, NULL);
21      check(status);
22
```

```
23      /* Print the log */
24      printf("%s\n", log);
25   }
```

LISTING 4.12

Source code to query a program object for a build log.

4.6.2 CREATING A PROGRAM STRING

In Chapter 3, we saw that program objects are created from character arrays (const char **strings) when using the API call clCreateProgramWithSource(). However, writing OpenCL C source code directly as a character array is very inconvenient. Therefore, a more common use case is to create a separate file containing the OpenCL C source, and read that file into a string within the host program.

When one writes C++ code (as shown in Listing 4.8), reading a file into a string is fairly straightforward. However, when one programs in C, the task is more involved. Listing 4.13 provides a C function for reading a file into a C string (character array).

```
1    char* readFile(const char *filename) {
2
3        FILE *fp;
4        char *fileData;
5        long fileSize;
6
7        /* Open the file */
8        fp = fopen(filename, "r");
9        if (!fp) {
10           printf("Could not open file: %s\n", filename);
11           exit(-1);
12       }
13
14       /* Determine the file size */
15       if (fseek(fp, 0, SEEK_END)) {
16           printf("Error reading the file\n");
17           exit(-1);
18       }
19       fileSize = ftell(fp);
20       if (fileSize < 0) {
21           printf("Error reading the file\n");
22           exit(-1);
23       }
24       if (fseek(fp, 0, SEEK_SET)) {
25           printf("Error reading the file\n");
26           exit(-1);
27       }
28
29       /* Read the contents */
30       fileData = (char*)malloc(fileSize + 1);
31       if (!fileData) {
32           exit(-1);
```

```
33      }
34      if (fread(fileData, fileSize, 1, fp) != 1) {
35          printf("Error reading the file\n");
36          exit(-1);
37      }
38
39      /* Terminate the string */
40      fileData[fileSize] = '\0';
41
42      /* Close the file */
43      if (fclose(fp)) {
44          printf("Error closing the file\n");
45          exit(-1);
46      }
47
48      return fileData;
49  }
```

LISTING 4.13

Source code to read an OpenCL C program from a file.

4.7 SUMMARY

This chapter discussed implementations of some well-known data-parallel algorithms while highlighting specific OpenCL functionality. The histogram example showed local memory usage, along with proper execution and memory synchronization. The rotation and convolution examples utilized image objects and samplers. The convolution example additionally utilized the C++ API, and its kernel took advantage of constant memory. Finally the producer-consumer example built on these techniques and implemented a multidevice application, with two kernels using pipes to communicate data.

Although these examples are correct OpenCL programs, their performance can be improved—in some cases significantly. Optimizing performance for specific hardware platforms is the goal of subsequent chapters.

OpenCL runtime and concurrency model

OpenCL supports a wide range of devices, ranging from discrete graphics processing unit (GPU) cards with thousands of "cores" to small embedded central processing units (CPUs). To achieve such wide support, it is vital that the memory and execution models for OpenCL be defined in such a way that we can achieve a high level of performance across a range of architectures without extraordinary programming effort. In this chapter, we discuss the different components of the execution model.

5.1 COMMANDS AND THE QUEUING MODEL

OpenCL is based on a task-parallel, host-controlled model, in which each task is data parallel. This is maintained through the use of thread-safe command-queues attached to each device. Kernels, data movement, and other operations are not simply executed by the user calling a runtime function. These operations are enqueued onto a specific queue using an asynchronous enqueue operation, to be executed at some point in the future. The synchronization points occur between commands in host command-queues and between commands in device-side command-queues.

The commands enqueued into OpenCL's command-queues can be kernel execution commands, memory transfer commands, or synchronization commands. Completion of a command from the point of view of the host program is guaranteed only at a command-queue synchronization point. The following are the primary command synchronization points:

- Waiting for the completion of a specific OpenCL event.
- A clFinish() call that blocks the host's execution until an entire queue completes execution.
- Execution of a blocking memory operation.

5.1.1 BLOCKING MEMORY OPERATIONS

Blocking memory operations are perhaps the most commonly used and easiest to implement method of synchronization. Instead of querying an event for completion, and blocking the host's execution until the memory operation has completed, most memory transfer functions simply provide a parameter that enables synchronous functionality. This option is the `blocking_read` parameter in `clEnqueueReadBuffer()`, and has synonymous implementations in the other data transfer application programming interface (API) calls.

```
cl_int
clEnqueueReadBuffer(
    cl_command_queue command_queue,
    cl_mem buffer,
    cl_bool blocking_read,
    size_t offset,
    size_t size,
    const void *ptr,
    cl_uint num_events_in_wait_list,
    const cl_event *event_wait_list,
    cl_event *event)
```

Enabling the synchronous functionality of a memory operation is commonly used when transferring data to or from a device. For example, when transferring data from a device to the host, the host should not try to access the data until the transfer is complete as the data will be in an undefined state. Therefore, the `blocking_read` parameter can be set to `CL_TRUE` to ensure that the transfer is complete before the call returns. Using this synchronous functionality allows host code that utilizes the data to be placed directly after the call with no additional synchronization steps. Blocking and nonblocking memory operations are discussed in detail in Chapter 6.

5.1.2 EVENTS

Recall from Chapter 3 that events are used to specify dependencies between commands. Each `clEnqueue` API call can generate an event representing the execution status of the command, and also takes an event list that specifies all of the dependencies that must be completed before execution of the command. Generating events and supplying them as dependencies are the mechanism that allows the OpenCL runtime to implement its execution task graph.

As the command moves into and out of the command-queue and through its stages of execution, its status is constantly updated within its event. The possible states that a command can be in are as follows:

- Queued: The command has been placed into a command-queue.
- Submitted: The command has been removed from the command-queue and submitted for execution on the device.
- Ready: The command is ready for execution on the device.
- Running: Execution of the command has started on the device.
- Ended: Execution of the command has finished on the device.
- Complete: The command and all of its child commands have finished execution.

Owing to the asynchronous nature of the OpenCL API, API calls cannot simply return error conditions or profiling data that relate to the execution of the OpenCL command. The API calls return error conditions relating information known at enqueue time (e.g., validity of parameters) However, OpenCL also provides a mechanism for checking error conditions relating to the execution of the command. The error conditions related to the execution of a command can be queried through the event associated with the command. Indeed, completion can be considered a condition similar to any other. Querying an event's status is done using the API call `clGetEventInfo()` and passing the argument `CL_EVENT_COMMAND_EXECUTION_STATUS` to the parameter `param_name`.

```
cl_int
clGetEventInfo(
    cl_event event,
    cl_event_info param_name,
    size_t param_value_size,
    void *param_value,
    size_t *param_value_size_ret)
```

Successful completion is indicated when the event status associated with a command is set to `CL_COMPLETE`. Notice that the description of "complete" specifies that the execution of a command and all of its child commands has finished. Child commands are relevant when a kernel enqueues child kernels for execution. This is discussed with device-side enqueuing later in this chapter.

Unsuccessful completion results in abnormal termination of the command, which is indicated by setting the event status to a negative value. In this case, the command-queue associated with the abnormally terminated command and all other command-queues in the same context may no longer be available.

The API call `clWaitForEvents()` can be used to have the host block execution until all events specified in the wave-list have finished executing.

```
cl_int
clWaitForEvents (
    cl_uint num_events,
    const cl_event *event_list)
```

5.1.3 COMMAND BARRIERS AND MARKERS

An alternative method of synchronizing without blocking the host is to enqueue a command barrier. A command barrier is conceptually similar to calling `clWaitForEvents()` from the host, but is managed internally to the runtime. Barriers are enqueued using the `clEnqueueBarrierWithWaitList()` command, which takes an optional list of events to wait on. If no events are provided, the barrier waits for completion of all preceding commands in the command-queue.

Markers are similar to barriers and are enqueued with the matching `clEnqueueMarkerWithWaitList()` command. The difference between a barrier and a marker is that the marker does not block the execution of subsequent commands in the queue. The marker therefore allows the programmer to query when the completion of all specified events occurs without inhibiting execution.

By combining these synchronization commands and the use of events, OpenCL provides the ability to produce sophisticated task graphs enabling highly complicated behavior. This ability is important when utilizing out-of-order command-queues, which allows the runtime to optimize command scheduling.

5.1.4 EVENT CALLBACKS

OpenCL allows a user to register callbacks that can be utilized by events. The callback functions are invoked when the event reaches a specified state. The clSetEventCallback() function is used to register a callback for an OpenCL event:

```
cl_int
clSetEventCallback(
   cl_event event,
   cl_int command_exec_callback_type,
   void (CL_CALLBACK *pfn_event_notify)
     (cl_event event,
      cl_int event_command_exec_status,
      void *user_data),
   void *user_data )
```

The parameter command_exec_callback_type is the parameter used to specify when the callback should be invoked. The possible arguments are limited to CL_SUBMITTED, CL_RUNNING, or CL_COMPLETE.

The guarantees related to the ordering of the callback functions are limited. For example, if different callbacks are registered for CL_SUBMITTED and CL_RUNNING, while the state changes are guaranteed to happen in successive order, the callback functions are not guaranteed to be processed in order. As we will discuss in Chapters 6 and 7, memory state cannot be guaranteed for any state other than CL_COMPLETE.

5.1.5 PROFILING USING EVENTS

Determining the execution time of a command is naturally expressed via events, as the transition through each state can be expressed by associating a timer value with each state. To enable the profiling of commands, creation of the command-queue must include providing the flag CL_QUEUE_PROFILING_ENABLE to the properties parameter of clCreateCommandQueueWithProperties().

Any command that generates an event can then be profiled using a call to clGetEventProfilingInfo():

```
cl_int
clGetEventProfilingInfo(
```

```
cl_event event,
cl_profiling_info param_name,
size_t param_value_size,
void *param_value,
size_t *param_value_size_ret)
```

By querying the timer value associated with the transition, the programmer can determine how long the command sat in the queue, when it was submitted to the device, etc. Most commonly, the programmer will want to know the actual duration that the command performed "useful" work (e.g., how long data transfer took, or how long the kernel took to execute). To determine the time that the command actually spent executing, the arguments CL_PROFILING_COMMAND_START and CL_PROFILING_COMMAND_END can be passed as the param_name parameter in subsequent calls to clGetEventProfilingInfo(). When a kernel enqueues child kernels, the total time including all child kernels can be obtained by passing CL_PROFILING_COMMAND_COMPLETE as the argument. OpenCL defines that the timer values returned must be in the nanosecond granularity.

5.1.6 USER EVENTS

So far we have seen events that are generated by passing an event pointer argument to various API calls. However, what if the programmer desires that an OpenCL command's execution wait for a host-based event? For example, the programmer may want his OpenCL data transfer to wait until a file has some new data. To enable this capability, *user events* were added to the specification in OpenCL 1.2.

```
cl_event
clCreateUserEvent(
    cl_context context,
    cl_int *errcode_ret)
```

Since the state transitions of user events are controlled by the application developer and not by the OpenCL runtime, the number of states possible for user events are limited. User events can be in a submitted state (CL_SUBMITTED), in a completed state (CL_COMPLETE), or in an error state. When a user event has been created, the execution status of the user event object's state is set to CL_SUBMITTED.

The state of a user event can be changed by clSetUserEventStatus().

```
cl_int clSetUserEventStatus(
    cl_event event,
    cl_int execution_status)
```

The execution_status parameter specifies the new execution status to be set. As this is a user event, the status can be CL_COMPLETE or a negative integer indicating an error. A negative integer value causes all enqueued commands that wait on this user event to be terminated. It should be noted that clSetUserEventStatus() can be called only once to change the execution status of an event.

5.1.7 OUT-OF-ORDER COMMAND-QUEUES

The command-queues in the OpenCL examples in Chapters 3 and 4 were created as default, in-order queues. In-order queues guarantee that commands will be executed in the order in which they have been enqueued to the device by the application. However, it is possible for a queue to execute out-of-order. An *out-of-order queue* has no default ordering of the operations defined in the queue. If the runtime decides that it has, for example, a direct memory access (DMA) engine that can execute in parallel with compute units, or the device can execute multiple kernels at once, it is at liberty to schedule those operations in parallel, with no guarantee that one command completes execution before another starts.

The command-queue creation API (`clCreateCommandQueueWithProperties()`) has as properties bit field, which we have not used until now. One of the properties available for this bit field is to enable out-of-order execution of the queue (`CL_QUEUE_OUT_OF_ORDER_EXEC_MODE_ENABLE`). Specifying this property will create an out-of-order queue on devices that support out-of-order execution.

The code in Listing 5.1 shows the host portion of a program that uses an out-of-order command queue to write an input buffer, execute two kernels, and read an output buffer back to the host. This series of commands is ordered by specifying event dependencies between successive commands. The task graph created by these event dependencies is what allows an out-of-order queue to determine which commands can be processed. In the example in Listing 5.1, the memory transfer functions are nonblocking and the final synchronization by the host is performed by using `clWaitForEvents()` on the read event. Performing nonblocking memory transfers is important when using out-of-order queues to expose the potential for overlapping transfers and execution.

```
1   // _____
2   // Relevant host program
3   // _____
4
5   // Create the command-queue
6   cl_command_queue_properties properties =
        CL_QUEUE_OUT_OF_ORDER_EXEC_MODE_ENABLE;
7   cl_command_queue queue = clCreateCommandQueueWithProperties(
8     context, devices[0], &properties, NULL);
9
10  // Declare the events
11  cl_event writeEvent, kernelEvent0, kernelEvent1, readEvent;
12
13  // Create the buffers
14  cl_mem input = clCreateBuffer(context, CL_MEM_READ_ONLY,
15    32*sizeof(float), NULL, NULL);
16  cl_mem intermediate = clCreateBuffer(context, CL_MEM_READ_WRITE,
17    32*sizeof(float), NULL, NULL);
```

```
18  cl_mem output = clCreateBuffer(context, CL_MEM_WRITE_ONLY,
19      32*sizeof(float), NULL, NULL);
20
21  // Write the input data
22  clEnqueueWriteBuffer(queue, input, CL_FALSE, 0, 32*sizeof(float),
23      (void*)hostInput, 0, NULL, &writeEvent);
24
25  // Set up the execution unit dimensions used by both kernels
26  size_t localws[1] = {8} ;
27  size_t globalws[1] ={32};
28
29  // Enqueue the first kernel
30  clSetKernelArg(kernel, 0, sizeof(cl_mem), (void *)&input);
31  clSetKernelArg(kernel, 1, sizeof(cl_mem), (void *)&intermediate);
32  clSetKernelArg(kernel, 2, 8*sizeof(float), NULL);
33  clEnqueueNDRangeKernel(queue, kernel, 1, NULL,
34      globalws, localws, 1, &writeEvent, &kernelEvent0);
35
36  // Enqueue the second kernel
37  clSetKernelArg(kernel, 0, sizeof(cl_mem), (void *)&intermediate);
38  clSetKernelArg(kernel, 1, sizeof(cl_mem), (void *)&output);
39  clSetKernelArg(kernel, 2, 8*sizeof(float), NULL);
40  clEnqueueNDRangeKernel(queue, kernel, 1, NULL,
41      globalws, localws, 1, &kernelEvent0, &kernelEvent1);
42
43  // Read output data
44  clEnqueueReadBuffer(queue, output, CL_FALSE, 0, 32*sizeof(float),
45      (void *)&hostOutput, 1, &kernelEvent1, &readEvent);
46
47  // Block until the read has completed
48  clWaitForEvents(1, &readEvent);
49
50  clReleaseEvent(writeEvent);
51  clReleaseEvent(kernelEvent);
52  clReleaseEvent(readEvent);
```

LISTING 5.1

Enqueuing two kernels on the same out-of-order command-queue, and using events to maintain dependencies.

Out-of-order command-queues do not guarantee out-of-order execution. In order to avoid deadlock in a robust application, it is important to enqueue commands while being aware that they could execute serially. We see in the code in Listing 5.1 that even if the commands enqueued were executed in order that they were enqueued, the program will execute correctly. However, if the commands to "enqueue input data" and "enqueue the first kernel" were reversed in the source code, the developer may still expect the queue to execute out-of-order. However, the program would deadlock if the queue behaves as an in-order queue since the kernel execution event would wait for the write data.

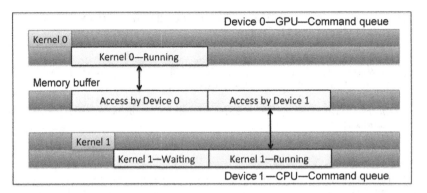

FIGURE 5.1

Multiple command-queues created for different devices declared within the same context. Two devices are shown, where one command-queue has been created for each device.

5.2 MULTIPLE COMMAND-QUEUES

If we have multiple devices in a system (e.g., a CPU and a GPU, or multiple GPUs), each device needs its own command-queue. However, OpenCL also allows multiple command-queues from a context to be mapped to the same device. This is potentially useful to overlap execution of independent commands or overlap commands and host-device communication, and is an alternative to out-of-order queues. Understanding the synchronization capabilities and the host and device memory models (Chapters 6 and 7) is necessary for the management of multiple command-queues.

Figure 5.1 shows an OpenCL context with two devices. Separate command-queues are created to access each device. Listing 5.2 shows the corresponding code to create two command-queues, with each command-queue targeting a different device. It is important to note that synchronization using OpenCL events can be done only for commands within the same context. If separate contexts were created for the different devices, then synchronization using events would not be possible, and the only way to share data between devices would be to use the host to explicitly copy data between buffer objects.

```
1
2  // Obtain devices of both CPU and GPU types
3  cl_device_id devices[2];
4  err_code = clGetDeviceIDs(NULL, CL_DEVICE_TYPE_CPU, 1, &devices[0],
       NULL);
5  err_code = clGetDeviceIDs(NULL, CL_DEVICE_TYPE_GPU, 1, &devices[1],
       NULL);
6
7  // Create a context including two devices
8  cl_context ctx;
9  ctx = clCreateContext(0, 2, devices, NULL, NULL, NULL);
10
11 // Create queues to each device
12 cl_command_queue queue_cpu, queue_gpu;
```

```
13   queue_cpu = clCreateCommandQueueWithProperties(context, devices[0],
        0, NULL);
14   queue_gpu = clCreateCommandQueueWithProperties(context, devices[1],
        0, NULL);
```

LISTING 5.2

Creating two command-queues for two devices present in the same context.

Multiple device programming with OpenCL can be summarized with two execution scenarios usually seen in parallel programming for heterogeneous devices:

- Pipelined execution: Two or more devices work in a pipeline manner such that one device waits on the results of another, shown in Figure 5.2.
- Independent execution: A scenario in which multiple devices work independently of each other, shown in Figure 5.3.

In the code in Listing 5.3, the wait-list orders execution such that the kernel on the GPU queue will complete it's execution before the CPU queue begins executing the kernel (showing the pipelined execution scenario).

```
1
2    cl_event event_cpu, event_gpu;
3
4    // Starts as soon as enqueued
5    err = clEnqueueNDRangeKernel(queue_gpu, kernel_gpu, 2, NULL, global,
        local, 0, NULL, &event_gpu);
6
7    // Starts after event_gpu is on CL_COMPLETE
8    err = clEnqueueNDRangeKernel(queue_cpu, kernel_cpu, 2, NULL, global,
        local, 1, &event_gpu, &event_cpu);
```

LISTING 5.3

A collaborative, pipelined model of multidevice execution. The enqueued kernel on the CPU command-queue waits for the kernel on the GPU command-queue to finish executing.

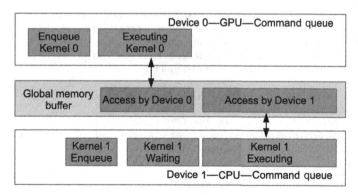

FIGURE 5.2

Multiple devices working in a pipelined manner on the same data. The CPU queue will wait until the GPU kernel has finished.

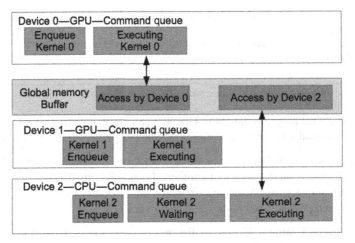

FIGURE 5.3

Multiple devices working in a parallel manner. In this scenario, both GPUs do not use the same buffers and will execute independently. The CPU queue will wait until both GPU devices have finished.

The code in Listing 5.4 shows an execution model in which the kernels are executed on different devices in parallel. The multidevice example in Figure 5.4 shows a case where two GPUs process kernels independently. The command enqueued on the CPU waits for both kernels on the GPU to complete execution.

```
1
2   cl_event events_gpu[2];
3
4   // Both of the GPU devices can execute concurrently as soon as they
        have
5   // their respective data since they have no events in their wait-lists
6   err = clEnqueueNDRangeKernel(queue_gpu_0, kernel_gpu, 2, NULL,
        global, local, 0, NULL, &events_gpu[0]);
7   err = clEnqueueNDRangeKernel(queue_gpu_1, kernel_gpu, 2, NULL,
        global, local, 0, NULL, &events_gpu[1]);
8
9   // The CPU will wait until both GPUs have finished executing their
        kernels.
10  // This requires two events in the CPU's wait-list
11  err = clEnqueueNDRangeKernel(queue_cpu, kernel_cpu, 2, NULL, global,
        local, 2, events_gpu, NULL);
```

LISTING 5.4

Parallel multidevice execution. The enqueued kernel on the CPU command-queue waits for the kernels on the GPU command-queues to finish.

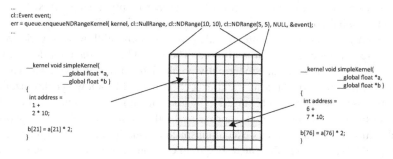

FIGURE 5.4

Executing the simple kernel shown in Listing 5.5. The different work-items in the NDRange are shown.

5.3 THE KERNEL EXECUTION DOMAIN: WORK-ITEMS, WORK-GROUPS, AND NDRanges

OpenCL execution is centered on the concept of a *kernel*. A kernel is a unit of code that represents a single instance of a kernel function executing on a compute device as written in the OpenCL C language. A kernel-instance is at first sight similar to a C function: In the OpenCL C language, a kernel looks like a C function. The OpenCL kernel takes a parameter list, has local variables (similarly to how Pthreads have their own local variables), and standard control flow constructs. What makes the OpenCL kernel different from a C function is its parallel semantics. We described in Chapter 3 how an OpenCL work-item defines just one sliver of a large parallel execution space. In this section, we expand on the previous discussion by providing the motivation for the hierarchical execution model of work-items, work-groups, and NDRanges.

A kernel dispatch is initiated when the runtime processes an entry in a command-queue created by a call to `clEnqueueNDRangeKernel()`. A kernel dispatch consists of a large number of work-items intended to execute together to carry out the operations specified in the kernel body. The enqueue call creates an NDRange (an *n*-dimensional range) worth of work-items. An NDRange defines a one-, two-, or three-dimensional grid of work-items, providing a simple and straightforward structure for parallel execution. When mapped to the hardware model of OpenCL, each work-item runs on a unit of hardware abstractly known as a processing element, where a given processing element may process multiple work-items in turn.

Within a kernel dispatch, each work-item is largely independent. In OpenCL, synchronization between work-items is intentionally limited. This relaxed execution model allows OpenCL programs to scale to devices possessing a large number of cores. As scalable devices are usually organized in a hierarchical manner—especially the memory system—OpenCL similarly provides a hierarchical structure of its execution space.

To flexibly support devices with a large number of processing cores, OpenCL divides the global execution space into a large number of equally sized one-, two-, or three-dimensional sets of work-items called work-groups. Within each work-group, some degree of communication is allowed. The OpenCL specification defines that an entire work-group can run concurrently on an element of the device known as a compute unit. This form of concurrent execution is vital to allow synchronization. Work-groups allow local synchronization by guaranteeing concurrent execution, but they also limit communication to improve scalability. An application that involves global communication across its execution space is usually inefficient to parallelize with OpenCL. To enable efficient work-group communication, a compute unit will likely be mapped to a core so that work-items of a work-group can communicate under a shared cache or scratchpad memory.

By defining larger dispatches with more work-groups, OpenCL kernels scale onto larger and more heavily threaded devices on which more work-groups and more work-items can execute at once. OpenCL work-items attempt to express parallelism that could be expressed using Win32 or POSIX threads. The hierarchical execution mode of OpenCL takes that a step further, because the set of work-items within a work-group can be efficiently mapped to a smaller number of hardware thread contexts. This can be viewed as a generalization of single instruction multiple data (SIMD) execution, where vectors execute multiple operations over multiple cycles. However, in the OpenCL case, subvectors (work-items) can maintain their own program counters until synchronization points. The best example of this is on the GPU, where as many as 64 work-items execute in lock step as a single hardware thread on an SIMD unit: on AMD architectures, this is known as a *wavefront*, and on NVIDIA architectures, it is called a *warp*. Even though the work-items execute in lockstep, different work-items can execute different instruction sequences of a kernel. This can occur if different work-items evaluate a conditional statement such as an *if-else* branch to different results. While work-items may proceed in lockstep through both blocks of the *if-else* branch, the hardware is responsible for squashing the results of the operations that should not have been executed. This phenomenon is commonly known as *divergence*, and can greatly affect kernel performance since work-items need to execute redundant operations and squash results.

This execution model where all work-items appear to have an independent program counter is a simpler development model than explicit use of SIMD instructions as developers are used to when using Streaming SIMD Extensions (SSE) intrinsics on x86 processors. Because of this SIMD execution, it is often noted that for a given device, an OpenCL work-group's size should be an even multiple of that device's SIMD width. This value can be queried from the runtime as the parameter `CL_KERNEL_PREFERRED_WORK_GROUP_SIZE_MULTIPLE` to the `clGetKernelWorkGroupInfo()` function.

OpenCL defines built-in functions callable from within a kernel to obtain the position of a given work-item in the execution range. Some of these functions take a dimension value, listed here as `uint dimension`. This refers to the zeroth, first, or second dimension in the iteration space as provided in the multidimensional NDRange parameters when enqueueing the kernel:

- `uint get_work_dim()`: Returns the number of dimensions in use in the dispatch.
- `size_t get_global_size(uint dimension)`: Returns the global number of work-items in the requested dimension.
- `size_t get_global_id(uint dimension)`: Returns the index of the current work-item in the global space in the requested dimension.
- `size_t get_local_size(uint dimension)`: Returns the size of work-groups in this dispatch in the requested dimension. If the kernel is executed with a nonuniform work-group size, remainder work-groups (discussed later in this chapter) may return different values for uniform work-groups.
- `size_t get_enqueued_local_size(uint dimension)`: Returns the number of work-items in the uniform region of the NDRange in the requested dimension.
- `size_t get_local_id(uint dimension)`: Returns the index of the current work-item as an offset from the beginning of the current work-group.
- `size_t get_num_groups(uint dimension)`: Returns the number of work-groups in the specified dimension of the dispatch. This is `get_global_size()` divided by `get_enqueued_local_size()`.
- `size_t get_group_id(uint dimension)`: Returns the index of the current work-group. That is, the global index of the first work-item in the work-group, divided by the work-group size.

As an example of execution of a simple kernel, take the trivial kernel in Listing 5.5 that executes over a two-dimensional execution space, multiplies an input array by two, and then assigns it to the output array. Figure 5.4 shows how this executes in practice. The call to `get_global_id()` returns different values for each work-item referring to different points in the iteration space. In this trivial example, we use the position in the space to directly map to a two-dimensional data structure. In real examples, more complicated mappings are possible, depending on the input and output structures and the way an algorithm will process the data.

```
1   __kernel void simpleKernel(
2       __global float *a,
3       __global float *b)
4   {
5       int address = get_global_id(0) +     get_global_id(1) *
            get_global_size(0);
6       b[address] = a[address] * 2;
7   }
```

LISTING 5.5

A simple kernel where each work-item of the kernel multiplies an element and then stores its result in an output buffer.

In previous versions of OpenCL, it was required that all dimensions of an NDRange were multiples of the corresponding work-group dimensions. For example, an NDRange of size 800×600 could not have work-groups sized 16×16, because $\frac{600}{16} = 37.5$. As work-groups should be sized to complement execution and memory hardware, this often required programmers to create NDRanges that were larger than the problem set. If we wanted work-groups to be sized 16×16, we would need to increase the NDRange size to 800×608. The difficulty with this approach is that work-items are created that do not map to the data set, and must be handled appropriately (e.g., checking the index and immediately returning for any out-of-range work-items). However, this technique creates headaches when one is performing operations such as barrier synchronizations that require all work-items in the group to perform the operation. To alleviate this problem, OpenCL 2.0 has removed the requirement that NDRange dimensions should be multiples of work-group dimensions. Instead, OpenCL 2.0 defines *remainder work-groups* as the boundaries of the NDRange, and the last work-group need not have the same dimensions as defined by the programmer. In the case of the 800×600 NDRange and 16×16 work-groups, the last row of work-groups will be sized 16×8. The functions `get_local_size()` and `get_enqueued_local_size()` can be used to get the size of the actual work-group (possibly with remainder dimensions), and the size of the uniform work-groups, respectively.

OpenCL 2.0 has also introduced built-in functions for linear indexing that simplifies a common calculation that programmers had to code by hand in prior versions of the specification. Linear indexing provides a well-defined, unique index for a work-item, regardless of the number of dimensions in the NDRange or work-group. These functions are `get_global_linear_id()` and `get_local_linear_id()`, which provide a global linear index within the NDRange, and a local linear index within the work-group, respectively:

- `size_t get_global_linear_id()`: Returns a one-dimensional global ID for the work-item.
- `size_t get_local_linear_id()`: Returns a one-dimensional local ID for the work-item.

5.3.1 SYNCHRONIZATION

"Synchronization" refers to mechanisms that constrain the order of execution between two or more execution units. In general, OpenCL intentionally limits synchronization between execution units. This is influenced by the desire for scalability, but also by the wide variety of devices that are targeted by OpenCL. For example, OpenCL runs on devices in which threading is managed by hardware, such as GPUs, in addition to operating-system-managed threading devices such as mainstream x86 CPUs. This can cause issues in enabling performance and correctness of concurrent programs. With an x86 thread, it is possible to attempt to lower a semaphore and block the thread If the semaphore is unavailable, the operating system will remove the thread from execution and is free to schedule anything in its place with little in the way of resource constraints. On a GPU, applying the same trick in the GPU equivalent of a thread (the wavefront on AMD hardware) is problematic because the resources occupied are fixed. For example, removing one wavefront from execution does not free its resources, so it is possible to reach a situation in which a wavefront that is not yet able to fit on the device is required to free the semaphore before one that is already on the device is able to continue. Because the wavefronts on the device are waiting for that semaphore, they never get to execute, and so the system deadlocks.

To circumvent this eventuality, OpenCL defines blocking synchronization (i.e., a barrier) only for work-items within the same work-group. In Chapter 7, we will see that OpenCL 2.0 now also provides lock-free memory ordering constraints using atomics and fences. However, their goal is to enable broader classes of algorithms based on memory visibility guarantees, and not to provide synchronization of execution order. The following sections deal with synchronization within a work-group using barriers, and synchronization of commands, respectively.

5.3.2 WORK-GROUP BARRIERS

A call to provide a barrier by a work-item within a work-group dictates that the work-item cannot continue past the barrier until all work-items in the group have also reached the barrier. This is a program-counter-level restriction, which means that each barrier in the code is treated as a different execution barrier. As a result, when a work-group barrier is placed within control flow in the kernel, all work-items within the group must encounter that barrier. The net effect of this is that behavior of barriers within control flow that diverges between different work-items in the group is undefined: on many devices, this leads to deadlock as work-items wait for others that will never reach the barrier.

A simple example of OpenCL synchronization is shown in Figure 5.5. In this diagram, we see an initial kernel enqueue with four work-groups of eight work-items each. Under the loosest interpretation of the OpenCL specification (i.e., disregarding hardware implementations), the work-items in each work-group proceed at differing rates. When the `work_group_barrier()` function is called, the most advanced work-item waits for all others to catch up, continuing only after all have reached that point. Different work-groups and work-items in other work-groups proceed with a schedule independent of the schedules of the other work-groups until the end of the kernel.

The signatures of the built-in functions to provide a work-group barrier are as follows:

```
void work_group_barrier(cl_mem_fence_flags flags)
```

```
void work_group_barrier(cl_mem_fence_flags flags, memory_scope scope)
```

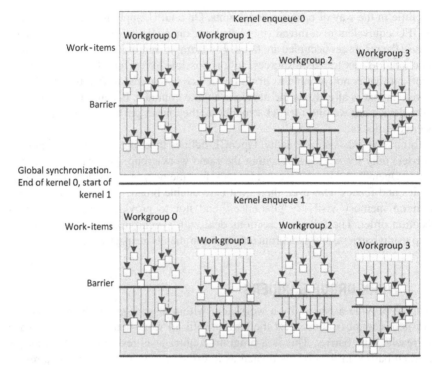

FIGURE 5.5

Within a single kernel dispatch, synchronization regarding execution order is supported only within work-groups using barriers. Global synchronization is maintained by completion of the kernel, and the guarantee that on a completion event all work is complete and memory content is as expected.

In Chapter 7, we will discuss the details regarding the scope parameter (as well as go into more detail regarding the flags parameter). However, for now it is sufficient to understand that the flags provided to the function determine which memory operations need to be visible to the other work-items in the group when the barrier operation completes.

The options for flags include the following:

- CLK_LOCAL_MEM_FENCE: Requires that all accesses to local memory become visible.
- CLK_GLOBAL_MEM_FENCE: Requires that all accesses to global memory become visible.
- CLK_IMAGE_MEM_FENCE: Requires that all accesses to images become visible.

In the following example, we will see work-items caching data into local memory, where each work-item reads a value from a buffer and requires that it become visible to all other work-items in the group. To do this, we will call `work_group_barrier()` and pass it the flag `CLK_LOCAL_MEM_FENCE`.

Between kernel dispatches, all work is guaranteed to be complete and all memory is guaranteed to be consistent. Then the next kernel launches with the same semantics. If we assume that the kernels enqueued as 0 and 1 in Figure 5.5 are produced from the same kernel object, the kernel code and API calls in Listing 5.6 could be expected to produce the behavior shown in Figure 5.5.

In this case, the behavior we see from the work-items is a simple wrapping neighborwise addition of elements in local memory, where availability of the data must be guaranteed before neighbors can read.

```
1  // _____
2  // Relevant host program
3  // _____
4
5  cl_mem input = clCreateBuffer(context, CL_MEM_READ_ONLY,
6      32*sizeof(float), 0, 0);
7
8  cl_mem intermediate = clCreateBuffer(context, CL_MEM_READ_WRITE,
9      32*sizeof(float), 0, 0);
10
11 cl_mem output = clCreateBuffer(context, CL_MEM_WRITE_ONLY,
12     32*sizeof(float), 0, 0);
13
14 clEnqueueWriteBuffer(queue, input, CL_TRUE, 0, 32*sizeof(float),
15     (void*)hostInput, 0, NULL, NULL);
16
17 clSetKernelArg(kernel, 0, sizeof(cl_mem), (void *)&input);
18 clSetKernelArg(kernel, 1, sizeof(cl_mem), (void *)&intermediate);
19 clSetKernelArg(kernel, 2, 8*sizeof(float), NULL);
20 size_t localws[1] = {8} ;
21 size_t globalws[1] ={32};
22
23 clEnqueueNDRangeKernel(queue, kernel, 1, NULL,
24     globalws, localws, 0, NULL, NULL);
25
26 clSetKernelArg(kernel, 0, sizeof(cl_mem), (void *)&intermediate);
27 clSetKernelArg(kernel, 1, sizeof(cl_mem), (void *)&output);
28 clSetKernelArg(kernel, 2, 8*sizeof(float), NULL);
29 clEnqueueNDRangeKernel(queue, kernel, 1, NULL,
30     globalws, localws, 0, NULL, NULL);
31
32 clEnqueueReadBuffer(queue, output, CL_TRUE, 0, 32*sizeof(float),
33     (void *)&hostOutput, 0, NULL, NULL);
34
35 // _____
36 // Kernel
37 // _____
38
39 __kernel void simpleKernel(
```

```
40        __global float *a,
41        __global float *b,
42        __local float *localbuf ) {
43
44        // Cache data to local memory
45        localbuf[get_local_id(0)] = a[get_global_id(0)];
46
47        // Wait until all work-items have read the data and
48        // it becomes visible
49        work_group_barrier(CLK_LOCAL_MEM_FENCE);
50
51        // Perform the operation and output the data
52        unsigned int otherAddress = (get_local_id(0) + 1) %
                get_local_size(0);
53        b[get_global_id(0)] = localbuf[get_local_id(0)] + localbuf[
                otherAddress];
54    }
```

LISTING 5.6

Enqueuing two kernels on the same command-queue.

5.3.3 BUILT-IN WORK-GROUP FUNCTIONS

The OpenCL C programming language implements built-in functions that operate on a work-group basis. As with the barrier operation, these built-in functions must be encountered by all work-items in a work-group executing the kernel. Thus, if the work-group function is within a conditional block, all the work-items in the work-group should have the same result of the conditional evaluation.

The work-group evaluation functions have been defined for all OpenCL C built-in data types, such as `half`, `int`, `uint`, `long`, `ulong`, `float`, and `double`. We have followed the terminology in the OpenCL specification, where `gentype` refers to the generic data types defined in the OpenCL C programming language. There are three types of built-in evaluation functions, categorized on the basis of their functionality:

1. predicate evaluation functions;
2. broadcast functions; and
3. parallel primitive functions (reduce and scan).

5.3.4 PREDICATE EVALUATION FUNCTIONS

The predicate evaluation functions evaluate a predicate for all work-items in the work-group and return a nonzero value if the associated condition is satisfied. The signatures of the predicate evaluation functions are as follows:

```
int work_group_any(int predicate)
```

```
int work_group_all(int predicate)
```

The function `work_group_any()` returns a nonzero value if any of the evaluations within the work-group result in a nonzero value. The function `work_group_all()` returns a nonzero value if all of the evaluations within the work-group result in nonzero values. An example of using the `work_group_all()` function is shown in Listing 5.7.

```
1  __kernel void compare_elements(int *input, int* output)
2  {
3          int tid = get_global_id(0);
4          int result = work_group_all((input[tid] > input[tid+1]));
5          output[tid] = result;
6  }
```
LISTING 5.7

Examples of using the predicate work-group functions in OpenCL kernels.

5.3.5 BROADCAST FUNCTIONS

The broadcast functions transmit data from one work-item within the work-group to all other work-items within the work-group. The function signature is overloaded on the basis of the number of work-group dimensions:

```
// Broadcast function for a 1D NDRange
gentype work_group_broadcast(gentype x, size_t local_id)

// Broadcast function for a 2D NDRange
gentype work_group_broadcast(gentype x, size_t local_id_x, size_t
local_id_y)

// Broadcast function for a 3D NDRange
gentype work_group_broadcast(gentype x, size_t local_id_x, size_t
local_id_y, size_t local_id_z)
```

Looking at the signatures, we see the value x is the variable to be broadcast by the work-item identified by the work-item indices specified as `local_id_*`. The function return value will return the broadcast value to each work-item.

5.3.6 PARALLEL PRIMITIVE FUNCTIONS

OpenCL supports two built-in parallel primitive functions: reduce and scan. These functions are common in many parallel applications, and requiring them to be implemented per device by the vendor will likely result in much higher performing code than if they were implemented by a programmer using a general algorithm. The signatures for the reduce and scan functions are as follows:

```
gentype work_group_reduce_<op>(gentype x)

gentype work_group_scan_inclusive_<op>(gentype x)

gentype work_group_scan_exclusive_<op>(gentype x)
```

In these functions, the `<op>` suffix can be replaced with `add`, `min`, or `max`. Therefore, to find the maximum value of a local array, the following OpenCL C code could be used:

```
float max;
max = work_group_reduce_max(local_data[get_local_id(0)]);
```

Most parallel programmers will be familiar with the prefix-sum operation, which can be implemented using `work_group_scan_inclusive_add()` or `work_group_scan_exclusive_add()`. The inclusive and exclusive versions of the scan operations specify whether or not the current element should be included in the computation. An inclusive scan of an array generates a new array where each element i is the sum of the elements up to and including i. Alternatively, an exclusive scan excludes the current element i. Each work-item provides and is returned the value corresponding to its linear index within the work-group.

The order of floating-point operations is not guaranteed for the parallel primitive functions, which can be a concern as floating-point operations are not associative.

5.4 NATIVE AND BUILT-IN KERNELS

OpenCL defines two additional types of mechanisms to enqueue execution on a compute device besides OpenCL `cl_kernel` objects. They are known as *native kernels* and *built-in kernels*. Native and built-in kernels both have orthogonal usage scenarios. Native kernels provide a mechanism to enqueue standard C functions for execution on a compute device. Built-in kernels are kernels that are specific to a particular device and provide a mechanism to allow an application developer to leverage special hardware that may be present on the device.

5.4.1 NATIVE KERNELS

Native kernels are an alternative to callbacks that are more cleanly integrated into the OpenCL execution model. Native kernels allow standard C functions compiled with a traditional compiler (rather than OpenCL kernels) to be executed within the OpenCL task graph, be triggered by events, and trigger further events. Native kernels can be queued for execution on a device and share memory objects with OpenCL kernels.

The difference between enqueuing a native kernel versus enqueuing an OpenCL kernel is that rather than taking a `cl_kernel` object as an argument, the native kernel

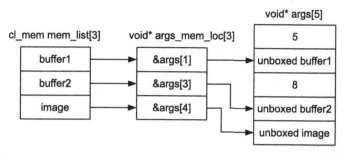

FIGURE 5.6

Example showing OpenCL memory objects mapping to arguments for
`clEnqueueNativeKernel()` in Listing 5.8.

enqueue function (`clEnqueueNativeKernel()`) takes a function pointer to a standard
C function. The argument list is provided separately along with its size.

```
cl_int
clEnqueueNativeKernel(
    cl_command_queue command_queue,
    void (CL_CALLBACK *user_func)(void *)
    void *args,
    size_t cb_args,
    cl_uint num_mem_objects,
    const cl_mem *mem_list,
    const void **args_mem_loc,
    cl_uint num_events_in_wait_list,
    const cl_event *event_wait_list,
    cl_event *event)
```

Regular OpenCL kernels use buffer and image objects passed as kernel arguments,
and it would be useful to pass these to native kernels as well. Passing arguments to
native kernels in OpenCL is done by a process called unboxing. Arguments are passed
to native kernels by passing in a list of memory objects, in the argument `mem_list`,
and a list of pointers, `args_mem_loc`, storing memory objects at addresses where the
unboxed memory pointers will be placed.

To illustrate the point, consider Listing 5.8, in which a native function `foo()`
expects an argument list containing five values, where the indices 0 and 2 are set
to integers 5 and 8, respectively, and the indices 1, 3, and 4 are two buffer objects and
an image object. This is shown in Figure 5.6.

```
1
2   // Native function that will be enqueued to device
3   void foo(void *args)
4   {
5       ...
```

```
 6   }
 7
 8   cl_command_queue queue = clCreateCommandQueue (...);
 9   cl_mem buffer1 = clCreateBuffer (...);
10   cl_mem buffer2 = clCreateBuffer (...);
11   cl_mem image = clCreateImage2D (...);
12
13   void *args[5] = { (void *)5, NULL, (void *)8, NULL, NULL };
14
15   num_mem_objects = 3;
16   cl_mem mem_list[3] = { buffer1, buffer2, image };
17   void *args_mem_loc[3] = { &args[1], &args[3], &args[4] };
18
19   clEnqueueNativeKernel(queue, foo, args, sizeof(args), num_mem_objects,
20       mem_list, args_mem_loc, 0, NULL, NULL);
```

LISTING 5.8

Enqueuing a native kernel function foo() to a device.

5.4.2 BUILT-IN KERNELS

Built-in kernels are tied to a particular device and are not built at runtime from source code in a program object. The common use of built-in kernels is to expose fixed-function hardware acceleration capabilities or embedded firmware associated with a particular OpenCL device or custom device. The semantics of a built-in kernel may be defined outside OpenCL, and hence are implementation defined.

An example of built-in kernel infrastructure is the motion estimation extension for OpenCL released by Intel. This extension depends on the OpenCL built-in kernel infrastructure to provide an abstraction for harnessing the domain-specific acceleration (for motion estimation in this case) in Intel devices that support OpenCL.

5.5 DEVICE-SIDE QUEUING

In prior versions of OpenCL, commands could be enqueued to a command-queue only from the host. OpenCL 2.0 has lifted this restriction by defining *device-side command-queues*, which allow a *child kernel* to be enqueued directly from a kernel executing on a device (referred to as the `parent kernel`).

The main benefit of a device-side command-queue is that it enables *nested parallelism*—a parallel programming paradigm where a thread executing a parallel task can spawn additional threads to execute additional tasks [1]. Nested parallelism is commonly seen in applications where the number of threads needed to execute an algorithm to completion may not be known when the threads are spawned. Nested parallelism can be contrasted with a single level of `fork-join` parallelism, where

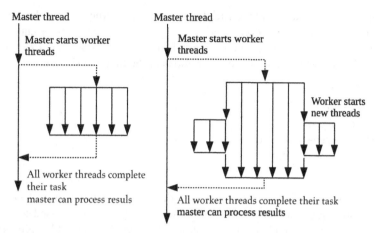

FIGURE 5.7

A single-level fork-join execution paradigm compared with nested parallelism thread execution.

threads are spawned, complete their task, and then exit. The main difference between single-level fork-join parallelism and nested parallelism is shown in Figure 5.7. In single-level fork-join parallelism (Figure 5.7), the parallel threads created for execution simply finish their task and then terminate. In the nested parallelism case shown in Figure 5.7, two threads create additional threads for execution.

Nested parallelism benefits applications with an irregular or data-driven loop structure. A common data-driven algorithm is the breadth-first search (BFS) graph algorithm. The BFS algorithm begins at a root node of a graph and inspects all the neighboring nodes. Then for each of the neighboring nodes, it inspects their unvisited neighboring nodes, and so on, until all nodes have been visited. While BFS is being parallelized, the number of new vertices that are discovered by each vertex is not known when the application is started. Device-side enqueuing allows application developers to implement OpenCL kernels with nested parallelism in a more natural manner without additional host-device communication.

To summarize, the main benefits of device-side queues are as follows:

- Kernels can be enqueued directly from the device. This removes the requirement of synchronization or communication with the host, and potentially eliminates expensive data transfers.
- Expressing algorithms naturally. Previously, algorithms containing recursion, irregular loop structures, or other constructs that do not fit a uniform single level of parallelism had to be redesigned for OpenCL.
- By their expressing algorithms naturally, finer granularities of parallelism may be exposed to schedulers and load balancers dynamically. This allows devices to efficiently adapt in response to data-driven decisions or workloads.

In order to enqueue a child kernel for execution, a kernel may make a call to the OpenCL C built-in function `enqueue_kernel()`. It is very important to note that `enqueue_kernel()` will enqueue a kernel for *each work-item* that executes the function. The following is one of four variations of the function signature:

```
int
enqueue_kernel(
    queue_t queue,
    kernel_enqueue_flags_t flags,
    const ndrange_t ndrange,
    void (^block)(void))
```

From the signature, we can see that as with host-side commands, a device-side enqueue also requires a command-queue. The `flags` parameter is used to specify when the child kernel should begin execution. There are three possible options with the following semantics:

- `CLK_ENQUEUE_FLAGS_NO_WAIT`: The child kernel can begin executing immediately.
- `CLK_ENQUEUE_FLAGS_WAIT_KERNEL`: The child kernel must wait for the parent kernel to reach the `ENDED` before executing. In this case, the parent kernel has finished executing. However, other child kernels could still be executing on the device.
- `CLK_ENQUEUE_FLAGS_WAIT_WORK_GROUP`: The child kernel must wait for the enqueuing work-group to complete its execution before starting.

It is also important to note that the parent kernel cannot wait for the child kernel to complete execution. A parent kernel's execution status is considered to be "complete" when the parent kernel itself and all its child kernels have completed execution. The execution status of a parent kernel will be `CL_COMPLETE` if this kernel and all its child kernels complete execution successfully. The execution status of the kernel will be an error code (given by a negative integer value) if it or any of its child kernels encounter an error, or are abnormally terminated.

Similarly to `clEnqueueNDRangeKernel()`, `enqueue_kernel()` also requires a parameter that defines the dimensions of the NDRange (specified by parameter `ndrange`). As with the host-side call, providing a global offset and work-group size is optional. Creating a variable of type `ndrange_t` to describe the execution unit configuration is done using permutations of the following built-in functions:

```
ndrange_t ndrange_<N>D(
const size_t global_work_size[<N>]),

ndrange_t ndrange_<N>D(
const size_t global_work_size[<N>],
const size_t local_work_size[<N>])
```

```
ndrange_t ndrange_<N>D(
const size_t global_work_offset[<N>],
const size_t global_work_size[<N>],
const size_t local_work_size[<N>])
```

where <N> is 1, 2, or 3. For example, creating a two-dimensional NDRange with dimensions 800 × 600 could be performed using

```
size_t globalSize[2] = {800, 600};
ndrange_t myNdrange = ndrange_2D(globalSize);
```

Finally, the last parameter of enqueue_kernel(), block, is the kernel that will be enqueued. The format for specifying the kernel is defined using Clang blocks. The following two sections describe in detail how device-side command-queues are utilized, and how a nested kernel is specified using the block syntax.

As with host API calls, enqueue_kernel() returns an integer status that indicates whether or not the enqueue succeeded. The function returns CLK_SUCCESS on success and CLK_ENQUEUE_FAILURE on failure. If the programmer desires a more specific error message regarding a failing enqueue, passing the option "-g" to clBuildProgram() or clCompileProgram() will enable finer-granularity error reporting, with values such as CLK_INVALID_NDRANGE or CLK_DEVICE_QUEUE_FULL.

5.5.1 CREATING A DEVICE-SIDE QUEUE

A device-side command-queue needs to be created on the host using the same API call as for host-side queues: clCreateCommandQueueWithProperties(). To specify that a queue should be created as a device-side queue, the properties parameter should be passed the parameter CL_QUEUE_ON_DEVICE. Additionally, when a device queue is being created, the specification requires that the argument CL_QUEUE_OUT_OF_ORDER_EXEC_MODE_ENABLE is also passed (using the OR-bitwise operator), since a device queue is treated as an out-of-order queue in OpenCL 2.0. The command-queue object can then be passed to the kernel as an argument, which will be specified as type queue_t in the kernel signature. An example showing a kernel with a command-queue parameter is provided in Listing 5.9.

```
1   //_____
2   // Relevant host program
3   //_____
4
5   // Specify the queue properties
6   cl_command_queue_properties properties =
7      CL_QUEUE_ON_DEVICE |
8      CL_QUEUE_OUT_OF_ORDER_EXEC_MODE_ENABLE;
9
10  // Create the device-side command-queue
11  cl_command_queue device_queue;
12  device_queue = clCreateCommandQueueWithProperties(
```

```
13                       context ,
14                       device ,
15                       &properties ,
16                       NULL);
17
18   ...
19
20   clSetKernelArg(kernel ,  0,  sizeof(cl_command_queue),  &device_queue);
21
22   ...
23
24
25   // _____
26   // Kernel
27   // _____
28
29   __kernel
30   void foo(queue_t myQueue,  ...)
31   {
32       ...
33   }
```

LISTING 5.9

Passing a device-side command-queue as a kernel argument.

Optionally, an additional argument, CL_QUEUE_ON_DEVICE_DEFAULT, can be supplied to clCreateCommandQueueWithProperties(), which will make the command-queue the "default" device-side command-queue for the device. This provides a simplification for the programmer, as the default queue can be accessed within a kernel using a built-in function, saving the developer the effort of passing the queue as a kernel argument.

5.5.2 ENQUEUING DEVICE-SIDE KERNELS

When enqueuing kernel execution commands using the host API (clEnqueueNDRangeKernel()), we must first set the kernel arguments with clSetKernelArg() before enqueuing the kernel onto a command-queue. When we enqueue kernels into a device-side command-queue with enqueue_kernel(), there is no equivalent mechanism to set arguments. A mechanism is required that can pass kernels and their arguments through the same signature. To perform this operation, OpenCL has chosen to represent kernels and kernel state using Clang block syntax.

Clang blocks have been introduced to the OpenCL specification as a method to encapsulate OpenCL kernels and their arguments in order to enqueue them onto device queues. Blocks are a way to pass code and scope as data. They are known in other languages as closures and anonymous functions. The block type is defined using a *result value type* and a list of *parameter types*. With this syntax, the declaration of a block ends up looking very similar to the declaration of a function type. The ∧ operator is used to declare a `block variable` (where the block references a defined kernel) or to indicate the beginning of a `block literal` (where the body of the kernel is coded directly in the declaration).

A simple example showing both declaration variations is provided in Listing 5.10.

```
1   __kernel
2   void child0_kernel ()
3   {
4       printf("Child0: Hello, world!\n");
5   }
6
7   void child1_kernel ()
8   {
9       printf("Child1: Hello, world!\n");
10  }
11
12  __kernel
13  void parent_kernel( )
14  {
15      kernel_enqueue_flags_t child_flags = CLK_ENQUEUE_FLAGS_NO_WAIT;
16      ndrange_t child_ndrange = ndrange_1D(1);
17
18      // Enqueue the child kernel by creating a block variable
19      enqueue_kernel(get_default_queue(), child_flags, child_ndrange,
20          ^{child0_kernel();});
21
22      // Create block variable
23      void (^child1_kernel_block)(void) = ^{child1_kernel();};
24      // Enqueue kernel from block variable
25      enqueue_kernel(get_default_queue(), child_flags, child_ndrange,
26          child1_kernel_block);
27
28      // Enqueue kernel from a block literal
29      // The block literal is bound by "^{" and "}"
30      enqueue_kernel(get_default_queue(), child_flags, child_ndrange,
31          ^{printf("Child2: Hello, world!\n";});
32  }
```

LISTING 5.10

A simple example showing child-kernel enqueues using block syntax.

Listing 5.10 shows three syntax options for enqueuing a kernel onto a device queue. However, none of the kernels we have shown required arguments to be passed from parent to child. With the block syntax, arguments are provided when the block is defined. Recall the kernel for a simple vector addition program we saw in Chapter 3:

```
__kernel
void vecadd(__global int *A, __global int *B, __global int *C)
{
    int idx = get_global_id(0);

    C[idx] = A[idx] + B[idx];
}
```

As a toy example to illustrate argument passing, we can modify the vector addition so that the parent enqueues a child kernel to execute the work. Listing 5.11 shows argument passing when we are creating a block variable, and Listing 5.12 shows argument passing when we are using a block literal. Notice that in Listing 5.11 arguments are provided similarly to standard function calls. However, when we are using a literal in Listing 5.12, no arguments are passed explicitly. Instead, the compiler establishes a new lexical scope within the parent for the literal. While global variables are bound in the expected manner, private and local data must be copied. Note that pointers to local or private address spaces are invalid, as they do not have scope outside their work-group or work-item, respectively. However, creation of local memory regions for child kernels is supported and is discussed next. Because the return type of a kernel is always void, it never needs to be explicitly defined when declaring a block.

```
1   __kernel
2   void child_vecadd(__global int *A, __global int *B, __global int *C)
3   {
4       int idx = get_global_id(0);
5
6       C[idx] = A[idx] + B[idx];
7   }
8
9   __kernel
10  void parent_vecadd(__global int *A, __global int *B, __global int *C)
11  {
12      kernel_enqueue_flags_t child_flags = CLK_ENQUEUE_FLAGS_NO_WAIT;
13      ndrange_t child_ndrange = ndrange_1D(get_global_size(0));
14
15      // Only enqueue one child kernel
16      if (get_global_id(0) == 0) {
17
18          enqueue_kernel(
19              get_default_queue(),
20              child_flags,
21              child_ndrange,
22              ^{child_vecadd(A, B, C);});   // Pass arguments to child
23      }
24  }
```

LISTING 5.11

Passing arguments using block syntax.

```
1    __kernel
2    void parent_vecadd(__global int *A, __global int *B, __global int *C)
3    {
4        kernel_enqueue_flags_t child_flags = CLK_ENQUEUE_FLAGS_NO_WAIT;
5        ndrange_t child_ndrange = ndrange_1D(get_global_size(0));
6
7        // Only enqueue one child kernel
8        if (get_global_id(0) == 0) {
9
10           // Enqueue kernel from block literal
11           enqueue_kernel(
12               get_default_queue(),
13               child_flags,
14               child_ndrange,
15               ^{int idx = get_global_id(0);  C[idx] = A[idx] + B[idx];";});
16       }
17   }
```

LISTING 5.12

Accessing arguments from lexical scope.

Dynamic local memory

When setting arguments using the host API, we can dynamically allocate local memory for a kernel by providing a NULL pointer to clSetKernelArg(). Since we do not have a similar mechanism for setting child-kernel arguments, the enqueue_kernel() function has been overloaded:

```
int
enqueue_kernel(
    queue_t queue,
    kernel_enqueue_flags_t flags,
    const ndrange_t ndrange,
    void (^block)(local void *, ...),
    uint size0, ...)
```

To create local memory pointers, the specification defines the block argument to be a variadic function (a function that receives a variable number of arguments). Each argument must be of type local void *. Notice that in the declaration that this argument list replaces the existing void type. The enqueue_kernel() function is also variadic, ending with a variable number of parameters that represent the size of each local array. Listing 5.13 modifies the toy vector addition example to use local memory in order to illustrate the use of dynamic local memory allocation with block syntax.

```
1    // When a kernel has been defined like this, then it can be
2    // enqueued from the host as well as from the device
3    __kernel
4    void child_vecadd(__global int *A, __global int *B, __global int *C,
```

```
 5                        __local int *local_A, __local int *local_B,
                          __local int *local_C)
 6   {
 7       int idx = get_global_id(0);
 8       int local_idx = get_local_id(0);
 9
10       local_A[local_idx] = A[idx];
11       local_B[local_idx] = B[idx];
12       local_C[local_idx] = local_A[local_idx] + local_B[local_idx];
13       C[idx] = local_C[local_idx];
14   }
15
16   __kernel
17   void parent_vecadd(__global int* A,__global int*B, __global int* C)
18   {
19           kernel_enqueue_flags_t child_flags = CLK_ENQUEUE_FLAGS_NO_WAIT;
20           ndrange_t child_ndrange = ndrange_1D(get_global_size(0));
21
22           int local_A_mem_size = sizeof(int)*1 ;
23           int local_B_mem_size = sizeof(int)*1 ;
24           int local_C_mem_size = sizeof(int)*1 ;
25
26           // Define a block with local memory for each local memory
                 argument of the kernel
27           void (^child_vecadd_blk)(local int *, local int *,
28                                    local int *) =
29               ^(local int *local_A, local int * local_B, local int *
30                 local_C)
31               {
32                       child_vecadd(A, B, C, local_A, local_B,
33                                    local_C);
34               };
35
36           //Only enqueue one child kernel
37           if(get_global_id(0)==0)
38           {
39                   // Variadic enqueue_kernel function takes in local
                         memory size of each argument in block
40                   enqueue_kernel(
41                           get_default_queue(),
42                           child_flags,
43                           child_ndrange,
44                           child_vecadd_blk,
45                           local_A_mem_size,
46                           local_B_mem_size,
47                           local_C_mem_size);
48           }
49   }
```

LISTING 5.13

Allocating dynamic local memory within a child kernel.

Enforcing dependencies using events

When introducing device-side command-queues, we mentioned that the queues always operate as out-of-order queues. This implies that there must be some mechanism provided to enforce dependency requirements. As on the host, events are used to satisfy this requirement when kernels are enqueued directly from a device. Once again, the `enqueue_kernel()` function is overloaded to provide this additional functionality:

```
int
enqueue_kernel(
  queue_t queue,
  kernel_enqueue_flags_t flags,
  const ndrange_t ndrange,
  uint num_events_in_wait_list,
  const clk_event_t *event_wait_list,
  clk_event_t *event_ret,
  void (^block)(void))
```

The reader should notice that the three additional parameters, `num_events_in_wait_list`, `event_wait_list`, and `event_ret`, mirror event-related parameters from the host API functions.

The final signature of `enqueue_kernel()` provides support for events and local memory to be utilized together:

```
int enqueue_kernel(
  queue_t queue,
  kernel_enqueue_flags_t flags,
  const ndrange_t ndrange,
  uint num_events_in_wait_list,
  const clk_event_t *event_wait_list,
  clk_event_t *event_ret,
  void (^block)(local void *, ...),
  uint size0, ...)
```

```
1   __kernel
2   void child0_kernel()
3   {
4       printf("Child0: I will run first.\n");
5   }
6
7   void child1_kernel()
8   {
9       printf("Child1: I will run second.\n");
10  }
11
12  __kernel
13  void parent_kernel( )
14  {
```

```
15    kernel_enqueue_flags_t child_flags = CLK_ENQUEUE_FLAGS_NO_WAIT;
16    ndrange_t child_ndrange = ndrange_1D(1);
17
18    clk_event event;
19
20    // Enqueue a kernel and initialize an event
21    enqueue_kernel(get_default_queue(), child_flags, child_ndrange,
22        0, NULL, &event, ^{child0_kernel();});
23
24    // Pass the event as a dependency between the kernels
25    enqueue_kernel(get_default_queue(), child_flags, child_ndrange,
26        1, &event, NULL, ^{child1_kernel();});
27
28    // Release the event. In this case, the event will be released
29    // after the dependency is satisfied (second kernel is ready
30    // to execute).
31    release_event(event);
32 }
```

LISTING 5.14

An example showing device-side enqueuing with events used to specify dependencies.

5.6 SUMMARY

In this chapter, we discussed a number of topics related to the runtime and execution model. The task-based execution that the runtime provides is based on a queuing model and a dependency mechanism provided by events. Events are also used for profiling OpenCL commands and executing user-defined callbacks associated with a command. The kernel execution domain comprises a hierarchical grouping of work-items into work-groups and NDRanges. A new feature of OpenCL 2.0 is the ability for devices to enqueue work into device-side queues. We introduced the method of generating kernel-instances from within a device using block syntax. While execution ordering and basic synchronization were discussed in this chapter, the following chapters describing the host-side and device-side memory models dive deeper into execution unit communication and synchronization.

REFERENCE

[1] J. Reinders, Intel Threading Building Blocks: Outfitting C++ for Multi-Core Processor Parallelism, O'Reilly Media, Inc., Sebastopol, 2007.

OpenCL host-side memory model

In order to be portable across a variety of hardware, OpenCL provides a well-defined abstract memory model. The abstract memory model is general enough to map to a wide range of devices, yet provides strong enough memory ordering guarantees to express classes of parallelism important to developers. Providing an abstract memory model also serves as a clean interface between programmers and hardware. Using the abstract memory model, programmers can write code that follows the rules of the model without being concerned about the memory system of the device that will eventually execute the kernel. Similarly, vendors implementing the runtime can map the abstract memory model to their hardware, and be sure that programmers will interact with it using only specific, predefined operations.

Previous chapters have already touched on some aspects of OpenCL's memory model. For instance, we have seen the use of memory object types such as buffers and images in the examples in Chapters 3 and 4. We have also been introduced to memory spaces such as global and local memory. This chapter and Chapter 7 will discuss the memory model in more detail. We will present the memory model as two parts, which we refer to as the *host-side memory model* and the *device-side memory model*. The host-side memory model is relevant within the host program, and involves allocation and movement of memory objects. The device-side memory model discussed in the next chapter is relevant within kernels (written in OpenCL C), and involves running computations using memory objects and other data.

OpenCL devices such as graphics processing units (GPUs) and other accelerators frequently operate with memory systems separate from the main memory associated with the computer's primary central processing unit (CPU). By default, OpenCL's host-side memory model supports a relaxed consistency in which global synchronization of memory is defined only on the completion of events. An important addition to the OpenCL 2.0 specification is optional support of consistency guarantees that closely mirror those of C/C++11 and Java.

To support systems with multiple discrete memories and various consistency models, OpenCL's memory objects are defined to be in a space separate from the host CPU's memory. Any movement of data in and out of OpenCL memory objects from a CPU pointer must be performed through application programming interface (API) functions. It is important to note that OpenCL's memory objects are defined within a context and not on a device. That is, in general, moving data in and out of a buffer need not move data to any specific device. It is the job of the runtime to ensure that data is in the correct place at the correct time.

This chapter begins by describing the types of memory objects defined by OpenCL, followed by a description of their management using the host API.

6.1 MEMORY OBJECTS

OpenCL defines three types of memory objects—*buffers*, *images*, and *pipes*—that are allocated using the host API. Buffers and images serve as data storage that is accessible from the host and randomly accessible from within a kernel. Unlike buffers and images, pipes serve only as a first in, first out (FIFO) mechanism between kernels. Data from within a pipe cannot be accessed by the host.

Buffer objects are one-dimensional arrays in the traditional CPU sense, and are similar to memory allocated through `malloc()` in a C program. Buffers can contain any scalar data type, vector data type, or user-defined structure. The data stored in a buffer is sequential, such that the OpenCL kernel can access it using pointers in a random access manner familiar to a C programmer.

Image objects take a different approach. The data layout transformations involved in optimizing image access make it difficult to define pointer access to this data because the relationship of one memory location to another becomes opaque to the developer. As a result, image structures are completely opaque not only to the developer but also to the kernel code, accessible only through specialized access functions. Because GPUs are designed for processing graphics workloads, they are heavily optimized for accessing image data. This has three main advantages:

1. GPU cache hierarchies and data flow structures are designed to optimize access to image-type data.
2. GPU drivers optimize data layouts to support the hardware in providing efficient access to the data, particularly when two-dimensional access patterns are used.
3. Image-access hardware supports sophisticated data conversions that allow data to be stored in a range of compressed formats.

The remainder of this section describes each type of memory object in more detail.

6.1.1 BUFFERS

Buffer objects are similar to arrays allocated using `malloc()`, so their creation is relatively simple. At the simplest level, creation requires a context in which to create the buffer, a size, and a set of creation flags. The API call `clCreateBuffer()` is used to create a buffer object.

```
cl_mem
clCreateBuffer(
    cl_context context,
    cl_mem_flags flags,
    size_t size,
    void *host_ptr,
    cl_int *err)
```

The function returns a buffer object, requiring the error code to be returned through a variable passed by reference as the last parameter. The `flags` parameter allows various combinations of read-only/write-only data access and allocation options. For example, in the following code, we create a read-only buffer that will use the same storage location as host array a, which is of the same size as the buffer. We will discuss allocation options (e.g., `CL_MEM_USE_HOST_PTR`) in more detail later in this chapter. Any error value will be returned in `err`, which can be any of a range of error conditions defined in the specification. As we have seen, `CL_SUCCESS` is returned by OpenCL functions upon successful completion.

```
cl_int err;
int a[16];

cl_mem newBuffer = clCreateBuffer(
    context,
    CL_MEM_READ_ONLY | CL_MEM_USE_HOST_PTR,
    16*sizeof(int),
    a,
    &err);

if( err != CL_SUCCESS ) {
    // Handle error as necessary
}
```

OpenCL also supports subbuffer objects that allow us to divide a single buffer into multiple smaller buffers that may overlap and that can be read, written, copied, and used in much the same way as their parent buffer object. Note that overlapping sub-buffers and the combination of subbuffers and their parent buffer objects constitutes aliasing, and behavior is undefined in these circumstances.

6.1.2 IMAGES

In OpenCL, images are storage objects that differ from buffers in three ways. Images are

1. opaque types that cannot be viewed directly through pointers in device code;
2. multidimensional structures; and
3. limited to a range of types relevant to graphics data rather than being free to implement arbitrary structures.

Image objects primarily exist in OpenCL to offer access to special function hardware on graphics processors that is designed to support highly efficient access to image data. These special function units do not always support the full range of access modes necessary to enable buffer access, but they may provide additional features such as filtering in hardware in a highly efficient manner. Filtering operations enable efficient transformations of image data based on collections of pixels. These operations would require long instruction sequences with multiple read operations, but can be performed very efficiently in dedicated hardware units.

Image data is accessed through specialized access functions in the kernel code, which are discussed Chapter 7 with the device-side memory model. Access to images from the host is not significantly different from access to buffers, except that all functions are expanded to support addressing in multiple dimensions. Thus, for example, `clEnqueueReadImage()` is more like `clEnqueueReadBufferRect()` than `clEnqueueReadBuffer()`.

The major difference between buffers and images from the host is in the formats that images can support. Whereas buffers support the basic OpenCL types and structures made from them, image formats are more subtle. Image formats are a combination of a channel order and a channel type. Channel order defines the number of channels and the order in which they occur—for example, `CL_RGB`, `CL_R`, or `CL_ARGB`. Channel type is selected from a wide range of storage formats from `CL_FLOAT` to less-storage-hungry formats such as `CL_UNORM_SHORT_565`, which packs into a single 16-bit word in memory. When they are accessed from kernel code, reading from any of these formats results in upconversion to a standard OpenCL C type. The list of image formats can be queried by the API call `clGetSupportedImageFormats()`.

Image objects are created using the API call `clCreateImage()`, which has the following signature:

```
cl_mem
clCreateImage (
    cl_context context,
    cl_mem_flags flags,
    const cl_image_format *image_format,
    const cl_image_desc *image_desc,
    void *host_ptr,
    cl_int *errcode_ret)
```

In the creation of an image, the `context`, `flags`, and `host_ptr` parameters are the same as in the creation of a buffer. The image format (`image_format`) and image descriptor (`image_desc`) parameters define image dimensions, data format, and data layout. These structures are described in detail in Chapter 4 along with an example initializing them for an image object.

6.1.3 PIPES

OpenCL 2.0 provides a new type of memory object called a pipe. A pipe organizes data in an FIFO structure, which facilitates the passing of processed data from one kernel to another. With the relaxed memory model defined in prior versions of the standard, this operation would not be possible, because there were no guarantees about the state of memory before a kernel was complete. The implication of a pipe is that within a device two kernels must be able to share a region of memory and guarantee protection of some shared state. This identifies an important trend in processors, as any device that can support pipes must at least have the ability to implement atomic operations on data shared between kernels, and must have a memory consistency model that supports acquire and release semantics.

One can imagine that given these device capabilities programmers could implement their own version of a pipe using a buffer. While this is feasible given the OpenCL 2.0 memory model, it would require a large amount of programming effort. Pipes are thus a nice abstraction that enables producer-consumer parallelism, and simplifies programmer effort in other scenarios that were difficult to program in prior versions of OpenCL (such as packing data when each work-item generates a variable number of outputs). The use of a pipe when running the producer and consumer on the same device also allows vendors to potentially map the pipe to specialized memories that may be lower latency than main memory. Pipe objects are not allowed to be read from or written to the host, so accesses to pipe objects are covered when we describe the device-side memory model.

The data in a pipe are organized as *packets*, where a packet can be any supported OpenCL C or user-defined type. The API to create a pipe is `clCreatePipe()`, with the following signature:

```
cl_mem
clCreatePipe(
    cl_context context,
    cl_mem_flags flags,
    cl_uint pipe_packet_size,
    cl_uint pipe_max_packets,
    const cl_pipe_properties *properties,
    cl_int *errcode_ret)
```

When a pipe is created, the packet size (`pipe_packet_size`) and the maximum number of packets (`pipe_max_packets`) must be supplied. As with other calls to create memory objects, there is a parameter to pass flags related to object allocation. In the case of a pipe, the only valid option related to access capability is

CL_MEM_READ_WRITE, which is the default. Further, since a pipe cannot be accessed by the host, CL_MEM_HOST_NO_ACCESS will also be used implicitly, even if this is not specified by the programmer.

6.2 MEMORY MANAGEMENT

When OpenCL creates memory objects, they are allocated in the global memory space that is visible to all devices in a context. Although OpenCL provides the abstraction of a single global memory, in reality many heterogeneous systems have multiple devices that may have restrictions about sharing address spaces and may have physically separate memories—as is the case in systems with a CPU and a discrete GPU. In these cases, the runtime may need to create multiple copies of the data for each device over the course of execution. Even in shared-memory systems where data does not need to be replicated between memories, almost all memory accesses by a device replicate data in a cache hierarchy or in hardware buffers. When data is replicated, it is possible that a copy on one device is inconsistent with memory that is visible to another device. Given the potential for replicated, nonconsistent views of a memory object, how do we ensure that we are working with the latest copy of data to obtain the expected results?

Later, we will discuss fine-grained memory ordering and visibility when dealing with shared virtual memory (SVM), but for now we will assume that we are working with memory objects with a default (non-SVM) allocation. When a default memory object is used, OpenCL's relaxed consistency model does not allow multiple kernels to modify the object at the same time. No modification is guaranteed to be visible until after the kernel completes execution, and since the runtime can create multiple copies of a memory object, two kernels updating different copies of the same object would likely result in the updates from one being completely masked by the other. If we take this a step further, the result of reading from a memory object while another kernel is modifying it is undefined, since there are no guarantees about when the data will become visible before the kernel completes execution. Aside from these responsibilities of the programmer, it is up to the runtime to ensure that data is in the correct place at the correct time. This combination of a relaxed memory model and the runtime's responsibility of memory management allows efficient execution with high portability and minimal programmer effort.

In addition to portability, the designers of the OpenCL specification also understood that in practice transfers are inefficient, and moving data only on demand would likely lead to poor performance. Therefore, OpenCL provides commands that allow the programmer to suggest how and where data is allocated, and where and when the data should be moved. Depending on the system that is running the OpenCL application, these choices may have a large impact on performance. The following two sections describe allocation and movement of memory objects—without and with memory allocation flags, respectively. The API calls that we discuss are based on buffer types, although in general operations described for buffers have synonymous implementations for images. Pipes are distinct from images and buffers, as the host does not have the ability to access the memory space allocated for a pipe.

6.2.1 MANAGING DEFAULT MEMORY OBJECTS

Recall that when a memory object is created, the call to create the object (e.g., clCreateBuffer()) takes a parameter called flags, and another called host_ptr. The signature of clCreateBuffer() is listed again below for convenience:

```
cl_mem
clCreateBuffer(
    cl_context context,
    cl_mem_flags flags,
    size_t size,
    void *host_ptr,
    cl_int *errcode_ret)
```

Some options passed to flags tell the runtime how and where the programmer would like the buffer's space to be allocated, and host_ptr can be used either to initialize the buffer or directly for storage. This section will describe working with memory objects when no allocation-related options are passed to flags, although we will discuss the option for initializing memory objects. The next section will describe the programmer's options that can affect where memory is physically allocated.

By default, OpenCL does not specify where the physical storage allocated for a memory object must reside—it specifies simply that the data is located in "global memory." For example, the runtime could decide to allocate space in CPU main memory or in video memory on a discrete GPU. Most likely it will create multiple allocations for the data and migrate the latest copy as needed.

When an object is created, it has the option of being initialized with host data by providing a valid pointer to host_ptr, and specifying the flag CL_MEM_COPY_HOST_PTR to flags. This combination of parameters will create a new allocation for the buffer and copy the data provided by host_ptr. Since the API call to create the buffer does not generate an event, we can assume that a copy of the data in host_ptr is complete when clCreateBuffer() returns. Figure 6.1 shows how the runtime may choose to migrate data if a buffer is initialized during creation, passed as an argument to a kernel, and then read back after the kernel execution.

In general, it is inefficient to move data allocated on one device to another device—in Chapter 8, we will describe the relative memory bandwidths in a modern CPU and GPU, and compare the interconnects used when transferring data. To allow programmers to perform data transfers as efficiently as possible, OpenCL provides a number of API calls dedicated to moving data in different ways. Keep in mind that the optimal choice will depend both on the algorithm and on the system characteristics.

The first set of commands that we will discuss are intended to be used to perform an explicit copying of data from the host to a device or vice versa, as shown in Figure 6.2. These commands are clEnqueueWriteBuffer() and clEnqueueReadBuffer(). The signature of clEnqueueWriteBuffer() is as follows:

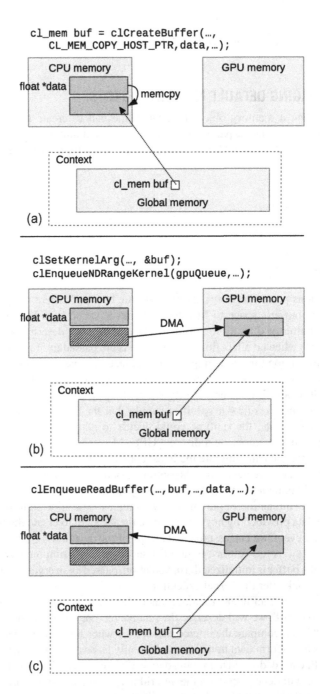

FIGURE 6.1

An example showing a scenario where a buffer is created and initialized on the host, used for computation on the device, and transferred back to the host. Note that the runtime could have also created and initialized the buffer directly on the device. (a) Creation and initialization of a buffer in host memory. (b) Implicit data transfer from the host to the device prior to kernel execution. (c) Explicit copying of data back from the device to the host pointer.

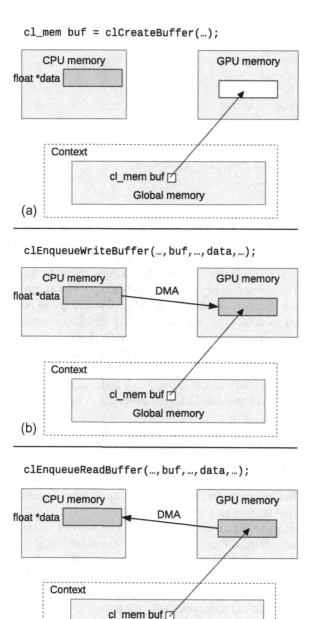

FIGURE 6.2

Data movement using explicit read-write commands. (a) Creation of an uninitialized buffer in device memory. (b) Explicit data transfer from the host to the device prior to execution. (c) Explicit data transfer from the device to the host following execution.

```
cl_int
clEnqueueWriteBuffer(
    cl_command_queue command_queue,
    cl_mem buffer,
    cl_bool blocking_write,
    size_t offset,
    size_t size,
    const void *ptr,
    cl_uint num_events_in_wait_list,
    const cl_event *event_wait_list,
    cl_event *event)
```

The signature of clEnqueueReadBuffer() is identical to that of clEnqueueWriteBuffer(), except that blocking_write is replaced with blocking_read. In the signature, a transfer will occur between the buffer and the host pointer ptr. The write call specifies a copy from the host to the device (technically just to global memory), and the read call specifies a copy from the device to the host. Notice that the signature includes a command-queue parameter. This is slightly awkward as there is no way to explicitly initialize a memory object after creation without also having to specify a target device. However, for most applications the programmer knows which device the data will target, and specifying a command-queue allows the runtime to target a device directly and avoid an additional copy. This design also allows the runtime to begin to transfer the data much sooner than if it had to wait until it had processed a kernel-execution command that required use of the buffer on a specific device.

If the programmer only wants to copy certain bytes to or from the buffer, the parameters offset and size can be used to specify the offset in the buffer to begin the copying and the number of bytes to copy, respectively. Notice that ptr is the starting location on the host for reading and writing data. The offset parameter only refers to the offset within the buffer object. It is up to the programmer to have ptr point to the desired starting location.

These data transfer functions are intended, like the rest of the OpenCL API, to be used asynchronously. That is, if we call clEnqueueReadBuffer(), we cannot expect to be able to read the data from the host array until we know that the read has completed—through the event mechanism, a clFinish() call, or by passing CL_TRUE to clEnqueueReadBuffer() to make it a blocking call. Thus, for example, the following host code sequence does not guarantee that the two printf() calls A and B will generate different values even if outputBuffer's content would suggest that it should. The printf() of C is the only point in the code where the printed value is guaranteed to be that copied from outputBuffer.

```
int returnedArray[16];
cl_mem outputBuffer;
cl_event readEvent;
```

```
// Some code that fills the returned array with 0s and invokes kernels
// that generates a result in outputBuffer
printf( "A: %d\n", returnedArray[3] );
clEnqueueReadBuffer(
    commandQueue,
    outputBuffer, /* buffer */
    CL_FALSE, /* nonblocking read */
    0,
    sizeof(int)*16,
    returnedArray, /* host ptr */
    0,
    0,
    &readEvent );

printf( "B: %d\n", returnedArray[3] );
clWaitForEvents(1, &readEvent);
printf( "C: %d\n", returnedArray[3] );
)))
```

This is a vital point about OpenCL's memory model. Changes to memory are not guaranteed to be visible, and hence memory is not guaranteed to be consistent, until an event reports that the command's execution has finished (we will discuss the differences with SVM later). This works both ways: in a transfer between a host pointer and a device buffer, you cannot reuse the data pointed to by the host pointer until you know that the event associated with the asynchronous copying of data into the device buffer has finished. Indeed, a careful reading of the OpenCL specification suggests that this is because buffers are associated with the context and not with a device. A clEnqueueWriteBuffer() enqueue, even on completion, does not guarantee that data have been moved to the device, and guarantees only that it has been moved out of the host pointer.

Unlike other API calls in OpenCL, data transfer calls generally allow us to specify synchronous execution. Had we replaced the previous call with

```
clEnqueueReadBuffer(
    commandQueue,
    outputBuffer,
    CL_TRUE, /* blocking read */
    0,
    sizeof(int)*16,
    returnedArray,
    0,
    0,
    &readEvent );
```

execution of the host thread would stall at the call to clEnqueueReadBuffer() until the copying finishes and all data is visible to the host.

In addition to transferring data between the host and the device, OpenCL provides a command, clEnqueueMigrateMemObjects(), to *migrate* data from its current location (wherever that may be) to a specified device. For example, if a buffer is created and initialized by passing CL_MEM_COPY_HOST_PTR to clCreateBuffer(), clEnqueueMigrateMemObjects() can be used to explicitly transfer the data to the device. It can also be used to transfer data between devices if an application is utilizing more than one device for computation. Notice that neither of these goals could be accomplished efficiently with clEnqueueReadBuffer() and clEnqueueWriteBuffer(), since both require the transfer to begin or end at the host. The signature of clEnqueueMigrateMemObjects() is as follows:

```
cl_int
clEnqueueMigrateMemObjects(
    cl_command_queue command_queue,
    cl_uint num_mem_objects,
    const cl_mem *mem_objects,
    cl_mem_migration_flags flags,
    cl_uint num_events_in_wait_list,
    const cl_event *event_wait_list,
    cl_event *event)
```

Unlike previous data transfer commands, clEnqueueMigrateMemObjects() takes an array of memory objects, allowing multiple objects to be migrated with a single command. As with all clEnqueue calls, the event produced should either be passed as a dependency to any dependent commands, or be queried directly for completion. When the event's status has been set to CL_COMPLETE, the memory objects will be located on the device associated with the command-queue that was passed as the argument to the command_queue parameter.

Aside from explicitly telling the runtime where memory objects should be migrated, this command has another subtle performance implication. If the programmer is able to enqueue this command such that it is processed during an unrelated operation (such as a kernel execution that does not include any of the specified memory objects), migration can potentially overlap the former operation and hide the transfer latency. Note that hiding the transfer latency can also occur in a similar manner with calls to clEnqueueWriteBuffer() and clEnqueueReadBuffer().

For migrating memory objects, the specification also provides a flag, CL_MIGRATE_MEM_OBJECT_HOST, that tells the runtime that the data should be migrated to the host. If CL_MIGRATE_MEM_OBJECT_HOST is supplied, the command-queue passed to the function will be ignored.

6.2.2 MANAGING MEMORY OBJECTS WITH ALLOCATION OPTIONS

The API calls described in the previous section were used to tell the OpenCL runtime to copy data between the host and a device, or to migrate data to a certain device. Alternatively, this section describes how the host and the device can directly access data that is physically located in the other's memory.

OpenCL provides two mechanisms for the programmer to specify that a memory object should be physically allocated in a place that allows the data to be mapped into the host's address space. Providing the option CL_MEM_ALLOC_HOST_PTR to flags in clCreateBuffer() tells the runtime to allocate new space for the object in "host-accessible" memory, and CL_MEM_USE_HOST_PTR tells the runtime to use the space pointed to by host_ptr directly. Since they represent two different allocation options, these flags are mutually exclusive and cannot be used together for the same memory object. Note that "host-accessible memory" is intentionally vague, and could include main memory connected to the host processor or a region of device memory that can be mapped into the host's address space.

As with default memory objects, the flag CL_MEM_COPY_HOST_PTR can be used with CL_MEM_ALLOC_HOST_PTR to allocate host-accessible memory and initialize it immediately. However, CL_MEM_COPY_HOST_PTR and CL_MEM_USE_HOST_PTR cannot be used together, as the argument passed to host_ptr will represent a pre-existing allocation, and it does not make sense to initialize it with itself.

It would be reasonable to assume that by specifying an option to allocate data in host-accessible memory that the data would be allocated in CPU main memory, and the compute device would access the data directly from there. In fact, when either of these flags is provided, this is what will occur on some systems. In a system with a CPU and a discrete GPU, this scenario would send GPU accesses to the memory object across the PCI Express bus. When a device accesses data directly from the host's memory in this way, the data is often referred to as *zero-copy* data.

Although using CL_MEM_USE_HOST_PTR or CL_MEM_ALLOC_HOST_PTR may result in the creation of zero-copy data on the host, it is not explicitly required by the specification. It is completely valid for the runtime to create storage in CPU memory and then copy it to device memory for a kernel execution. In this scenario, a discrete GPU would be able to access the buffer directly from its own video memory. In fact, if CL_MEM_ALLOC_HOST_PTR is used, it is also completely valid for the runtime to allocate storage solely in device memory as long as it can be mapped into the host's address space. Remember that the specification says that passing CL_MEM_ALLOC_HOST_PTR creates space in host-accessible memory, and not necessarily in host memory itself.

In shared-memory systems, or when a CPU is being used as the device, CL_MEM_USE_HOST_PTR may prevent unnecessary copies of data from being created and lead to better performance. For example, imagine that the device selected to execute a kernel is the same CPU as the host: if the option CL_MEM_USE_HOST_PTR is not specified, then the application will incur the overhead of allocating additional space for the buffer and making a copy of the data. One could imagine a similar situation for heterogeneous shared-memory processors, such as accelerated processing units (APUs). If the CPU and GPU share the same memory, does it make sense to use `CL_MEM_USE_HOST_PTR` for APUs as well? As with many optimization-related considerations, the answer depends on a number of factors.

In the case of APUs, the OpenCL runtime or device driver may optimize memory accesses for a certain device by allocating data with system-specific flags (e.g., cached vs. uncached) or may have other performance considerations, such as nonuniform memory accesses (NUMA). For example, when running on some APUs, `CL_MEM_USE_HOST_PTR` may lead to the buffer being treated as cacheable and fully coherent. This can cause inefficient accesses by the GPU, which must now probe the CPU cache hierarchy prior to accesses. Especially when using APUs, the programmer should understand the device-specific performance implications of creating memory objects with the `CL_MEM_USE_HOST_PTR` and `CL_MEM_ALLOC_HOST_PTR` flags.

Since `CL_MEM_USE_HOST_PTR` and `CL_MEM_ALLOC_HOST_PTR` specify that data should be created in host-accessible memory, the OpenCL specification provides a mechanism for the host to access the data without going through the explicit read and write API calls. In order for the host to access the data storage of a memory object, it must first *map* the memory object into its address space. Note that mapping does not necessarily imply creating a copy, unlike a call to `clEnqueueReadBuffer()` which would always result in a copy of the data. In systems where zero-copy memory objects are supported, a call to map the data into host memory would simply require that all in-flight updates to the data have finished and are visible to the host.

The call to map memory objects is type specific. For a buffer, the call is `clEnqueueMapBuffer()`, with the following signature:

```
void*
clEnqueueMapBuffer(
    cl_command_queue command_queue,
    cl_mem buffer,
    cl_bool blocking_map,
    cl_map_flags map_flags,
    size_t offset,
    size_t size,
    cl_uint num_events_in_wait_list,
    const cl_event *event_wait_list,
    cl_event *event,
    cl_int *errcode_ret)
```

When `clEnqueueMapBuffer()` is called, it returns a pointer that is valid on the host. When the event returned by `clEnqueueMapBuffer()` is set to `CL_COMPLETE`, it is safe for the host to access the data, which is mapped to the pointer returned by the call. As with `clEnqueueWriteBuffer()` and `clEnqueueReadBuffer()`, this call has a blocking parameter, `blocking_map`, which when passed `CL_TRUE` will turn the call into a blocking call. If `blocking_map` is set, then the host is able to access the returned pointer as soon as the call completes.

When `clEnqueueMapBuffer()` is called, there are three different flags that can be passed to the `map_flags` parameter: `CL_MAP_READ`, `CL_MAP_WRITE`, and `CL_MAP_WRITE_INVALIDATE_REGION`. The flag `CL_MAP_READ` tells the runtime that the host will be reading the data, and `CL_MAP_WRITE` and `CL_MAP_WRITE_INVALIDATE_REGION` tell the runtime that the host will be modifying the data. `CL_MAP_WRITE_INVALIDATE_REGION` is an optimization that specifies that the entire region will be modified or disregarded, and so the runtime does not need to map the latest values before it can be modified. By there not being a requirement that the data is in a consistent state, the runtime can potentially allow access to the region much sooner with `CL_MAP_WRITE_INVALIDATE_REGION` than with `CL_MAP_WRITE`.

When the host has finished modifying the mapped data, it needs to tell the runtime that it has finished using the complementary unmap call. While the command to map a memory object is type specific, the command to unmap is the same for all memory objects: `clEnqueueUnmapMemObject()`.

```
cl_int
clEnqueueUnmapMemObject(
    cl_command_queue command_queue,
    cl_mem memobj,
    void *mapped_ptr,
    cl_uint num_events_in_wait_list,
    const cl_event *event_wait_list,
    cl_event *event)
```

Unmapping a memory object requires passing the memory object itself, along with the host pointer (`mapped_ptr`) that was returned by the call that mapped the data. As with all previous data management commands, when the event returned by `clEnqueueUnmapMemObject()` is set to `CL_COMPLETE`, updates to the data are considered complete. Unlike most other calls, there is no parameter that turns `clEnqueueUnmapMemObject()` into a blocking call. Figure 6.3 shows the process of mapping and unmapping a memory object. Undefined behavior occurs if an object that is currently mapped for reading by the host is written to by a device. Similarly, undefined behavior occurs if an object that is currently mapped for writing by the host is read by a device.

As we have mentioned a number of times throughout this section, the actual behavior associated with these flags is implementation defined, and in practice is highly device specific. To give programmers an idea of how data would be allocated in practice, we will briefly describe the AMD-specific treatment of flags. For default memory objects (no flags supplied) data will likely be allocated in device memory directly. When `CL_MEM_USE_HOST_PTR` or `CL_MEM_ALLOC_HOST_PTR` is supplied, if devices in the context support virtual memory, data will be created as pinned (nonpageable) host memory and will be accessed by the device as zero-copy

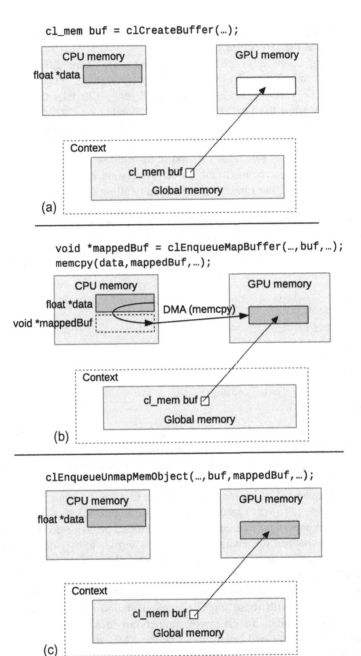

FIGURE 6.3

Data movement using map/unmap. (a) Creation of an uninitialized buffer in device memory. (b) The buffer is mapped into the host's address space. (c) The buffer is unmapped from the host's address space.

data. If virtual memory is not supported, data will be allocated in device memory as with default memory objects. If the programmer desires data allocation on the device and direct access to data in device memory by the host, AMD provides a vendor-specific extension called CL_MEM_USE_PERSISTENT_MEM_AMD. When this flag is supplied, accesses to a memory object that is mapped into the host's address space will occur directly from device memory.

6.3 SHARED VIRTUAL MEMORY

One of the most significant updates to OpenCL in the 2.0 standard is the support of *SVM*. SVM extends global memory into the host's memory region, allowing virtual addresses to be shared between the host and all devices in a context. An obvious benefit of SVM is the ability to pass pointer-based data structures as arguments to OpenCL kernels. For example, prior to support of SVM, there was no way to have a kernel operate on a linked-list that was created on the host, since each node of the list points to the next node, and the pointers were valid only in the host's address space. Further, how would one even go about copying a linked list onto the device? Small objects spread across memory were not suited for OpenCL's memory model, and would have to be marshaled to be suitable for processing by a kernel. SVM removes these limitations and more.

There are three types of SVM in OpenCL:

1. Coarse-grained buffer SVM.
2. Fine-grained buffer SVM.
3. Fine-grained system SVM.

The reader can refer to Table 6.1 for a summary of the characteristics as we discuss each type of SVM.

Coarse-grained buffer SVM allows virtual address sharing to occur at the granularity of OpenCL buffer memory objects. The difference between a coarse-grained SVM buffer and a non-SVM buffer is simply that the host and device share virtual memory pointers. Buffer objects that are allocated to use coarse-grained SVM should

Table 6.1 Summary of Options for SVM

	Coarse-Grained Buffer SVM	Fine-Grained Buffer SVM	Fine-Grained System SVM
OpenCL object	Buffer	Buffer	None (host memory)
Sharing granularity	Buffer	Bytes	Bytes
Allocation	clSVMAlloc	clSVMAlloc	malloc (or similar)
Consistency	Sync points	Sync points and optional atomics	Sync points and optional atomics
Explicit updates between host and device?	Map/unmap commands	No	No

be mapped into and unmapped from the host's address space to guarantee that the latest updates made by a device are visible. To do this, the host thread can call `clEnqueueMapBuffer()` specify a blocking command to map the buffer region. Recall that by specifying a blocking command, the function will wait for an event to signal the kernel's completion before returning. When `clEnqueueMapBuffer()` returns, any memory operations performed by the kernel in that buffer region will be visible to the host.

While non-SVM buffers are created using the API call `clCreateBuffer()`, the command to create an SVM buffer is `clSVMAlloc()`, with the following signature:

```
void*
clSVMAlloc(
    cl_context context,
    cl_svm_mem_flags flags,
    size_t size,
    unsigned int alignment)
```

As with non-SVM buffers, the `flags` parameter takes read-only, write-only, and read-write options (we will describe the remaining options shortly). The `alignment` parameter is the minimum byte alignment for this object required by the system. Passing an alignment of zero uses the default alignment, which will be the size of the largest data type supported by the OpenCL runtime. Notice that instead of a `cl_mem` object, a call to `clSVMAlloc()` returns a `void` pointer. As with a call to `malloc()` from a regular C program, `clSVMAlloc()` will return a non-`NULL` value on a successful allocation, or `NULL` on a failure.

Freeing an SVM buffer allocated with `clSVMAlloc()` is done using a call to `clSVMFree()`, which simply takes the context and SVM pointer as parameters.

```
void
clSVMFree(
    cl_context context,
    void* svm_pointer)
```

A call to `clSVMFree()` is instantaneous, and does not wait for currently enqueued or executing commands to finish. Calling `clSVMFree()` and then accessing a buffer can therefore result in a segmentation fault as can happen in a normal C program. To allow SVM buffers to be freed after completion of enqueued commands, the specification supplies a command to enqueue a free operation: `clEnqueueSVMFree()`.

Unlike coarse-grained buffer SVM, *fine-grained buffer SVM* supports sharing at a byte-level granularity within an OpenCL buffer memory object. If (optional) SVM atomic operations are supported, fine-grained buffer SVM can be used by the host and the device to concurrently read and update the same region of the buffer. Fine-grained buffer SVM also enables kernels running on the same or different devices to concurrently access the same region of a buffer as well. Among their other benefits, SVM atomics provide synchronization points to ensure that data is updated according to OpenCL's memory consistency model. If SVM atomics are not supported, reads from the host and the device can still occur from the same region of the buffer, and updates can occur to nonoverlapping regions.

In order to create a buffer with a fine-grained SVM, the flag CL_MEM_SVM_FINE_ GRAIN_BUFFER needs to be passed to the flags parameter of clSVMAlloc(). Using atomic operations on an SVM buffer requires additionally passing CL_MEM_SVM_ATOMICS to the flags parameter. Note that CL_MEM_SVM_ATOMICS is valid only if CL_MEM_SVM_FINE_GRAIN_BUFFER is also specified.

Fine-grained system SVM extends fine-grained buffer SVM to the host's entire address space—this includes regions of memory outside the OpenCL context that were allocated using the regular system malloc(). If fine-grained system SVM is supported, buffer objects are no longer necessary for OpenCL programs, and kernels can simply be passed pointers that were allocated on the host.

Determining the type of SVM supported by a device is done by passing the flag CL_DEVICE_SVM_CAPABILITIES to clGetDeviceInfo(). At minimum, OpenCL requires that coarse-grained buffer SVM must be supported by all devices.

6.4 SUMMARY

This chapter presented OpenCL's memory model from the point of view of the host. The host's role in the memory model is largely related to the allocation and management of memory objects (buffers, images, and pipes) in global memory. We described in detail the allocation flags that allow the programmer to guide how and where data is allocated, and the management flags that can be used to guide where and when to move data. The chapter concluded with an introduction to the support of SVM, which will be continued in the next chapter that discusses the device-side memory model.

OpenCL device-side memory model

7

The device-side memory model defines the abstract memory spaces that work-items within an OpenCL application may target when executing a kernel. The memory model also defines the memory consistency that work-items can expect in each memory space. This chapter discusses each memory space in detail, describes the mapping of memory objects to memory spaces, and introduces synchronization and memory ordering.

On OpenCL devices, the memory space is classified into four categories:

1. global memory
2. local memory
3. constant memory
4. private memory

These memory spaces are visualized in Figure 7.1. As discussed in Chapter 2, OpenCL is designed to run on a range of architectures. The purpose of arranging a memory hierarchy of this form is to allow OpenCL programs to perform efficiently on such architectures. The actual meaning of each memory space in terms of a hardware mapping is very much implementation dependent. Regardless of how they are mapped to hardware, as a programming construct, these memory spaces are disjoint. Furthermore, as shown in Figure 7.1, local memory and private memory are divided into disjoint blocks across work-groups and work-items. When separate layers of address space are defined in this way, the mapping to hardware can efficiently use anything from relaxed memory consistency models with programmatically controlled scratchpad buffers, as seen on most graphics processing unit (GPU) devices, to fully coherent memory systems such as x86-based architectures.

The default address space for function arguments and local variables within a function or block is private. Pointer arguments can be placed in one of the other address spaces depending on where the data comes from or where it is to be used. The pointer itself is always in the private address space wherever the data lies. The address spaces are strictly disjoint when used through pointers. Casting from one address space to another is not legal because this would imply either that the data lives at a globally accessible address or that the compiler would have to generate a copy to go with the cast, which is not feasible in practice. However,

163

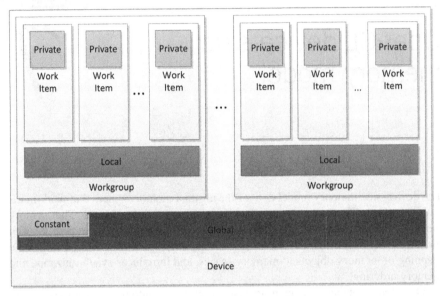

FIGURE 7.1

The memory spaces available to an OpenCL device.

as we will see later in this chapter, OpenCL 2.0 has introduced a generic address space, which does allow address spaces to be inferred automatically in some cases. Image arguments always live in the global address space, so we discuss images in those terms.

Before the memory spaces are discussed in detail, the following section outlines the capabilities of work-items to synchronize and communicate. This information will be useful when discussing the qualities of each memory space.

7.1 SYNCHRONIZATION AND COMMUNICATION

When describing the host memory model, we said that by default OpenCL does not guarantee that writes will be visible to the host until the kernel completes. Similarly, regular accesses by work-items are not required to be visible to other work-items during a kernel's execution. However, the OpenCL C language (combined with the memory model) does provide certain synchronization operations to allow visibility within various memory spaces using barriers, memory fences, and atomics. The hierarchy of consistency is as follows:

- Within a work-item, memory operations are ordered predictably: any two reads from and writes to the same address will not be reordered by hardware or the compiler. Specifically for image accesses, synchronization is required for any read-after-write operation, even when it is performed by the same work-item.

- Between work-items and within a work-group, memory is guaranteed to be consistent only after synchronization using an atomic operation, memory fence, or barrier.
- Between work-groups, memory is guaranteed to be consistent only after a synchronization operation using an atomic operation or memory fence. Work-items from different work-groups cannot synchronize using a barrier.

7.1.1 BARRIERS

Within a work-group, the programmer may require all work-items in the work-group to synchronize at a barrier using a call to `work_group_barrier()`. The two versions of the barrier function are as follows:

```
void
work_group_barrier (
   cl_mem_fence_flags flags)

void
work_group_barrier (
   cl_mem_fence_flags flags,
   memory_scope scope)
```

The barrier requires that all work-items in the work-group reach it and that visibility requirements are met before any is allowed to continue execution. As barrier operations are often used to ensure data visibility within the work-group (e.g., after manually caching a subset of global memory into local memory), the `flags` parameter to `work_group_barrier()` is used to specify which types of accesses must be visible after the barrier completes. The three options are `CLK_LOCAL_MEM_FENCE`, `CLK_GLOBAL_MEM_FENCE`, and `CLK_IMAGE_MEM_FENCE`, which ensure that all local memory, global memory, or image accesses are visible to the entire work-group, respectively.

The second version of `work_group_barrier()` also allows a memory scope to be specified. The memory scope can be used in combination with the `flags` argument for fine-grained control of data visibility. Two possible options for memory scope are `memory_scope_work_group` and `memory_scope_device`. If `CLK_GLOBAL_MEM_FENCE` and `memory_scope_work_group` are used together, the barrier will ensure that all global memory accesses from every work-item in the work-group are visible to all other work-items in the work-group before any proceed past the barrier. If `CLK_GLOBAL_MEM_FENCE` and `memory_scope_device` are used, then the barrier will ensure that its accesses are visible to the entire device. The flag `CLK_LOCAL_MEM_FENCE` can be used only with `memory_scope_work_group`, as work-items outside the group do not have access to the memory space.

7.1.2 ATOMICS

The atomics defined in OpenCL 2.0 are based on C/C++11 atomics and are used to provide atomicity and synchronization. Atomicity safely allows a series of operations (such as read-modify-write) to execute without another work-item or host thread being able to view or modify the memory location in between. When used for synchronization, atomics are used to access special variables (called *synchronization variables*) that enforce parts of the memory consistency model. There are different flavors of atomic operations, including variations of atomic read-modify-writes, atomic loads, and atomic stores.

As we have mentioned, atomics are used to ensure that threads do not see partial results in a series of events—this is a problem in shared-memory, concurrent programming. Consider the example where we have two threads and both are trying to increment a shared value. Thread 0 must read the value from memory, increment the value, and write the new value to memory. Thread 1 must do the same. Figure 7.2 shows that the ordering of operations will produce different results. This is referred to as a *data race*. The same data race occurs even when the threads are running on a single core, as thread 0 can be preempted in the middle of performing the operation.

For similar reasons, atomic load and store operations are required. The C/C++11 standards, and likewise OpenCL, do not guarantee any load or store operations to be atomic. Imagine a scenario where a 64-bit store to memory is broken into two machine instructions. It is feasible that at some point in time the first store operation has finished but the second has not. At this time, another thread performs a load, reading 32 bits of the new stored value, and 32 bits of the old stored value. The value read by the second thread would be nonsensical and lead to unexpected results. In practice, most architectures do guarantee that loading or storing data at some granularity will

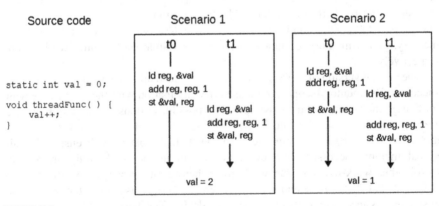

FIGURE 7.2

Data race when incrementing a shared variable. The value stored depends on the ordering of operations between the threads.

be atomic (usually aligned types that fit within a cache line). However, portable code should never assume that any operation on shared memory is implicitly guaranteed to be atomic.

Atomic operations have changed considerably in the OpenCL 2.0 specification. The OpenCL C language defines atomic types that correspond to basic types, and requires support for integer and single-precision floating-point atomics:

```
atomic_int
atomic_uint
atomic_float¹
```

Additional types are provided if optional 64-bit atomic extensions are supported:

```
atomic_long
atomic_ulong
atomic_double
atomic_size_t
atomic_intptr_t
atomic_uintptr_t
atomic_ptrdiff_t
```

The atomic pointer types require only 64-bit extension support if the compute device uses a 64-bit address space.

There are many variations of atomic operations specified in the OpenCL C language. Floating-point operands are supported only for the *compare-and-swap* class of atomic operations (e.g., `atomic_exchange()`). The operations that perform arithmetic and bitwise operations are referred to as atomic *fetch-and-modify* functions. The basic signature for operations of this type is as follows:

```
C atomic_fetch_key(volatile A *object, M operand)
```

Here *key* can be `add`, `sub`, `or`, `xor`, `and`, `min`, or `max`. The parameter `object` is a pointer to a variable of one of the atomic types, and `operand` is the value to be applied. The return value, `C`, is the nonatomic version of type `A`, and holds the value pointed to by `object` immediately prior to the atomic operation. As an example use of an atomic function, suppose a work-item wants to find the minimum of a shared variable, `atomic_int curMin`, and a value in one of its variables, `int myMin`. The atomic function could be called as follows:

```
int oldMin = atomic_fetch_min(&curMin, myMin);
```

The new minimum will be stored in `curMin`. Specifying a variable to hold the return value is optional, and not specifying a variable for the return value is a potential

---

[1] `atomic_float` is only supported for compare-and-swap type operations, not general fetch-and-modify (Section 7.7.1)

performance optimization. On some GPU architectures, for example, atomics are performed by hardware units within the memory system. Thus, certain types of atomic operations can be considered complete as soon as they are issued to the memory hierarchy. However, utilizing the return value requires data to be sent back to the compute unit, potentially adding dozens to hundreds of cycles of latency.

The reason why atomics are being discussed as part of the memory model chapter is that they now play a fundamental role in synchronization. Whenever an atomic operation is performed, the programmer has the ability to specify whether the atomic should be treated as a synchronization operation that serves as an acquire operation, a release operation, or both. Using this mechanism allows work-items to control the visibility of their data accesses, enabling communication paradigms that were not possible in prior versions of OpenCL.

7.2 GLOBAL MEMORY

Global memory is identified in OpenCL C code by a pointer with the type qualifier __global (or global), by one of the image types, or by the pipe type. Data in the global memory space are accessible by all work-items executing a kernel (i.e., by all compute units in the device). The types of objects differ in their scope and use cases. The following sections discuss each global memory object type in detail.

7.2.1 BUFFERS

The __global address space qualifier refers to a pointer referencing data in a buffer object. A buffer can carry any scalar data type, vector data type, or user-defined structure. Whatever the type of buffer, it is accessed at the end of a pointer and can be read/write accessible as well as read only or write only.

Buffer objects map very easily to the standard array representation that programmers expect in the host C program. Consider the following host code, which is legal C:

```
float a[10], b[10];
for (int i = 0; i < 10; ++i) {
    *(a+i) = b[i];
}
```

The example shows that we can access a and b either through pointers or using array access syntax. This is important because it implies that data is allocated sequentially, such that the ith element of array a, a[i], is stored at location $(a + i)$. We can use sizeof() operations on array elements to calculate offsets into arrays to cast to pointers of different types. In low-level code, it is useful to have these features, and it is a natural expectation for OpenCL, a C-derived language.

Thus, the following trivial operation code is an example of valid use of a buffer:

```
typedef struct AStructure
{
    float a;
    float b;
```

```
} AStructure;

__kernel void aFunction(
    __global AStructure *inputOutputBuffer )
{
    __global AStructure* inputLocation =
        inputOutputBuffer + get_global_id(0);
    __global AStructure* outputLocation =
        inputOutputBuffer + get_global_size(0) + get_global_id(0);

    outputLocation->a = inputLocation->a * -1;
    outputLocation->b = (*inputLocation).b + 3.f;
}
```

7.2.2 IMAGES

Image objects, although conceptually in the __global memory space, are treated differently from buffers, and are not mappable to __global pointers. Image objects can be one-dimensional, two-dimensional, or three-dimensional, and are specified using the image1d_t, image2d_t, or image3d_t type qualifiers. Prior to OpenCL 2.0, images could be either read only or write only, but never both within the same kernel. This was a result of the design of GPU hardware supporting very high performance caching and filtering. Beginning in the 2.0 version of the specification, reading and writing the same image is supported.

Images are opaque memory objects. Although we can read or write the data on the basis of coordinates, we do not really know the relative memory locations of two different values in the image. As a result, and to support parameterization of the style of read, rather than accessing images through pointers, we use a set of built-in functions. The built-in functions to read an image are read_imagef(), read_imagei(), and read_imageui(), for floating-point, integer, and unsigned-integer data, respectively. Each of the image read functions takes three parameters: the image object, the image sampler, and the coordinates to sample.

The coordinates may be specified as integer or floating-point values. The output always returns a four-element vector type based on the type of the built-in read function. For example, the two signatures for reading floating-point data from a two-dimensional image are as follows:

```
float4
read_imagef (
    image2d_t image,
    sampler_t sampler,
    int2 coord)

float4
read_imagef (
```

```
image2d_t image,
sampler_t sampler,
float2 coord)
```

Notice that the coordinates in the listed signatures are of type `int2` and `float2`, respectively. This is because these signatures are specific to the two-dimensional image type, `image2d_t`. The functions for one-dimensional images (`image1d_t`) take `int` and `float` coordinates, and three-dimensional images (`image3d_t`) take `int4` and `float4` coordinates with the last component of the vector ignored.

If the image contains data that has less than four channels, most image types will return 0 for the values of the unused color channels and 1 in the alpha channel. For example, if a single channel image (`CL_R`) is read, then the `float4` vector will contain (`r, 0.0, 0.0, 1.0`).

The second parameter to the read function is a sampler object. It is the sampler object that defines how the image is interpreted by the hardware or runtime system. The sampler can be defined either by declaring a constant variable of `sampler_t` type within the OpenCL C source or by passing as a kernel parameter a sampler created in host code using the `clCreateSampler()` function. The following is an example of using a constant-variable-declared sampler:

```
__constant sampler_t sampler =
   CLK_NORMALIZED_COORDS_FALSE |
   CLK_FILTER_NEAREST          |
   CLK_ADDRESS_CLAMP;

__kernel void samplerUser(
   __read_only image2d_t sourceImage,
   __global float *outputBuffer ) {

   float4 a = read_imagef(
      sourceImage,
      sampler,
      (float2)(
         (float)(get_global_id(0)),
         (float)(get_global_id(1))) );

   outputBuffer[get_global_id(1) * get_global_size(0) +
      get_global_id(0)] = a.x + a.y + a.z + a.w;
}
```

The sampler object determines the addressing and filtering modes used when accessing an image, and whether or not the coordinates being passed to the function are normalized.

Specifying normalized coordinates (`CLK_NORMALIZED_COORDS_TRUE`) tells the sampler that the dimensions of the image will be addressed in the range of [0, 1].

Use of nonnormalized (CLK_NORMALIZED_COORDS_FALSE) coordinates specifies that the coordinates will be used to index into a location within the image as if it were a multidimensional array.

The addressing mode options specify what to do on out-of-bounds accesses. These can sometimes be very useful for programmers who may otherwise have to write specific bounds checks within a program (e.g., a convolution where apron pixels reside out-of-bounds). The options include clamping to the value at the image's border (CLK_ADDRESS_CLAMP) and wrapping around the image (CLK_ADDRESS_REPEAT).

The filtering mode has two options: return the image element nearest to the supplied coordinates (CLK_FILTER_NEAREST), or linearly interpolate the surrounding elements on the basis of the coordinates' relative location (CLK_FILTER_LINEAR). For linear filtering of a two-dimensional image, a 2 × 2 square of image elements will be interpolated. For a three-dimensional image, a 2 × 2 × 2 cube of elements will be interpolated.

To facilitate more succinct use of image objects, the OpenCL C language also supplies samplerless read functions:

```
float4
read_imagef (
    image2d_t image,
    int2 coord)
```

These simplified functions use a predefined sampler with fixed attributes: coordinates are unnormalized, there is no filtering with surrounding pixels, and results of out-of-bounds accesses are undefined. Accessing an image using this type of sampler is comparable to how we would access one- or multi-dimensional arrays in C; however, the opaque access function still allows for hardware optimizations.

Unlike reads, write functions do not take a sampler object. Instead the sampler is replaced with the value to be written:

```
void
write_imagef(
    image2d_t image,
    int2 coord,
    float4 color)
```

When an image is being written to, the coordinates provided must be unnormalized and in the range between 0 and the size of the image dimension −1.

As we have mentioned, implementing images as opaque types enables optimizations in the runtime system and hardware that buffers cannot support. Take one common optimization as an example. Any given multidimensional data structure, of which an image is an example, must be mapped to a one-dimensional memory address at some point. The obvious method, and indeed the method applied to multidimensional arrays in most programming languages, is a dictionary order in either a row-major or a column-major pattern. If data is stored in row-major order, (x, y) comes before $(x + 1, y)$, which comes long before $(x, y + 1)$, and so on. The long distance in memory between (x, y) and $(x, y + 1)$ means that an access of consecutive addresses in the y-dimension strides inefficiently through memory, hitting a large number of cache lines. In contrast, the fact that (x, y) is adjacent to $(x + 1, y)$ means consecutive accesses in the x-dimension stride efficiently (and cause memory accesses to coalesce).

Z-order, or Morton-order, memory layouts apply a mapping that preserves spatial locality of data points. Figure 7.3 shows that the data is stored in order $(0, 0)$, $(1, 0)$, $(0, 1)$, $(1, 1)$, $(2, 0)$, and so on. By storing data according to its position in a Z-ordered mapping, we may hit the same cache line repeatedly when performing a vertical read. If we go further by laying out our computational work in a two-dimensional layout (as we see in the graphics pipeline), we further improve this data locality. This sort of optimization is possible transparently (and hence different optimizations can be performed on different architectures) only if we offer the kernel programmer no guarantees about the relative locations of memory elements.

We can go a step further with this approach. If for execution we are using an architecture that does not have vector registers and does not perform vector reads from memory, we might wish `float4 a = read_imagef( sourceImage, imageSampler, location)` to compile down to four scalar reads instead of a single vector read. In these circumstances, it might be a more efficient use of the memory system to read

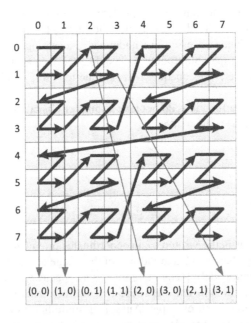

FIGURE 7.3

Applying Z-order mapping to a two-dimensional memory space.

from the same offset into four separate arrays instead of four times from the single array because the data in each separate array would exhibit better locality on each individual read operation.

7.2.3 PIPES

Recall that a pipe is an ordered sequence of data items that are stored in a first in, first out (FIFO) structure. Declaration of a pipe is slightly different than declaration of both buffers and images. An address space qualifier is not required for a pipe: since pipes are meant to communicate between kernel-instances, they implicitly store their data in global memory. Similarly to images, the keyword `pipe` is used to specify that a kernel argument is a pipe. Unlike images, a type must be provided that specifies the data type of the packets that are stored in the pipe. The data type can be any OpenCL C supported type (scalar or vector, floating point or integer), or a user-defined type built from the supported types. Along with the type, the programmer should supply an access qualifier that tells the kernel whether the pipe is readable (`__read_only` or `read_only`) or writable (`__write_only` or `write_only`) during its execution. The default is readable. A pipe cannot be both read by and written from the same kernel, so specifying the read/write access qualifier (`__read_write` or `read_write`) is invalid and will cause a compilation error.

An example of a kernel declaration containing one input pipe and one output pipe is as follows:

```
kernel
void foo(
    read_only pipe int pipe0,
    write_only pipe float4 pipe1)
```

Similarly to images, pipe objects are opaque. This makes sense because the purpose of the pipe is to provide FIFO functionality, and therefore pipes should not be randomly accessed. OpenCL C provides functions in order to read packets from or write packets to a pipe. The most basic way to interact with a pipe is with the following read and write commands:

```
int
read_pipe(
    pipe gentype p,
    gentype *ptr)

int
write_pipe(
    pipe gentype p,
    const gentype *ptr)
```

The function calls both take a pipe object, and a pointer to the location where the data should be written to (when reading from the pipe) or read from (when writing to the pipe). For both reading from and writing to a pipe, the function calls return 0 upon success. In some cases, these function calls may not complete successfully: `read_pipe()` returns a negative value if the pipe is empty, and `write_pipe()` returns a negative value if the pipe is full.

The programmer can ensure that reads from and writes to a pipe will always be successful by reserving space in the pipe ahead of time. The commands `reserve_read_pipe()` and `reserve_write_pipe()` both have a pipe object and number of packets as parameters, and return a *reservation identifier* of type `reserve_id_t`.

```
reserve_id_t
reserve_read_pipe(
    pipe gentype p,
    uint num_packets)


reserve_id_t
reserve_write_pipe(
    pipe gentype p,
    uint num_packets)
```

The reservation identifier returned by `reserve_read_pipe()` and `reserve_write_pipe()` can then be used to access overloaded versions of `read_pipe()` and `write_pipe()`. The signature for the version of `read_pipe()` that takes a reservation identifier is as follows:

```
int
read_pipe(
    pipe gentype p,
    reserve_id_t reserve_id,
    uint index,
    gentype *ptr)
```

When reservation identifiers are used, OpenCL C provides blocking functions to ensure that reads or writes have finished: `commit_read_pipe()` and `commit_write_pipe()`, respectively. These functions take a pipe object and a reservation identifier as parameters, and have no return value. Once the function call has returned, it is safe to assume that all reads and writes have committed.

```
void
commit_read_pipe(
    pipe gentype p,
    reserve_id_t reserve_id)
```

In addition to individual work-items reading from or writing to a pipe, some kernels may produce or consume data from the pipe on a work-group granularity. In order to remove some of the need to mask off individual work-items, OpenCL C provides intrinsic functions to reserve and commit accesses to the pipe per work-group. These functions are `work_group_reserve_read_pipe()` and `work_group_reserve_write_pipe()`. Similarly, the functions to guarantee that accesses have completed are `work_group_commit_read_pipe()` and `work_group_commit_write_pipe()`. In both cases, the work-group functions have signatures that mirror those for individual work-items. Note that all work-items must encounter these work-group-based functions, otherwise the behavior produced is undefined. Actual accesses to the pipe still occur using `read_pipe()` and `write_pipe()`. In Chapter 4, we demonstrated using pipes and their associated application programming interface (API).

7.3 CONSTANT MEMORY

The constant address space, described by the `__constant` qualifier, intends to cleanly separate small sets of constant values from the global address space such that the runtime can allocate caching resources or utilize efficient constant memory banks if possible. Data can be created for the constant address space in two ways:

1. A buffer may be allocated and passed as a kernel argument. The kernel signature should specify the pointer using the `__constant` qualifier.
2. Variables within the kernel may be specified using the `__constant` qualifier as long as they are initialized and compile-time constant.

Architectures differ in how they treat this data. For example, in AMD GPUs, constant data is stored in a cache separate from the cache where general-purpose data is stored. This cache has lower latency than the level 1 (L1) cache, and can greatly reduce memory traffic within the GPU. Depending on the pattern of the access, the address may even be stored within the instruction, freeing up other functional units, and leading to even lower latency.

OpenCL defines a limited number of constant arguments for each device that, along with the constant buffer size, can be queried with `CL_DEVICE_MAX_CONSTANT_ARGS` and `CL_DEVICE_MAX_CONSTANT_BUFFER_SIZE` arguments to `clDeviceInfo()`. Chapter 8 describes the implementation of constant memory on a modern GPU.

7.4 LOCAL MEMORY

A subset of the architectures supported by OpenCL, including many of the GPUs and the Cell Broadband Engine, possess small scratchpad memory buffers distinct from the primary DRAM and caching infrastructure. Local memory in these cases is disjoint from global memory, and is often accessed using separate memory operations. As a result, data must be copied into and out of it programmatically. Depending on the architecture, this occurs either through direct memory access transfers (most efficiently accessed using the `async_work_group_copy()` function) or by memory-to-memory copies. Local memory is also supported in central processing unit (CPU) implementations, but it sits in standard cacheable memory; in such cases, use of local memory can still be beneficial because it encourages cache-aware programming.

Local memory is most useful because it provides the most efficient method of communication between work-items in a work-group. Any allocated local memory buffer can be accessed at any location by an entire work-group, and hence writes to the local array will be visible to other work-items. Remember that OpenCL work-items are conceptually, if not literally, executed independently. Local memory is defined by the `__local` address space qualifier, and can either be defined within the kernel or passed as a parameter. Both examples are shown in the following code:

```
__kernel void localAccess(
    __global float* A,
    __global float* B,
    __local float* C )
{
    __local float aLocalArray[1];
    if( get_local_id(0) == 0 ) {
        aLocalArray[0] = A[0];
    }
    C[get_local_id(0)] = A[get_global_id(0)];

    work_group_barrier(CLK_LOCAL_MEM_FENCE);

    float neighborSum = C[get_local_id(0)] + aLocalArray[0];

    if( get_local_id(0) > 0 )
        neighborSum = neighborSum + C[get_local_id(0)-1];

    B[get_global_id(0)] = neighborSum;
}
```

Figure 7.4 shows a diagrammatic representation of the data flow in the previous code sample. Note that data will be read from global memory and written to the two local arrays `C` and `aLocalArray` at unpredictable times as the work-items execute independently in an undefined order. The reality will be slightly more predictable on a given device because implementations will map to hardware in predictable ways. For example, on AMD GPUs, execution occurs in lockstep over a wide single instruction multiple data (SIMD) vector, meaning that the read and write operations will have an ordering guarantee over the entire vector in the same way that they would over a single

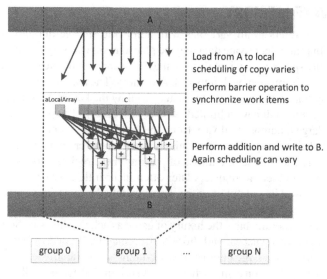

Load from A to local scheduling of copy varies

Perform barrier operation to synchronize work items

Perform addition and write to B. Again scheduling can vary

FIGURE 7.4

The pattern of data flow for the example shown in the localAccess kernel.

work-item. However, this feature does not apply generally. In the general case, we must insert the barrier operation: only at this barrier can we guarantee that all writes to local arrays, and the global memory reads that fed them, will have been completed across the work-group such that the data is visible to all work-items. Beyond this barrier, the data can be used by the entire work-group as shown in the lower part of the diagram.

In the kernel code, aLocalArray is at function scope lexically but is visible to the entire work-group. That is, there is only one 32-bit variable in local memory per work-group, and any work-item in the group using the name aLocalArray has access to the same 32-bit value. In this case, after the barrier we know that work-item 0 has written to aLocalArray, and hence all work-items in the group can now read from it.

The alternative method for creating local arrays is through a kernel parameter, as we see for array C. This version is created by a runtime API call. To allocate the memory, we call clSetKernelArg() as we would for passing a global array to the kernel, but we leave the final pointer field as NULL. We therefore allocate a per-work-group amount of memory on the basis of the third parameter but with no global object to back it up, so it sits in local memory:

```
ciErrNum = clSetKernelArg(
    kernel object,
    parameter index,
    size in bytes,
    NULL);
```

7.5 PRIVATE MEMORY

Private memory refers to all variables with automatic storage duration and kernel parameters. In principle, private data may be placed in registers, but owing to either a lack of capacity spilling or an inability for the hardware to dynamically index register arrays, data may be pushed back into global memory. The amount of private memory allocated may impact the number of registers used by the kernel. Like local memory, a given architecture will have a limited number of registers. The performance impact of using too large a number will vary from one architecture to another.

CPUs of the x86 type have a relatively small number of registers. However, because of large caches, the operations of pushing these registers to memory on the stack and returning them to registers later often incur little overhead. Variables can be efficiently moved in and out of scope, keeping only the most frequently used data in registers.

GPUs do not generally have the luxury of using a cache in this way. Some devices do not have read/write caches, and those that do may be limited in size, and hence spilling registers from a large number of work-items would rapidly lead to filling this cache, leading to stalling on a miss when the data is required again. Spilling to DRAM on such a device causes a significant performance degradation, and is best avoided.

When registers are not spilled, the capacity of the register bank of a GPU trades against the number of active threads in a manner similar to that of local data shares (LDS) as described in Chapter 8. The AMD Radeon HD R9 290X architecture has 256 kB of registers on each compute unit. This is four banks (one per SIMD) of 256 registers, with each register a 64-wide vector with 4 bytes per lane. If we use 100 registers per work-item, only two waves will fit per SIMD, which is not enough to cover anything more than instruction latency. If we use 49 registers per work-item, we can fit five waves, which helps with latency hiding.

Moving data into registers may appear to improve performance, but if the cost is that one fewer wavefront can execute on the core, less latency hiding occurs, and we may see more stalls and more wasted GPU cycles.

7.6 GENERIC ADDRESS SPACE

In all prior versions of OpenCL, the use of named address spaces required programmers to write multiple versions of callable OpenCL C functions based on the address space of where the arguments resided. Consider the following example that doubles the data in a buffer, either directly within global memory, or after first caching the data in local memory. While doubling a value is trivial, it is easy to imagine functions that may prefer to use a global memory pointer directly (e.g., when executing on a CPU with an automatic caching system), or sometimes prefer to work from local memory (e.g., when executing on a GPU with fast scratchpad storage). Prior to OpenCL 2.0, the function to perform the doubling operation would have to be written twice, once per address space as shown in Listing 7.1.

```
1
2   void doDoubleGlobal(__global float *data, int index) {
3
4       data[index] *= 2;
5   }
6
7   void doDoubleLocal(__local float *data, int index) {
8
9       data[index] *= 2;
10  }
11
12  __kernel
13  void doubleData(
14      global float *globalData,  // the data
15      local float *localData, // local storage
16      int useLocal) // whether or not to use local memory
17  {
18      int globalId = get_global_id(0);
19      int localId = get_local_id(0);
20
21      if (useLocal) {
22          // copy data to local memory
23          localData[localId] = globalData[globalId];
24
25          doDoubleLocal(localData, localId);
26
27          globalData[globalId] = localData[localId];
28      }
29      else {
30
31          doDoubleGlobal(globalData, globalId);
32      }
33  }
```

LISTING 7.1

Multiple versions of functions for named address spaces as required by OpenCL 1.x.

Starting in OpenCL 2.0, pointers to a named address spaces can be implicitly converted to the generic address space as shown in Listing 7.2.

```
1
2   void doDouble(float *data, int index) {
3
4       data[index] *= 2;
5   }
6
7   __kernel
8   void doubleData(
9       global float *globalData,  // the data
10      local float *localData, // local storage
11      int useLocal) // whether or not to use local memory
12  {
13      int globalId = get_global_id(0);
```

```
14      int localId = get_local_id(0);
15
16      generic float *data;  // generic keyword not required
17      int myIndex;
18
19      if (useLocal) {
20          // copy data to local memory
21          localData[localId] = globalData[globalId];
22
23          // set data to local address space
24          data = localData;
25          myIndex = localId;
26      }
27      else {
28          // set data to global address space
29          data = globalData;
30          myIndex = globalId;
31      }
32
33      doDouble(data, myIndex);
34
35      if (useLocal) {
36          globalData[globalId] = localData[localId];
37      }
38  }
```

LISTING 7.2

A single version of the function using the generic address space in OpenCL 2.0.

The generic address space subsumes the global, local, and private address spaces. The specification states that the constant address cannot be either cast or implicitly converted to the generic address space. Even though the constant address space is logically considered a subset of the global address space, in many processors (especially graphics processors), constant data is mapped to special hardware units that cannot be targeted dynamically by the instruction set architecture.

7.7 MEMORY ORDERING

A very important part of the memory model provided by any programming language is the ordering guarantees that threads can expect. When we are working with multiple threads and shared data, the memory consistency model defines how threads can interact to generate "correct" results. With OpenCL, a language that provides portability of highly parallel applications to multiple classes of devices, the formal specification of these requirements is very significant.

As we have discussed, work-items executing a kernel have shared access to data in global memory. Additionally work-items within a work-group have shared access to data in local memory. Until now, we have dealt largely with the case of what is referred to as OpenCL's "relaxed" consistency model. For global memory, we have simplified the more complicated memory model away, and said that by default work-items from different work-groups cannot expect to see updates to global memory. In regard to updates to a memory object, we have said that updates cannot be assumed to be complete until the correspond command utilizing the object is set to CL_COMPLETE. Indeed, this simplification is largely correct and will likely cover the majority of OpenCL kernels. As we saw in Chapter 4, this view of the memory consistency model was enough to support applications such as a histogram and a convolution.

In recent years, languages such as C, C++, and Java have all converged to support acquire-release operations to enable lock-free synchronization between threads. These operations help support additional classes of parallel applications, such as those that require critical sections of code. OpenCL 2.0 has also added support for acquire-release operations based on the C11 specification. In addition to allowing OpenCL developers to expand the classes of problems that they can solve, support for these synchronization operations also makes it easier for higher-level languages to target OpenCL.

The most intuitive way for programmers to reason about memory is using the *sequential consistency* model. If a system were to implement sequential consistency, memory operations from each processor would appear to execute in program order, and operations from all processors would appear in a sequential order. However, sequential consistency would greatly restrict optimizations that have no effect on program correctness (e.g., reordering of instructions by the compiler or using a store buffer in the processor). Therefore, memory models often "relax" the requirements of sequential consistency while producing the equivalent output. Relaxing sequential consistency requires hardware and software to adhere to certain rules. For the programmer, this comes at the cost of sometimes telling the hardware when data needs to be made visible to other threads.

Although sometimes required for program correctness, synchronization operations have more overhead than does working with the relaxed memory model. OpenCL therefore provides options to be specified with each synchronization operation that allow the programmer to specify only the required strength and scope of synchronization. These options are referred to as *memory order* and *memory scope*, respectively.

OpenCL provides options to specify three different degrees of consistency (from weakest to strongest): relaxed, acquire-release, and sequential. These options are specified as memory order options with the following semantics:

- *Relaxed* (memory_order_relaxed): This memory order does not impose any ordering constraints—the compiler is free to reorder this operation with preceding or subsequent load and store operations, and no visibility guarantees are enforced regarding preceding or subsequent side effects. Atomic operations in previous versions of the OpenCL standard were implied to have a relaxed memory order. Because of their limited guarantees, programmers may find using relaxed ordering provides the best performance for operations such as incrementing counters.

- *Acquire* (`memory_order_acquire`): Acquire operations are paired with loads. When this memory order is specified for a synchronization operation, any shared memory stores that have been "released" by other units of execution (e.g., other work-items, or the host thread) are guaranteed to be visible. The compiler has the liberty to move preceding load and store operations to be executed after the synchronization; however, it may not move subsequent load and store operations to execute prior to the synchronization.
- *Release* (`memory_order_release`): Complementary to acquire operations, release operations are paired with stores. When a release memory order is specified for a synchronization operation, the effects of any preceding stores must be made visible, and all preceding loads must have completed before the synchronization operation can complete. Complementary to acquire operations, the compiler has the liberty to move subsequent load and store operations prior to the synchronization; however, it may not move any prior load or store operations after the synchronization.
- *Acquire-release* (`memory_order_acq_rel`): This memory order has the properties of both the acquire and release memory orders: it will acquire any released side effects from other units of execution, and will then immediately release its own side effects. It is typically used to order read-modify-write operations.
- *Sequential* (`memory_order_seq_cst`): This memory order implements sequential consistency for data-race-free programs.[1] With sequential consistency, the loads and stores of each unit of execution appear to execute in program order, and the loads and stores from different units of execution appear to be simply interleaved. This is stronger than `memory_order_acq_rel` because it imposes a single total ordering of accesses.

When synchronization operations to global memory are performed, specifying only a memory order may introduce more overhead than is strictly required by the program. For instance, imagine a system that includes multiple devices, sharing a context that contains a fine-grained shared virtual memory (SVM) buffer. If a work-item performed a synchronization operation with a release, the device executing the work-item would need to ensure that all stores performed by the work-item were first visible to all devices in the system—incurring significant overhead if not required for algorithmic correctness. Therefore, for many operations, memory order arguments are optionally accompanied by a memory scope, which limits the visibility of operations to the specified units of execution.

The options that can be specified as a memory scope are as follows:

- *Work-item* (`memory_scope_work_item`): Specifies that memory ordering applies only to the work-item. This is required for RAW operations on image objects.

---

[1] Multiple threads/work-items accessing a variable concurrently constitutes a data race.

- *Work-group* (`memory_scope_work_group`): Specifies that memory ordering applies to work-items executing within a single work-group. This could potentially be used as a lighter-weight synchronization than the barrier with memory fence that we have needed in the past for work-group synchronization.
- *Device* (`memory_scope_device`): Specifies that memory ordering applies to work-items executing on a single device.
- *All devices* (`memory_scope_all_svm_devices`): Specifies that memory ordering applies to work-items executing across multiple devices and the host (when using fine-grained SVM with atomics).

Unlike accesses to global memory, specifying a memory scope for accesses to local memory is not required (and in fact will be ignored)—local atomics will always have a scope of `memory_scope_work_group`. Since local memory is accessible only by work-items from a work-group, trying to provide ordering guarantees to execution units outside the work-group with `memory_scope_device` or `memory_scope_all_svm_devices` does not make sense.

7.7.1 ATOMICS REVISITED

Earlier in this chapter we briefly described support for atomics in OpenCL 2.0. Now that we have been introduced to memory ordering and scope, we will briefly revisit atomics.

Recall that we introduced groups of atomic operations, such as atomic loads, atomic stores, and atomic fetch-and-modify operations. We showed the following signature for fetch-and-modify operations:

```
C atomic_fetch_key(volatile A *object, M operand)
```

Here, *key* could be replaced by operations such as `add`, `min`, and `max`. Recall that for these type of operations, the parameter `object` is a pointer to a variable of one of the atomic types, and `operand` is the value to be applied. The return value, `C`, is the nonatomic version of type `A`, and holds the value pointed to by `object` immediately before the atomic operation.

In addition to the aforementioned properties regarding atomics, C/C++11 and OpenCL 2.0 utilize them for enforcing memory ordering. Thus, all atomic functions provide multiple signatures that support order and scope arguments. For example, fetch-and-modify functions also include the following signatures:

```
C atomic_fetch_key_explicit(volatile A *object, M operand,
memory_order order)
```

```
C atomic_fetch_key_explicit(volatile A *object, M operand,
memory_order order, memory_scope scope)
```

This, by design, makes atomic operations the primary mechanism for synchronization between threads. The reason that synchronization was implemented as a property of atomics is that atomic operations on a flag are a common way for one thread to let another know that data is ready or to permit access to a region of code. It therefore becomes natural that when one thread wants another to be able to see some data, it should (atomically) set a flag and then release its shared data. The other thread should be able to read the flag, and upon finding a success condition, should have acquired the latest copy of any shared data.

Notice that atomic operations that include the parameter for memory order have `explicit` appended to their name. Functions that do not end in `explicit` are implemented to have the same semantics as if the memory order were specified as `memory_order_seq_cst`, and the memory scope were specified as `memory_scope_device`.

In addition to the load, store, and fetch-and-modify classes of atomic instructions, OpenCL C also supports functions for atomic exchange, compare-and-exchange (i.e., compare-and-swap), and test-and-set functionality. One version of the compare-and-swap function has the following signature:

```
bool
atomic_compare_exchange_strong_explicit(
    volatile A *object,
    C *expected,
    C desired,
    memory_order success,
    memory_order failure,
    memory_scope scope)
```

Unlike any previous signature we have seen, `atomic_compare_exchange_strong_explicit()` has memory order arguments `success` and `failure`. These arguments specify what ordering should be performed when the compare operation succeeds (i.e., the exchange happens) and when it fails. This can enable the programmer to limit potentially expensive synchronizations to occur only when necessary. For example, the programmer may want to pass `memory_order_relaxed` as an argument to the `failure` parameter in the case that a work-item is waiting for a successful exchange operation before proceeding.

So far we have discussed the use of atomic operations, but have not described how they are initialized. OpenCL C has two options for initializing atomics depending on the scope of their declaration. Variables declared with a program scope can be initialized with the macro `ATOMIC_VAR_INIT()`, with the following signature:

```
#define ATOMIC_VAR_INIT(C value)
```

This macro initializes atomic objects that are declared in program scope and allocated in the global address space. For example,

```
global atomic_int sync = ATOMIC_VAR_INIT(0);
```

Atomic variables declared with automatic storage should be initialized using the (nonatomic) function `atomic_init()`. Notice that because `atomic_init()` is nonatomic itself, it cannot be called concurrently by multiple work-items. Instead, initialization requires serialization and synchronization, such as in the following code:

```
local atomic_int sync;
if (get_local_id(0) == 0)
   atomic_init(&sync, 0);
work_group_barrier(CLK_LOCAL_MEM_FENCE);
```

7.7.2 FENCES

A synchronization operation without an associated memory location is a fence. Although we have seen some practical use of fences for work-group synchronization, we have not yet detailed their use for memory ordering. In OpenCL C, a fence operation is performed by calling `atomic_work_item_fence()`, with the following signature:

```
void
atomic_work_item_fence(
   cl_mem_fence_flags flags,
   memory_order order,
   memory_scope scope)
```

The `flags` parameter can be set to `CLK_GLOBAL_MEM_FENCE`, `CLK_LOCAL_MEM_FENCE`, or `CLK_IMAGE_MEM_FENCE`, or a combination of these using a bitwise OR. A combination of these values has the same effect as if the fence were called with each parameter individually. The memory order and memory scope parameters have the effect of defining ordering constraints and setting the scope of the fence, as we have seen previously.

Recall that on many systems image objects are still subject to the constraints of non-general-purpose graphics hardware. The OpenCL specification recognizes this, and requires `atomic_work_item_fence()` to be called with `CLK_IMAGE_MEM_FENCE` to ensure that image writes are visible to later reads—even by the same work-item. If multiple work-items will be synchronizing and reading data that were previously written by a different work-item from the group, then `work_group_barrier()` called with `CLK_IMAGE_MEM_FENCE` should be used instead. Another subtle case where work-item fences are required is for ordering accesses to local and global memory together.

We previously introduced the combination of a work-group barrier and memory fence to be used as a synchronization function. More formally, this can be thought of as two fence operations—referred to as entry and exit fences. The entry fence is a release fence with the specified flags and scope. Likewise, the exit fence is an acquire fence with the specified flags and scope.

7.8 SUMMARY

This chapter provided details on the abstract memory model used by work-items when executing OpenCL kernels. The memory model includes memory spaces, memory object types, and the consistency models for these spaces and types supported by the specification. Combined with the host-side memory model presented in Chapter 6, the reader should now have a solid understanding of the management and manipulation of data within an OpenCL application.

Dissecting OpenCL on a heterogeneous system

In Chapter 2, we discussed trade-offs present in different architectures, many of which support the execution of OpenCL programs. The design of OpenCL is such that the models map capably to a wide range of architectures, allowing for tuning and acceleration of kernel code. In this chapter, we discuss OpenCL's mapping to a real system in the form of a high-end central processing unit (CPU) combined with a discrete graphics processing unit. Although AMD systems have been chosen to illustrate this mapping and implementation, each respective vendor has implemented a similar mapping for their own CPUs and GPUs.

8.1 OpenCL ON AN AMD FX-8350 CPU

AMD's OpenCL implementation is designed to run on both x86 CPUs and AMD GPUs in an integrated manner. All host code executes as would be expected on the general-purpose x86 CPUs in a machine, along with operating system and general application code. However, AMD's OpenCL implementation is also capable of compiling and executing OpenCL C code on x86 devices using the queuing mechanisms provided by the OpenCL runtime. Figure 8.1 shows a diagram of an AMD FX-8350 CPU, which will be used to illustrate the mapping of OpenCL onto an x86 CPU.

The entire chip in Figure 8.1 is consumed by the OpenCL runtime as a single device that is obtained using `clGetDeviceIDs()`. The device is then passed to API calls such as `clCreateContext()`, `clCreateCommandQueue()`, and `clBuildProgram()`. The CPU device requires the `CL_DEVICE_TYPE_CPU` flag (or `CL_DEVICE_TYPE_ALL` flag) to be passed to the device types parameter of `clGetDeviceIDs()`.

Within the CPU, OpenCL can run on each of the eight cores. If the entire CPU is treated as a single device, parallel workloads can be spread across the CPU cores from a single queue, efficiently using the parallelism present in the system. It is possible to split the CPU into multiple devices using the device fission extension.

187

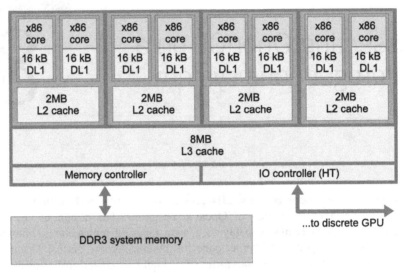

FIGURE 8.1

High-level design of AMD's Piledriver-based FX-8350 CPU.

8.1.1 RUNTIME IMPLEMENTATION

The OpenCL CPU runtime creates a thread to execute on each core of the CPU (i.e., a worker pool of threads) to process OpenCL kernels as they are generated. These threads are passed work by a core management thread for each queue that has the role of removing the first entry from the queue and setting up work for the worker threads. Any given OpenCL kernel may comprise thousands of work-groups, for which arguments must be appropriately prepared, and memory must be allocated and possibly initialized.

OpenCL utilizes barriers and fences to support fine-grained synchronization. On a typical CPU-based system, in which the operating system is responsible for managing interthread communication, the cost of interacting with the operating system is a barrier to achieving efficient scaling of parallel implementations. In addition, running a single work-group across multiple cores could create cache-sharing issues. To alleviate these issues, the OpenCL CPU runtime executes a work-group within a single operating system thread. The OpenCL thread will run each work-item in the work-group in turn before moving on to the next work-item. After all work-items in the work-group have finished executing, the worker thread will move on to the next work-group in its work queue. As such, there is no parallelism between multiple work-items within a work-group, although between work-groups multiple operating system threads allow parallel execution when possible. Given this approach to scheduling work-groups, a diagram of the mapping of OpenCL to the FX-8350 CPU is shown in Figure 8.2.

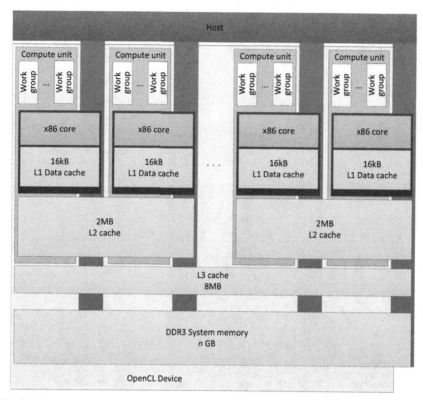

FIGURE 8.2

OpenCL mapped onto an FX-8350 CPU. The FX-8350 CPU is both the OpenCL host and the device in this scenario.

In the presence of barrier synchronization, OpenCL work-items within a single work-group execute concurrently. Each work-item in the group must complete the section of the code that precedes the barrier operation, wait for other work-items to reach the barrier, and then continue execution. At the barrier operation, one work-item must terminate and another continue; however, it is impractical for performance reasons to let the operating system handle this with thread preemption (i.e., interrupting one thread to allow another to run). Indeed, as the entire work-group is running within a single thread, preemption would have no effect. In AMD's OpenCL CPU runtime, barrier operations are supported using setjmp and longjmp. The setjmp call stores the system state and longjmp restores it by returning to the system state at the point where setjmp was called [1]. The runtime provides custom versions of these two functions because they need to work in cooperation with the hardware branch predictor and maintain proper program stack alignment. Figure 8.3 shows the execution flow of work-groups by CPU threads.

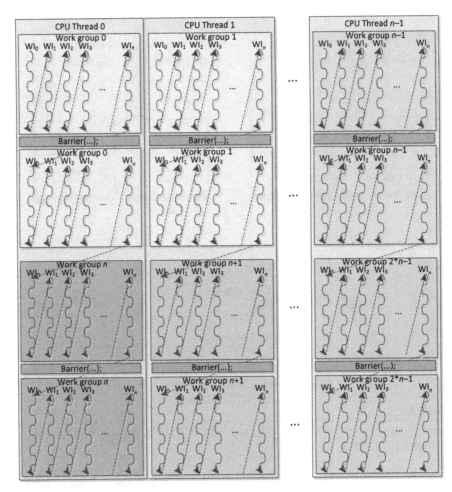

FIGURE 8.3

Implementation of work-group execution on an x86 architecture.

Note that although a CPU thread eventually executes multiple work-groups, it will complete one work-group at a time before moving on to the next. When a barrier is involved, it will execute every work-item of that group up to the barrier, then every work-item after the barrier, hence providing correct barrier semantics and reestablishing concurrency—if not parallelism—between work-items in a single work-group.

Work-item data stored in registers are backed into a work-item stack in main memory during the `setjmp` call. This memory is carefully laid out to behave well in the cache, reducing cache contention and hence conflict misses and improving the utilization of the cache hierarchy. In particular, the work-item stack data is staggered in memory to reduce the chance of conflicts, and data is maintained in large pages to ensure contiguous mapping to physical memory and to reduce pressure on the CPU's translation lookaside buffer.

8.1.2 VECTORIZING WITHIN A WORK-ITEM

The AMD Piledriver microarchitecture includes 128-bit vector registers and operations from various Streaming SIMD Extensions (SSE) and Advanced Vector Extensions (AVX) versions. OpenCL C includes a set of vector types: float2, float4, int4, and other data formats. Mathematical operations are overloaded on these vector types, enabling the following operations:

```
float4 a = input_data[location];
float4 b = a + (float4)(0.f, 1.f, 2.f, 3.f);
output_data[location] = b;
```

These vector types are stored in vector registers, and operations on them compile to SSE and AVX instructions on the AMD Piledriver architecture. This offers an important performance optimization. Vector load and store operations, as we also see in our low-level code discussions, improve the efficiency of memory operations. Currently, access to single instruction, multiple data (SIMD) vectors are entirely explicit within a single work-item: we will see how this model differs on AMD GPU devices when we discuss a GPU in Section 8.2.

8.1.3 LOCAL MEMORY

The AMD Piledriver design does not provide dedicated hardware for scratchpad memory buffers. CPUs typically provide multiple levels of memory caching in order to hide main memory access latency. The data localization provided by local memory supports efficient mapping onto the CPU cache hierarchy and allows the kernel developer to improve cache performance even in the absence of a true hardware scratchpad. To improve cache locality, local memory regions are allocated as an array per CPU thread and are reused for each work-group executed by that thread. For a sequence of work-groups, barring any data races or memory conflicts, there is then no need for this local memory to generate further cache misses. As an additional benefit, there is no overhead from repeated calls to memory allocation routines. Figure 8.4 shows how we would map local memory to the AMD CPU cache.

Despite the potential advantages of the use of local memory on the CPU, it can also have a negative impact on performance for some applications. If a kernel is written such that its data accesses have good locality (e.g., a blocked matrix multiplication), then using local memory as storage will effectively perform an unnecessary copying of data while increasing the amount of data that needs to fit in the level 1 (L1) cache. In this scenario, performance can possibly be degraded from smaller effective cache size, unnecessary cache evictions from the added contention, and the data copying overhead.

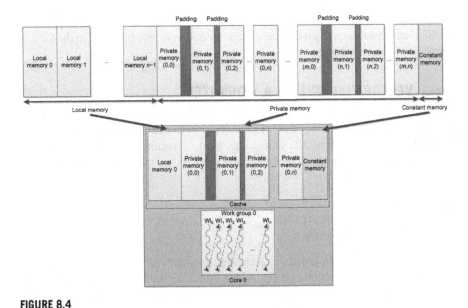

FIGURE 8.4

Mapping the memory spaces for a work-group (work-group 0) onto a Piledriver CPU cache.

8.2 OpenCL ON THE AMD RADEON R9 290X GPU

In this section, we will use the term "wavefront" when referring to hardware threads running on AMD GPUs (also called "warp" by NVIDIA). This helps avoid confusion with software threads—work-items in OpenCL and threads in CUDA. However, sometimes use of the term "thread" is unavoidable (e.g., multithreading) or preferable when describing GPU characteristics in general. In this context, we will always use "threads" when referring to hardware threads. Although this section includes many specifics regarding the Radeon R9 290X GPU, the approach of mapping work-items to hardware threads, scheduling and occupancy considerations, and the layout of the memory system are largely similar across device families and between vendors.

A GPU is a significantly different target for OpenCL code compared with the CPU. The reader must remember that a graphics processor is primarily designed to render three-dimensional graphics efficiently. This goal leads to significantly different prioritization of resources, and thus a significantly different architecture from that of the CPU. On current GPUs, this difference comes down to a few main features, of which the following three were discussed in Chapter 2:

1. Wide SIMD execution: A far larger number of execution units execute the same instruction on different data items.
2. Heavy multithreading: Support for a large number of concurrent thread contexts on a given GPU compute core.

3. Hardware scratchpad memory: Physical memory buffers purely under the programmer's control.

The following are additional differences that are more subtle, but that nevertheless create opportunities to provide improvements in terms of latency of work dispatch and communication:

- Hardware synchronization support: Supporting fine-grained communication between concurrent threads.
- Hardware managed tasking and dispatch: Work queue management and load balancing in hardware.

Hardware synchronization support reduces the overhead of synchronizing execution of multiple wavefronts on a given compute unit, enabling fine-grained communication at low cost.

GPUs provide extensive hardware support for task dispatch because of their deep roots in the three-dimensional graphics world. Gaming workloads involve managing complicated task graphs arising from interleaving of work in a graphics pipeline. As shown in the high-level diagram of the AMD Radeon R9 290X in Figure 8.5, the architecture consists of a command processor and work-group generator at the front that passes constructed work-groups to hardware schedulers. These schedulers arrange compute workloads onto the 44 cores spread throughout the device. The details of each compute unit are described in Section 8.2.2.

To obtain the high degree of performance acceleration associated with GPU computing, scheduling must be very efficient. For graphics, wavefront scheduling overhead needs to remain low because the chunks of work may be very small

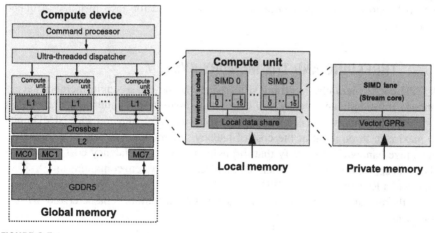

FIGURE 8.5

High-level Radeon R9 290X diagram labeled with OpenCL execution and memory model terms.

(e.g., a single triangle consisting of a few pixels). Therefore, when writing kernels that we want to achieve high performance on a GPU, we need to

- provide a lot of work for each kernel dispatch;
- batch multiple launches together if kernels are small.

By providing a sufficient amount of work in each kernel, we ensure that the work-group generation pipeline is kept occupied so that it always has more work to give to the schedulers and the schedulers always have more work to push onto the SIMD units. In essence, we wish to create a large number of wavefronts to occupy the GPU since it is a throughput machine.

The second point refers to OpenCL's queuing mechanism. When the OpenCL runtime chooses to process work in the work queue associated with the device, it scans through the tasks in the queue with the aim of selecting an appropriately large chunk to process. From this set of tasks, it constructs a command buffer of work for the GPU in a language understood by the command processor at the front of the GPU's pipeline. This process consists in (1) constructing a queue, (2) placing it somewhere in memory, (3) telling the device where it is, and (4) asking the device to process it. Such a sequence of operations takes time, incurring a relatively high latency for a single block of work. In particular, as the GPU runs behind a driver running in kernel space, this process requires a number of context switches into and out of kernel space to allow the GPU to start running. As in the case of the CPU, where context switches between short-running threads becomes a significant overhead, switching into kernel mode and preparing queues for overly small units of work is inefficient. There is a fairly constant overhead for dispatching a work queue and further overhead for processing depending on the amount of work in it. This overhead must be overcome by providing very large kernel launches, or long sequences of kernels. In either case, the goal is to increase the amount of work performed for each instance of queue processing.

8.2.1 THREADING AND THE MEMORY SYSTEM

A CPU cache hierarchy is arranged to reduce latency of a single memory access stream: any significant latency will cause that stream to stall and reduce execution efficiency. Alternatively, because the GPU cores use threading and wide SIMD units to maximize throughput at the cost of latency, the memory system is designed to maximize bandwidth to satisfy that throughput, with some latency cost. Figure 8.6 shows an approximation of the memory hierarchy for a system containing an FX-8350 CPU and a Radeon R9 290X GPU.

With relevance to the memory system, GPUs can be characterized by the following:

- A large number of registers.
- Software-managed scratchpad memory called *local data shares* (LDS) on AMD hardware.

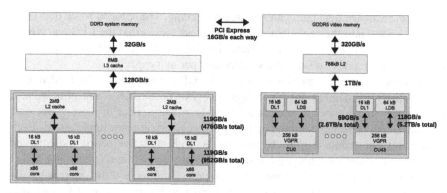

FIGURE 8.6

Memory bandwidths in the discrete system.

- A high level of on-chip multithreading.
- A single level 2 (L2) cache.
- High-bandwidth memory.

As mentioned previously, graphics workloads fundamentally differ from compute workloads, and have led to the current GPU execution and memory models. Fundamentally, the GPU relies much less heavily on data reuse than does the CPU, and thus has much smaller caches. Even though the size of the L1 data caches are similar between x86 cores and Radeon R9 290X compute units, up to 40 wavefronts execute concurrently on a compute unit, providing a much smaller effective cache size per wavefront. The lack of reliance on caching is based on a number of factors, including less temporal reuse of data in graphics, and owing to the large data sets and amount of multithreading, the inability to realistically cache a working set. When data reuse does occur, multithreading and high-bandwidth memory helps overcome the lack of cache.

Also of note in the memory system is that there is a single, multibanked L2 cache, which must supply data to all compute units. This single-L2-cache design allows the GPU to provide coherence between caches by writing through the L1 caches and invalidating any data that may potentially be modified by another cache. The write-through design makes register spilling undesirable, as every access would require a long-latency operation and would create congestion at the L2 cache.

To avoid spilling, GPUs provide much larger register files than their CPU counterparts. For example, unlike the x86 architecture, which has a limited number of general-purpose registers (16 architectural registers per thread context), the Radeon R9 290X allows a single wavefront to utilize up to 16,384 registers! Wavefronts try to compute using only registers and LDS for as long as possible, and try to avoid generating traffic for the memory system whenever possible.

LDS allows high-bandwidth and low-latency programmer-controlled read/write access. This form of programmable data reuse is less wasteful and also more area/power efficient than hardware-controlled caching. The reduced waste data (data that are loaded into the cache but not used) access means that the LDS can have a smaller capacity than an equivalent cache. In addition, the reduced need for control logic and tag structures results in a smaller area per unit capacity.

Hardware-controlled multithreading in the GPU cores allows the hardware to cover latency to memory. To reach high levels of performance and utilization, a sufficiently large number of wavefronts must be running. Four or more wavefronts per SIMD unit or 16 per compute unit may be necessary in many applications. Each SIMD unit can maintain up to 10 wavefronts, with 40 active across the compute unit. To enable fast switching, wavefront state is maintained in registers, not cache. Each wavefront in flight is consuming resources, and as a result increasing the number of live wavefronts to cover latency must be balanced against register and LDS use.

To reduce the number of requests generated by each wavefront, the caches that are present in the system provide a filtering mechanism to combine complicated gathered read and scattered write access patterns in vector memory operations into the largest possible units—this technique is referred to as *coalescing*. The large vector reads that result from well-structured memory accesses are far more efficient for a DRAM-based system, requiring less temporal caching than the time-distributed smaller reads arising from the most general CPU code.

Figure 8.6 shows the PCI Express bus as the connection between the CPU and GPU devices. All traffic between the CPU, and hence main memory, and the GPU must go through this pipe. Because PCI Express bandwidth is significantly lower than access to DRAM and even lower than the capabilities of on-chip buffers, this can become a significant bottleneck on a heavily communication-dependent application. In an OpenCL application, we need to minimize the number and size of memory copy operations relative to the kernels we enqueue. It is difficult to achieve good performance in an application that is expected to run on a discrete GPU if that application has a tight feedback loop involving copying data back and forth across the PCI Express bus.

8.2.2 INSTRUCTION SET ARCHITECTURE AND EXECUTION UNITS

A simplified version of a Radeon R9 290X compute unit based on AMD's Graphics Core Next (GCN) architecture is shown in Figure 8.7. Compute units in the Radeon R9 290X have four SIMD units. When a wavefront is created, it is assigned to a single SIMD unit within the compute unit (owing to register allocation) and is also allotted the amount of memory it requires within the LDS. As wavefronts contain 64 work-items and the SIMD unit contains 16 lanes, vector instructions executed by a wavefront are issued to the SIMD unit over four cycles. Each cycle, wavefronts belonging to one SIMD unit are selected for scheduling. This way, every four cycles, a new instruction can be issued to the SIMD unit, exactly when the previous instruction is fully submitted to the pipeline.

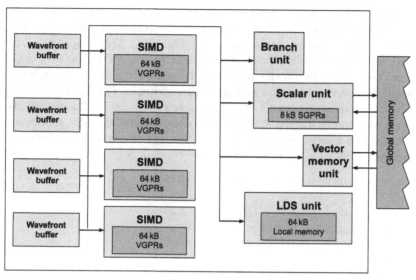

FIGURE 8.7

Radeon R9 290X compute unit microarchitecture.

Recall that within a compute unit, the Radeon R9 290X has a number of additional execution units in addition to the SIMD unit. To generate additional instruction-level parallelism (ILP), the Radeon R9 290X compute unit looks at the wavefronts that did not schedule an instruction to the SIMD, and considers them for scheduling instructions to the other hardware units. In total, the scheduler may select up to five instructions on each cycle onto one of the SIMD units, the scalar unit, memory unit, LDS, or other hardware special function devices [2]. These other units have scheduling requirements different from those of the SIMD units. The scalar unit, for example, executes a single instruction for the entire wavefront and is designed to take a new instruction every cycle.

In previous devices, such as the Radeon HD 6970 architecture presented in Chapter 2, control flow was managed automatically by a branch unit. This design led to a very specialized execution engine that looked somewhat different from other vector architectures on the market. The Radeon R9 290X design is more explicit in integrating scalar and vector code instruction-by-instruction, much as an x86 CPU will when integrating SSE or AVX operations. Recall that each wavefront (64 work-items) executes a single instruction stream (i.e., a single program counter is used for all 64 work-items), and that all branching is performed at wavefront granularity. In order to support divergent control flow on the Radeon R9 290X, the architecture provides an execution mask used to enable or disable individual results from being written. Thus, any divergent branching between work-items in a wavefront requires restriction of instruction set architecture (ISA) to a sequence of mask and unmask operations. The result is a very explicit sequence of instruction blocks that execute until all necessary paths have been covered. Such execution divergence creates inefficiency as only part of the vector unit is active at any given time. However, being able to support such control flow improves the programmability by removing the need for the programmer to manually vectorize code. Very similar issues arise when developing code for competing architectures, such as NVIDIA's GeForce GTX 780, and are inherent in software production for wide-vector architectures, whether manually, compiler, or hardware vectorized, or somewhere in between.

The following is an example of code designed to run on the Radeon R9 290X compute unit (see the Radeon R9 290X family Sea Islands series ISA specification; [3]). Let us take a very simple kernel that will diverge on a wavefront of any width greater than one:

```
kernel void foo(const global int* in, global int *out)
{
    if( get_global_id(0) == 0 ) {
        out[get_global_id(0)] = in[get_global_id(0)];
    }
    else {
        out[get_global_id(0)] = 0;
    }
}
```

While this is a trivial kernel, it will allow us to see how the compiler maps this to ISA, and indirectly how that ISA will behave on the hardware. When we compile this for the Radeon R9 290X, we get the following:

```
1    s_buffer_load_dword s0, s[4:7], 0x04
2    s_buffer_load_dword s1, s[4:7], 0x18
3    s_waitcnt lgkmcnt(0)
4    s_min_u32 s0, s0, 0x0000ffff
5    v_mov_b32 v1, s0
6    v_mul_i32_i24 v1, s12, v1
7    v_add_i32 v0, vcc, v0, v1
8    v_add_i32 v0, vcc, s1, v0
9    s_buffer_load_dword s0, s[8:11], 0x00
10   s_buffer_load_dword s1, s[8:11], 0x04
11   v_cmp_eq_i32 s[4:5], v0, 0
12   s_and_saveexec_b64 s[4:5], s[4:5]
13   v_lshlrev_b32 v1, 2, v0
14   s_cbranch_execz label_0016
15   s_waitcnt lgkmcnt(0)
16   v_add_i32 v1, vcc, s0, v1
17   s_load_dwordx4 s[8:11], s[2:3], 0x50
18   s_waitcnt lgkmcnt(0)
19   tbuffer_load_format_x v1, v1, s[8:11], 0 offen
20        format:[BUF_DATA_FORMAT_32,BUF_NUM_FORMAT_FLOAT]
21   label_0016:
22   s_andn2_b64 exec, s[4:5], exec
23   v_mov_b32 v1, 0
24   s_mov_b64 exec, s[4:5]
25   v_lshlrev_b32 v0, 2, v0
26   s_waitcnt lgkmcnt(0)
```

```
27        v_add_i32 v0, vcc, s1, v0
28        s_load_dwordx4 s[0:3], s[2:3], 0x58
29        s_waitcnt vmcnt(0) & lgkmcnt(0)
30        tbuffer_store_format_x v1, v0, s[0:3], 0 offen
31            format:[BUF_DATA_FORMAT_32,BUF_NUM_FORMAT_FLOAT]
32        s_endpgm
```

LISTING 8.1

Radeon R9 290X ISA divergent execution example.

This code may be viewed, like OpenCL code, as representing a single lane of execution: a single work-item. However, unlike the higher-level language, here we see a combination of scalar operations (prefixed with s_), intended to execute on the scalar unit of the GPU core in Figure 8.7, and vector operations (prefixed with v_) that execute across one of the vector units.

If we look at Line 11 of Listing 8.1, we see a vector comparison operation that tests the work-item ID (stored in v0) against the constant 0 for each work-item in the wavefront. The result of the operation is stored as a 64-bit Boolean bitmask in two consecutive scalar registers (s[4:5]). The resulting bitmask will be used to determine which work-items will execute each conditional path in the OpenCL C kernel.

Next, Line 12 implicitly manipulates the execution mask by ANDing the current execution mask with the comparison bitmask. In this case, the resulting execution mask will be used to compute the if clause of the conditional. The previous execution mask is stored in the destination scalar registers (in this example, s[4:5], which previously held the comparison bitmask, now holds the previous execution mask). The previous execution mask will be used when determining which work-items will execute the else clause of the conditional and will also be used again to reset the execution mask after the conditional completes. Additionally, this operation ensures that the scalar condition code (SCC) register is set: this is what will trigger the conditional branch.

Setting the SCC register is an optimization, which allows an entire branch of the conditional to be skipped if it has been determined that no work-items will enter it (in this case, if the bitmask is zero, the s_cbranch_execz instruction on Line 14 could potentially allow the if conditional clause to be skipped). If the conditional branch does not happen, the code will enter the else clause of the conditional. In the current example, work-item 0 will generate a 1 for its entry of the bitmask, so the if conditional will be executed—just by a single SIMD lane (starting on Line 16).

When the if clause is executed, a vector load (a load from the tbuffer or texture buffer, showing the graphics heritage of the ISA) on Line 19 pulls the expected data into a vector register, v1. Line 19 is the last operation for the if clause. Note that while the original OpenCL C code also had a store following the load, the compiler factored out the store to later in the program in the compiled code.

Next, Line 22 takes the original execution mask and ANDs it with the bitwise-negated version of the current execution mask. The result is that the new execution mask represents the set of work-items that should execute the else clause of the conditional. Instead of loading a value from memory, these work-items move the constant value 0 into v1 on Line 23. Notice that the values to be stored to memory from both control flow paths are now stored in the v1 register. This will allow us to execute a single store instruction later in the program.

Attentive readers may have noticed that there is no branch to skip the else clause of the conditional in the program listing. In this case, the compiler has decided that, as there is no load to perform in the else branch, the overhead of simply masking out the operations and treating the entire section as predicated execution is an efficient solution, such that the else branch will always execute and may simply not update v1.

Obviously this is a very simple example. With deeply nested conditionals, the mask code can be complicated with long sequences of storing masks and ANDing with new condition codes, narrowing the set of executing lanes at each stage until finally scalar branches are needed. At each stage of narrowing, efficiency of execution decreases, and as a result, well-structured code that executes the same instruction across the vector is vital for efficient use of the architecture. It is the sophisticated set of mask management routines and other vector operations that differentiates this ISA from a CPU ISA such as SSE, not an abstract notion of having many more cores.

Finally, on Line 24, the execution mask is reset to its state before diverging across the conditional, and the data currently stored in v1 are written out to memory using the tbuffer store instruction on Line 30.

8.2.3 RESOURCE ALLOCATION

Each SIMD unit on the GPU includes a fixed amount of register and LDS storage space. There is 256 kB of registers on each compute unit. These registers are split into four banks such that there are 256 registers per SIMD unit, each 64 lanes wide and 32 bits per lane. These registers are divided on the basis of the number of wavefronts executing on the compute unit. There is 64 kB of LDS on each compute unit, accessible as a random-access 32-bank SRAM. The LDS is divided between the number of work-groups executing on the compute unit, on the basis of the local memory allocation requests made within the kernel and through the OpenCL runtime parameter-passing mechanism.

When executing a single kernel on each compute unit, as is the standard mapping when running an OpenCL program, we might see a resource bottleneck, as seen in Figure 8.8. In this diagram, we see two work-groups each containing two wavefronts, where each work-item (and hence wavefront scaled up) needs 42 vector registers and a share in 50 scalar registers, and the work-group needs 24 kB of LDS. This allocation of four wavefronts per compute unit is limited by the LDS requirements of the work-group and is below the minimum number of wavefronts we need to run on the device to keep the device busy, as with only one wavefront per SIMD unit we have no capacity to switch in a replacement when the wavefront is executing scalar code or memory operations. A general expression for determining the work-group occupancy on a compute unit within the Radeon R9 290X is given in Equation 8.1:

$$\frac{WG}{CU} = \min \left(\frac{\frac{40\ WF}{CU}}{\frac{WF}{WG}}, \frac{\frac{64k\ VGPR}{CU}}{\frac{VGPR}{WI} \times \frac{WI}{WG}}, \frac{\frac{8k\ SGPR}{CU}}{\frac{SGPR}{WF} \times \frac{WF}{WG}}, \frac{\frac{64kB\ LDS}{CU}}{\frac{local\ memory}{WG}} \right). \qquad (8.1)$$

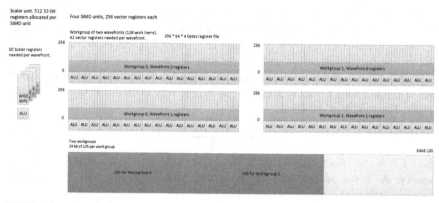

FIGURE 8.8

Mapping OpenCL's memory model onto a Radeon R9 290X GPU.

In Equation 8.1, VGPR is vector general purpose register, SGPR is scalar general purpose register, WI is work-item, WG is work-group, and WF is wavefront. The parameters based on the compiled OpenCL kernel are those shown in bold.

In the example in Figure 8.8, if we can increase the number of wavefronts running on the SIMD unit (empirically four or more wavefronts), we have a better chance of keeping the scalar and vector units busy during control flow and, particularly, memory latency, where the more wavefronts running, the better our latency hiding. Because we are LDS limited in this case, increasing the number of wavefronts per work-group to three would be a good start if this is practical for the algorithm. Alternatively, reducing the LDS allocation would allow us to run a third work-group on each compute unit, which is very useful if one wavefront is waiting for barriers or memory accesses and hence not for the SIMD unit at the time.

Each wavefront runs on a single SIMD unit and stays there until completion. Any set of wavefronts that are part of the same work-group stay together on a single compute unit. The reason for this should be clear when we see the amount of state storage required by each group: in this case, we see 24 kB of LDS and just over 21 kB of registers per work-group. This would be a significant amount of data to have to flush to memory and move to another core. As a result, when the memory controller is performing a high-latency read or write operation, if there is not another wavefront with arithmetic logic unit (ALU) work to perform ready to be scheduled onto the SIMD unit, hardware will lie idle.

8.3 MEMORY PERFORMANCE CONSIDERATIONS IN OpenCL

8.3.1 GLOBAL MEMORY

Issues related to memory in terms of temporal and spatial locality were discussed in Chapter 2. Obtaining peak performance from an OpenCL program depends heavily on utilizing memory efficiently. Unfortunately, efficient memory access is highly dependent on the particular device on which the OpenCL program is running. Access patterns that may be efficient on the GPU may be inefficient when run on a CPU. Even when we move an OpenCL program to GPUs from different manufacturers, we can see substantial differences. However, there are common practices that will produce code that performs well across multiple devices.

In all cases, a useful way to start analyzing memory performance is to judge what level of throughput a kernel is achieving. A simple way to do this is to calculate the memory bandwidth of the kernel:

$$EB = \frac{B_r + B_w}{t}, \tag{8.2}$$

where EB is the effective bandwidth, B_r is the number of bytes read from global memory, B_w is the number of bytes written to global memory, and t is the time required to run the kernel.

The time, t, can be measured using profiling tools such as the AMD CodeXL Profiler. B_r and B_w can often be calculated by multiplying the number of bytes each work-item reads or writes by the global number of work-items. Of course, in some cases, this number must be estimated because we may branch in a data-dependent manner around reads and writes.

Once we know the bandwidth measurement, we can compare it with the peak bandwidth of the execution device and determine how far away we are from peak performance: The closer to the peak, the more efficiently we are using the memory system. If our numbers are far from the peak, then we can consider restructuring the memory access pattern to improve utilization.

Spatial locality is an important consideration for OpenCL memory access. Most architectures on which OpenCL runs are vector based at some level (whether SSE-like vector instructions or automatically vectorized from a lane-oriented input language such as AMD IL or NVIDIA PTX), and their memory systems benefit from issuing accesses together across this vector. In addition, localized accesses offer caching benefits.

There is a vector instruction set on most modern CPUs; the various versions of SSE and the AVX are good examples. For efficient memory access, we want to design code such that full, aligned, vector reads are possible using these instruction sets. Given the small vector size, the most efficient way to perform such vector reads is to give the compiler as much information as possible by using vector data types such as float4. Such accesses make good use of cache lines, moving data between the cache and registers as efficiently as possible. However, on these CPUs, caching helps cover some of the performance loss from performing smaller, unaligned, or more randomly addressed reads. Figures 8.9 and 8.10 provide a simple example of the difference between a single contiguous read and a set of four random reads. Not only do the narrower reads hit multiple cache lines (creating more cache misses if they do not hit in the cache), but they also cause less efficient transfers to be passed through the memory system.

GPU memory architectures differ significantly from CPU memory architectures, as discussed in Chapter 2 and earlier in this chapter. GPUs use multithreading to cover some level of memory latency, and are biased in favor of ALU capability

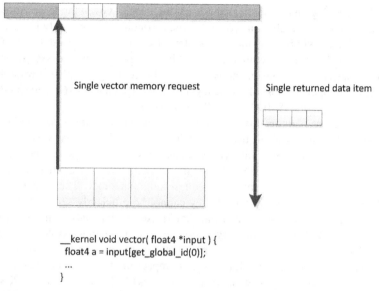

Contiguous data in memory

Single vector memory request

Single returned data item

```
__kernel void vector( float4 *input ) {
    float4 a = input[get_global_id(0)];
    ...
}
```

FIGURE 8.9

Using vector reads provides a better opportunity to return data efficiently through the memory system. When work-items access consecutive elements, GPU hardware can achieve the same result through coalescing.

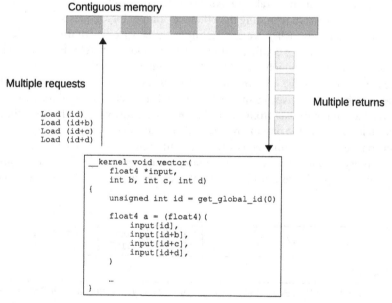

Contiguous memory

Multiple requests

Multiple returns

```
Load (id)
Load (id+b)
Load (id+c)
Load (id+d)
```

```
__kernel void vector(
    float4 *input,
    int b, int c, int d)
{
    unsigned int id = get_global_id(0)

    float4 a = (float4)(
        input[id],
        input[id+b],
        input[id+c],
        input[id+d],
    )

    ...
}
```

FIGURE 8.10

Accesses to nonconsecutive elements return smaller pieces of data less efficiently.

rather than caching and sophisticated out-of-order logic. Given the large amount of compute resources available on typical GPUs, it becomes increasingly important to provide high bandwidth to the memory system if we do not want to starve the GPU. Many modern GPU architectures, particularly high-performance desktop versions such as the latest AMD Radeon and NVIDIA GeForce designs, utilize a wide SIMD architecture. Imagine the loss of efficiency if Figure 8.10 scaled to a 64-wide hardware vector, as we see in the AMD Radeon R9 architecture.

Efficient access patterns differ even among these architectures. For an x86 CPU with SSE, we would want to use 128-bit float4 accesses, and we would want as many accesses as possible to fall within cache lines to reduce the number of cache misses. For the AMD Radeon R9 290X GPU architecture, consecutive work-items in a wavefront will issue a memory request simultaneously. These requests will be delayed in the memory system if they cannot be efficiently serviced. For peak efficiency, the work-items in a wavefront should issue 32-bit reads such that the reads form a contiguous 256-byte memory region so that the memory system can create a single large memory request. To achieve reasonable portability across different architectures, a good general solution is to compact the memory accesses as effectively as possible, allowing the wide-vector machines (AMD and NVIDIA GPUs) and the narrow vector machines (x86 CPUs) to both use the memory system efficiently. To achieve this, we should access memory across a whole work-group starting with a base address aligned to work-groupSize * loadSize, where loadSize is the size of the load issued by each work-item, and which should be reasonably sized—preferably 32 bits on AMD GCN-based architectures, 128 bits on x86 CPUs and older GPU architectures, and expanding to 256 bits on AVX-supported architectures. The reason that 32-bit accesses are preferable on AMD GCN-based architectures is explained in the following discussion regarding the efficiency of memory requests.

Complications arise when we are dealing with the specifics of different memory systems, such as reducing conflicts on the off-chip links to DRAM. For example, let us consider the way in which the AMD Radeon architecture allocates its addresses. Figure 8.11 shows that the low 8 bits of the address are used to select the byte within the memory bank; this gives us the cache line and subcache line read locality. If we try to read a column of data from a two-dimensional array, we already know that we are inefficiently using the on-chip buses. It also means that we want multiple groups running on the device simultaneously to access different memory channels and banks. Each memory channel is an on-chip memory controller corresponding to a link to an off-chip memory (Figure 8.12). We want accesses across the device to be spread

[47:x]	bank [x:12]	channel [11:8]	offset [7:0]

FIGURE 8.11

Mapping the Radeon R9 290X address space onto memory channels and DRAM banks.

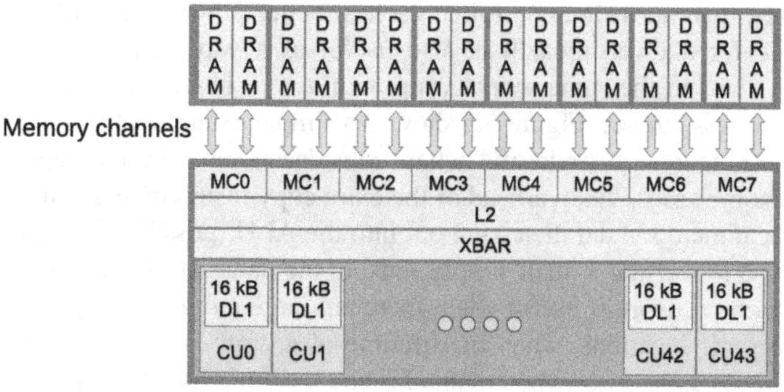

FIGURE 8.12

Radeon R9 290X memory subsystem.

across as many banks and channels in the memory system as possible, maximizing concurrent data access. However, a vector memory access from a single wavefront that hits multiple memory channels (or banks) occupies those channels, blocking access from other wavefronts and reducing overall memory throughput. Optimally, we want a given wavefront to be contained with a given channel and bank, allowing multiple wavefronts to access multiple channels in parallel. This will allow data to stream in and out of memory efficiently.

To avoid using multiple channels, a single wavefront should access addresses from within a 64-word (256-byte) region, which is achievable if all work-items read 32 bits from consecutive addresses. The worst possible situation is if each work-item in multiple wavefronts reads an address with the same value above bit 8: each one hits the same channel and bank, and accesses are serialized, achieving a small fraction of peak bandwidth. More details on this subject for AMD architectures can be found in AMD's OpenCL programming guide [4]. Similar information is provided to cover the differences in competing architectures from the respective vendors—for example, NVIDIA's CUDA programming guide [5].

8.3.2 LOCAL MEMORY AS A SOFTWARE-MANAGED CACHE

Most OpenCL-supporting devices have some form of cache support. Owing to their graphics-oriented designs, many GPUs have read-only data caches that enable some amount of spatial reuse of data.

The easiest way to guarantee the use of caches on a wide range of devices is to use OpenCL image types (discussed in Chapters 6 and 7). On GPUs, images map data sets to the texture read hardware and, assuming that complicated filtering and two-dimensional access modes are not needed, improve memory efficiency on the GPU. However, GPU caches are small compared with the number of active wavefront contexts reading data. Programmer-controlled scratchpad memory in the local address space is an efficient approach for caching data with less overhead from wasted space than hardware-controlled caches, better power efficiency, and higher performance for a given area. It is also useful as a way to exchange data with other work-items in the same work-group with a very low and, barring collisions, guaranteed access latency. Figure 5.5 showed a simple example of this approach.

Of course, there are trade-offs when considering how best to optimize data locality. In some cases, the overhead of the extra copy instructions required to move data into local memory and then back out into the ALU (possibly via registers) will sometimes be less efficient than simply reusing the data out of cache. Moving data into local memory is most useful when there are large numbers of reads and writes reusing the same locations, when the lifetime of a write is very long with a large number of reads using it, or when manual cache blocking offers a way to correct for conflict misses that can often be problematic in two-dimensional data access patterns.

In the case of read/write operations, the benefit of local memory becomes even more obvious, particularly given the wide range of architectures with read-only caches. Consider, for example, the following relatively naive version of a prefix sum code:

```
1   void localPrefixSum(
2       __global unsigned *input,
3       __global unsigned *output,
4       __local  unsigned *prefixSums,
5                unsigned numElements)
6   {
7
8       /* Copy data from global memory to local memory */
9       for (unsigned index = get_local_id(0);
10          index < numElements;
11          index += get_local_size(0))
12      {
13          prefixSums[index] = input[index];
14      }
15
16      /* Run through levels of tree, each time halving the size
17       * of the element set performing reduction phase */
18      int offset = 1;
19      for (unsigned level = numElements/2; level > 0; level /= 2)
20      {
21          barrier(CLK_LOCAL_MEM_FENCE);
22
23          for (int sumElement = get_local_id(0);
24              sumElement < level;
25              sumElement += get_local_size(0))
26          {
27              int ai = offset*(2*sumElement+1)-1;
28              int bi = offset*(2*sumElement+2)-1;
29              prefixSums[bi] = prefixSums[ai] + prefixSums[bi];
30          }
31          offset *= 2;
32
33      }
```

```
34            barrier (CLK_LOCAL_MEM_FENCE) ;
35
36            /* Need to clear the last element */
37            if ( get_local_id (0) == 0 )
38            {
39                 prefixSums [ numElements−1 ] = 0;
40            }
41
42            /* Push values back down the tree */
43            for( int level = 1; level < numElements; level *= 2 )
44            {
45                 offset /= 2;
46                 barrier (CLK_LOCAL_MEM_FENCE) ;
47
48                 for( int sumElement = get_local_id (0);
49                     sumElement < level ;
50                     sumElement += get_local_size (0) )
51                 {
52                     int ai = offset *(2* sumElement+1)−1;
53                     int bi = offset *(2* sumElement+2)−1;
54                     unsigned temporary = prefixSums [ ai ];
55                     prefixSums [ ai ] = prefixSums [ bi ];
56                     prefixSums [ bi ] = temporary + prefixSums [ bi ];
57                 }
58            }
59            barrier (CLK_LOCAL_MEM_FENCE) ;
60
61            /* Write the data out to global memory */
62            for (unsigned index = get_local_id (0);
63                 index < numElements ;
64                 index += get_local_size (0))
65            {
66                 output [ index ] = prefixSums [ index ];
67            }
68      }
```

LISTING 8.2

Single work-group prefix sum.

Although the previous code is not optimal for many architectures, it does effectively share data between work-items using a local array. The data flow of the first loop (Line 19) is shown in Figure 8.13. Note that each iteration of the loop updates a range of values that a different work-item will need to use on the next iteration. Note also that the number of work-items collaborating on the calculation decreases on each iteration. The inner loop masks excess work-items off to avoid diverging execution across the barrier. To accommodate such behavior, we insert barrier operations to ensure synchronization between the work-items and so that we can guarantee that the data will be ready for the execution of the next iteration.

The prefix sum code in Listing 8.2 uses local memory in a manner that is inefficient on most wide SIMD architectures, such as high-end GPUs. As mentioned

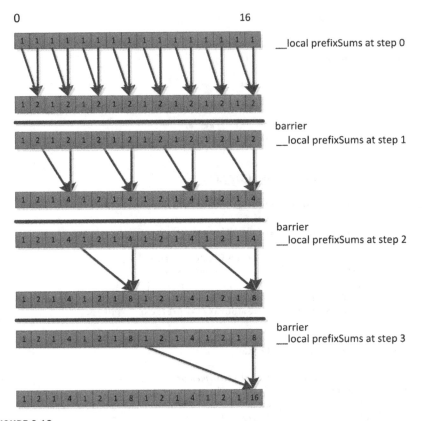

0   16

__local prefixSums at step 0

barrier
__local prefixSums at step 1

barrier
__local prefixSums at step 2

barrier
__local prefixSums at step 3

FIGURE 8.13

The accumulation pass of the prefix sum shown in Listing 8.2 over a 16-element array in local memory using 8 work-items.

in the discussion on global memory, memory systems tend to be banked to allow a large number of access ports without requiring multiple ports at every memory location. As a result, scratchpad memory hardware (and caches, similarly) tends to be built such that each bank can perform multiple reads or concurrent reads and writes (or some other multiaccess configuration), where multiple reads will be spread over multiple banks. This is an important consideration when we are using wide SIMD hardware to access memory. Each cycle, the Radeon R9 290X GPU can process local memory operations from two of the four SIMD units. As each SIMD unit is 16 lanes wide, up to 32 local reads or writes may be issued every cycle to fit with the 32 banks on the LDS. If each bank supports a single access port, then we can achieve this throughput only if all accesses target different memory banks, because each bank can provide only one value. Similar rules arise on competing architectures; NVIDIA's Fermi architecture, for example, also has a 32-banked local memory.

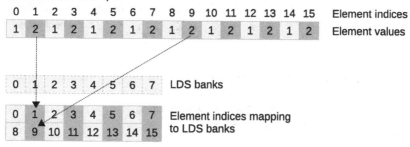

FIGURE 8.14

Step 1 in Figure 8.13 showing the behavior of an LDS with eight banks.

The problem for local memory is not as acute as that for global memory. In global memory, we saw that widely spread accesses would incur latency because they might cause multiple cache line misses. In local memory, at least on architectures with true scratchpads, the programmer knows when the data is present because he or she put it there manually. The only requirement for optimal performance is that we issue 16 accesses that hit different banks.

Figure 8.14 shows accesses from step 1 of the prefix sum in Figure 8.13 to a simplified eight-bank LDS, where each work-item can perform a single local memory operation per cycle. In this case, our local memory buffer can return up to eight values per cycle from memory. What performance result do we obtain when performing the set of accesses necessary for step 1 of the prefix sum?

Note that our 16-element local memory (necessary for the prefix sum) is spread over two rows. Each column is a bank, and each row is an address within a bank. Assuming (as is common in many architectures) that each bank is 32 bits wide, and assuming, for simplicity, that the current wavefront is not competing with one from another SIMD unit, our memory address would break down as shown at the top of Figure 8.14. Two consecutive memory words will reside in separate banks. As with global memory, an SIMD vector that accesses consecutive addresses along its length will efficiently access the local memory banks without contention. In Figure 8.13, however, we see a different behavior. Given the second access to local memory, the read from `prefixSums[bi]` in

`prefixSums[bi] = prefixSums[ai] + prefixSums[bi]` on Line 29; tries to read values from locations 3, 7, 11, and 15. As shown in Figure 8.14, 3 and 11 both sit in bank 3, and 7 and 15 both sit in bank 7. There is no possible way to read two rows from the same bank simultaneously, so these accesses will be serialized

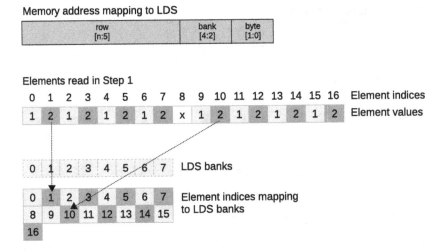

FIGURE 8.15

Step 1 in Figure 8.14 with padding added to the original data set to remove bank conflicts in the LDS.

on GPUs by the hardware, incurring a read delay. For good performance, we might wish to restructure our code to avoid this conflict. One useful technique is to add padding to the addresses, and an example of this is shown in Figure 8.15. By shifting addresses after the first set (aligning to banks), we can change evenly strided accesses to avoid conflicts. Unfortunately, this adds address computation overhead, which can be more severe than the bank conflict overhead; hence, this trade-off is an example of architecture-specific tuning.

Local memory should be carefully rationed. Any device that uses a real scratchpad region that is not hardware managed will have a limited amount of local memory. In the case of the Radeon R9 290X GPU, this space is 64 kB. It is important to note that this 64 kB is shared between all work-groups executing simultaneously on the core. Also, because the GPU is a latency hiding throughput device that utilizes multithreading on each core, the more work-groups that can fit, the better the hardware utilization is likely to be. If each work-group uses 16 kB, then only four can fit on the core. If these work-groups contain a small number of wavefronts (one or two), then there will be barely enough wavefronts to cover latency. Therefore, local memory allocation will need to balance efficiency gains from sharing and efficiency losses from reducing the number of hardware threads to one or two on a multithreaded device.

The OpenCL application programming interface includes calls to query the amount of local memory the device possesses, and this can be used to parameterize kernels before the programmer compiles or dispatches them. The first call in the following code queries the type of the local memory so that it is possible to determine if it is dedicated or in global memory (which may or may not be cached; this can also be queried), and the second call returns the size of each local memory buffer:

```
cl_int err;
cl_device_local_mem_type type;
err = clGetDeviceInfo(
    deviceId,
    CL_DEVICE_LOCAL_MEM_TYPE,
    sizeof(cl_device_local_mem_type),
    &type,
    0);

cl_ulong size;
err = clGetDeviceInfo(
    deviceId,
    CL_DEVICE_LOCAL_MEM_SIZE,
    sizeof(cl_ulong),
    &size,
    0);
```

8.4 SUMMARY

The aim of this chapter was to show a very specific mapping of OpenCL to an architectural implementation. In this case, it was shown how OpenCL maps slightly differently to a CPU architecture and a GPU architecture. The core principles of this chapter apply to competing CPU and GPU architectures, but significant differences in performance can easily arise from variation in vector width (32 on NVIDIA GPUs, 64 on AMD GPUs, and much smaller on CPUs), variations in thread context management, and instruction scheduling. It is clear that in one book we cannot aim to cover all possible architectures, but by giving one example, we hope that further investigation through vendor documentation will lead to efficient code on whatever OpenCL device is being targeted.

REFERENCES

[1] J. Gummaraju, L. Morichetti, M. Houston, B. Sander, B.R. Gaster, B. Zheng, Twin peaks: a software platform for heterogeneous computing on general-purpose and graphics processors, in: PACT 2010: Proceedings of the Nineteenth International Conference on Parallel Architectures and Compilation Techniques, September 1115, 2010, Vienna, Austria. Association for Computing Machinery, 2010.
[2] Advanced Micro Devices, GCN Whitepaper. AMD Graphics Core Next (GCN) Architecture, 2013. http://www.amd.com/Documents/GCN_Architecture_whitepaper.pdf.

[3] Advanced Micro Devices, AMD Sea Islands Series Instruction Set Architecture, 2013. http://developer.amd.com/wordpress/media/2013/07/AMD_Sea_Islands_Instruction_Set_Architecture.pdf.

[4] Advanced Micro Devices, The AMD Accelerated Parallel Processing-OpenCL Programming Guide, Advanced Micro Devices, Inc., Sunnyvale, CA, 2012.

[5] NVIDIA, CUDA C Programming Guide, NVIDIA Corporation, Santa Clara, CA, 2012.

Case study: Image clustering

The bag-of-words (BoW) model is one of the most popular approaches to image classification and forms an important component of image search systems. The BoW model treats an image's features as words, and represents the image as a vector of the occurrence counts of image features (words). This chapter discusses the OpenCL implementation of an important component of the BoW model—namely, the histogram builder. We discuss the OpenCL kernel and study the performance impact of various source code optimizations.

9.1 INTRODUCTION

Image classification refers to a process in computer vision that can classify an image according to its visual content. For example, an image classification algorithm may be designed to tell if an image contains a human figure or not. While detecting an object is trivial for humans, robust image classification is still a challenge in computer vision applications.

The BoW model is a commonly used method in document classification and natural language processing. In the BoW model, the frequency of the occurrence of each word in the document is used as a parameter for training a machine learning algorithm. In addition to document classification, the BoW model can also be applied to image classification. To apply the BoW model to classify images, we need to extract a set of *words* (just like in document classification) from the image and count their occurrence. In computer vision, the words extracted from an image are commonly known as *features*. A feature generation algorithm reduces an image to a set of features that can serve as a signature for an image. A high-level algorithm for image classification is shown in Figure 9.1, and consists of feature generation, clustering, and histogram building steps, which are briefly described below:

1. **Feature generation:** The feature generation algorithm we have applied in the BoW model is the speeded up robust features (SURF) algorithm. SURF was first introduced in 2006 by Bay et al. [1], and is a popular algorithm that is invariant to various image transformations. Given an input image, the SURF algorithm returns a list of *features* illustrated in Figure 9.2. Each feature includes a location

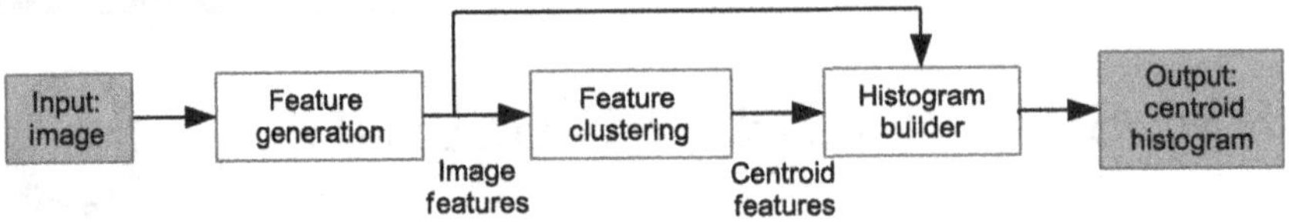

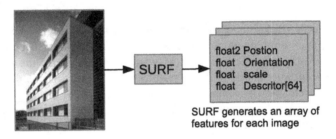

FIGURE 9.1

An image classification pipeline. An algorithm such as SURF is used to generate features. A clustering algorithm such as k-means then generates a set of centroid features that can serve as a set of visual words for the image. The generated features are assigned to each centroid by the histogram builder.

FIGURE 9.2

Feature generation using the SURF algorithm. The SURF algorithm accepts an image as an input and generates an array of features. Each feature includes position information and a set of 64 values known as a `descriptor`.

in the image and a descriptor vector. The descriptor vector (also referred to as a *descriptor*) is a 64-dimension vector for each feature. The descriptor contains information about the local color gradients around the feature's location. In the context of this chapter, *feature* refers to the 64 element descriptor which is a part of each feature. The remainder of this chapter does not focus on the location information generated as part of the feature.

2. **Image clustering:** The descriptors generated from the SURF algorithm are usually quantized, typically by k-means clustering, and mapped into clusters. The centroid of each cluster is also known as a *visual word*.

3. **Histogram builder:** The goal of this stage is to convert a list of SURF descriptors into a histogram of visual words (centroids). To do this, we need to determine to which centroid each descriptor belongs. In this case, both the descriptors of the SURF features and the centroid have 64 dimensions. We compute the Euclidean distance between the descriptor and all the centroids, and then assign each SURF descriptor to its closest centroid. The histogram is formed by counting the number of SURF descriptors assigned to each centroid.

Using this approach, we can represent images by histograms of the frequency of the centroids (visual words) in a manner similar to document classification. Machine learning algorithms such as a support vector machine can then be used for classification. A diagram of this execution pipeline is shown in Figure 9.1.

In this chapter, we explore the parallelization of the histogram-building stage in Figure 9.1. We first introduce the sequential central processing unit (CPU) implementation and its parallelized version using OpenMP. Then we move to multiple parallel implementations using OpenCL that are targeted toward a graphics processing unit (GPU) architecture. Several implementations are discussed, including a naive implementation, a version that uses more optimal accesses to global memory, and additional versions that utilize local memory. At the end of the chapter, an evaluation of performance is provided using an AMD Radeon HD 7970 GPU.

> **NOTE**
>
> This chapter focuses on the histogram-building section of the image classification application. Readers interested in feature generation can access an open-source version of the SURF algorithm implemented in OpenCL at https://code.google.com/p/clsurf/.

9.2 THE FEATURE HISTOGRAM ON THE CPU

In this section, we first introduce the algorithm for converting SURF features into a histogram and implement a sequential version for execution on a CPU. We then parallelize the algorithm using OpenMP to target a multicore CPU.

9.2.1 SEQUENTIAL IMPLEMENTATION

Listing 9.1 shows the procedure for converting the array of SURF features into a histogram of cluster centroids (visual words). Line 2 loops through the SURF descriptors and line 7 loops through the cluster centroids. Line 12 loops through the 64 elements of the current descriptor to compute the Euclidean distance between the SURF feature and the cluster centroid. Line 18 finds the closest cluster centroid for the SURF descriptor and assigns its membership to the cluster.

```
1   // Loop over all the descriptors generated for the image
2   for(int i = 0; i < n_desc; i++)
3   {
4     membership = 0;
5     min_dist = FLT_MAX;
6     // Loop over all the cluster centroids available
7     for(j = 0 ; j < n_cluster; j++)
8     {
9       dist = 0;
10      // n_features: No. of elements in each descriptor (64)
11      // Calculate the distance between the descriptor and the centroid
12      for(k = 0 ; k < n_features; k++)
13      {
14        dist_temp = surf[i][k]-cluster[j][k];
15        dist += dist_temp * dist_temp;
16      }
```

```
17      // Update the minimum distance
18      if(dist < min_dist)
19      {
20        min_dist = dist;
21        membership = j;
22      }
23    }
24    // Update the histogram location of the closest centroid
25    histogram[membership] += 1;
26  }
```

LISTING 9.1

Convert a list of SURF features to a histogram of clusters sequentially.

9.2.2 OpenMP PARALLELIZATION

To take advantage of the cores present on a multicore CPU, we use OpenMP to parallelize Listing 9.1. The OpenMP application programming interface supports multiplatform shared-memory parallel programming in C/C++ and Fortran. It defines a portable, scalable model with a simple and flexible interface for developing parallel applications on platforms from desktops to supercomputers [2]. In C/C++, OpenMP uses pragmas (#pragma) to direct the compiler on how to generate the parallel implementation.

Using OpenMP, we can distribute the histogram-building step across the multiple CPU cores by dividing the task of processing SURF descriptors between multiple threads. Each thread computes the distance from its descriptor to the cluster centroids and assigns membership to a centroid. Although the computation for each descriptor can be done independently, assigning membership to the histogram creates a *race condition*: if multiple threads try to update the same location simultaneously, the results will be undefined. This race condition can be solved by using an atomic addition operation (line 26). The histogram algorithm using OpenMP parallelization is showing in Listing 9.2.

```
1   // All the descriptors for the image can be handled in parallel
2   #pragma omp parallel for schedule(dynamic)
3   for(int i = 0; i < n_desc; i++)
4   {
5     membership = 0
6     min_dist = FLT_MAX
7     for(j = 0 ; j < n_cluster; j++)
8     {
9       dist = 0;
10      // n_features: No. of elements in each descriptor (64)
11      //Calculate the distance between the descriptor and the centroid
12      for(k = 0 ; k < n_features; k++)
13      {
14        dist_temp = surf[i][k]-cluster[j][k];
15        dist += dist_temp * dist_temp;
16      }
17      // Update the minimum distance
```

```
18        if(dist < min_dist)
19        {
20          min_dist = dist;
21          membership = j;
22        }
23      }
24      // The histogram needs to be updated atomically since multiple
25      // descriptors could update the same element
26      #pragma omp atomic
27      histogram[membership] += 1
28    }
```

LISTING 9.2

Convert a list of SURF features to a histogram of clusters using OpenMP.

In Listing 9.2, the pragma on line 2 is used to create threads and divide the loop iterations among them. The pragma on line 18 tells the compiler to use an atomic operation when updating the shared memory location.

9.3 OpenCL IMPLEMENTATION

In this section, we discuss the OpenCL implementation of the histogram builder. We first implement a naive OpenCL kernel based on the sequential and OpenMP versions of the algorithm. Then we explain how this naive implementation can be improved for execution on GPUs by applying optimizations such as coalesced memory accesses and using local memory.

9.3.1 NAIVE GPU IMPLEMENTATION: GPU1

Given the parallel algorithm shown in Listing 9.2, the simplest way to parallelize the algorithm in OpenCL would be to decompose the computation across the outermost loop iterations: where each OpenCL work-item is responsible for computing the membership of a single descriptor.

However, as with the OpenMP example, this implementation creates a race condition as multiple work-items update the histogram in global memory. To solve this issue, we use an atomic addition to update the histogram as we did for the OpenMP parallelization. The code for this naive OpenCL kernel is shown in Listing 9.3. We refer to this implementation as GPU1.

```
1   __kernel
2   void kernelGPU1(
3       __global float *descriptors,
4       __global float *centroids,
5       __global int *histogram,
6       int n_descriptors,
7       int n_centroids,
8       int n_features)
9   {
10      // Global ID identifies SURF descriptor
```

```
11      int desc_id = get_global_id(0);
12
13      int membership = 0;
14      float min_dist = FLT_MAX;
15
16      // For each cluster, compute the membership
17      for(int j = 0; j < n_centroids; j++) {
18
19          float dist = 0;
20
21          // n_features: No. of elements in each descriptor (64)
22          // Calculate the distance between the descriptor and the
                 centroid
23          for(int k = 0; k < n_features; k++) {
24              float temp = descriptors[desc_id*n_features+k] -
25                  centroids[j*n_features+k];
26              dist += temp*temp;
27          }
28
29          // Update the minimum distance
30          if(dist < min_dist) {
31              min_dist = dist;
32              membership = j;
33          }
34      }
35
36      // Atomic increment of histogram bin
37      atomic_fetch_add_explicit(&histogram[membership], 1,
38          memory_order_relaxed, memory_scope_device);
39  }
```

LISTING 9.3

Kernel for GPU1, the baseline histogram kernel.

Notice that in Listing 9.3, the atomic increment on line 37 is performed using a relaxed memory order. We chose this option because we are performing only a simple counter update, so enforcing stronger ordering requirements is not needed. See Chapter 7 for more details.

9.3.2 COALESCED MEMORY ACCESSES: GPU2

Recall that successive work-items are executed in lockstep when running on GPU single instruction, multiple data (SIMD) hardware. Also recall that SURF descriptors and cluster centroids comprise vectors of 64 consecutive elements. Keeping this information in mind, take a look at line 24 of Listing 9.3, and notice the access to descriptors. Given what we know about GPU hardware, would line 24 result in high-performance access to memory?

Suppose there are four work-items running in parallel with global IDs ranging from 0 to 3. When looping over the features in the innermost loop, these four work-items would be accessing memory at a large stride—in this kernel, the stride will be n_features elements. Assuming that we are processing centroid 0 (j = 0), when

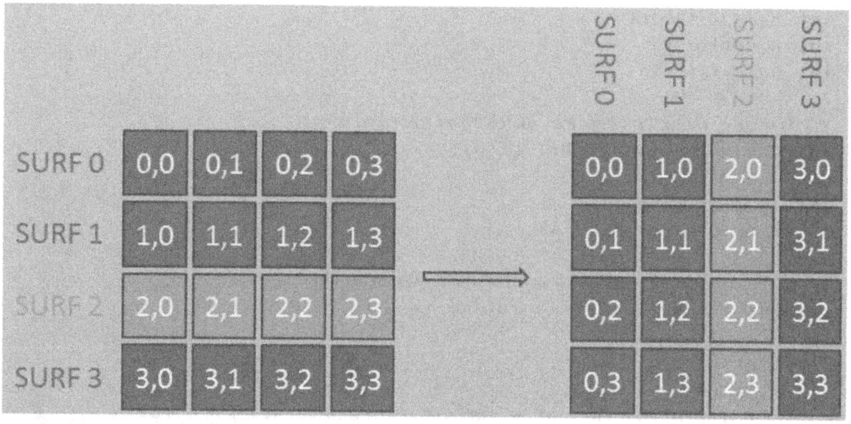

FIGURE 9.3

The data transformation kernel used to enable memory coalescing is the same as a matrix transpose kernel.

computing the distance for feature 0 (k = 0), the work-items would produce accesses to descriptors[0], descriptors[64], descriptors[128], and descriptors[192]. Computing the distance for the next feature would generate accesses to descriptors[1], descriptors[65], descriptors[129], and descriptors[193], and so on.

Recall from Chapter 8 that accesses to consecutive elements can be *coalesced* into fewer requests to the memory system for higher performance, but that strided accesses generate multiple requests, resulting in lower performance. This strided pattern when accessing the buffers is uncoalesced and suboptimal.

To improve the memory bandwidth utilization by increasing the memory coalescing, we need to adjust the order in which elements are stored in the descriptors buffer. This can be done by using a data layout transformation known as a *transpose*, which is demonstrated in Figure 9.3. In a transpose, the rows and column positions of each element are exchanged. That is, for an element $A_{i,j}$ in the original matrix, the corresponding element in the transposed matrix is $A_{j,i}$. We create a simple transformation kernel where each thread reads one element of the input matrix from global memory and writes back the same element at its transposed index in the global memory.

Since we are using a one-dimensional array for the input buffers, an illustration of applying a transpose kernel is shown in Figure 9.4. After the transformation, descriptors[0], descriptors[64], descriptors[128], and descriptors[192] are stored in four consecutive words in memory and can be accessed by four work-items using only one memory transaction.

```
1   __kernel
2   void kernelGPU2(
3       __global float *descriptors,
4       __global float *centroids,
5       __global int *histogram,
```

```
6      int n_descriptors,
7      int n_centroids,
8      int n_features)
9  {
10     // Global ID identifies SURF descriptor
11     int desc_id = get_global_id(0);
12
13     int membership = 0;
14     float min_dist = FLT_MAX;
15
16     // For each cluster, compute the membership
17     for(int j = 0; j < n_centroids; j++) {
18
19         float dist = 0;
20
21         // n_features: No. of elements in each descriptor (64)
22         // Calculate the distance between the descriptor and the
                centroid
23         for(int k = 0; k < n_features; k++) {
24             float temp = descriptors[k*n_descriptors+desc_id] -
25                 centroids[j*n_features+k];
26             dist += temp*temp;
27         }
28
29         // Update the minimum distance
30         if(dist < min_dist) {
31             min_dist = dist;
32             membership = j;
33         }
34     }
35
36     // Atomic increment of histogram bin
37     atomic_fetch_add_explicit(&histogram[membership], 1,
38         memory_order_relaxed, memory_scope_device);
39 }
```

LISTING 9.4

Kernel for GPU2 with coalesced memory accesses.

After the transformation, line 24 of Listing 9.4 shows that descriptors is now indexed by k*n_descriptors+desc_id. As k and n_descriptors have the

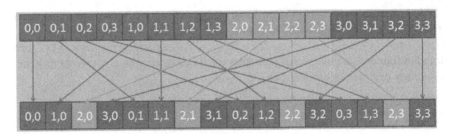

FIGURE 9.4

A transpose illustrated on a one-dimensional array.

same value for all work-items executing in lockstep, the work-item accesses will be differentiated solely by their ID (desc_id). In our previous example of four work-items, k = 0 would produce accesses to descriptors[0], descriptors[1], descriptors[2], and descriptors[3]. When k = 1, accesses would be generated for descriptors[64], descriptors[65], descriptors[66], and descriptors[67]. This access pattern is much more favorable, and allows GPU coalescing hardware to generate highly efficient accesses to the memory system.

9.3.3 VECTORIZING COMPUTATION: GPU3

Since each SURF descriptor is a fixed-sized vector with 64 dimensions, vectorization with float4 has the ability to substantially increase the utilization of the processing elements. This type of vectorization on a CPU would allow the compiler to take advantage of Streaming SIMD Extensions instructions for higher-throughput execution. Some families of GPUs (e.g. AMD Radeon 6xxx series) could also take advantage of vectorized operations. Newer GPUs from AMD and NVIDIA do not explicitly execute vector instructions; however, in some scenarios this optimization could lead to high performance from improved memory system utilization or improved code generation.

```
float a[4], b[4], c[4];

a[0] = b[0] + c[0]
a[1] = b[1] + c[1]
a[2] = b[2] + c[2]
a[3] = b[3] + c[3]
```

Vectorization can allow us to generalize operations on scalars transparently to vectors, matrices, and higher-dimensional arrays. This can be done explicitly by the developer in OpenCL using the float4 type. The listing below is an explicit vectorization of the addition operations in the listing above.

```
float a[4], b[4], c[4];

float4 b4 = (float4)(b[0], b[1], b[2], b[3])
float4 c4 = (float4)(c[0], c[1], c[2], c[3])
float4 a4 = b4 + c4
```

To introduce vectorization into our algorithm, the OpenCL kernel is updated as shown in Listing 9.5, named as implementation GPU3.

```
1  __kernel
2  void kernelGPU3(
3      __global float *descriptors,
4      __global float *centroids,
5      __global int *histogram,
6      int n_descriptors,
7      int n_centroids,
8      int n_features)
```

```
 9   {
10       // Global ID identifies SURF descriptor
11       int desc_id = get_global_id(0);
12
13       int membership = 0;
14       float min_dist = FLT_MAX;
15
16       // For each cluster, compute the membership
17       for(int j = 0; j < n_centroids; j++) {
18
19           float dist = 0;
20           // n_features: No. of elements in each descriptor (64)
21           // Calculate the distance between the descriptor and the
                  centroid
22           // The increment of 4 is due to the explicit vectorization where
23           // the distance between 4 elements is calculated in each
24           // loop iteration
25           for (int k = 0; k < n_feature; k += 4) {
26               float4 surf_temp =(float4)(
27                   descriptors[(k+0)*n_surf + surf_id],
28                   descriptors[(k+1)*n_surf + surf_id],
29                   descriptors[(k+2)*n_surf + surf_id],
30                   descriptors[(k+3)*n_surf + surf_id]);
31
32               float4 cluster_temp =(float4)(
33                   centroids[j*n_feature+k],
34                   centroids[j*n_feature+k+1],
35                   centroids[j*n_feature+k+2],
36                   centroids[j*n_feature+k+3]);
37
38               float4 temp = surf_temp - cluster_temp;
39               temp = temp * temp;
40
41               dist += temp.x + temp.y + temp.z + temp.w;
42           }
43
44           // Update the minimum distance
45           if(dist < min_dist) {
46               min_dist = dist;
47               membership = j;
48           }
49       }
50
51       // Atomic increment of histogram bin
52       atomic_fetch_add_explicit(&histogram[membership], 1,
53           memory_order_relaxed, memory_scope_device);
54   }
```

LISTING 9.5

Kernel for GPU3 using vectorization.

9.3.4 MOVE SURF FEATURES TO LOCAL MEMORY: GPU4

The following snippet shows the memory accesses to `descriptors` and `centroids` from Listing 9.4:

```
for(int k = 0; k < n_features; k++) {
    float temp = descriptors[k*n_descriptors+desc_id] —
        centroids[j*n_features+k];
    dist += temp*temp;
}
```

Notice that the data in both of these buffers is accessed multiple times. Is it possible to take advantage of one of the other OpenCL memory spaces to improve performance? When `centroids` are accessed, the address used to index the buffer is independent of the work-item's ID. This type of access pattern is favorable for constant memory, which we will discuss in the next iteration of the algorithm. For this version, we will focus on optimizing accesses to `descriptors`. Since addressing `descriptors` is dependent on the work-item ID, it is not well suited for constant memory. However, can we take advantage of local memory instead?

Recall that when running applications on most GPUs, local memory is a high-bandwidth, low-latency memory used for sharing data among work-items within a work-group. On GPUs with dedicated local memory, access to local memory is usually much faster than accesses to global memory. Also, unlike accesses to global memory, accesses to local memory usually do not require coalescing, and are more forgiving than global memory when having nonideal access patterns (such as patterns that cause large numbers of memory bank conflicts). However, local memory has limited size—on the AMD Radeon HD 7970 GPU there is 64 KB of local memory per compute unit, with the maximum allocation for a single work-group limited to 32 KB. Allocating large amounts of local memory per work-group has the consequence of limiting the number of in-flight threads. On a GPU, this can reduce the scheduler's ability to hide latency, and potentially leave execution resources vacant.

Initially, this data does not seem to be a good candidate for local memory, as local memory is primarily intended to allow communication of data between work-items, and no data is shared when accessing `descriptors`. However, for some GPUs such as the Radeon HD 7970, local memory has additional advantages. First, local memory is mapped to the local data store (LDS), which provides four times more storage than the general-purpose level 1 (L1) cache. Therefore, placing this buffer in the LDS may provide low-latency access to data that could otherwise result in cache misses. The second benefit is that even assuming a cache hit, LDS memory has a lower latency than the L1 cache. Therefore, with enough reuse, data resident in the LDS could provide a speedup over the L1 cache even with a high hit rate. The trade-off, of course, is that the use of local memory will limit the number of in-flight work-groups, potentially underutilizing the GPU's execution units and memory system. This is an optimization that needs to be considered on a per-architecture basis. A version of the kernel utilizing local memory to cache `descriptors` is shown in Listing 9.6.

```
1   __kernel
2   void kernelGPU4(
3       __global float *descriptors,
4       __global float *centroids,
5       __global int *histogram,
6       int n_descriptors,
7       int n_centroids,
8       int n_features)
9   {
10
11      // Global ID identifies SURF descriptor
12      int desc_id = get_global_id(0);
13      int local_id = get_local_id(0);
14      int local_size = get_local_size(0);
15
16      // Store the descriptors in local memory
17      __local float desc_local[4096]; // 64 descriptors * 64 work-items
18      for(int i = 0; i < n_features; i++) {
19          desc_local[i*local_size + local_id] =
20              descriptors[i*n_descriptors + surf_id];
21      }
22      barrier(CLK_LOCAL_MEM_FENCE);
23
24      int membership = 0;
25      float min_dist = FLT_MAX;
26
27      // For each cluster, compute the membership
28      for(int j = 0; j < n_centroids; j++) {
29
30          float dist = 0;
31          // n_features: No. of elements in each descriptor (64)
32          // Calculate the distance between the descriptor and the
                centroid
33          for(int k = 0; k < n_features; k++) {
34              float temp = desc_local[k*local_size+local_id] -
35                  centroids[j*n_features+k];
36              dist += temp*temp;
37          }
38
39          // Update the minimum distance
40          if(dist < min_dist) {
41              min_dist = dist;
42              membership = j;
43          }
44      }
45
46      // Atomic increment of histogram bin
47      atomic_fetch_add_explicit(&histogram[membership], 1,
48          memory_order_relaxed, memory_scope_device);
49  }
```

LISTING 9.6

Kernel for GPU4, with descriptor data stored in local memory.

When `descriptors` are accessed, `n_descriptors` and `desc_id` are fixed per work-item for the entire duration of the kernel. The index simply varies on the basis of `k`. Therefore, each work-item will access the `n_feature` elements (64) of `descriptors` a total of `n_centroids` times (the `j` iterator). Given the small L1 cache sizes on GPUs, it is very likely that many of these accesses will generate L1 cache misses and cause redundant accesses to global memory.

Moving `descriptors` to LDS would require $64 \times 4 = 256$ bytes per descriptor. With a wavefront size of 64 work-items, each wavefront requires 16 KB of LDS to cache its portion of descriptors. This would allow at most four work-groups to be executed at a time per compute unit (one wavefront per work-group). On the Radeon HD 7970, each compute unit comprises four SIMD units, limiting our execution to one work-group per SIMD unit and removing the ability to hide latency on a given SIMD unit. Any benefit we see from performance will be a trade-off between lower-latency memory accesses and decreased parallelism. We refer to this implementation as GPU4.

9.3.5 MOVE CLUSTER CENTROIDS TO CONSTANT MEMORY: GPU5

As shown in the convolution example in Chapter 4, and the memory model discussion in Chapter 7, constant memory is a memory space that it intended to hold data that is accessed simultaneously by all work-items. Data typically stored in constant memory would include convolution filters and constant variables such as π. In the case of our histogram kernel, the descriptors for each centroid also fit this characteristic. Notice that when `centroids` are accessed, the address depends on two of the loop iterators, but never on the work-item ID. Therefore, work-items executing in lockstep will generate identical addresses.

The trade-off for mapping `centroids` to constant memory is that on GPUs constant memory usually maps to specialized caching hardware that is a fixed size. In the case of the Radeon HD 7970, the largest buffer size that can be mapped to constant memory is 64 KB. For this example, the features for each centroid consume 256 bytes. Therefore, we can map at most 256 centroids at a time to constant memory.

Alert readers may also question the effectiveness of mapping `centroids` to constant memory. If all work-items are accessing the same address, will not the accesses be coalesced and generate only a single request to global memory? On most modern GPUs, the answer is yes: only a single request will be generated. However, similarly to mapping `descriptors` to LDS, there are additional benefits to mapping `centroids` to constant memory. The first benefit of utilizing constant memory is to remove pressure from the GPU's L1 cache. With the small L1 cache capacity, removing up to 64 KB of recurring accesses could lead to a significant performance improvement. The second benefit is that the GPU's constant cache also has a much lower latency than does accessing the general-purpose L1 cache. As long as our data set has few enough centroids to fit into constant memory, this will likely lead to a significant performance improvement.

Mapping the `centroids` buffer to constant memory is as simple as changing the parameter declaration from `__global` to `__constant`, as shown in Listing 9.7.

```
1   __kernel
2   void kernelGPU5(
3       __global float *descriptors,
4       __constant float *centroids,
5       __global int *histogram,
6       int n_descriptors,
7       int n_centroids,
8       int n_features)
9   {
10      // Global ID identifies SURF descriptor
11      int desc_id = get_global_id(0);
12      int local_id = get_local_id(0);
13      int local_size = get_local_size(0);
14
15      // Store the descriptors in local memory
16      __local float desc_local[4096]; // 64 descriptors * 64 work-items
17      for(int i = 0; i < n_features; i++) {
18          desc_local[i*local_size + local_id] =
19              descriptors[i*n_descriptors + surf_id];
20      }
21      barrier(CLK_LOCAL_MEM_FENCE);
22
23      int membership = 0;
24      float min_dist = FLT_MAX;
25
26      // For each cluster, compute the membership
27      for(int j = 0; j < n_centroids; j++) {
28
29          float dist = 0;
30
31          // Calculate the distance between the descriptor and the
                centroid
32          for(int k = 0; k < n_features; k++) {
33              float temp = desc_local[k*local_size+local_id] -
34                  centroids[j*n_features+k];
35              dist += temp*temp;
36          }
37
38          // Update the minimum distance
39          if(dist < min_dist) {
40              min_dist = dist;
41              membership = j;
42          }
43      }
44
45      // Atomic increment of histogram bin
46      atomic_fetch_add_explicit(&histogram[membership], 1,
47          memory_order_relaxed, memory_scope_device);
48  }
```

LISTING 9.7

Kernel for GPU5, with centroid data stored in constant memory.

9.4 PERFORMANCE ANALYSIS

To illustrate the performance impact of the various kernel implementations, we executed the kernels on a Radeon HD 7970 GPU. To additionally provide insight into the impact of data sizes on the optimization, we generated inputs with various combinations of SURF descriptors and cluster centroids. We varied the number of SURF descriptors between 4096, 16,384, and 65,536. At the same time, we varied the number of cluster centroids between 16, 64, and 256. We picked large numbers of SURF features because a comprehensive high-resolution images can usually contains thousands of features. However, for cluster centroids, the numbers are relatively small since a large number of clusters could reduce the accuracy of image classification.

The performance experiments described in this section can be carried out using performance profiling tools such as AMD's CodeXL, which is described in detail in Chapter 10. The performance discussed in this chapter is used only for illustrating the benefits of source code optimization of OpenCL kernels. The performance impact of each optimization will vary depending on the targeted architecture.

9.4.1 GPU PERFORMANCE

We evaluate performance, and keep in mind that GPU1 requires only a single OpenCL kernel. However, the rest of the implementations require a transpose kernel to be called before execution of the histogram kernel, and thus consist of two kernels. The transpose kernel overhead is based solely on the number of SURF descriptors, and will not be impacted by other changes. Therefore, we separate out the transpose timing in Table 9.1, so that the impact from the other performance results can be viewed in isolation. The execution time for the second kernel from each implementation is shown in Table 9.2.

Table 9.1 The Time Taken for the Transpose Kernel

No. of Features	Transform Kernel (ms)
4096	0.05
16,384	0.50
65,536	2.14

All implementations other than GPU1 execute this kernel. To make an accurate comparison between GPU1 and all other kernels, these values should be added to the execution time of the histogram kernel (shown in Table 9.2).

Table 9.2 Kernel Running Time (ms) for Different GPU Implementations

# of Clusters	# of SURF Descriptors	GPU Implementations				
		GPU1	GPU2	GPU3	GPU4	GPU5
8	4096	0.41	0.27	0.10	0.17	0.09
	16,384	3.60	0.28	0.17	0.69	0.19
	65,536	15.36	1.05	0.59	1.31	0.74
16	4096	0.77	0.53	0.19	0.28	0.14
	16,384	7.10	0.53	0.32	0.57	0.29
	65,536	30.41	1.47	1.17	2.26	1.12
64	4096	6.00	3.53	1.34	1.00	0.43
	16,384	28.28	2.11	1.20	2.96	0.86
	65,536	122.09	5.80	4.65	9.04	3.87
128	4096	4.96	4.04	1.47	1.95	0.81
	16,384	55.70	4.27	2.40	5.89	1.61
	65,536	243.30	11.63	9.29	17.46	6.43
256	4096	10.49	8.06	2.84	4.35	1.57
	16,384	109.67	8.62	4.77	11.44	3.13
	65,536	488.54	23.28	18.71	34.73	13.97

9.5 CONCLUSION

In this chapter, we performed various source code optimizations on a real-world OpenCL kernel. These optimizations included improving memory accesses using a data transformation, implementing vectorized mathematical operations, and mapping data to local and constant memory for improved performance. We evaluated the implementations on a GPU to observe the performance impact of each optimization.

REFERENCES

[1] H. Bay, T. Tuytelaars, L.V. Gool, SURF: speeded up robust features, in: ECCV, 2006, pp. 404-417.
[2] L. Dagum, R. Menon, OpenMP: an industry standard API for shared-memory programming, IEEE Comput. Sci. Eng. 5 (1) (1998) 46-55.

OpenCL profiling and debugging

10

10.1 INTRODUCTION

Our motivation for writing programs in OpenCL is not limited to writing isolated high-performance kernels but is to speed up parallel applications. Previous chapters have discussed how we can optimize kernels running on OpenCL devices by targeting features of the architecture. An OpenCL application can include many kernels and a large amount of input/output data movement between the host and the device. We need to measure the performance and study an application as a whole to understand bottlenecks. Profiling an application can help us to improve performance by answering some of the following questions regarding an application:

- Which kernel should be optimized when multiple kernels exist in an application?
- How much time is spent by the kernels waiting in command-queues versus actually executing?
- What is the ratio between execution time and the time spent initializing the OpenCL runtime and compiling kernels for an application?
- What is the ratio of time spent in host-device input-output to computation time for an application?

Answering the performance questions above can help a developer quickly determine why an application is not performing as expected and, in combination with the debugging features described later in this chapter, can greatly improve the development process.

We conclude this chapter by discussing debugging OpenCL code. Debugging parallel programs is traditionally more complicated than debugging conventional serial code owing to subtle bugs such as race conditions, which are difficult to detect and reproduce.

10.2 PROFILING OpenCL CODE USING EVENTS

OpenCL supports 64-bit timing of commands submitted to command-queues using `clEnqueueXX()` commands, such as `clEnqueueNDRangeKernel()`. Generally, commands are enqueued into a queue asynchronously, and as described in previous chapters, the developer uses events to track a command's status and enforce dependencies. Events provide a gateway to a command's history. Events contain information detailing when the corresponding command was placed in the queue, when it was submitted to the device, and when it started and ended execution. Access to an event's profiling information is through the application programming interface (API) clGetEventProfilingInfo(), which provides an interface for queuing timing information:

Profiling of OpenCL programs using events has to be enabled explicitly on a per command-queue basis. Profiling is enabled when creating a command-queue by setting the CL_QUEUE_PROFILING_ENABLE flag. Once a command-queue has been created, it is not possible to turn event profiling on and off.

```
cl_int clGetEventProfilingInfo (
  cl_event event,
  cl_profiling_info param_name,
  size_t param_value_size,
  void *param_value,
  size_t *param_value_size_ret)
```

Table 10.1 The Command States that can be Used to Obtain Timestamps from OpenCL Events

Event State	Information Returned in param_value
CL_PROFILING_COMMAND_QUEUED	A 64-bit value that describes the current device time counter in nanoseconds when the command identified by the event is enqueued in a command-queue by the host.
CL_PROFILING_COMMAND_SUBMIT	A 64-bit value that describes the current device time counter in nanoseconds when the command identified by the event that has been enqueued is submitted by the host to the device associated with the command-queue.
CL_PROFILING_COMMAND_START	A 64-bit value that describes the current device time counter in nanoseconds when the command identified by event starts execution on the device.
CL_PROFILING_COMMAND_END	A 64-bit value that describes the current device time counter in nanoseconds when the command identified by event has finished execution on the device.
CL_PROFILING_COMMAND_COMPLETE	A 64-bit value that describes the current device time counter in nanoseconds when the command identified by event and any child commands enqueued by this command on the device have finished execution.

The first argument, event, is the event being queried, and the second argument is an enumeration value describing the query. Valid values for the enumeration are given in Table 10.1.

As discussed previously, OpenCL command-queues work asynchronously—that is, the functions return as soon as the command is enqueued. For this reason, querying an OpenCL event for timestamps after a kernel enqueue necessitates a clFinish() call or other event synchronization before the call to clGetEventProfilingInfo() to ensure that the task associated with the event has completed execution. The following is a simple example of the use of events to profile a kernel execution:

```
1   // Sample code that can be used for timing kernel execution duration
2   // Using different parameters for cl_profiling_info allows us to
3   // measure the wait time
4   cl_event timing_event;
5   cl_int err_code;
6
7   //! We are timing the clEnqueueNDRangeKernel call and timing
8   //information will be stored in timing_event
9   err_code = clEnqueueNDRangeKernel ( command_queue, kernel,
10  work_dim, global_work_offset, global_work_size, local_work_size,
11  0, NULL, &timing_event);
12  clFinish(command_queue);
13
14  cl_ulong starttime;
15  cl_ulong endtime;
16  err_code = clGetEventProfilingInfo( timing_event,
        CL_PROFILING_COMMAND_START,
17      sizeof(cl_ulong), &starttime, NULL);
18  kerneltimer = clGetEventProfilingInfo( timing_event,
        CL_PROFILING_COMMAND_END,
19      sizeof(cl_ulong), &endtime, NULL);
20  unsigned long elapsed = (unsigned long)(endtime - starttime);
21  printf("Kernel Execution\t%ld ns\n",elapsed);
```

LISTING 10.1

Using OpenCL events to get timing information for a kernel.

10.3 AMD CodeXL

The previous section demonstrated how the OpenCL API provides some basic features for application profiling by obtaining timing information of OpenCL commands. The following sections discuss how AMD's CodeXL tool can help with profiling and debugging an OpenCL application. CodeXL is a popular tool developed by AMD to enable application developers to study the performance of OpenCL applications and debug OpenCL applications executing on AMD platforms.

CodeXL can operate in multiple modes, with each mode fulfilling a different role to support the application developer. On the basis of the selected mode, CodeXL can be used as a profiler, a debugger, or a static kernel analysis tool. The main modes for CodeXL are briefly described below:

- **Profile mode:** In profile mode, CodeXL provides performance profiling functionality for OpenCL applications. In profile mode, CodeXL gathers performance data from the OpenCL runtime and AMD Radeon graphics processing units (GPUs) during the execution of an OpenCL application.
- **Analysis mode:** In analysis mode, CodeXL can be used as a static analysis tool to compile, analyze, and disassemble OpenCL kernels for AMD GPUs. CodeXL can be used as an kernel prototyping tool in analysis mode.
- **Debug mode:** In debug mode, CodeXL can be used as a debugger for OpenCL applications. CodeXL allows the developer to debug an application by stepping through OpenCL API calls and kernel source code. Debug mode can also be used to view function parameters and reduce memory consumption.

CodeXL is distributed by AMD in two different forms:

1. **Visual Studio plug-in:** When used as a Microsoft Visual Studio plug-in, CodeXL uses the same settings as the active project in the solution. CodeXL will query Visual Studio for all the project settings required to run the application.
2. **Stand-alone:** CodeXL is also available as a stand-alone application that is available for Windows and Linux. One of the main benefits of the stand-alone application is that it does not require the application source code. The developer can create a CodeXL project by specifying only the application binary, command line arguments, and the kernel source location.

All three modes of CodeXL are available with both the Visual Studio plug-in and the stand-alone application. The reader can download CodeXL from the AMD developer website at `http://developer.amd.com`. The remainder of this chapter is focused on CodeXL 1.5. The reader should also refer to the user guide for the features available in the latest version of CodeXL.

10.4 PROFILING USING CodeXL

In profile mode, CodeXL can be used as a performance analysis tool that gathers performance data from the OpenCL runtime and from AMD GPUs during the execution of an OpenCL application. We can use this information to discover bottlenecks in an application and find ways to optimize the application's performance for AMD platforms. Hereafter, we refer to the CodeXL's profile mode as the *profiler*.

To start the profiler in the CodeXL Visual Studio plug-in, simply load a solution into Visual Studio. By default, the CodeXL Session Explorer panel will be docked in the same window panel as the Visual Studio Solution Explorer panel. No code or project modifications are required to profile the application. Select a C/C++ project as the startup project, and choose Profile Mode from the CodeXL menu bar. The modes of operation supported by the profiler are listed below:

- GPU application timeline traces
- GPU performance counters during kernel execution
- Collecting central processing unit (CPU) performance information

From the menu bar, we can collect an Application Timeline Trace or GPU performance counters. When the application completes execution, the profiler will
process and display the profile information. The CodeXL profiler can also be
used from within the CodeXL stand-alone application or from within a command
line utility tool, sprofile, included within the CodeXL install directory. Use of
sprofile is a popular way of scripting multiple performance analysis runs, using
a command line interface and in cases where the application source code is not
available.

Each time the application has been run with the profiler, the resultant performance
data is saved as a separate session. Figure 10.1 shows three sessions of the CodeXL
profiler.

10.4.1 COLLECTING OpenCL APPLICATION TRACES

The OpenCL application trace lists all the OpenCL API calls made by the application.
For each API call, the profiler records the input parameters and output results. In
addition, the profiler also records the CPU timestamps for the host code and device
timestamps retrieved from the OpenCL runtime. The output data is recorded in a
text-based file format called an application trace profile file.

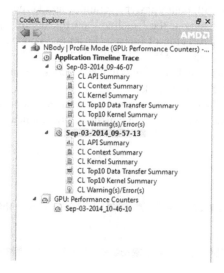

FIGURE 10.1

The session explorer for CodeXL in profile mode. Two application timeline sessions and one
GPU performance counter session are shown.

The OpenCL application trace is especially useful in helping to understand the high-level structure of a complex application. The OpenCL application trace data allows us to study the following:

- Discover the high-level structure of the application with the Timeline View. From this view, we can determine the number of OpenCL contexts and command-queues created and their usage in the application. The kernel execution and data transfer operations are shown in a timeline.
- The Summary Pages can help us to determine if the application is bound by kernel execution or data transfer operations. We can find the top 10 most expensive kernel and data transfer operations, and the API hot spots (most frequent API call or most expensive API call) in the application.
- View and debug the input parameters and output results for all API calls made by the application with the API Trace View.
- View warnings and best practices with reference to how the application uses the OpenCL runtime.

The Application Timeline View (Figure 10.2) provides a visual representation of the execution of the application. Along the top of the timeline is the time grid, which shows the total elapsed time for the application. Timing begins when the first OpenCL call is made by the application and ends when the final OpenCL call is made. Directly below the timeline, each host (operating system) thread that made at least one OpenCL call is listed. For each host thread, the OpenCL API calls are plotted along the time grid, showing the start time and duration of each call.

Below the host threads, the OpenCL tree shows all contexts and queues created by the application, along with data transfer operations and kernel execution operations for each queue. We can navigate the Timeline View by zooming, panning, collapsing/expanding, or selecting a region of interest. From the Timeline View, we can also navigate to the corresponding API call in the API Trace View, and vice versa. An important feature of the Timeline View is that right-clicking on an API call opens the function's location in the source code.

The Application Timeline View can be useful for debugging your OpenCL application. The following are the main benefits of the application timeline trace:

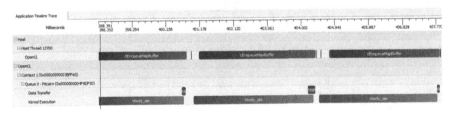

FIGURE 10.2

The Timeline View of CodeXL in profile mode for the Nbody application. We see the time spent in data transfer and kernel execution.

- You can confirm that the high-level structure of your application is correct. By examining the timeline, you can verify that the queues and contexts created match your expectations for the application.
- You can gain confidence that synchronization has been performed properly in the application. For example, if kernel A execution is dependent on a buffer operation and outputs from kernel B, then kernel A's execution should appear after the completion of kernel B's execution in the timeline. It can be difficult to find these synchronization errors using traditional debugging techniques.
- Finally, you can see that the application has been utilizing hardware efficiently. The timeline should show that independent kernel executions and data transfer operations occur simultaneously.

10.4.2 HOST API TRACE VIEW

The host API Trace View (Figure 10.3) lists all the OpenCL API calls made by each host thread in the application. We have used the Nbody application in the AMD accelerated parallel processing (APP) software development kit (SDK) throughout this chapter. Each host thread that makes at least one OpenCL call is listed in a separate tab.

The host API Trace contains a list of all the API calls made by a host thread. For each call, the list displays the index of the call (representing execution order), the name of the API function, a list of parameters passed to the function, and the value returned by the function. When displaying parameters, the profiler will attempt to dereference pointers and decode enumeration values to give as much information as possible about the data being passed in or returned from the function. Double-clicking an item in the Host API trace will display and zoom into that API call in the Host Thread row in the Timeline View.

The host API Trace allows us to analyze the input parameters and output results for each API call. For example, we can easily check that all the API calls return CL_SUCCESS or that all the buffers are created with the correct flags. We can also identify redundant API calls using this view.

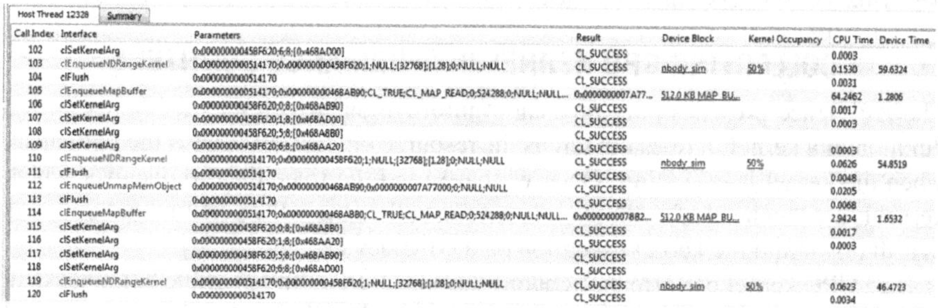
Host Thread 12328 | Summary

Call Index	Interface	Parameters	Result	Device Block	Kernel Occupancy	CPU Time	Device Time
102	clSetKernelArg	0x000000000458F620;6;8;[0x468AD00]	CL_SUCCESS			0.0003	
103	clEnqueueNDRangeKernel	0x0000000000514170;0x000000000458F620;1;NULL;[32768];[128];0;NULL;NULL	CL_SUCCESS	nbody_sim	50%	0.1530	59.6324
104	clFlush	0x0000000000514170	CL_SUCCESS			0.0031	
105	clEnqueueMapBuffer	0x0000000000514170;0x000000000468AB90;CL_TRUE;CL_MAP_READ;0;524288;0;NULL;NULL...	0x000000007A77...	512.0 KB MAP_BU...		64.2462	1.2806
106	clSetKernelArg	0x000000000458F620;0;8;[0x468AB90]	CL_SUCCESS			0.0017	
107	clSetKernelArg	0x000000000458F620;1;8;[0x468AD00]	CL_SUCCESS			0.0003	
108	clSetKernelArg	0x000000000458F620;5;8;[0x468A8B0]	CL_SUCCESS				
109	clSetKernelArg	0x000000000458F620;6;8;[0x468AA20]	CL_SUCCESS			0.0003	
110	clEnqueueNDRangeKernel	0x0000000000514170;0x000000000458F620;1;NULL;[32768];[128];0;NULL;NULL	CL_SUCCESS	nbody_sim	50%	0.0626	54.8519
111	clFlush	0x0000000000514170	CL_SUCCESS			0.0048	
112	clEnqueueUnmapMemObject	0x0000000000514170;0x000000000468AB90;0x000000007A77000;0;NULL;NULL	CL_SUCCESS			0.0205	
113	clFlush	0x0000000000514170	CL_SUCCESS			0.0068	
114	clEnqueueMapBuffer	0x0000000000514170;0x000000000468ABB0;CL_TRUE;CL_MAP_READ;0;524288;0;NULL;NULL...	0x000000007882...	512.0 KB MAP_BU...		2.9424	1.6532
115	clSetKernelArg	0x000000000458F620;0;8;[0x468A8B0]	CL_SUCCESS			0.0017	
116	clSetKernelArg	0x000000000458F620;1;8;[0x468AA20]	CL_SUCCESS			0.0003	
117	clSetKernelArg	0x000000000458F620;5;8;[0x468AB90]	CL_SUCCESS				
118	clSetKernelArg	0x000000000458F620;6;8;[0x468AD00]	CL_SUCCESS				
119	clEnqueueNDRangeKernel	0x0000000000514170;0x000000000458F620;1;NULL;[32768];[128];0;NULL;NULL	CL_SUCCESS	nbody_sim	50%	0.0623	46.4723
120	clFlush	0x0000000000514170	CL_SUCCESS			0.0034	

FIGURE 10.3

The API Trace View of CodeXL in profile mode for the Nbody application.

10.4.3 SUMMARY PAGES VIEW

The Application Timeline Trace also provides a number of summary pages to show various statistics for your OpenCL application. It can provide a general idea of the location of the application's bottlenecks. The summary pages for each profiling session can be viewed from within the CodeXL profiler, as shown in Figure 10.1. The main summary pages are described below:

- **API Summary page:** This page shows statistics for all OpenCL API calls made in the application for API hot spot identification.
- **Context Summary page:** This page shows the statistics for all the kernel dispatch and data transfer operations for each context. It also shows the number of buffers and images created for each context.
- **Kernel Summary page:** This page shows statistics for all the kernels that are created in the application.
- **Top 10 Data Transfer Summary page:** This page shows a sorted list of the 10 most expensive individual data transfer operations.
- **Top 10 Kernel Summary page:** This page shows a sorted list of the 10 most expensive individual kernel execution operations.
- **Warning(s)/Error(s) Page:** This page shows potential problems in your OpenCL application. It can report unreleased OpenCL resources and OpenCL API failures and provide suggestions to achieve better performance. Clicking on a hyperlink takes you to the corresponding OpenCL API that generates the message.

From the context summary page, it is possible to determine whether the application is bound by kernel execution or data transfers. If the application is bound by data transfers, it is possible to determine the most expensive data transfer type (read, write, copy, or map). We can investigate whether we can minimize this type of data transfer by modifying the algorithm if possible. With the Timeline and Summary views, we can investigate whether data transfers have been executed in the most efficient way—that is, concurrently with a kernel's execution.

If the application is bound by kernel execution, we can determine which kernel is the bottleneck. If the kernel execution on a GPU device is the bottleneck, the GPU performance counters can then be used to investigate the bottleneck inside the kernel.

10.4.4 COLLECTING GPU KERNEL PERFORMANCE COUNTERS

The API Trace provides only timestamp information, which tells us the execution duration of a kernel. It does not tell us the resource on the GPU that is the bottleneck when the kernel is executing. Once we have used the trace data to discover which kernel is most in need of optimization, we can collect the GPU performance counters to drill down into the kernel execution on a GPU device.

The GPU kernel performance counters can be used to find possible bottlenecks in the kernel execution. The performance counters on the GPU gather data as the kernel executes. This data is presented to the developer to analyze which resource on the GPU is the bottleneck. A list of performance counters supported by AMD Radeon GPUs can be found in the CodeXL documentation.

	Method	tion	ThreadID	Time	VGPRs	SGPRs	FCStacks	:ernelOccupanc	Wavefronts	VALUInsts	SALUInsts	VFetchInsts	SFetchInsts
1	nbody_sim_k1 ...	1	12616	61.77452	46	48	NA	50	512	626723	53279	2	32781

VWriteInsts	VALUUtilization (%)	VALUBusy (%)	SALUBusy (%)	FetchSize	WriteSize	CacheHit (%)	MemUnitBusy (%)	CallIndex
2	100	59.79	6.55	27685.63	1105.63	66.52	0.49	103

FIGURE 10.4

CodeXL Profiler showing the different GPU kernel performance counters for the Nbody kernel.

The GPU performance counters results for the Nbody kernel are shown in Figure 10.4. Using the performance counters, we can do the following:

- Determine the number of resources (general-purpose registers, local memory size) allocated for the kernel. These resources affect the possible number of in-flight wavefronts in the GPU. A higher number of wavefronts better hides data latency.
- Determine the number of arithmetic logic unit (ALU), global, and local memory instructions executed by the GPU.
- View the cache hit percentage and the number of bytes fetched from and written to the global memory.
- Determine the utilization of the vector ALU units and the memory units.
- View any local memory (local data share) bank conflicts where multiple lanes within a single instruction, multiple data (SIMD) unit attempt to read from or write to the same local data share bank and have to be serialized, causing increased access latency.

The output data is recorded in a comma-separated-variable (csv) format. You can also click on the kernel name entry in the "Method" column to view the OpenCL kernel source, AMD intermediate language (IL), GPU instruction set architecture (ISA), or CPU assembly code for that kernel. From the data in Figure 10.4, we can try to determine optimizations that would improve the kernel's performance. For example, despite having a large number of vector instructions (626723/work-item) and no divergence (VALU utilization is 100%), the vector ALU is only busy for 59% of the execution time. There are only 2 fetch instructions per work-item, so the kernel is not memory bound given the large number of ALU instructions. For this kernel, which executes such a large number of instructions, the cause is likely due to misses in the instruction cache. This would explain the low utilization despite otherwise favorable statistics. Refactoring the code to have a smaller footprint, or increasing the number of waves in flight to cover the miss latency are two possible paths to optimization.

10.4.5 CPU PERFORMANCE PROFILING USING CodeXL

CodeXL provides several modes of CPU profiling. CodeXL's CPU profiling capabilities let you assess program performance using instruction-based sampling or time-based sampling. The CPU profiling capabilities allow a developer to investigate branching, data access, instruction access, or level 2 (L2) cache behavior.

Since this chapter focuses on OpenCL developer tools, we direct the reader to the latest CodeXL User Guide. The CodeXL User Guide can be found at http://developer. amd.com/tools-and-sdks/opencl-zone/codexl/

10.5 ANALYZING KERNELS USING CodeXL

In analysis mode, CodeXL can be used as a static analysis tool. Analysis mode can be used to compile, analyze, and disassemble an OpenCL kernel for AMD Radeon GPUs. It can be used as a graphical user interface tool for interactive tuning of an OpenCL kernel or in command line mode. Hereafter, we refer to CodeXL in analysis mode as *KernelAnalyzer*. CodeXL's KernelAnalyzer can also be accessed from within a command line tool, `CodeXLAnalyzer.exe`, which is located in the CodeXL install directory.

KernelAnalyzer is an offline compiler and an analysis tool, which means it can compile a kernel for any GPU supported by the installed Catalyst driver regardless of the GPU present in the system. To use KernelAnalyzer, the AMD OpenCL runtime is required to be installed on the system. To carry out static analysis of an OpenCL kernel it must be compiled by KernelAnalyzer. To compile an OpenCL kernel in KernelAnalyzer, simply drop the source containing the OpenCL kernel anywhere within CodeXL's main window (Figure 10.6). The application is not required to compile or analyze the OpenCL kernel. The main benefits of KernelAnalyzer can be grouped into the following categories:

1. **Prototyping OpenCL kernels:** Since KernelAnalyzer does not require host code to compile OpenCL kernels, it is a useful tool to prototype an OpenCL kernel. KernelAnalyzer includes an offline compiler that allows us to compile and disassemble OpenCL kernels and view the ISA code. The compilation errors generated by the OpenCL driver will be shown in the output tab for different GPU devices. Since different GPU devices support different OpenCL extensions and built-in functions, KernelAnalyzer can efficiently check if the kernel can be compiled on various GPU devices.

2. **Generating OpenCL binaries:** Very often, a developer would not desire to distribute an OpenCL kernel's source code as plain text. In this case, the OpenCL kernel would be distributed as a binary accompanying the main executable. While the OpenCL provides an API to generate kernel binaries and save them, it can generate binaries only for devices present on the platform. KernelAnalyzer's command line can greatly simplify the process of generating OpenCL kernel binaries since the user can simply supply a kernel file and then compile a binary for AMD-supported platforms. Additionally, KernelAnalyzer also provides options to generate the kernel binary such that it will contain only some ELF sections. This allows developers to avoid distributing OpenCL kernels as text even within a binary. The binary could contain just ISA or LLVM intermediate representation (IR), or source, etc. The role of the different sections of an OpenCL kernel binary are as follows:

- ISA sections: If the developer includes only a particular GPU device's ISA in the kernel binary, then a different binary would be needed for each OpenCL device.
- LLVM IR sections: An OpenCL kernel binary with LLVM IR (or AMD IL) would support multiple AMD devices since the OpenCL runtime compilation calls will translate the IR to the appropriate GPU's ISA.

3. **Early performance evaluation of kernels:** An OpenCL kernel can be executed only once the relevant host-device interaction has been implemented. This delays performance evaluation and prototyping since a kernel's performance cannot be studied independently of the host code. KernelAnalyzer allows a developer to perform preliminary studies of the performance of an OpenCL kernel before the host-side OpenCL has been implemented by carrying out detailed emulation of the kernel execution on a model of the target device.

Once kernel source code has been loaded into KernelAnalyzer, KernelAnalyzer can build the OpenCL kernel and carry out its analysis of the kernel. When we run the `Build and Analyze` step, KernelAnalyzer shows a list of Graphics IP versions in the CodeXL session explorer (Figure 10.5). For each of the Graphics IP versions, the AMD IL and the ISA is shown for the selected kernel. For the example Nbody kernel, the AMD IL and the GPU ISA code are shown in Figure 10.6.

The following sections expand on the above benefits of KernelAnalyzer and discuss the possible benefits of analyzing a kernel's IL and ISA. KernelAnalyzer consists of the ISA view, the Statistics view, and the Analysis view.

10.5.1 KERNELANALYZER STATISTICS AND ISA VIEWS

Just like the x86 ISA, GPU ISAs are also complex instruction sequences. Sometimes the meaning of each instruction is hard to understand even by an expert developer. However, even basic high-level analysis of the generated GPU ISA code in KernelAnalyzer can greatly help performance tuning of an application in the early stages of OpenCL development. Device-specific kernel optimizations are commonly performed by analyzing the ISA code. Some of the benefits of studying the ISA code are described below:

- Viewing the number of general-purpose registers used and the registers spilled to memory by the compiler. Spilled registers can greatly reduce application performance since spilled registers are usually stored in high-latency global memory. Register usage statistics can guide an application developer to refactor his or her kernel to use fewer registers or more local memory.
- Viewing the number of loads and stores for different graphics architectures in the ISA can guide the developer with regard to possible optimizations by tuning the load or store size of each work-item.
- Viewing the effect of source code optimizations such as loop unrolling on the ISA code generated. Viewing the ISA code also allows a developer to examine the ISA code for built-in OpenCL functions such as atomic operations.

It should be noted when observing the analysis and the ISA that the OpenCL compiler can carry out source optimizations when compiling OpenCL kernels. The result of such optimizations can be that branch statements may appear or disappear in the final ISA seen in KernelAnalyzer. This can make it difficult to build correspondence between OpenCL source and ISA code. The developer can supply -00 as a build option to KernelAnalyzer to minimize the number of optimization passes carried out by the compiler.

KernelAnalyzer also presents a Statistics view (Figure 10.7). The Statistics view can help the developer understand the resource usage of an OpenCL kernel. The AMD OpenCL compiler gathers information regarding the GPU resources that would be required to run an OpenCL kernel. The resource usage of a kernel is commonly known as the *occupancy* of the kernel since it decides the number of wavefronts that can be scheduled to a compute unit. Modern AMD GPUs run up to 10 concurrent wavefronts per SIMD in order to hide latency. The number of wavefronts that can be scheduled to

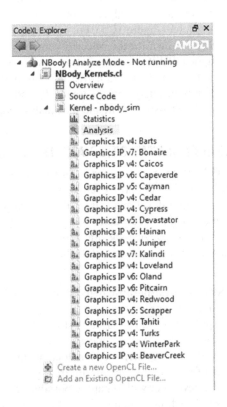

FIGURE 10.5

AMD CodeXL explorer in analysis mode. The NBody OpenCL kernel has been compiled and analyzed for a number of different graphics architectures.

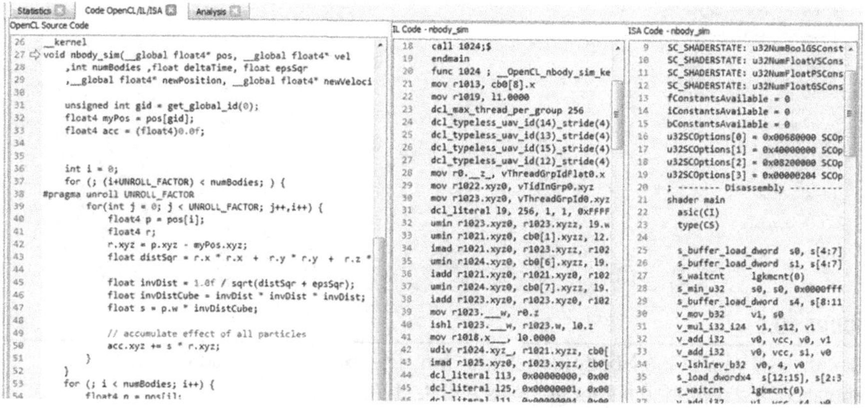

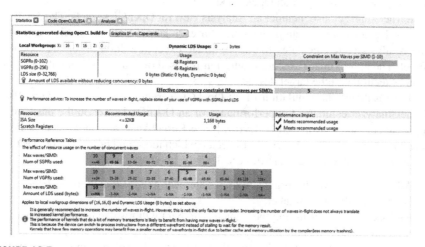

FIGURE 10.6

The ISA view of KernelAnalyzer. The NBody OpenCL kernel has been compiled for multiple graphics architectures. For each architecture, the AMD IL and the GPU ISA can be evaluated.

FIGURE 10.7

The Statistics view for the Nbody kernel shown by KernelAnalyzer. We see that the number of concurrent wavefronts that can be scheduled is limited by the number of vector registers.

the compute unit is limited by the resources present (local memory, vector and scalar registers) on a compute unit. The occupancy of the Nbody kernel is seen in Figure 10.7. We see that the Nbody kernel is limited by the number of vector registers present in the compute unit.

Statistics | Code OpenCL/IL/ISA | Analysis

Analysis generated by emulated execution

Family	Graphics IP v7												Graphics IP v6		
Device	Bonaire			Kalindi			Capeverde			Hainan			Oland		
	True	False	Both	True	False	Both	True	False	Both	True	False	Both	True	False	Both
ISA branches executed	88	5692	5692	88	5692	5692	88	5692	5692	88	5692	5692	88	5692	5692
Clock cycles per wavefront	88	5692	5692	176	11384	11384	88	5692	5692	88	5692	5692	88	5692	5692
Total clock cycles	12	1913	1914	12	1913	1914	12	1913	1914	12	1913	1914	12	1913	1914
SALU instructions	13	913	913	13	913	913	13	913	913	13	913	913	13	913	913
SFetch instructions	25	16125	16128	25	16125	16128	25	16125	16128	25	16125	16128	25	16125	16128
VALU instructions	2	2	2	2	2	2	2	2	2	2	2	2	2	2	2
VFetch instructions	2	2	2	2	2	2	2	2	2	2	2	2	2	2	2
VWrite instructions	0	0	0	0	0	0	0	0	0	0	0	0	0	0	0
LDS instructions	0	0	0	0	0	0	0	0	0	0	0	0	0	0	0
GDS instructions	0	0	0	0	0	0	0	0	0	0	0	0	0	0	0
Atomic instructions	0	0	0	0	0	0	0	0	0	0	0	0	0	0	0
SGPRs	48	48	48	48	48	48	48	48	48	48	48	48	48	48	48
VGPRs	46	46	46	46	46	46	46	46	46	46	46	46	46	46	46
Wavefronts	4096	4096	4096	4096	4096	4096	4096	4096	4096	4096	4096	4096	4096	4096	4096
Code Length	1168	1168	1168	1168	1168	1168	1168	1168	1168	1168	1168	1168	1168	1168	1168

FIGURE 10.8

The Analysis view of the Nbody kernel is shown. The execution duration calculated by emulation is shown for different graphics architectures.

10.5.2 KERNELANALYZER ANALYSIS VIEW

The Statistics and ISA views of KernelAnalyzer show us the output IL code, the ISA code, and the occupancy of an OpenCL kernel.

KernelAnalyzer also includes an Analysis view for OpenCL kernels. The Analysis view of KernelAnalyzer can be launched for each kernel from the session explorer. The Analysis view calculates the approximate execution duration of the OpenCL kernel. The approximate execution duration is based on a detailed emulation of the kernel execution on the target device.

The results of the emulation of an OpenCL kernel are shown in Figure 10.8. KernelAnalyzer estimates the performance of an OpenCL kernel on the basis of an approximate model of the GPU device. Since KernelAnalyzer cannot accept input data for execution, it uses heuristics to decide which loops and branches are executed and how many times. The heuristics are described below:

- **All true:** All waves hitting the branch statement will resolve to true—hence, jump to the designated label.
- **All false:** All waves hitting the branch statement will resolve to false—hence, perform the next statements.
- **Both:** Some waves hitting the branch statement will resolve to false—perform both statements. It is enough that some waves will fall into the "else" statement.

The estimated execution time for the OpenCL kernel is calculated by applying the heuristics defined above. Figure 10.8 shows the estimated execution time for the Nbody kernel for different graphics architectures. The True, False, and Both columns show each heuristic and can be used to form an approximate upper and lower bound on the kernel's execution duration.

Additionally, the Analysis view also provides other statistics, such as the vector and scalar instructions executed and the number of scalar fetch instructions. These statistics can be used for performance evaluation by developers who may not have a particular OpenCL device installed in their system.

10.6 DEBUGGING OPENCL KERNELS USING CodeXL

From the previous sections, we have seen how we can optimize the performance of our OpenCL code. However, the paramount requirement of any program is correctness. Debugging parallel programs is traditionally more complicated than debugging conventional serial code owing to subtle bugs such as race conditions, which are difficult to detect and reproduce. The difficulties of debugging parallel applications running on heterogeneous devices are exacerbated by the complexity and "black box" nature of the accelerated parallel platform.

In OpenCL, the developer works on top of an API that hides the parallel platform's implementation. Debuggers transform the developer's view into a "white box" model, letting the developer see how individual commands affect the parallel computing system. This allows developers to find bugs caused by incorrect OpenCL usage and optimize their applications for the system on which it runs. In this section, we discuss debugging in a heterogeneous environment using CodeXL's debug mode. In debug mode, CodeXL behaves as an OpenCL and OpenGL debugger and memory analyzer. It helps developers find bugs and optimize OpenCL performance and memory consumption.

Figure 10.9 shows a simplified high-level overview of how CodeXL interacts with OpenCL devices in debug mode. It shows some of the important modules/components. CodeXL intercepts the API calls between the application and the OpenCL installable client driver (ICD). This enables CodeXL to log API calls, identify all OpenCL objects, and gather data on these objects. In the following sections, we briefly describe the debugging capabilities of CodeXL to demonstrate its usage in

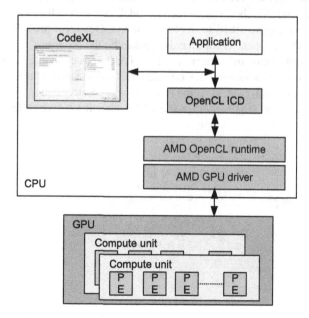

FIGURE 10.9

A high-level overview of how CodeXL interacts with an OpenCL application.

development environments. In this section, for the sake of brevity, we will refer to CodeXL in debug mode as simply CodeXL.

As previously discussed, there are two distinct regions of code in heterogeneous applications:

1. API-level code (e.g., clCreateBuffer(), clEnqueueNDRangeKernel()). <note to copyeditor: please use true type for the function call names> These calls run on the host.
2. The OpenCL commands, which involve devices for execution or data transfers.

CodeXL allows developers to debug OpenCL applications by setting breakpoints on both API function calls and within OpenCL kernels. We give brief details about the debugging capabilities of CodeXL for both API-level host-code and compute kernels.

10.6.1 API-LEVEL DEBUGGING

We will discuss API-level debugging in context using the NBody example. In order to launch API-level debugging, CodeXL must be switched to debug mode. API-level debugging is provided by CodeXL to view the parameters that a runtime function is called with. The following are features provided by API-level debugging:

- **API function breakpoints:** CodeXL will break the debugged application before the function is executed. This allows one to view the call stack that led to the function call, as well as the function's parameters.
- **Record the OpenCL API call history:** When the debugged process is suspended, CodeXL shows us the last OpenCL function call and its parameters in the context. Figure 10.10 shows how CodeXL Debugger provides a back-trace of the OpenCL commands invoked by the program.
- **Program and kernel information:** OpenCL contexts contain multiple program and kernel objects within them. CodeXL allows us to verify which programs are associated with each context. If the program was created using clCreateProgramWithSource(), we can also view the source code passed to this function.

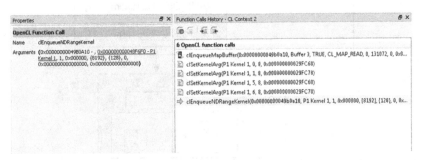

FIGURE 10.10

CodeXL API trace showing the history of the OpenCL functions called.

- **Image and buffer data:** An OpenCL context will contain buffers and images. CodeXL allows us to view the object's data. For image types, CodeXL allows us to see the image data visualized in the "Image view."
- **Memory checking:** CodeXL allows us to view the memory consumption for a specific context's buffers. The memory checking functionality provided by CodeXL Debugger can be used to trace memory leaks and unneeded objects that were created or were not released in time, consuming device memory and making debugging more difficult.
- **API usage statistics:** CodeXL shows statistical information about the currently selected context's API usage. By viewing a breakdown of the API calls made in this context, we can see the number of times a function is called.

10.6.2 KERNEL DEBUGGING

The API-level view allows you to view the parameters and break on different OpenCL API function calls. CodeXL also lets you debug your OpenCL kernels at runtime, inspect variable values across different work-items and work-groups, inspect the kernel call stack, and more. There are multiple ways to start debugging an OpenCL kernel with CodeXL Debugger:

1. **OpenCL kernel breakpoints:** The developer can set a breakpoint in the kernel source code file.
2. **Stepping in from API-level debugging:** The developer can step into debugging a kernel's execution from the corresponding `clEnqueuNDRangeKernel()` call.
3. **Kernel function breakpoints:** Adding the kernel function's name as a function breakpoint in the breakpoints dialog. When a kernel matching the function name starts executing, the debugged process stops at the kernel's beginning.

Figure 10.11 shows the appearance of OpenCL kernel code while debugging is being done with CodeXL. A common concern when debugging an OpenCL application is keeping track of state in the presence of a large number of work-items. A kernel on a GPU device will commonly be launched with many thousands of work-items. CodeXL assists the developer by allowing us to focus on a particular active work-item by displaying the work-item's variable's values and enforcing possible breakpoints for the work-item.

CodeXL also provides a unified breakpoints dialog box that allows a developer to view all the active API and kernel execution breakpoints by clicking on Add / Remove Breakpoints in the Debug menu. In this dialog box, the developer can also configure CodeXL to break automatically on any OpenCL API call.

Multi-watch—viewing data during kernel debugging
CodeXL allows us to set breakpoints and step through the execution of a GPU kernel. This allows us to evaluate whether the program is following the expected execution sequence. However, to study the correctness of a program, it is also important to view the input, output, and intermediate data of the executing kernel. The debugger provides support for viewing data using the Multi-Watch window.

The Multi-Watch window is shown in Figure 10.12. We see that the Multi-Watch window allows us to view the global memory buffers present on the device. It also provides options to visualize the data as an image. The Multi-Watch window also provides a convenient method to view the state of the variables across multiple work-items.

10.7 DEBUGGING USING printf

The OpenCL C kernel programming language implements the well-known C and C++ printf() function. The printf() function is an invaluable debugging tool for C and C++ developers for tracking program data.

When a kernel invocation has completed execution, the output of all printf() calls executed by this kernel invocation is flushed to the implementation-defined output stream. Calling clFinish() on a command-queue flushes all pending output by printf in previously enqueued and completed commands to a output stream. It should be noted that printf() does not guarantee that output will be ordered. This is similar to the behavior seen when debugging a multithreaded program with printf() where the order of the data to the output stream is not defined.

The OpenCL-C specification explains some of the subtle differences in the interpretation of the printf() format string between OpenCL-C and C99.

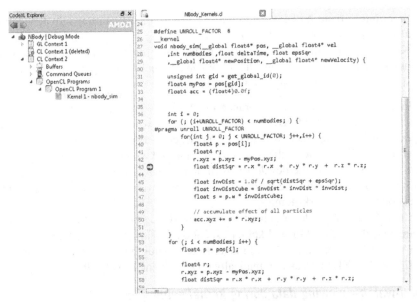

FIGURE 10.11

A kernel breakpoint set on the Nbody kernel.

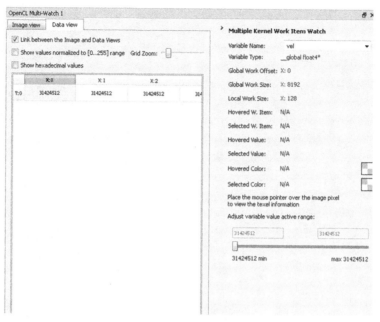

FIGURE 10.12

The Multi-Watch window showing the values of a global memory buffer in the Nbody example. The values can also be visualized as an image.

10.8 SUMMARY

In this chapter we have provided a brief overview of the developer tools available in OpenCL. We have shown how OpenCL events can be used to obtain timing information for an OpenCL command. We have shown how CodeXL's profiling mode can be used to study the performance of OpenCL kernels. We have seen how the analysis mode of CodeXL can be used to prototype OpenCL kernels and do preliminary performance evaluations of kernels without requiring host code. We have also shown how the debug mode can be used to debug OpenCL API calls and kernels. CodeXL is a rapidly improving tool and the user should visit http://developer.amd.com/tools-and-sdks/opencl-zone/codexl/ for information about the newest features in CodeXL.

Mapping high-level programming languages to OpenCL 2.0

11

A compiler writer's perspective

I-Jui (Ray) Sung, Wen-Heng (Jack) Chung, Yun-Wei Lee, Wen-Mei Hwu

11.1 INTRODUCTION

High-level programming languages and domain-specific languages can often benefit from the increased power efficiency of heterogeneous computing. However, it should not require the compiler writers for these languages to deal with vendor-specific intricacies across graphics processing unit (GPU) platforms and the complexity of generating code for them. Instead, OpenCL itself can serve as a compiler target for portable code generation and runtime management. By using OpenCL as the target platform, compiler writers can focus on more important, higher-level problems in language implementation. Such improved productivity can enable a proliferation of high-level programming languages for heterogeneous computing systems.

In this chapter we use C++ Accelerated Massive Parallelism (AMP), a parallel programming extension to C++, as an example to show how efficient OpenCL code can be generated from a higher-level programming model. The C++ language provides several high-level, developer-friendly features that are missing from OpenCL. These high-level features support software engineering practices and improve developer productivity. It is the compiler writer's job to translate these features into the OpenCL constructs without incurring an excessive level of overhead. We present some important implementation techniques in this translation process; for compiler writers interested in mapping other programming models to OpenCL these implementation techniques can be useful too.

We will start with a brief introduction of C++ AMP, and a simple vector addition "application" will serve as the running example. With the example, subsequent sections illustrates how C++ AMP features are mapped to OpenCL. The actual, working implementation consists of a compiler, a set of header files, and a runtime library, which together are publicly accessible as an open source project.[1]

---

[1] https://bitbucket.org/multicoreware/cppamp-driver-ng/.

11.2 A BRIEF INTRODUCTION TO C++ AMP

C++ AMP is a programming model that supports expression of data-parallel algorithms in C++. Compared with other GPU programming models such as OpenCL and CUDA C, C++ AMP encapsulates many low-level details of data movement so the program looks more concise. But it still contains features to let programmers address system intricacies for performance optimization.

Developed initially by Microsoft and released in Visual Studio 2012, C++ AMP is defined as an open specification. Based on open source Clang and LLVM compiler infrastructure, MulticoreWare[2] has published Clamp, a C++ AMP implementation which targets OpenCL for GPU programs. It runs on Linux and Mac OS X, and supports all major GPU cards from vendors such as AMD, Intel, and NVIDIA.

C++ AMP is an extension to the C++11 standard. Besides some C++ header files which define classes for modeling data-parallel algorithms, it adds two additional rules to the C++ programming language. The first one specifies additional language restrictions for functions to be executed on GPUs, and the second one allows cross-thread data sharing among GPU programs. This chapter does not aim to be a comprehensive introduction to C++ AMP. We will highlight the most important core concepts and show how a C++ AMP compiler can implement such features based on OpenCL. For those who are interested in a comprehensive tutorial on C++ AMP itself, Microsoft has published a book on C++ AMP [1] that serves as a good starting point.

Let us start from a simple vector addition program in C++ AMP (Figure 11.1).

```
1.  #include <amp.h>
2.  #include <vector>
3.  using namespace concurrency;
4.  int main(void) {
5.    const int N = 10;
6.    std::vector<float> a(N);
7.    std::vector<float> b(N);
8.    std::vector<float> c(N);
9.    float sum = 0.f;
10.   for (int i = 0; i < N; i++) {
11.     a[i] = 1.0f * rand() / RAND_MAX;
12.     b[i] = 1.0f * rand() / RAND_MAX;
13.   }
14.   array_view<const float, 1> av(N, a);
15.   array_view<const float, 1> bv(N, b);
16.   array_view<float, 1> cv(N, c);
17.   parallel_for_each(cv.get_extent(),
18.             [=] (index<1>idx) restrict(amp)
19.             {
20.                 cv[idx] = av[idx] + bv[idx];
21.             });
22.   cv.synchronize();
23.   return 0;
24. }
```

FIGURE 11.1

C++ AMP code example—vector addition.

[2]https://bitbucket.org/multicoreware/cppamp-driver-ng/.

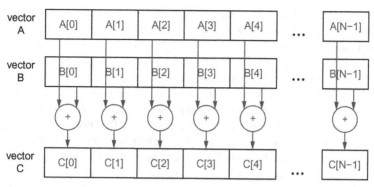

FIGURE 11.2

Vector addition, conceptual view.

Conceptually, the C++ AMP code here computes vector addition as shown in Figure 11.2.

Line 1 in Figure 11.1 includes the C++ AMP header, amp.h, which provides the declarations of the core features. The C++ AMP classes and functions are declared within the concurrency namespace. The "using" directive on the next line makes the C++ AMP names visible in the current scope. It is optional but helps avoid the need to prefix C++ AMP names with a *concurrency::* scope specifier.

This main function in line 4 is executed by a thread running on the host, and it contains a data-parallel computation that may be accelerated. The term "host" has the same meaning in the C++ AMP documentation as in OpenCL. While OpenCL uses the term "device" to refer to the execution environment used for accelerated execution, C++ AMP uses the term "accelerator" for the same purpose. One high-level feature in C++ AMP and commonly seen in other high-level languages is Lambda. Lambda enables C++ AMP host and accelerator code to be collocated in the same file and even within same function. So there is no separation of flow in the source of device code and host code in C++ AMP. Later we will talk about how a C++11-ish Lambda is compiled into OpenCL in the context of C++ AMP.

11.2.1 C++ AMP array_view

In C++ AMP, the primary vehicle for reading and writing large data collections is the class template *array_view*. An *array_view* provides a multidimensional reference to a rectangular collection of data locations. This is not a new copy of the data but rather a new way to access the existing memory locations. The template has two parameters: the type of the elements of the source data, and an integer that indicates the dimensionality of the *array_view*. Throughout C++ AMP, template parameters that indicate dimensionality are referred as the rank of the type or object. In this example, we have a 1-dimensional *array_view* (or "an *array_view* of rank 1") of C++ float values.

For example, in line 14 in Figure 11.1, *array_view* av(a) provides a one-dimensional reference to the C++ vector a. It tells the C++ AMP compiler that accesses to a vector through av will use it only as an input (const), treat it as a one-dimensional array (1), and assume that the size of the array is given by a variable (N).

The constructor for *array_view* of rank 1, such as cv on line 16, takes two parameters. The first is an integer value which is the number of data elements. In the case of av, bv, and cv, the number of data elements is given by N. In general the set of per-dimension lengths is referred to as an extent. To represent and manipulate extents, C++ AMP provides a class template, *extent*, with a single integer template parameter which captures the rank. For objects with a small number of dimensions, various constructors are overloaded to allow specification of an *extent* as one or more integer values, as is done for cv. The second parameter for the cv constructor is a standard container storing the host data. In vecAdd the host data is expressed as a C-style pointer to contiguous data.

11.2.2 C++ AMP *parallel_for_each*, OR KERNEL INVOCATION

Line 16 in Figure 11.1 illustrates the *parallel_for_each* construct, which is the C++ AMP code pattern for a data-parallel computation. This corresponds to the kernel launch in OpenCL. In OpenCL terminology, the *parallel_for_each* creates an "*NDRange* of work items." In C++ AMP, the set of elements for which a computation is performed is called the **compute domain**, and is defined by an extent object. Like in OpenCL, each thread will invoke the same function for every point, and threads are distinguished only by their location in the domain (*NDRange*).

Similarly to the standard C++ STL algorithm for_each, the *parallel_for_each* function template specifies a function to be applied to a collection of values. The first argument to a *parallel_for_each* is a C++ AMP *extent* object which describes the domain over which a data-parallel computation is performed. In this example, we perform an operation over every element in an *array_view*, and so the *extent* passed into the *parallel_for_each* is the *extent* of the cv *array_view*. In the example, this is accessed through the *extent* property of the *array_view* type (cv.get_extent()). This is a one-dimensional *extent*, and the domain of the computation consists of integer values $0 \ldots n - 1$.

Functors as kernels

The second argument to a *parallel_for_each* is a C++ function object (or functor). In Figure 11.1, we use the C++11 Lambda syntax as a convenient way to build such an object. The core semantics of a *parallel_for_each* is to invoke the function defined by the second parameter exactly once for every element in the compute domain defined by the *extent* argument.

Captured variables as kernel arguments

The leading [=] indicates that variables declared inside the containing function but referenced inside the Lambda are "captured" and copied into data members of the function object built for the Lambda. In this case this will be the three *array_view* objects. The function invoked has a single parameter that is initialized to the location of a thread within the compute domain. This is again represented by a class template, *index*, which represents a short vector of integer values. The rank of an *index* is the length or number of elements of this vector, and is the same as the rank of the *extent*. The *index* parameter idx values can be used to select elements in an *array_view*, as illustrated on line 20.

The restrict(amp) modifier

A key extension to C++ is shown in this example: the *restrict(amp)* modifier. In C++ AMP, the existing C99 keyword "restrict" is borrowed and allowed in a new context: it may trail the formal parameter list of a function (including Lambda functions). The *restrict* keyword is then followed by a parenthesized list of one or more restriction specifiers. While other uses are possible, in C++ AMP only two such specifiers are defined: *amp* and *cpu*. They more or less work like markers to guide the compiler to generate either central processing unit (CPU) code or accelerator code out of a function definition and whether the compiler should enforce a subset of the C++ language. Details follow.

As shown in line 18, the function object passed to *parallel_for_each* must have its call operator annotated with a *restrict(amp)* specification. Any function called from the body of that operator must similarly be restricted. The *restrict(amp)* specification identifies functions that may be invoked on a hardware accelerator. Analogously, *restrict(cpu)* indicates functions that may be invoked on the host. When no restriction is specified, the default is *restrict(cpu)*. A function may have both restrictions, *restrict(cpu,amp)*, in which case it may be called from either host or accelerator contexts and must satisfy the restrictions of both contexts.

As mentioned earlier, the restrict modifier allows a subset of C++ to be defined for use in a body of code. In the first release of C++ AMP, the restrictions reflect current common limitations of GPUs when used as accelerators of data-parallel code. For example, the C++ operator *new*, recursions. and calls to virtual methods are prohibited. Over time we can expect these restrictions to be lifted. and the open specification for C++ AMP includes a possible road map of future versions which are less restrictive. The *restrict(cpu)* specifier, of course, permits all of the capabilities of C++ but, because some functions that are part of C++ AMP are accelerator specific they do not have *restrict(cpu)* versions and so may be used only in *restrict(amp)* code.

Inside the body of the *restrict(amp)* Lambda, there are references to the *array_view* objects declared in the containing scope. These are "captured" into the function object that is created to implement the Lambda. Other variables from the function scope may also be captured by value. Each of these other values is made available to each invocation of the function executed on the accelerator. As for any C++11 nonmutable Lambda, variables captured by value may not be modified in the body of the Lambda. **However, the elements of an *array_view* may be modified, and those modifications will be reflected back to the host.** In this example, any changes to cv made inside the *parallel_for_each* will be reflected in the host data vector c.

11.3 OpenCL 2.0 AS A COMPILER TARGET

Clamp is an open source implementation of C++ AMP contributed by Multicore-Ware. It consists of the following components:

- C++ AMP compiler: derived from open source Clang and LLVM projects, the compiler supports C++ AMP language extensions to C++ and emits kernel codes in OpenCL C or the Standard Portable Intermediate Representation (SPIR) format.
- C++ AMP headers: a set of C++ header files which implement classes defined in the C++ AMP specification. Some functions are simply wrappers around OpenCL built-in functions, but some require careful deliberation.
- C++ AMP runtime: a small library acts as a bridge between host programs and kernels. Linked with built executables, it would load and build kernels, set kernel arguments, and launch kernels.

SPIR is a subset of the LLVM intermediate representation (IR) that is specified to support the OpenCL C programming language. It is a portable, nonsource representation for device programs. It enables application developers to avoid shipping kernels in source form, while managing the proliferation of devices and drivers from multiple vendors. An application that uses a valid SPIR IR instance should be capable of being run on any OpenCL platform supporting the cl_khr_spir extension and the matching SPIR version (CL_DEVICE_SPIR_VERSIONS). To build program objects from kernels in SPIR format, clCreateProgramWithBinary() should be used.

There are two versions of SPIR available. SPIR 1.2 defines an encoding of an OpenCL C version 1.2 device program into LLVM (version 3.2), and SPIR 2.0 defines an encoding of OpenCL version 2.0 into LLVM. Since there is a direct correspondence between SPIR and OpenCL C, we will use code examples expressed in OpenCL C in this chapter for better readability.

Based on the vector addition example code, the rest of the chapter will show the design of the main components of the Clamp compiler. We will omit some details which are irrelevant to OpenCL and focus on how OpenCL is used to enable critical C++ AMP features. The focus is to provide insight into the use of OpenCL as an implementation platform for C++ AMP.

11.4 MAPPING KEY C++ AMP CONSTRUCTS TO OpenCL

To map a new programming model to OpenCL, one can start with a mapping of the key constructs. Table 11.1 shows a mapping of the key C++ AMP constructs to their counterparts in OpenCL. As we showed in Figure 11.1, a Lambda in a *parallel_for_each* construct represents a C++ functor whose instances should be executed in parallel. This maps well to OpenCL kernel functions, whose instances should be executed in parallel by the work-items. Although not shown in the vector addition example, one can also pass a functor to a *parallel_for_all* construct for

Table 11.1 Mapping Key C++ AMP Constructs to OpenCL

OpenCL	C++AMP
Kernel	Lambda defined in *parallel_for_each*, or a functor passed to *parallel_for_each*
Kernel name	Mangled name for the C++ *operator()* of the Lambda/functor object
Kernel launch	*parallel_for_each*
Kernel arguments	Captured variables in Lambda
cl_mem buffers	*concurrency::array_view* and *array*

execution in parallel. As a result, we show how C++ AMP Lambdas defined in *parallel_for_each* or functors passed to *parallel_for_each* are mapped to OpenCL kernels.

As for the names to be used for each generated OpenCL kernel, we can used the mangled names of the C++ *operator()* of the Lambda/functor. C++ mangling rules will eliminate undesirable name conflicts and enforce correct scoping rules for the generated kernels.

The rest of the mapping has to do with the interactions between host code and device code. The C++ AMP construct *parallel_for_each* corresponds to the sequence of OpenCL application programming interface (API) calls for passing arguments and launching kernels. For Lambda functors such as the one shown in Figure 11.1, the arguments to be passed to the OpenCL kernels should be automatically captured according to the C++ Lambda rules. On the other hand, all *array_views* used in the Lambda should become explicit *cl_mem* buffers.

To summarize, with this conceptual mapping, we can see that the output of the C++ AMP compiler should provide the following:

1. A legitimate OpenCL kernel whose arguments present values of the captured variables from the surrounding code.
2. Host code that is able to locate, compile, prepare arguments and buffers for, and launch the kernel produced in the previous step at runtime.

Since a C++ Lambda can be viewed as an anonymous functor, we can close the gap further by conceptually rewriting the Lambda into a functor version as in Figure 11.3. The code makes the Lambda into an explicit functor; all the captured variables, va, vb, and vc, are now spelled out in the class, and the body of the Lambda becomes an *operator()* member function. Finally, a constructor is supplied to populate these captured variables on the host side.

However, we still see the following gaps or missing parts:

1. The *operator()* still needs to be mapped to an OpenCL kernel. In particular, the C++ AMP *parallel_for_each* construct is not accounted for in this conceptual code. Also, this functor is a class, but we need an instance to be created.
2. How does the runtime on the host side infer the name of the kernel?

```
1.    class vecAdd {
2.    private:
3.        array_view<const float, 1> va, vb;
4.        array_view<float, 1> vc;
5.    public:
6.        vecAdd(array_view<const float, 1> a,
7.            array_view<const float, 1> b,
8.            array_view<float, 1> c) restrict(cpu)
9.          : va(a), vb(b), vc(c) {};
10.       void operator() (index<1> idx) restrict(amp) {
11.           cv[idx] = av[idx] + bv[idx];
12.       }
13.   };
```

FIGURE 11.3

Functor version for C++AMP vector addition (conceptual code).

3. The *array_view* on the host side may contain *cl_mem*, but on the device side it should be operating on raw pointers as OpenCL *cl_mem* is not allowed on the device side. It is not clear yet how these diverging needs should be fulfilled.

To close the gap further, we need to conceptually bring the functor class further as well. See the parts below the comments on lines 1, 21, 29, and 31 in Figure 11.4.

With the version shown in Figure 11.4, we can see how these three remaining gaps are closed. Line 1 defines a simplified version of *concurrency::array_view* to show the high-level idea, and is not meant to represent the exact semantics of a standard *concurrency::array_view*. The trick here is to provide two slightly different definitions of the same container type for the host and the device. Note we treat an *array_view* as an OpenCL buffer here, and without going too much into the C++ AMP specification, let us for now consider that an *array_view* is backed by an OpenCL memory object as its backing storage (hence the name `backing_storage`). Also we have to add two member functions and a new constructor to the functor, and these functions would have to be automatically injected by the C++ AMP compiler (eventually):

- One is compiled only in host code that provides the mangled kernel name.
- The other is an OpenCL kernel, and is compiled only in device code. It acts as a trampoline, whose mangled name can be queried and used by the host code at runtime. The trampoline function populates a clone of the functor object on the device side with the kernel arguments, and also an index object based on the global indices. Finally, the cloned version of the functor object is invoked in the trampoline.
- The new constructor defined in line 22 is also compiled only in device code, and is part of the trampoline. The purpose of that new constructor is to construct an almost identical copy of the Lambda on the GPU side on the basis of the arguments received by the trampoline. That almost identical copy of the Lambda lives in the function scope, and usually will not have its address visible outside the scope. This gives the compiler freedom for more optimization later.

```
1.   // This is used to close the gap #3
2.   template <class T>
3.   class array_view {
4.   #ifdef HOST_CODE
5.       cl_mem _backing_storage;
6.       T *_host_ptr;
7.   #else
8.       T *_backing_storage;
9.   #endif
10.      size_t _sz;
11.  };
12.  class vecAdd {
13.  private:
14.      array_view<const float, 1> va, vb;
15.      array_view<float, 1> vc;
16.  public:
17.      vecAdd(array_view<const float, 1> a,
18.          array_view<const float, 1> b,
19.          array_view<float, 1> c) restrict(cpu)
20.          : va(a), vb(b), vc(c) {};
21.      // This new constructor is for closing gap #1
22.  #ifndef HOST_CODE
23.      vecAdd(__global float *a, size_t as, __global float *b, size_t bs, __global float *c,
     size_t cs) restrict(amp)
24.          : va(a, as), vb(b, bs), vc(c, cs) {};
25.      void operator() (index<1> idx) restrict(amp) {
26.          cv[idx] = av[idx] + bv[idx];
27.      }
28.  #endif
29.  // The following parts are added to close the gap #1 and #2
30.  #ifdef HOST_CODE
31.  // This is to close the gap #2
32.      static const char * __get_kernel_name(void) {
33.          return mangled name of "vecAdd::trampoline(const __global float *va, const
     __global float *vb, __global float *vc)"
34.      }
35.  #else // This is to close the gap #1
36.      __kernel void trampoline(const __global float *va, size_t vas, const __global float
     *vb, size_t vbs, __global float *vc, size_t vcs) {
37.          vecAdd tmp(va, vas, vb, vbs, vc, vcs); // Calls the new constructor at line 20
38.          index<1> i(get_global_id(0));
39.          tmp(i);
40.      }
41.  #endif
42.  };
```

FIGURE 11.4

Further expanded version for C++AMP vector addition (conceptual code).

However, the main point of the conceptual code in Figure 11.4 is to illustrate the way Clamp creates a mangled name of each kernel (i.e. trampoline that calls operator()), a trampoline as well as a new constructor that constructs a *slightly* different Lambda object on the device side, and two definitions of the same array container depending on the current mode (host or device). Ultimately in the output OpenCL code, we want the trampoline to receive these *cl_mem* buffers through *clSetKernelArg()* OpenCL

API calls and take them in the same order, but appear as device memory pointers (i.e. `__global float *` for this case) in the device code. To satisfy this requirement, we need to implement the following capabilities in the compiler:

- Systematically pass *cl_mem* from the host side Lambda object to the trampoline via OpenCL *clSetKernelArg()* calls.
- Also, systematically recover these as pointer arguments of the trampoline, which will in turn call the new constructor and instantiate a slightly different Lambda from the device side along with other arguments (see the next point).
- The rest of the captured variables should not be affected, and their values should be passed opaquely. For example, in line 35, the values of the `_sz` member for *array_view*s should be passed directly from the host to the device.

In order to systematically implement these capabilities, it is desirable to clearly specify the output code arrangements needed for each type of data member of a Lambda. Table 11.2 shows such conceptual layout arrangements of the Lambda data members in Figure 11.1 on both the device side and the host side.

With this mapping, we are ready to generate the OpenCL code sequence for a C++ AMP *parallel_for_each*. This can be done through the C++ template as shown in Figure 11.4. On the basis of the mapping defined so far, a conceptual implementation of *parallel_for_each* in Figure 11.1 is shown in Figure 11.5.

In general, in order to generate the type of OpenCL code sequence shown in Figure 11.5, we need to perform object introspection and enumerate the data members in the functor prior to kernel invocation (lines 6-11 in Figure 11.5). In particular, they need to appear in the same order as they appear in the argument list of the trampoline.

As stated earlier, functors are the way C++ AMP passes data to and from the kernels, but kernel function arguments are the way OpenCL passes data to and from kernels. Essentially an instance of the functor in CPU address space will have to be copied and converted to an instance in the GPU address space: most data members of the functor are copied (i.e. by value), and that is what our initial implementation does.

Table 11.2 Conceptual Mapping of Data Members on the Host Side and on the Device Side

Data Members	Host Side	Device Side	Note
array_view<const float, 1> va;	cl_mem va._backing_storage	__global float * va._backing_storage	Translated by clSetKernelArg
(more of va)	size_t va._sz	size_t va._sz	Passed verbatim
array_view<const float, 1> vb;	cl_mem vb._backing_storage	__global float * vb._backing_storage	Translated by clSetKernelArg
(more of vb)	size_t vb._sz	size_t vb._sz	Passed verbatim
array_view<float, 1> vc;	cl_mem vc._backing_storage	__global float * vc._backing_storage	Translated by clSetKernelArg
(more of vc)	size_t va._sz	size_t va._sz	Passed verbatim

```
1.    template <class T>
2.    void parallel_for_each(T k) {
3.      // Locate the kernel source file or SPIR
4.      // Construct an OpenCL kernel named  k::__get_kernel_name()
5.      // We need to look into the objects
6.      clSetKernelArg(.., 0, k.va._backing_storage); // cf. line 5 of Figure 3
7.      clSetKernelArg(.., 1, k.va._sz);
8.      clSetKernelArg(.., 2, k.vb._backing_storage);
9.      clSetKernelArg(.., 3, k.vb._sz);
10.     clSetKernelArg(.., 4, k.vc._backing_storage);
11.     clSetKernelArg(.., 5, k.vc._sz);
12.     // Invoke the kernel
13.     // We need to copy the results back if necessary from vc
14.   }
```

FIGURE 11.5

Host code implementation of *parallel_for_each* (conceptual code).

Remember that we are going to pass an OpenCL buffer by value. But the tricky part is that we also need to pass opaque handles (i.e. *cl_mem*) and rely on the underlying OpenCL runtime to convert them to pointers in the GPU address space and perform the memory copy. This is the case for all pre-OpenCL 2.0 runtimes.

At this point, the reader may recognize that the code sequence in Figure 11.5 is quite similar to that for object serialization,[3] except that this time it is not for external storage and retrieval, but is more for squeezing the object contents through a channel implemented by *clSetKernelArg()*, which does some translation on *cl_mem*s into device-side pointers ready to be used in kernels. We need to make sure class instances are stored in a format that is available to the GPU side so that these objects can be properly reconstructed on the GPU side.

Note that in languages such as Java, serialization and deserialization code sequences can be generated through reflection, but reflection is not yet possible at the C++ source level without major modifications to the compiler (and the language itself). In the actual C++ AMP compiler, these serialization and deserialization code sequences are generated as more or less straightforward enumeration of member data and calls to appropriate *clSetKernelArgs()*.

11.5 C++ AMP COMPILATION FLOW

With the conceptual mapping of C++ AMP to OpenCL defined above, it is easier to understand how to compile and link a C++ AMP program. The Clamp compiler employs a multistep process:

---

[3]http://en.wikipedia.org/wiki/Serialization.

1. As a first step, the input C++ AMP source code is compiled in a special "device mode" so that all C++ AMP-specific language rules will be checked and applied. The Clamp compiler will emit OpenCL kernels (based on AMP-restricted functions called from the *parallel_for_each* function) into an LLVM bitcode file. All functions called from a kernel will be inlined into the kernel. The host program will also be compiled and emitted into the same bitcode file in order to fulfill C++ function name mangling rules.

2. The LLVM bitcode file will then go through some transformation passes to ensure that it can be lowered into correct OpenCL programs. All host codes will be pruned first, then all pointers in the kernels and instructions which use them will be declared with the correct address space (_ _ *global*, _ _ *constant*, _ _ *local*, _ _ *private*) per the OpenCL specification. It is worth noting that there is a fundamental difference between OpenCL and C++ AMP on the address spaces. In OpenCL, the address space is part of the pointer type, whereas in C++ AMP it is part of the pointer value. Hence, a static compiler analysis is necessary to infer the address space of pointers from how they are assigned and used. Additional metadata will also be provided by the transformation so the resulting LLVM bitcode is compatible with the OpenCL SPIR format.

3. The transformed LLVM bitcode is now an OpenCL SPIR bitcode and can be linked and executed on platforms which support the *cl_khr_spir* extension. It is saved as an object file which would be linked against host programs. An additional, optional step could be applied to lower it to OpenCL C format so the resultant kernel can be used on any OpenCL platforms that may not support SPIR.

4. The input C++ AMP source code will be compiled again in "host mode" to emit host codes. C++ AMP headers are designed so that none of the kernel codes will be directly used in host mode. Instead, calls to C++ AMP runtime API functions will be used instead to launch kernels.

5. Host codes and device codes are linked to produce the final executable file.

11.6 COMPILED C++ AMP CODE

Let us revisit the C++ AMP Lambda in the vector addition example (line 17 in Figure 11.1), shown again in Figure 11.6 for easy reference.

The OpenCL kernel code after it has been compiled by the Clamp compiler is shown in Figure 11.7.

```
1. [=] (index<1> idx) restrict(amp) { cv[idx] = av[idx] + bv[idx]; }
```

FIGURE 11.6

C++ AMP Lambda—vector addition.

```
1.  __kernel void
    ZZ6vecAddPfS_S_iEN3_EC__019__cxxamp_trampolineEiiS_N11Concurrency11acce
    ss_typeEiiS_S2_iiS_S2_(
2.      __global float *llvm_cbe_tmp__1,
3.      unsigned int llvm_cbe_tmp__2,
4.      __global float *llvm_cbe_tmp__3,
5.      unsigned int llvm_cbe_tmp__4,
6.      __global float *llvm_cbe_tmp__5,
7.      unsigned int llvm_cbe_tmp__6) {
8.      unsigned int llvm_cbe_tmp__7;
9.      float llvm_cbe_tmp__8;
10.     float llvm_cbe_tmp__9;
11.     llvm_cbe_tmp__7 = /*tail*/ get_global_id(0u);
12.     llvm_cbe_tmp__10 = *((&llvm_cbe_tmp__1[((signed int )llvm_cbe_tmp__7)]));
13.     llvm_cbe_tmp__11 = *((&llvm_cbe_tmp__3[((signed int )llvm_cbe_tmp__7)]));
14.     *((&llvm_cbe_tmp__5[((signed int )llvm_cbe_tmp__7)])) = (((float
        )(llvm_cbe_tmp__10 + llvm_cbe_tmp__11)));
15.     return;
16. }
```

FIGURE 11.7

Compiled OpenCL SPIR code—vector addition kernel.

The compiled code may seem daunting at first, but it is actually not hard to understand with the following mapping:

- Line 1: name of trampoline, mangled
- Lines 2-3: serialized *array_view* va
- Lines 4-5: serialized *array_view* vb
- Lines 6-7: serialized array_view vc
- Line 11: get global work-item index, `idx` in C++ AMP Lambda
- Line 12: load `va[idx]`
- Line 13: load `vb[idx]`
- Line 14: calculate `va[idx]` + `vb[idx]` and store to `vc[idx]`

11.7 HOW SHARED VIRTUAL MEMORY IN OpenCL 2.0 FITS IN

One of the most important new features of OpenCL 2.0 is shared virtual memory (SVM). It is an address space exposed to both the host and the devices within the same context. It supports the use of shared pointer-based data structures between OpenCL host code and kernels. It logically extends a portion of the device global memory into the host address space, therefore giving work-items access to the host address space.

According to the OpenCL 2.0 specification, there are three types of SVM:

1. Coarse-grained buffer SVM: sharing occurs at the granularity of OpenCL buffer memory objects. Consistency happens only at synchronization points—for example, kernel launch, mapping/unmapping.
2. Fine-grained buffer SVM : sharing occurs at the granularity of OpenCL buffer memory objects. Consistency happens not only at synchronization points but also at atomic operations performed on either the host side or the device side.
3. Fine-grained system SVM : sharing occurs at the granularity of individual loads/stores into bytes occurring anywhere within the host memory.

The difference between fine-grained and coarse-grained buffer SVM is best illustrated with a small example. Suppose we have a chunk of data to be made visible to a kernel running on an OpenCL 2.0 GPU, and let us say the kernel is computing some sort of histogramming and will update the chunk of data atomically. Table 11.3 shows how this data sharing can be done on pre-2.0, 2.0 coarse-grained, and 2.0 fine-grained operations and the implications.

The unique aspect of OpenCL 2.0 fine-grained buffer SVM is that it enables concurrent host and device atomic operations. In an histogramming example, fine-grained buffer SVM means the histogramming can be done concurrently by the host and the devices; all of them may share the same buffer, and changes made by all entities will be visible to the others as long as they are done through atomics.

Only coarse-grained buffer SVM is mandatory in OpenCL 2.0, and the two other types are optional. In this section, we demonstrate how to adopt coarse-grained buffer SVM in C++ AMP. Note that coarse-grained buffer SVM is similar to the OpenCL 1.x type of buffers, except that there is no need for explicit copying through *clEnqueueWriteBuffer()* API calls. Because of that similarity, in Clamp we mainly treat coarse-grained buffer SVM as a performance improvement venue for the implementation of *concurrency::array_view*s.

Table 11.3 Data Sharing Behavior and Implications of OpenCL 2.0 SVM Support

Steps	Pre-2.0	2.0/Coarse-Grained Buffer SVM	2.0/Fine-Grained Buffer SVM
Copy to device	clEnqueueWriteBuffer	No need	No need
Device atomic updates visible to host?	NA	No	Yes
When would changes from the device side be visible to the host	Not until copy back	After kernel has finished	After kernel has finished or after device-side atomics
Copy from device	clEnqueueReadBuffer	No need	No need

NA, not applicable.

To utilize coarse-grained buffer SVM, a host program needs to use *clSVMAlloc()* to allocate SVM buffers that can be shared by hosts and devices. *cl_mem* buffers are then created by calling *clCreateBuffer()* with CL_MEM_USE_HOST_PTR with the pointers to the buffers that are allocated by *clSVMAlloc()* supplied as host_ptr.

The contents of these buffers are automatically shared between host codes and device codes. There is no need for calls to *clEnqueueWriteBuffer()* and *clEnqueueReadBuffer()* for the device to access these shared buffers.

Once an SVM buffer is no longer needed, *clReleaseMemObject()* is used to release it. After that, *clSVMFree()* is used to deallocate the SVM buffer.

11.8 COMPILER SUPPORT FOR TILING IN C++AMP

Tiling is one of the most important techniques in optimizing GPU programs. Depending on the level of abstraction, a programming model can provide either implicit or explicit support for tiling. An implicit approach may involve automatically deducing the part of memory accesses to be tiled from a given kernel, and generate appropriate code to either transparently or semitransparently tile the memory access pattern to achieve better memory locality and usually better performance. Conversely, an explicit approach relies on the user to explicitly define memory objects in different address spaces that correspond to on-chip and off-chip memory, and also the data movement between them. C++ AMP, CUDA, and OpenCL are all examples of such explicit programming models. The rest of this section considers supporting explicit tiling in C++ AMP from a compiler writer's perspective.

For programming models that explicitly support tiling, one can usually find the following traits:

* A way to divide the compute domain into fixed-sized chunks.
* A way to explicitly specify the address space where a data buffer resides, usually on-chip, off-chip, or thread-private. These map to OpenCL __ *local*, __ *global*, and __ *private* respectively.
* A way to provide barrier synchronization within these fixed-sized chunks of computation (i.e. work-items in a work-group) to coordinate their execution timing.

We first review some background knowledge for readers who are not familiar with tiling in C++ AMP. In C++ AMP, an extent describes the size and the dimension of the compute domain. In addition, *tile_extent* describes how to divide the compute domain. The division is analogous to how OpenCL work-group sizes divide the OpenCL work-item dimensions.

11.8.1 DIVIDING THE COMPUTE DOMAIN

In C++ AMP, a template method "tile" in the class extent is used to compute a *tile_extent*. Its template parameters indicate the tiling size. From here it becomes clear that unlike tiling in OpenCL, tiling in C++ AMP is parameterized statically.

To notify the library and compiler about tiling, we use a Lambda kernel that has a slightly different signature (line 13 in the following listing), which in turn uses *tiled_index*. A *tiled_index* is analogous to a tuple that represents values of OpenCL *get_global_id( )*, *get_local_id( )*, and *get_group_id( )*.

```
1    void mxm_amp_tiled(int M, int N, int W,
2                       const std::vector<float>& va,
3                       const std::vector<float>& vb,
4                       std::vector<float>& result)
5    {
6        extent<2> e_a(M, N), e_b(N, W), e_c(M, W);
7
8        array_view<const float, 2> av_a(e_a, va);
9        array_view<const float, 2> av_b(e_b, vb);
10       array_view<float, 2> av_c(e_c, vresult);
11
12       extent<2> compute_domain(e_c);
13       parallel_for_each(compute_domain.tile<TILE_SIZE, TILE_SIZE>(),
14                   [=] (tiled_index<TILE_SIZE, TILE_SIZE> tidx) restrict(amp)
15                   { mxm_amp_kernel(tidx, av_a, av_b, av_c); });
16   }
```

11.8.2 SPECIFYING THE ADDRESS SPACE AND BARRIERS

In a C++ AMP kernel function, the *tile_static* qualifier is used to declare a memory object that resides in on-chip memory (local memory in OpenCL terms). To force synchronization across threads in a C++ AMP tile, the *barrier.wait* method of a *tile_static* object is used. As in OpenCL, threads in the same tiling group will stop at the same program point where wait is called.

An interesting difference between OpenCL and C++ AMP lies in how the address space information is carried in pointers. In OpenCL, it is part of the pointer's type: for a pointer that is declared with _ _*local*, it cannot point to a buffer declared using the _ _*private* qualifier. In C++ AMP, however, the address space information is part of the pointer's value. One could have a general pointer such as

```
float *foo
```

and the pointer foo can point to a buffer declared using *tile_static* (which is equivalent to _ _*local* in OpenCL), and with certain limitations[4] the same pointer can point to a value in global memory.

One could attempt to define C++ AMP's *tile_static* as a macro that expands to Clang/LLVM's _ _*attribute_ _((address_space()))* qualifier, which is an extension

---

[4]For current C++ AMP 1.2, these limitations do allow a compiler to statically derive the address space information through dataflow analysis.

made for Embedded C that goes to part of the pointer and memory object *type*. However, the approach would fail to generate the correct address space information for the pointer foo in the following code snippet:

```
tile_static float bar;
float *foo = &bar;
```

That is, we cannot embed the address space qualifier as part of the pointer type, but we need to be able to propagate that information as part of variable definitions. The template approach does not allow proper differentiation between these values within the compiler.

An alternative approach is to specify the address space as variable attributes, which are special markers that go with a particular variable, but not part of its type. An example of such an attribute would be compiler extensions that specify in which section of the object file a variable is defined. Attributes of this kind go with the variable definition but not its type: one can have two integers of the same type but each staying in a different section, and a pointer can be pointing to either of these two without type errors. In Clamp we follow this approach—a simple mapping that allows a dataflow analysis to deduce address space information but the code would still look like largely legitimate C++ code:

- Define C++ AMP's *tile_static* as a variable attribute.
- All pointers are initially without an address space.
- A static-single-assignment-based analysis is introduced to deduce the point-to variable attributes.

The analysis aims only at essentially an easy subset of the much harder pointer analysis problems, which are generally undecidable. The next section describes in detail how the address space deduction is done.

11.9 ADDRESS SPACE DEDUCTION

As stated in the previous section, each OpenCL variable declaration has its own address space qualifier, indicating which memory region an object should be allocated. The address space is an important feature of OpenCL. By putting data into different memory regions, OpenCL programs can achieve high performance while maintaining data coherence. This feature, however, is typically missing from high-level languages such as C++ AMP. High-level languages put data into a single generic address space, and there is no need to indicate the address space explicitly. A declaration without an address space will be qualified as private to each work-item in OpenCL, which violates the intended behavior enforced by C++ AMP. For example, if a *tile_static* declaration is qualified as private, the data will no longer be shared among work-groups, and the execution result will be incorrect. To resolve this discrepancy, a special transformation is required to append a correct address space designation for each declaration and memory access.

In Clamp, after OpenCL bitcode has been generated, the generated code will go through a llvm transformation pass to decide on and promote (i.e. adding type qualifiers to) the declaration to the right address space. In theory, it is impossible to always conclusively deduce the address space for each declaration, because the analyzer lacks the global view identifying how the kernels will interact with each other. However, there are clues we can use to deduce the correct address space in practical programs.

The implementation of *array* and *array_view* provides a hint to deduce the correct address space. In C++ AMP, the only way to pass bulk data to the kernel is to wrap them by *array* and *array_view*. The C++ AMP runtime will append the underlying pointer to the argument list of the kernel. Those data will be used in the kernel by accessing the corresponding pointer on the argument of the kernel function. Those pointers, as a result, should be qualified as global, because the data pointed to by them should be visible to all the threads. The deduction process will iterate through all such arguments of the kernel function, promote pointers to global, and update all the memory operations that use the pointers.

The *tile_static* data declarations cannot be identified through pattern analysis, so they need to be preserved from the Clamp front end. In the current Clamp implementation, declarations with *tile_static* qualifiers are placed into a special section in the generated bitcode. The deduction process will propagate the *tile_static* attribute to any pointers that receive the address of these variables, append it to the corresponding OpenCL declarations.

Let us use a tiny C++ AMP code example to illustrate this transformation:

```
void mm_kernel(int *p, int n)
{
        tile_static int tmp[30];
        int id = get_global_id(0);
        tmp[id] = 5566;
        barrier(0);
        p[id] = tmp[id];
}
```

After the initial Clamp pass, the code will be transformed to pure LLVM IR. An address space is lacking at this stage, and this code will produce an incorrect result. Notice that the variable tmp is put to a special ELF section ("clamp_opencl_local"):

```
@mm_kernel.tmp = internal unnamed_addr global [30 x i32] zeroinitializer, align
16, section "clamp_opencl_local"

define void @mm_kernel(i32* nocapture %p, i32 %n) {
   %1 = tail call i32 bitcast (i32 (...)* @get_global_id to i32 (i32)*)(i32 0)
   %2 = sext i32 %1 to i64
   %3 = getelementptr inbounds [30 x i32]* @mm_kernel.tmp, i64 0, i64 %2
   store i32 5566, i32* %3, align 4, !tbaa !1
   %4 = tail call i32 bitcast (i32 (...)* @barrier to i32 (i32)*)(i32 0) #2
   %5 = load i32* %3, align 4, !tbaa !1
```

```
%6 = getelementptr inbounds i32* %p, i64 %2
store i32 %5, i32* %6, align 4, !tbaa !1
ret void
}
```

After the deduction pass in Clamp, the correct address spaces are deduced and appended to the associated declaration of mm_kernel.tmp memory operations. The generated code can now be executed correctly, as illustrated in the following refined LLVM IR:

```
@mm_kernel.tmp = internal addrspace(3) unnamed_addr global [30 x i32] zeroinitializer, align 4

define void @mm_kernel(i32 addrspace(1)* nocapture %p, i32 %n) {
  %1 = tail call i32 bitcast (i32 (...)* @get_global_id to i32 (i32)*)(i32 0)
  %2 = getelementptr inbounds [30 x i32] addrspace(3)* @mm_ kernel.tmp, i32 0,
  i32 %1 store i32 5566, i32 addrspace(3)* %2, align 4, !tbaa !2
  %3 = tail call i32 bitcast (i32 (...)* @barrier to i32 (i32)*)(i32 0)
  %4 = load i32 addrspace(3)* %2, align 4, !tbaa !2
  %5 = getelementptr inbounds i32 addrspace(1)* %p, i32 %1
  store i32 %4, i32 addrspace(1)* %5, align 4, !tbaa !2
  ret void
}
```

11.10 DATA MOVEMENT OPTIMIZATION

As the speed of processors becomes faster and faster, computation power is no longer the major bottleneck for high-performance systems. Instead, for data-intensive computation, the bottleneck mainly lies in memory bandwidth. In many cases, the time spent moving data between the accelerator and the host system can be much greater than the time spent performing computation. To minimize the overhead, OpenCL provides various ways to create a buffer object in the accelerator. In OpenCL, CL_MEM_READ_ONLY indicates that the data will not be modified during the computation. If the object is created with CL_MEM_READ_ONLY, the data will be put into the constant memory region and need not be copied back to the host system after computation has been done. Conversely, CL_MEM_WRITE_ONLY indicates that the buffer is only used to store result data. If the object is created with CL_MEM_WRITE_ONLY, the data on the host does not need to be copied to the accelerator before computation starts. In mapping C++ AMP to OpenCL, we can utilize these features to further improve the performance.

11.10.1 discard_data()

In C++ AMP, *discard_data* is a member function of *array_view*. Calling this function tells the runtime that the current data in the array will be discarded (overwritten), and therefore there is no need to copy the data to the device before computation starts. In this case, we can create a buffer object with CL_MEM_WRITE_ONLY.

11.10.2 array_view<const T, N>

If an *array_view*'s first template parameter is qualified as const, we can create the buffer object with CL_MEM_READ_ONLY. This way, the OpenCL runtime knows that underlying data will not be changed during the computation, and therefore there is no need to copy the data back from the device after computation has finished.

11.11 BINOMIAL OPTIONS: A FULL EXAMPLE

In this section we present a nontrivial application, from an application programmer's view, that requires all the techniques described above to compile it into a valid and well-optimized OpenCL implementation. The application chosen is binomial options. Note we will not dive into the mathematical aspects nor the financial side of this application, but will present it as a "put-it-all-together" example for compiler writers.

```
void binomial_options_gpu(std::vector<float>& v_s,
                std::vector<float>& v_x,
                std::vector<float>& v_vdt,
                std::vector<float>& v_pu_by_df,
                std::vector<float>& v_pd_by_df,
                std::vector<float>& call_value)
```

The code snippet above is the prototype of the binomial options function. v_s, v_x, v_vdt, v_pu_by_df, and v_pd_by_df hold the input data separately; call_value is used to store the result.

```
extent<1> e(data_size);
array_view<float, 1> av_call_value(e, call_value);
av_call_value.discard_data();
```

In order to use input data in the kernel function, data should be wrapped by the containers provided by C++ AMP. In this example, *concurrency::array_view* is used. *discard_data* is called for av_call_value here to tell the runtime not to copy data from the host to the device.

```
array_view<const float, 1> av_s(e, v_s);
array_view<const float, 1> av_x(e, v_x);
array_view<const float, 1> av_vdt(e, v_vdt);
array_view<const float, 1> av_pu_by_df(e, v_pu_by_df);
array_view<const float, 1> av_pd_by_df(e, v_pd_by_df);

extent<1> ebuf(MAX_OPTIONS*(NUM_STEPS + 16));
array<float, 1> a_call_buffer(ebuf);
```

Notice that `av_s`, `av_x`, `av_vdt`, `av_pi_by_df`, and `av_pd_by_df` are wrapped by const *array_view*s and will not be copied back after computation has finished.

```
extent<1> compute_extent(CACHE_SIZE * MAX_OPTIONS);
parallel_for_each(compute_extent.tile<CACHE_SIZE>(),
            [=, &a_call_buffer](tiled_index<CACHE_SIZE> ti) restrict(amp)
            {
                  binomial_options_kernel(ti, av_s, av_x, av_vdt, av_pu_by_df, av_pd_
by_df, av_call_value, a_call_buffer);
            });
av_call_value.synchronize();
```

After the calculation of the computation range, the C++ AMP code calls *parallel_for_each* to do the calculation. After the computation has finished, the synchronize member function is called to ensure the result is synchronized back to the source container. All the data in use will be handled by the runtime implicitly. Programmers do not need to explicitly pass or copy the data between the host and the device. Note that the *parallel_for_each* construct uses explicit tiling for locality control.

```
void binomial_options_kernel(tiled_index<CACHE_SIZE> &tidx,
            array_view<const float, 1> s,
            array_view<const float, 1> x,
            array_view<const float, 1> vdt,
            array_view<const float, 1> pu_by_df,
            array_view<const float, 1> pd_by_df,
            array_view<float, 1> call_value,
            array<float, 1> &call_buffer) restrict(amp)
{
 index<1> tile_idx = tidx.tile;
 index<1> local_idx = tidx.local;

 tile_static float call_a[CACHE_SIZE + 1];
 tile_static float call_b[CACHE_SIZE + 1];

 int tid = local_idx[0];
 int i;

 for(i = tid; i <= NUM_STEPS; i += CACHE_SIZE)
 {
    index<1> idx(tile_idx[0] * (NUM_STEPS + 16) + (i));
    call_buffer[idx] = expiry_call_value(s[tile_idx], x[tile_idx], vdt[tile_idx], i);
 }

 for(i = NUM_STEPS; i > 0; i -= CACHE_DELTA)
    for(int c_base = 0; c_base < i; c_base += CACHE_STEP)
    {
      int c_start = min(CACHE_SIZE - 1, i - c_base);
```

```
        int c_end = c_start - CACHE_DELTA;

        tidx.barrier.wait();
        if(tid <= c_start)
        {
          index<1> idx(tile_idx[0] * (NUM_STEPS + 16) + (c_base + tid));
          call_a[tid] = call_buffer[idx];
        }

        for(int k = c_start - 1; k >= c_end;)
        {
          tidx.barrier.wait();
          call_b[tid] = pu_by_df[tile_idx] * call_a[tid + 1] + pd_by_df[tile_idx]
          * call_a[tid];
          k--;

          tidx.barrier.wait();
          call_a[tid] = pu_by_df[tile_idx] * call_b[tid + 1] + pd_by_df[tile_idx]
          * call_b[tid];
          k--;
        }

        tidx.barrier.wait();
        if(tid <= c_end)
        {
          index<1> idx(tile_idx[0] * (NUM_STEPS + 16) + (c_base + tid));
          call_buffer[idx] = call_a[tid];
        }
      }

  if (tid == 0)
      call_value[tile_idx] = call_a[0];
}
```

The declarations stating with *tile_static* declare shared arrays that will be shared among work-items in the same tiling group. To ensure memory data consistency of the shared array, the `tidx.barrier.wait` function call is used. Work-items in same tiling group will stop and wait at the same program point where wait is called until all work-items in the same tiling group have arrived at that point.

11.12 PRELIMINARY RESULTS

In order to assess the efficiency of our C++ AMP implementation, we measure the execution time of the binomial options benchmark[5] in two ways. The first way is to implement the benchmark directly in OpenCL and execute it on a particular OpenCL implementation. The second way is to implement the benchmark in C++ AMP, compile it through Clamp, and execute the translated OpenCL code on the same platform In this experiment, we use the following configuration:

---

[5]https://bitbucket.org/UncleHandsome/benchmark.

- GPU: AMD Radeon R7 260X
- Linux kernel: 3.16.4-1-ARCH
- AMD Catalyst driver: 14.301.1001
- AMD OpenCL accelerated parallel processing (APP) software development kit (SDK): v2.9-1

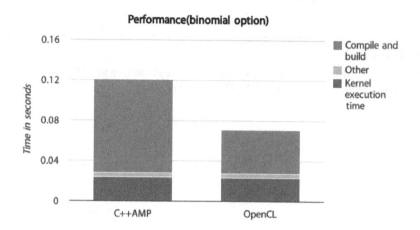

The chart shows that the C++ AMP-generated kernel execution time is almost the same as the OpenCL kernel execution time, but the time spent compiling the automatically generated OpenCL kernel code is much longer. This is because the current implementation appends mathematical built-in functions to the kernel, making the kernel source code about 10 times larger for this benchmark. "Other" includes the time to write OpenCL buffers and pass arguments. Because CL_MEM_USE_HOST_PTR is used in the benchmark, there is almost no performance overhead in these activities for the C++ AMP version.

Because the kernel compilation time is incurred only when a kernel is launched the first time in an application, the compile time is typically amortized across many launches in real applications. For these applications, users will experience comparable execution times between the two versions of the benchmark.

For the binomial options benchmark, the host off-loading code plus the kernel code is 160 lines of OpenCL code versus 80 lines of C++ AMP code. This clearly shows the higher-level programming nature of C++ AMP as compared with OpenCL.

11.13 CONCLUSION

In this chapter, we presented a case study of implementing C++ AMP on top of OpenCL. In C++ AMP, users can leave the data movement between the host and the device to the compiler. We showed the key transformations for compiling high-level, object-oriented C++ AMP code into OpenCL host code and device kernels. Using the binomial options benchmark, we showed that Clamp, the MulticoreWare C++ AMP implementation achieves comparable execution time between automatically generated kernels and hand-written OpenCL ones. This shows that OpenCL is an effective platform for implementing high-level programming languages such as C++ AMP for data-parallel algorithms.

REFERENCE

[1] K. Gregory, A. Miller, C++ Amp: Accelerated Massive Parallelism with Microsoft Visual C++, Microsoft, 2012, 326 pp., ISBN: 9780735664739.

WebCL: Enabling OpenCL acceleration of Web applications

12

Mikaël Bourges-Sévenier, Rémi Arnaud

12.1 INTRODUCTION

Web applications are gaining popularity as ubiquitous Web browsers and cloud servers are becoming the main way we access our personal and professional data. The ability to update and maintain Web applications without distributing and installing software on millions of client computers is very attractive to developers, as is the Inherent cross-platform support. Thanks to wide availability of fast Internet access, and constant mobile connectivity, end users are able to access their data and applications from anywhere, on any device.

With the rapid advance in graphics and computing power of devices, and in particular mobile devices, new application programming interfaces (APIs) such as WebGL and WebCL are making their way into Web browser. Those API are very important as they provide access to hardware acceleration on the device itself, providing the end user with faster rendering and computing, as well as longer battery life. This also enables better experience in general as the interactivity of the Web application does not rely solely on the quality of the network connection, and enables off-line Web applications. Thanks to WebGL and WebCL, the Web browser is able to reach a level of performance that was before accessible only to native applications, opening up a whole new era of Web applications.

12.2 PROGRAMMING WITH WebCL

WebCL 1.0 is a JavaScript representation of OpenCL 1.2. WebCL exposes the underlying object-oriented nature of OpenCL in JavaScript. This allows a simplified programming of OpenCL while maintaining the very same API design, semantic, and runtime. We will often compare the relationship of WebCL with browsers with that of since the integration is similar. However, WebCL does not require knowledge or usage of WebGL.

As with OpenCL, programming with WebCL is composed of two parts:

1. The host side (e.g. in the Web browser) that sets up and controls the execution of the JavaScript program
2. The device side (e.g. on a GPU) that runs computations—that is, kernels in OpenCL

As with WebGL, WebCL is a property of a Window object. First, we need to check if WebCL is available, and then if a context can be created:

```
// First check if the WebCL extension is installed at all
if (window.webcl == undefined) {
 alert("Unfortunately your system does not support WebCL. " +
  "Make sure that you have both the OpenCL driver " +
  "and the WebCL browser extension installed.");
}
// Get a list of available CL platforms, and another list of the
// available devices on each platform. If there are no platforms,
// or no available devices on any platform, then we can conclude
// that WebCL is not available.
webcl = window.webcl
try {
 var platforms = webcl.getPlatforms();
 var devices = [];
 for (var i in platforms) {
  var p = platforms[i];
  devices[i] = p.getDevices();
 }
 alert("Excellent! Your system does support WebCL.");
} catch (e) {
 alert("Unfortunately platform or device inquiry failed.");
}
// Setup WebCL context using the default device
var ctx = webcl.createContext ();
```

Figure 12.1 illustrates the WebCL objects. Note that WebCL is the name of the interface, while `webcl` is the name of the JavaScript object. For more information please consult the WebCL specification [1].

The application can not only query the platforms to list the available devices, but can also query devices for additional information and make a specific choice of platform and/or device.

```
// find appropriate device
for (var j = 0, jl = devices.length; j < jl; ++j) {
 var d = devices[j];
 var devExts = d.getInfo(cl.DEVICE_EXTENSIONS);
 var devGMem = d.getInfo(cl.DEVICE_GLOBAL_MEM_SIZE);
 var devLMem = d.getInfo(cl.DEVICE_LOCAL_MEM_SIZE);
 var devCompUnits = d.getInfo(cl.DEVICE_MAX_COMPUTE_UNITS);
 var devHasImage = d.getInfo(cl.DEVICE_IMAGE_SUPPORT);

 // select device that matches your requirements
 platform = ...
 device = ...
}

// assuming we found the best device, we can create the context
var context = webcl.createContext( platform, device );
```

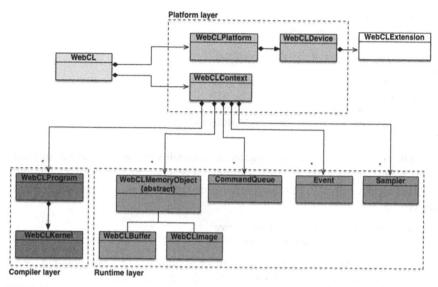

FIGURE 12.1

WebCL objects.

The application runtime manages OpenCL objects such as command-queues, memory objects, program objects. and kernel objects in a program and calls that allow you to enqueue commands to a command-queue. such as executing a kernel, reading a memory object, or writing a memory object.

WebCL defines the following objects:

- **Command-queues**
- Memory objects (**buffers** and **images**)
- **Sampler** objects, which describe how to sample an image being read by a kernel
- **Program** objects, which contain a set of kernel functions identified with the _ _kernel qualifier in the program source
- **Kernel** objects, which encapsulate the specific _ _kernel functions declared in a program source and its argument values to be used when executing the _ _ kernel function
- **Event** objects, which are used to track the execution status of a command as well as to profile a command
- Command synchronization objects such as **markers** and **barriers**

The first thing to do is to create a program. WebCL, like WebGL 1.0, assumes a program is provided in source code form (a string). Currently, a WebCL device is required to have an internal compiler. The source code is first loaded to the device, and then compiled. As with any compiler, the OpenCL compiler defines standard compilation options.

```
// Create the compute program from the source strings
program = context.createProgram(source);

// Build the program executable with relaxed math flag
try {
 program.build(device, "-cl-fast-relaxed-math");
} catch (err) {
throw 'Error building program: ' + err
 + program.getBuildInfo(device, cl.PROGRAM_BUILD_LOG));
}
```

At this point, our program is compiled, and contains one or more kernel functions. These kernel functions are the entry points of our program, and are similar to the entry points of a shared library. To refer to each kernel function, we create a *WebCLKernel* object:

```
// Create the compute kernels from within the program
var kernel = program.createKernel('kernel_function_name');
```

A kernel function may have one or more arguments, like any function. Since JavaScript offers only the type Number for numerical values, *typed arrays* [2] are used to pass function arguments of various numerical types (see Table 12.1). For other types of values, we must use WebCL objects:

- *WebCLBuffer* and *WebCLImage*, which in-turn wrap a typed array
- *WebCLSampler* for sampling an image

A *WebCLBuffer* object stores a one-dimensional collection of elements. Elements of a buffer can be of scalar type (e.g. int, float), of vector data type, or have a user-defined structure.

```
// create a 1D buffer
var buffer = webcl.createBuffer(flags, sizeInBytes, optional srcBuffer);

// flags:
//webcl.MEM_READ_WRITE Default. Memory object is read and written by kernel
//webcl.MEM_WRITE_ONLY Memory object only written by kernel
//webcl.MEM_READ_ONLY Memory object only read by kernel
//webcl.MEM_USE_HOST_PTR Implementation uses storage memory in srcBuffer.
srcBuffer must be specified.
//webcl.MEM_ALLOC_HOST_PTR Implementation requests OpenCL to allocate
host memory.
//webcl.MEM_COPY_HOST_PTR Implementation request OpenCL to allocate host
memory and copy
data from srcBuffer memory. srcBuffer must be specified.
```

Note that only reading from a buffer object and its subbuffer objects or reading from multiple overlapping subbuffer objects is defined. All other concurrent reading or writing is undefined.

A WebCL image is used to store a one-, two-, or three-dimensional texture, renderbuffer, or image. The elements of an image object are selected from a predefined list of image formats. However, currently, WebCL supports only two-dimensional images.

Table 12.1 Relationships Between C Types Used in Kernels and *setArg()*'s *webcl.type*

Kernel Argument Type	setArg() Value	setArg() Typed Array	Remarks
char, uchar	scalar	Uint8Array, Int8Array	1 byte
short, ushort	scalar	Uint16Array, Int16Array	2 bytes
int, uint	scalar	Uint32Array, Int32Array	4 bytes
long, ulong	scalar	Uint64Array, Int64Array	8 bytes
float	scalar	Float32Array	4 bytes
half, double	scalar	Float32Array, Float64Array	Not on all implementations
			2 bytes (half), 8 bytes (double)
<char...double>N	vector	Int8Array for (u)char$N$	$N = 2, 3, 4, 8, 16$
		Int16Array for (u)short$N$	
		Int32Array for (u)int$N$	
		Int64Array for (u)long$N$	
		Float32Array	
		for float$N$ and half$N$	
		Float64Array for double$N$	
char,..., double *	WebCLBuffer		
image2d_t	WebCLImage		
sampler_t	WebCLSampler		
__local		Int32Array ([size_in_bytes])	Size initialized in kernel

```
// create a 32-bit RGBA WebCLImage object
// first, we define the format of the image
var imageFormat = {
 // memory layout in which pixel data channels are stored in the image.
 'channelOrder' : webcl.RGBA,
 // type of the channel data
 'channelType' : webcl.UNSIGNED_INT8,
 // image size
 'width': image_width,
 'height': image_height,
 // scan-line pitch in bytes.
 // If imageBuffer is null, it must be 0. Otherwise, it must be at least image_ width *
sizeInBytesOfChannelElement, which is the default if rowPitch is not specified.
 'rowPitch': image_pitch
};

// Image on device
// imageBuffer is a typed array that contain the image data already allocated by the
application.
```

```
// imageBuffer.byteLength >= rowPitch * image_height. The size of each element
in bytes must be a
power of 2.
```

```
var image = context.createImage(webcl.MEM_READ_ONLY | webcl.MEM_
USE_ HOST_PTR,
imageFormat, imageBuffer);
```

A *WebCLSampler* describes how to sample an image when the image is read in a kernel function. It is similar to WebGL samplers.

```
// create a sampler object
var sampler = context.createSampler(normalizedCoords, addressingMode, filterMode);
// normalizedCoords indicates if image coordinates specified are normalized.
// addressingMode indicated how out-of-range image coordinates are handled when
reading an image.
// This can be set to webcl.ADDRESS_MIRRORED_REPEAT,
webcl.ADDRESS_REPEAT, webcl.ADDRESS_CLAMP_TO_EDGE,
webcl.ADDRESS_CLAMP and webcl.ADDRESS_NONE.
// filterMode specifies the type of filter to apply when reading an image. This can be
webcl.FILTER_NEAREST or webcl.FILTER_LINEAR
```

Passing arguments is done using *WebCLKernel.setArg()*, with scalars, vectors, or memory objects. When passing values referring to local memory, we use an *Int32Array* of length 1 with the number of bytes to be allocated because local variables cannot be initialized by the host or the device but the host can tell the device how many bytes to allocate for a kernel argument.

As a rule of thumb, all values passed to a kernel by *setArg()* are objects. Scalars must be wrapped into a typed array of size 1. Vectors are typed arrays with size of the number of elements in the vector. Buffers, images, and samplers are WebCL objects. Memory object (buffers and images) content must be transferred from host memory to device memory by enqueue commands before execution of the kernel.

Here are some examples:

```
// Sets value of kernel argument idx with value as memory object or sampler
kernel.setArg(idx, a_buffer);
kernel.setArg(idx, a_image);
kernel.setArg(idx, a_sampler);
```

```
// Sets value of argument 0 to the integer value 5
kernel.setArg(0, new Int32Array([5]));
```

```
// Sets value of argument 1 to the float value 1.34
kernel.setArg(1, new Float32Array([1.34]));
```

```
// Sets value of argument 2 as a 3-float vector
// buffer should be a Float32Array with 3 floats
kernel.setArg(2, new Float32Array([1.0,2.0,3.0]));
```

```
// Allocate 4096 bytes of local memory for argument 4
kernel.setArg(4, new Int32Array([4096]));
```

When a scalar is passed, the type is used to tell what specific type is expected by the program. JavaScript has only one type—Number—so we need to provide the information in the *setArg* call using typed arrays.

Notes:

- Long integers are 64-bit integers that have no representation in JavaScript. They must be represented as two 32-bit integers: the low-order 32 bits are stored in the first element of each pair, and the high-order 32 bits are stored in the second element.
- If the argument of a kernel function is declared with the _ _constant qualifier, the size in bytes of the memory object cannot exceed `webcl.DEVICE_MAX_CONSTANT_BUFFER_SIZE`.
- OpenCL allows the passing of structures as byte arrays to kernels but, for portability, WebCL currently does not allow this. The main reason is that endianness between the host and devices may be different, and this would require developers to format their data for each device's endianness even on the same machine.
- All WebCL API calls are thread-safe, except *kernel.setArg()*. However, *kernel.setArg()* is safe as long as concurrent calls operate on different WebCLKernel objects. Behavior is undefined if multiple threads call on the same *WebCLKernel* object at the same time.

Operations on WebCL objects such as memory, program, and kernel objects are performed using command-queues. A command-queue contains a set of operations or commands. Applications may use multiple independent command-queues without synchronization as long as commands do not apply on shared objects between command-queues. Otherwise, synchronization is required.

Commands are queued in order, but execution may be in order (default) or out of order on the devices that support it (it is optional in OpenCL). Out of order means that if a command-queue contains command A and command B, an in-order command-queue object guarantees that command B is executed when command A finishes. If an application configures a command-queue to be out of order, there is no guarantee that commands finish in the order they were queued. For out-of-order queues, a wait for events or a barrier command can be enqueued in the command-queue to guarantee previous commands finish before the next batch of commands is executed. Out-of-order queues are an advanced topic we will not cover in this chapter. Interested readers should refer to [3]. Beware that many underlying OpenCL implementations do not support out-of-order queues. You should first test if you can create a command-queue with QUEUE_OUT_OF_ORDER_EXEC_MODE_ENABLE flag. If the INVALID_QUEUE_PROPERTIES exception is thrown, the device does not support out-of-order queues.

```
// Create an in-order command-queue (default)
var queue = context.createCommandQueue(device);
```

```
// Create an in-order command-queue with profiling of commands enabled
var queue = context.createCommandQueue(device, webcl.QUEUE_PROFILING_
ENABLE);

// Create an out-of-order command-queue
var queue = context.createCommandQueue(device,
webcl.QUEUE_OUT_OF_ORDER_EXEC_MODE_ENABLE);
```

A command-queue is attached to a specific device. Multiple command-queues can be used per device. One application is to overlap kernel execution with data transfers between the host and the device. Figure 12.2 shows the timing benefit if a problem can be separated in half:

- The first half of the data is transferred from the host to the device, taking half the time needed for the full data set. Then, the kernel is executed, possibly in half the time needed with the full data set. Finally, the result is transferred back to the device in half the time needed for the full result set.
- Just after the first half has been transferred, the second half is transferred from the host to the device, and the same process is repeated.

Once a set of commands have been queued, WebCL provides *enqueueNDRange(kernel, offsets, globals, locals)* to execute them:

- kernel—the kernel to be executed.
- offsets—offsets to apply to globals. If null, then offsets=[0, 0, 0].
- globals—the problem size per dimension.
- locals—the number of work-items per work-group per dimension. If null, the device will choose the appropriate number of work-items.

For example, if we want to execute a kernel over an image of size (width, height), then globals may be [width, height] and locals may be [16, 16]. Note that *enqueue NDRange()* will fail if the locals size is more than *webcl.KERNEL_WORK_GROUP_SIZE*.

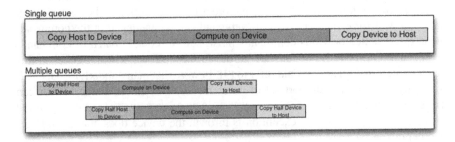

FIGURE 12.2

Using multiple command-queues for overlapped data transfer.

12.3 SYNCHRONIZATION

Just like C/C++ OpenCL programs, the device can process the commands in the queue in an asynchronous manner. The host submits commands to the command-queue and can then wait for the completion of all the enqueued commands by using a *clFinish*.

Nearly all commands available in the *WebCLCommandQueue* class have two final parameters:

1. *event_list*—an array of *WebCLEvents*
2. *event*—an event returned by the device to monitor the execution status of a command

By default, the *event_list* and *event* parameters are null for any command. However, if an event is passed to a command, then the host can wait for the execution of the particular command using *clWaitForEvents*. The programmer can also use event callback functions to be notified when a certain command completes. The host code would need to register a callback function in order to be notified once the command completes. If an *event_list* is passed to the command, then the command will not start executing until all the commands corresponding to each event have reached *webcl.COMPLETE*.

For the commands an application wishes to be notified of their *webcl.COMPLETE* status, we first create a *WebCLEvent* object, pass it to the command, then register a JavaScript callback function. Note that the last argument of *WebCLEvent.setCallback()* can be anything, as this argument is passed untouched as the last argument of the callback function. Also note that in the case of enqueue read/write *WebCLBuffers* or *WebCLImages*, *clBuffer* ownership is transferred from the host to the device. Thus, when the *read_complete()* callback is called, *clBuffer* ownership is transferred back from the device to the host. This means that once the ownership of *clBuffer* has been transferred, the host cannot access or use this buffer anymore. Once the callback has been called, the host can use the buffer again. See the example code below:

```
// Enqueue kernel
try {
kernel_event=new cl.WebCLEvent();
queue.enqueueNDRange(kernel, 2, null, globals, locals, null, kernel_event);
} catch(ex) {
throw "Couldn't enqueue the kernel. "+ex;
}
// Set kernel event handling routines: call kernel_complete()
try {
kernel_event.setCallback(webcl.COMPLETE, kernel_complete, "The kernel
finished successfully.");
} catch(ex) {
throw "Couldn't set callback for event. "+ex;
}
```

```
// Read the buffer
var data=new Float32Array(4096);
try {
read_event=new webcl.WebCLEvent();
queue.enqueueReadBuffer(clBuffer, false, 0, 4096*4, data, null, read_event);
} catch(ex) {
throw "Couldn't read the buffer. "+ex;
}

// register a callback on completion of read_event: calls read_complete()
read_event.setCallback(webcl.COMPLETE, read_complete, "Read complete");

// wait for both events to complete
queue.waitForEvents([kernel_event, read_event]);

// kernel callback
function kernel_complete(event, data) {
 // event.status = webcl.COMPLETE or error if negative
 // event.data is null
 // data should contain "The kernel finished successfully."
}
// read buffer callback
function read_complete(event, data) {
 // event.status = cl.COMPLETE or error if negative
 // event.data contains a WebCLMemoryObject with values from device
 // data contains "Read complete"
}
```

12.4 INTEROPERABILITY WITH WebGL

Recall that WebCL is for computing, not for rendering. However, if your data already resides in the graphics processing unit (GPU) and you need to render it, would it not be faster to tell OpenGL to use it rather than reading it from the GPU memory to central processing unit (CPU) memory and send it again to OpenGL on your GPU? This is where the WebGL interoperability extension comes in.

Since WebCL is using data from WebGL, the WebGL context must be created first. Then, a shared WebCL context can be created. This WebGL shared group object manages shared WebGL and WebCL resources such as the following (Figure 12.3):

- Textures objects—contain texture data in image form,
- Vertex buffers objects—contain vertex data such as coordinates, colors, and normal vectors,
- Renderbuffer objects—contain images used with WebGL framebuffer objects [4].

12.5 EXAMPLE APPLICATION

Applications such as image processing and ray tracing produce an output image whose pixels are drawn onto the screen. For such applications, it suffices to map the

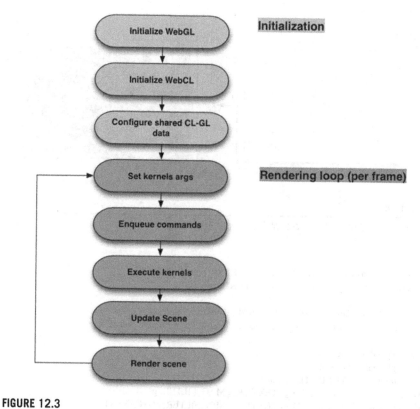

Initialization

Rendering loop (per frame)

FIGURE 12.3

Typical runtime involving WebCL and WebCL.

output image onto two unlit screen-aligned triangles rendered by WebGL. A compute kernel provides more flexible ways to optimize generic computations than a fragment shader. More importantly, texture memory is cached and thus provides a faster way to access data than regular (global) CPU memory. However, in devices without image memory support, one should use *WebCLBuffers* and update WebGL textures with pixel buffer objects.

In this section, we use Iñigo Quilez's excellent ShaderToy's Mandelbulb fragment shader [5] converted as a WebCL kernel, depicted in Figure 12.4. The whole WebGL scene consists of two textured triangles filling a canvas. WebCL generates the texture at each frame. Therefore, for a canvas of dimension (width, height), WebCL will generate width × height pixels.

Since WebCL uses WebGL buffers for compute, WebGL context must first be initialized, and then WebCL context is created by sharing that WebGL context. Once both contexts have been initialized, it is possible to create shared objects by creating first the WebGL object, and then the corresponding WebCL object from the WebGL object. The following illustrates how a WebGL texture is created and can be used as target by WebCL:

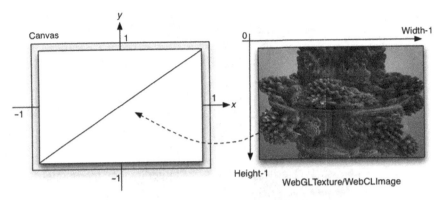

FIGURE 12.4

Two triangles in WebGL to draw a WebCL-generated image.

```
// retrieve a <canvas> object with id glcanvas in HTML page
var canvas = document.getElementById("glcanvas");

// Try to grab the standard context. If it fails, fallback to experimental.
var gl = canvas.getContext("webgl") || canvas.getContext("experimental-webgl");

// Create OpenGL texture object
Texture = gl.createTexture();
gl.bindTexture(gl.TEXTURE_2D, Texture);
gl.texParameteri(gl.TEXTURE_2D, gl.TEXTURE_MAG_FILTER, gl.NEAREST);
gl.texParameteri(gl.TEXTURE_2D, gl.TEXTURE_MIN_FILTER, gl.NEAREST);

gl.texImage2D(gl.TEXTURE_2D, 0, gl.RGBA, TextureWidth, TextureHeight, 0,
gl.RGBA,
gl.UNSIGNED_BYTE, null);
gl.bindTexture(gl.TEXTURE_2D, null);

// Create OpenCL representation (a WebCLImage) of OpenGL texture
try {
clTexture = context.createFromGLTexture2D(cl.MEM_
WRITE_ONLY, gl.TEXTURE_2D, 0, Texture);
}

catch(ex) {
throw "Error: Failed to create WebCLImage. "+ex;
}

// To use this texture, somewhere in your code, do as usual:
glBindTexture(gl.TEXTURE_2D, Texture)
```

Simply use this texture as an argument to the program

```
kernel.setArg(0, clTexture);
kernel.setArg(1, new Uint32Array([TextureWidt]));
```

```
kernel.setArg(2, new Uint32Array([TextureHeight]));
```

Finally, here is how to use this WebCLImage inside the kernel code:

```
__kernel
void compute(__write_only image2d_t pix, uint width, uint height)
{
const int x = get_global_id(0);
const int y = get_global_id(1);

// compute pixel color as a float4

write_imagef(pix, (int2)(x,y), color);
}
```

12.6 SECURITY ENHANCEMENT

Security is at the forefront of concerns for Web browser vendors. Remember when nobody had JavaScript turned on in their Web browser by default? The justified fear is that an unknown program, hiding inside a webpage may be able to access operating system resources and, for example, steal data from your computer, or install viruses and other trojans. A malicious script could also bring a computer down by utilizing all the resources, or crashing the computer.

In the case of WebGL and WebCL, the code is destined to run on the GPU to get maximum performance, and currently GPUs are lacking hardware mechanisms to make sure a program cannot access anything other than what it is supposed to: memory protection and reading uninitialized data are required.

A mechanism has been created to make sure the kernels sent to WebCL cannot access data outside their boundaries. Recall that WebCL mandates kernels are sent in text form, which enables the WebCL compiler to analyze and annotate a kernel before it is sent to the compiler. Alternatively, it would also have been possible to allow for precompiled programs provided there is a way to validate the safety of a program and a digital signature process, but there are no binary standard formats for compile kernels at this point in time.

The two principles of this protection are that the memory allocated in the program has to be initialized (prevent access to old data from other programs) and that untrusted code must not access invalid memory.

The mechanism to guarantee this level of security is as follows:

* Keep track of memory allocations (also in runtime if the platform supports dynamic allocation)
* Trace valid ranges for reads and writes
* Validate them efficiently while compiling the program or at runtime

The kernels are passed through a validator, which annotates the code to make sure that there is no possible out-of-bounds access, which does impact performance (measurements suggest less than 30% performance degradation), but ensure safety. For more information, please read [6].

12.7 WebCL ON THE SERVER

Since WebCL is all about computing, it can be used on Web browsers as well as by stand-alone applications and servers programmed with JavaScript. Node.js is a platform built on Chrome's JavaScript runtime for easily building fast and scalable network applications. Node.js uses an event-driven, nonblocking input/output model that makes it lightweight and efficient, perfect for data-intensive real-time applications that run across distributed devices [7]. Node.js is very modular, and more than 80,000 modules exist, one of which is *node-webcl* [8], a cross-platform module implementing the WebCL specification on top of OpenCL. *node-webcl* also extends the specification with features specific to node.js (e.g. using node.js's buffers as well as typed arrays) and other features that may be considered in future releases of the WebCL specification.

Installing *node-webcl* is more complex than installing a browser. This is a development tool, and it requires third-party libraries and it needs to be recompiled.

- First, make sure the OpenCL software development kit (SDK) is installed for your GPU and/or your CPU:
  - For Intel GPUs, install it from https://software.intel.com/en-us/vcsource/tools/opencl-sdk.
  - For AMD GPUs, install it from http://developer.amd.com/tools-and-sdks/opencl-zone/amd-accelerated-parallel-processing-app-sdk/.
  - For NVIDIA GPUs, install it from https://developer.nvidia.com/opencl.
- Install node.js from http://nodejs.org.
- Install node-gyp: npm install -g node-gyp.
- Install node-image:
  - Download the FreeImage library and headers from http://freeimage.sourceforge.net/.
  - npm install node-image.

If you want to develop applications with the WebGL interoperability extension, you need to install node-webgl and node-glfw:

- Install GLEW from http://glew.sourceforge.net/.
- Install GLFW 3.x from http://www.glfw.org/.
- Install the AntTweakBar library and headers from http://anttweakbar.sourceforge.net/.
- npm install node-glfw node-webgl.

Finally, compile and install node-webcl:

- npm install node-webcl

We recommend installation of GLEW, AntTweakBar, FreeImage, and GLFW in your include and library paths so node-gyp can find them easily while building each node.js module, otherwise you will need to edit each module's binding.gyp file. These four libraries are available on all desktop platforms (Mac, Windows, Linux) and can be installed on Linux and Mac machines using package managers such as apt-get and Homebrew [9].

To use node-webcl in your code, open your favorite JavaScript text editor. You require node-webcl so that the WebCL API is added to the global namespace. The webcl object below is exactly the same as a browser's window.webcl object.

```
// add WebCL API
var webcl = require('node-webcl');

// rest of the code is identical to that in a browser
```

Removing the "require" line and using webcl = window.webcl will make your code work on any WebCL-enabled browser. With node-webcl, one can now take advantage of operating system access and all node.js modules.

One possible use case is to use node.js with node-webcl to perform accelerated computations on a server and communicate the results to browsers via Web sockets [10], which in turn can render it in a meaningful way [11].

Likewise, many numerical applications require the use of various frameworks, such as Python, R, and MATLAB. These scripting languages provide similar features also available in JavaScript. And, given the speed of the JavaScript runtime and that many of these numerical libraries have already been ported to JavaScript (even tools to transcode these languages directly to JavaScript), JavaScript with node.js becomes a much faster platform unifying frameworks and languages.

Because *node-webcl* is less restrictive than browsers, applications can be developed more quickly and typically run faster. Enhanced with the node.js fast evented runtime, very dynamic and multithreaded applications can be developed in JavaScript that may not be possible in browsers. This is ideal for server-side applications that need to schedule complex workloads on all OpenCL-enabled devices in a platform.

With node.js and node-webcl, JavaScript-based applications can be developed and deployed rapidly on the server side and on the client side. Complex, data-intensive real-time applications are now possible from JavaScript.

Recently, a new node.js module appeared, called node-opencl [18]. While developed by the same authors as node-webcl, node-opencl is a complete rewrite. node-opencl is lower-level than node-webcl and is a direct representation of OpenCL features in JavaScript. Contrary to WebCL that supports OpenCL 1.1, node-opencl supports all versions of OpenCL. One could make a pure JavaScript representation of WebCL on top of node-opencl. While all other WebCL implementations have sporadic maintenance, node-opencl and node-webcl are actively supported.

12.8 STATUS AND FUTURE OF WebCL

WebCL 1.0 was released on March 14, 2014, and the group has been developing the conformance tests [12], white papers, and tutorials [13]. At the time of writing, there are four implementations of WebCL 1.0:

1. Nokia's WebCL implementation for the Firefox browser [14]
2. Samsung's WebCL implementation for WebKit-based browsers [15]
3. AMD's WebCL implementation for Chromium-based browsers [16]
4. Motorola Mobility's WebCL implementation for node.js (not a browser) [17], [19]
5. AMD's node-opencl, a node.js wrapper to OpenCL for servers [18]

The conformance was finalized by the end of 2014, which should help Web browser vendors release updated versions of their browsers with WebCL support.

REFERENCES

[1] WebCL 1.0 Specification, http://www.khronos.org/registry/webcl/specs/latest/1.0/.
[2] Typed Array Specification, https://www.khronos.org/registry/typedarray/specs/latest/.
[3] Derek Gerstmann Siggraph Asia 2009 on Advanced OpenCL Event Model Usage, http://sa09.idav.ucdavis.edu/docs/SA09-opencl-dg-events-stream.pdf.
[4] http://learningwebgl.com/blog/?p$=$1786.
[5] Iñigo Quilez. ShaderToy with Mandelbulb shader, http://www.iquilezles.org/apps/shadertoy/?p$=$mandelbulb.
[6] Vincit Ltd: Mikael Lepistö, Rami Ylimäki, http://learningwebcl.com/wp-content/uploads/2013/11/WebCLMemoryProtection.pdf.
[7] https://www.nodejs.org.
[8] https://github.com/Motorola-Mobility/node-webcl.
[9] http://brew.sh/.
[10] http://dev.w3.org/html5/websockets/.
[11] http://superconductor.github.io/superconductor/.
[12] https://github.com/KhronosGroup/WebCL-conformance.
[13] http://learningwebcl.com/.
[14] http://webcl.nokiaresearch.com/.
[15] https://github.com/SRA-SiliconValley/webkit-webcl.
[16] https://github.com/amd/Chromium-WebCL.
[17] https://github.com/Motorola-Mobility/node-webcl.
[18] https://github.com/mikeseven/node-opencl.
[19] https://github.com/mikeseven/node-webgl.

WORKS CITED

The Khronos Group—A Non-profit Industry Consortium to Develop, Publish and Promote Open Standard, Royalty-free Media Authoring and Acceleration Standards for Desktop and Handheld Devices, Combined with Conformance Qualification Programs for Platform and Device Interoperability, The Khronos Group Inc., Web, 21 August 2014, http://www.khronos.org/.

Typed Array Specification, Web, 27 August 2014, https://www.khronos.org/registry/typedarray/specs/latest/.

WebGL Specification, WebGL 1.0.2 Specification, Web, 1 March 2013, http://www.khronos.org/registry/webgl/specs/1.0/.

WebCL Specification, Web, 27 August 2014, http://www.khronos.org/registry/webcl/specs/latest/1.0/.

Foreign lands
Plugging OpenCL in

13

13.1 INTRODUCTION

Up to this point, we have considered OpenCL in the context of the system programming languages C and C++; however, there is a lot more to OpenCL. In this chapter, we look at how OpenCL can be accessed from a selection of different programming language frameworks, including Java, Python, and the functional programming language Haskell.

13.2 BEYOND C AND C++

For many developers, C and C++ are the programming languages of choice. For many others, this is not the case: for example, a large amount of the world's software is developed in Java or Python. These high-level languages are designed with productivity in mind, often providing features such as automatic memory management, and performance has not necessarily been at the forefront of the minds of system designers. An advantage of these languages is that they are often highly portable, think of Java's motto "write once, run everywhere," and reduce the burden on the developer to be concerned with low-level system issues. However, it is often the case that it is not easy, sometimes it is even impossible, to get anything close to peak performance for applications written in these languages.

To address the performance gap and also to allow access to a wide set of libraries not written in a given high-level language, a foreign function interface (FFI) is provided to allow applications to call into native libraries written in C, C++, or other low-level programming languages. For example, Java provides the Java Native Interface, while Python has its own mechanism. Both Java (e.g. JOCL (Java bindings for OpenCL) [1]) and Python (e.g. PyOpenCL [2]) have OpenCL wrapper application programming interfaces (APIs) that allow the developer to directly access the compute capabilities offered by OpenCL. These models are fairly low level, and provide the plumbing between the managed runtimes and the native, unmanaged, aspects of OpenCL. To give a flavor of what is on offer, Listing 13.1 is a PyOpenCL implementation of vector addition.

```
1   import pyopencl as cl
2   import numpy
3   import numpy.linalg as la
4
5   a = numpy.random.rand(50000).astype(numpy.float32)
6   b = numpy.random.rand(50000).astype(numpy.float32)
7
8   ctx = cl.create_some_context()
9   queue = cl.CommandQueue(ctx)
10
11  mf =cl.mem_flags
12  a_buf=cl.Buffer(ctx,mf.READ_ONLY|mf.COPY_HOST_PTR,hostbuf=a)
13  b_buf=cl.Buffer(ctx,mf.READ_ONLY|mf.COPY_HOST_PTR,hostbuf=b)
14  dest_buf =cl.Buffer(ctx,mf.WRITE_ONLY,b.nbytes)
15
16  prg =cl.Program(ctx, " " "
17     __kernel void vecadd(__global const float *a,
18     __global const float *b, __global float *c)
19     {
20        int gid =get_global_id(0);
21        c[gid] =a[gid] + b[gid];
22     }
23     " " ").build()
24
25  prg.vecadd(queue, a.shape, None, a_buf, b_buf, dest_buf)
26
27  a_plus_b = numpy.empty_like(a)
28  cl.enqueue_copy(queue, a_plus_b, dest_buf)
29
30  print la.norm(a_plus_b - (a+b))
```

LISTING 13.1

PyOpenCL implementation of a vector addition.

An example of moving beyond simple wrapper APIs is Aparapi [3]. Originally developed by AMD but now a popular open source project, Aparapi allows Java developers to take advantage of the computing power of graphics processing units (GPUs) and other OpenCL devices by executing data-parallel code fragments on the GPU rather than confining them to the local central processing unit (CPU). The Aparapi runtime system achieves this by converting Java bytecode to OpenCL at runtime and executing on the GPU. If for any reason Aparapi cannot execute on the GPU, it will execute in a Java thread pool. An important goal of Aparapi is to stay within the Java language both from a syntax point of view and from one of spirit. This design requirement can be seen from the source code to perform a vector addition, given in Listing 13.2, where there is no OpenCL C code or OpenCL API calls.

```
1   package com.amd.aparapi.sample.add;
2   import com.amd.aparapi.Kernel;
3   import com.amd.aparapi.Range;
4   public class Main{
5     public static void main(String[] _args) {
6        final int size = 512;
```

```
7       final float[] a = new float[size];
8       final float[] b = new float[size];
9       for (int i = 0; i < size; i++) {
10          a[i] = (float)(Math.random()*100);
11          b[i] = (float)(Math.random()*100);
12      }
13      final float[] sum = new float[size];
14      Kernel kernel = new Kernel(){
15        @Override public void run() {
16            int gid = getGlobalId();
17            sum[gid] = a[gid] + b[gid];
18        }
19      };
20      kernel.execute(Range.create(512));
21      for (int i = 0; i < size; i++) {
22          System.out.printf("%6.2f + %6.2f = %8.2f\n", a[i], b[i],
23              sum[i]);
24      }
25      kernel.dispose();
26   }
27 }
```

LISTING 13.2

Java implementation of vector addition, using Aparapi to target OpenCL.

Instead, the Aparapi developer expresses OpenCL computations by generating instances of Aparapi classes, overriding methods that describe the functionality of a kernel that will be dynamically compiled to OpenCL at runtime from the generated Java bytecode.

Aparapi is an example of a more general concept of embedding a domain-specific language (DSL) within a hosting programming language: in this case, Java. DSLs focus on providing an interface for a domain expert, and commonly a DSL will take the form of a specific set of features for a given science domain—for example, medical imaging. In this case, the domain is that of data-parallel computations and in particular that of general-purpose computing on GPUs.

13.3 HASKELL OpenCL

Haskell is a pure functional language, and along with Standard ML (SML) and its variants is one of the most popular modern functional languages. Unlike many of the other managed languages, Haskell (and SML) programming consists in describing functions, in terms of expressions, and evaluating them by application to argument expressions. In general, the model differs from imperative programming by not defining sequencing of statements and not allowing side effects. There is usually no assignment outside declarations. This is often seen as both a major advantage and a major disadvantage of Haskell. Combining side-effect free programming with Haskell's large and often complex type system can often be an off-putting experience for the newcomer used to the imperative models of C, C++, or Java. However, side-effect free can be liberating in the presence of parallel programming, as in this case evaluating an expression will produce a single isolated result, which is thread-safe by definition. For this reason, Haskell has recently gained a lot of interest in the parallel programming research community. The interested reader new to Haskell would do well to read Hutton's excellent book on programming in Haskell [4] and Meijer's companion video series on Microsoft's Channel 9 [5].

Owing to certain aspects of Haskell's type system, it has proven to be an excellent platform for the design of embedded DSLs, which in turn provide abstractions that automatically compile the source code to GPUs. See, for example, Accelerate [6] or Obsidian [7] for two excellent examples of this approach. However, this is a book about low-level programming with OpenCL, and so here we stay focused, instead considering how the Haskell programmer can get direct access to the GPU via OpenCL. The benefits of accessing OpenCL via Haskell are many-fold but in particular

- OpenCL brings a level of performance to Haskell not achievable by existing CPU threading libraries;
- the high-level nature of Haskell significantly reduces the complexity of OpenCL's host API and leads to a powerful and highly productive development environment.

There has been more than one effort to develop wrapper APIs for OpenCL in Haskell; however, we want more than a simple FFI binding for OpenCL. In particular, we want something that makes accessing OpenCL simpler, while still providing full access to the power of OpenCL. For this, we recommend HOpenCL [8], which is an open source library providing both a low-level wrapper to OpenCL and a higher-level interface that enables Haskell programmers to access the OpenCL APIs in an idiomatic fashion, eliminating much of the complexity of interacting with the OpenCL platform and providing stronger static guarantees than other Haskell OpenCL wrappers. For the remainder of this chapter, we focus on the latter higher-level API; however, the interested reader can learn more about the low-level API in the HOpenCL documentation. It should be noted that HOpenCL presently only supports the OpenCL 1.2 API. The advanced OpenCL 2.0 features such as device-queues and pipe objects have not yet been ported to HOpenCL.

As a simple illustration we again consider the vector addition described in Chapter 3. The kernel code is unchanged and is again embedded as a string, but the rest is entirely Haskell.

13.3.1 MODULE STRUCTURE

HOpenCL is implemented as a small set of modules all contained under the structure `Langauge.OpenCL`.

- `Language.OpenCL.Host.Constants`—defines base types for the OpenCL core API
- `Langauge.OpenCL.Host.Core`—defines the low-level OpenCL core API

- `Language.OpenCL.GLInterop`—defines the OpenGL interoperability API
- `Language.OpenCL.Host`—defines the high-level OpenCL API

For the most part, the following sections introduce aspects of the high-level API, and in the cases where reference to the core is necessary, it will be duly noted. For details of the low-level API, the interested reader is referred to the HOpenCL documentation [8].

13.3.2 ENVIRONMENTS

As described in early chapters, many OpenCL functions require either a context, which defines a particular OpenCL execution environment, or a command queue, which sequences operations for execution on a particular device. In much OpenCL code, these parameters function as "line noise"—that is, technically necessary, they do not change over large portions of the code. To capture this notion, HOpenCL provides two type classes, `Contextual` and `Queued`, to qualify operations that require contexts and command queues, respectively.

In general, an application using HOpenCL will want to embed computations that are qualified into other qualified computations—for example, embedding `Queued` computations within `Contextual` computations and thus tying the knot between them. The `with` function is provided for this purpose:

```
with :: Wraps t m n => t -> m u -> n u
```

13.3.3 REFERENCE COUNTING

For OpenCL objects whose life is not defined by a single C scope, the C API provides operations for manual reference counting (e.g. `clRetainContext`/`clReleaseContext`). HOpenCL generalizes this notion with a type class `LifeSpan` which supports the operations `retain` and `release`:

```
retain  :: (LifeSpan t, MonadIO m) => t -> m ()
release :: (LifeSpan t, MonadIO m) => t -> m ()
```

The `using` function handles construction and release of new reference-counted objects. It introduces the ability to automatically manage OpenCL object lifetimes:

```
using :: (Lifespan t m, CatchIO m) => m t -> (t -> m u) -> m u
```

To simplify the use of OpenCL contexts (`Context`) and command queues (`CommandQueue`), which are automatically reference counted in HOpenCL, the operation `withNew` combines the behavior of the `with` function and the `using` function:

```
withNew :: (Wraps t m n, Lifespan t, CatchIO n) => n t -> m u -> n u
```

13.3.4 PLATFORM AND DEVICES

The API function `platforms` is used to discover the set of available platforms for a given system.

```
platforms :: MonadIO m => m [Platform]
```

Unlike the C API, there is no need to call `platforms` twice, first to determine the number of platforms and second to get the actual list of platforms; HOpenCL manages all of the plumbing automatically. The only complicated aspect of the definition of `platforms` is that the result is returned within a monad `m`, which is constrained to be an instance of the type class `MonadIO`. This constraint enforces that the particular OpenCL operation happens within a monad that can perform input/output. This is true for all OpenCL actions exposed by HOpenCL, and is required to capture the fact that the underlying API may perform unsafe operations and thus needs sequencing.

After platforms have been discovered, they can be queried, using the overloaded `(?)` operator, to determine which implementation (vendor) the platform was defined by. For example, the following code selects the first platform and displays the vendor:

```
(p:_) <- platforms
putStrLn . ("Platform is by: " ++)   =<< p ? PlatformVendor
```

In general, any OpenCL value that can be queried by a function of the form `clGetXXXInfo`, where **XXX** is the particular OpenCL type, can be queried by an instance of the function:

```
(?) :: MonadIO m => t -> qt u -> m u
```

For platform queries, the type of the operator `(?)` is

```
(?) :: MonadIO m => Platform -> PlatformInfo u -> m u
```

Similarly to the OpenCL C++ wrapper API's implementation of `clGetXXXInfo`, the type of the value returned by the operator `(?)` is dependent on the value being queried, providing an extra layer of static typing. For example, in the case of `PlatformVendor`, the result is the Haskell type `String`.

The `devices` function returns the set of devices associated with a platform. It takes the arguments of a platform and a device type. The device type argument can be used to limit the devices to GPUs only (`GPU`), CPUs only (`CPU`), all devices (`ALL`), or other options. As with platforms, the operator `(?)` is called to retrieve information such as name and type:

```
devicesOfType :: MonadIO m => Platform -> [DeviceType] -> m [Device]
```

13.3.5 THE EXECUTION ENVIRONMENT

As described earlier, a host can request that a kernel be executed on a device. To achieve this, a context must be configured on the host that enables it to pass commands and data to the device.

Contexts

The function `context` creates a context from a platform and a list of devices:

```
context :: MonadIO m => Platform -> [Device] -> m Context
```

If it is necessary to restrict the scope of the context—for example, to enable graphics interoperability—then properties may be passed using the `contextFromProperties` function:

```
contextFromProperties :: MonadIO m =>
ContextProperties -> [Device] -> m Context
```

Context properties are built with the operations `noProperties`, which defines an empty set of properties, and `pushContextProperty`, which adds a context property to an existing set. The operations `noProperties` and `pushContextProperty` are defined as part of the core API in `Language.OpenCL.Host.Core`:

```
noProperties :: ContextProperties
pushContextProperty :: ContextProperty t u =>
t u -> u -> ContextProperties -> ContextProperties
```

Command queues

Communication with a device occurs by submitting commands to a **command queue**. The function `queue` creates a command queue within the current `Contextual` computation:

```
queue :: Contextual m => Device -> m CommandQueue
```

As `CommandQueue` is reference counted and defined within a particular `Contextual` computation, a call to `queue` will often be combined with `withNew`, embedding the command queue into the current context:

```
withNew (queue gpu) $
  __computation dependent on newly created command queue
```

Buffers

The function `buffer` allocates an OpenCL buffer, assuming the default set of flags. The function `bufferWithFlags` allocates a buffer with the associated set of user-supplied memory flags (`MemFlag` is defined in `Language.OpenCL.Host.Constants`):

```
buffer :: (Storable t, Contextual m) => Int -> m (Buffer t)
bufferWithFlags :: (Storable t, Contextual m) =>
                                    Int -> [MemFlag] -> m (Buffer t)
```

As buffers are associated with a `Contextual` computation (a `Context`), the `using` function can be used to make this association.

Data contained in host memory is transferred to and from an OpenCL buffer using the commands `writeTo` and `readFrom`, respectively:

```
readFrom :: (Readable cl hs, Storable t, Queued m) =>
                                    cl t -> Int -> Int -> m (hs t)
writeTo :: (Writable cl hs, Storable t, Queued m) =>
                                    cl t -> Int -> hs t -> m Event
```

Creating an OpenCL program object

OpenCL programs are compiled at runtime through two functions, programFromSource
and buildProgram, that create a program object from the source string and build a
program object, respectively:

```
programFromSource :: Contextual m => String -> m Program
buildProgram :: MonadIO m => Program -> [Device] -> String -> m ()
```

The OpenCL kernel

Kernels are created with the function kernel:

```
kernel :: MonadIO m => Program -> String -> m Kernel
```

Arguments can be individually set with the function fixArgument. However, often the
arguments can be set at the point when the kernel is invoked, and HOpenCL provides
the function invoke for this use case:

```
fixArgument :: (KernelArgument a, MonadIO m) => Kernel ->
    Int -> a -> m ()
invoke :: KernelInvocation r => Kernel -> r
```

Additionally, it is possible to create a kernel invocation, which one can think of as a
kernel closure, from a kernel and a set of arguments using the function setArgs (this
can be useful in a multithreaded context):

```
setArgs :: Kernel -> [Co.Kernel -> Int -> IO ()] -> Invocation
```

A call to invoke by itself is not enough to actually enqueue a kernel; for this, an
application of invoke is combined with the function overRange, which describes the
execution domain and results in an event representing the enqueue, within the current
computation:

```
overRange :: Queued m => Invocation -> ([Int], [Int], [Int]) -> m Event
```

Full source code example for vector addition

The following example source code implements the vector addition OpenCL application, originally given in Chapter 3, and is reimplemented here using HOpenCL:

```
module VecAdd where

import Language.OpenCL.Host
import Language.OpenCL.Host.FFI

import Control.Monad.Trans (liftIO)
```

```
source =
  "__kernel void vecadd(                                    \n" ++
  "    __global int *C, __global int* A, __global int *B) {  \n" ++
  "    int tid = get_global_id(0);                          \n" ++
  "    C[tid] = A[tid] + B[tid];                            \n" ++
  "}                                                         "

elements = 2048 :: Int;

main = do (p:_) <- platforms
          [gpu] <- devicesOfType p [GPU]
          withNew (context p [gpu]) $
            using (programFromSource source) $ \p ->
            using (buffer elements) $ \inBufA ->
            using (buffer elements) $ \inBufB ->
            using (buffer elements) $ \outBuf ->
              do { buildProgram p [gpu] ""
                 ; using (kernel p "vecadd") $ \vecadd ->
                   withNew (queue gpu) $
                     do writeTo inBufA 0 [0.. elements — 1 ]
                        writeTo inBufB 0 [0.. elements - 1 ]
                        invoke vecadd outBuf inBufA inBufB
                           'overRange' ([0], [elements], [1])
                        (x::[Int]) <- readFrom outBuf 0 elements
                        liftIO (if and $ zipWith (\a b -> a == b+b)
                                            x [0.. elements — 1 ]
                        then print "Output is correct"
                        else print "Output is incorrect") }
```

This is the complete program!

13.4 SUMMARY

In this chapter, we have shown that accessing OpenCL's compute capabilities need not be limited to the C or the C++ programmer. We highlighted that there are production-level bindings for OpenCL for many languages, including Java and Python, and focused on a high-level abstraction for programming OpenCL from the functional language Haskell.

REFERENCES

[1] Java bindings for OpenCL (JOCL), 2012, http://www.jocl.org/.
[2] A. Klöckner, *PyOpenCL*, 2012, http://mathema.tician.de/software/pyopencl.
[3] Aparapi, 2012, http://Aparapi.googlecode.com.
[4] G. Hutton, Programming in Haskell, Cambridge University Press, Cambridge, 2007.
[5] E. Meijer, Functional Programming Fundamentals. Channel 9 Lectures, 2009, http://channel9.msdn.com/Series/C9-Lectures-Erik-Meijer-Functional-Programming-

Fundamentals/Lecture-Series-Erik-Meijer-Functional-Programming-Fundamentals-Chapter-1.

[6] M.M. Chakravarty, G. Keller, S. Lee, T.L. McDonell, V. Grover, Accelerating Haskell array codes with multicore GPUs, in: Proceedings of the Sixth Workshop on Declarative Aspects of Multicore Programming, ACM DAMP'11, New York, NY, 2011, pp. 3-14.

[7] J. Svensson, M. Sheeran, K. Claessen, Obsidian: a domain specific embedded language for parallel programming of graphics processors. in: S.-B. Scholz, O. Chitil (Eds.), Implementation and Application of Functional Languages, Lecture Notes in Computer Science, vol. 5836, Springer, Berlin/Heidelberg, 2011, pp. 156-173.

[8] B.R. Gaster, J. Garrett Morris, HOpenCL, 2012, https://github.com/bgaster/hopencl.git.

Index

Note: Page numbers followed by *f* indicate figures and *t* indicate tables.

A

Accelerated processing units (APUs), 26, 27, 37, 37*f*, 38*f*
A10-7850K APU, 37, 37*f*
AMD FX-8350 CPU
  AMD Piledriver architecture, 191
  barrier operations, 189
  fine-grained synchronization, 188
  high-level design, 187, 188*f*
  local memory, 191, 192*f*
  runtime, thread creation, 188
  work-group execution, x86 architecture, 189, 190*f*
  work-groups scheduling, 188, 189*f*
  work-item stack data storage, 190
AMD Radeon HD 6970 GPU architecture, 25, 27*f*
AMD Radeon R9 290X GPU
  architecture, 34, 35*f*
  control flow management, 197
  hardware threads, 192
  high-level diagram, 193, 193*f*
  ISA divergent execution, 198, 199
  queuing mechanism, 194
  SCC register, 199
  SIMD unit, 196, 197*f*
  threading and memory system, 194
  three-dimensional graphics, 192, 193
  unit microarchitecture, 196, 197*f*
  wavefront scheduling, 193, 194
Aparapi, 292, 293
API. *See* Application programming interface (API)
API-level debugging, 244
Application programming interface (API), 12, 43, 291
APUs. *See* Accelerated processing units (APUs)

B

Bag-of-words (BoW) model
  document classification, 213
  image classification, 213, 214*f*
    feature generation algorithm, 213, 214*f*
    histogram builder, 214, 215, 217
    image clustering, 214
  natural language processing, 213

BFS algorithm. *See* Breadth-first search (BFS) algorithm
Blocking memory operations, 111
BoW model. *See* Bag-of-words (BoW) model
Breadth-first search (BFS) algorithm, 133
Broadcast functions, 129

C

C++ Accelerated Massive Parallelism (C++ AMP)
  address space deduction, 265
  array_view, 250*f*, 251
  binomial functions, 268, 270
  Clamp compiler
    compilation flow, 259
    components, 254
    SPIR code, 254, 260
  data movement optimization, 267
  data-parallel algorithms, 250
  features, 249
  Lambda, 251
  mapping, 254, 255*t*
    C++ mangling rules, 255
    functor version, 255, 256*f*
    host and device code, 250*f*, 255, 258*t*
    host code implementation, 258, 259*f*
    missing parts, 255
    trampoline, 256, 257*f*
  parallel_ for_each construct, 252
    captured variables, 252
    compute domain, 252
    extent object, 252
    functors, 252
    restrict(amp) modifier, 253
  SVM (*see* Shared virtual memory (SVM))
  tiling
    address space qualifier, 264
    compute domain division, 263
    explicit approach, 263
    implicit approach, 263
  vector addition, 250, 250*f*, 251, 251*f*
Callback functions, 114
C++ AMP. *See* C++ Accelerated Massive Parallelism (C++ AMP)
Central processing unit (CPU), 16, 77
  ARM Cortex, 30
  Atom, 30, 31
  EPIC, 31, 32

Central processing unit (CPU)(*Continued*)
  FX-8350
    AMD Piledriver architecture, 191
    barrier operations, 189
    C code compilation and execution, 187
    fine-grained synchronization, 188
    high-level design, 187, 188*f*
    local memory, 191, 192*f*
    runtime, thread creation, 188
    work-group execution, x86 architecture, 189,
      190*f*
    work-groups scheduling, 188, 189*f*
    work-item stack data storage, 190
  Haswell, 31
  low-power, 30
  mainstream desktop, 31
  Niagara, 32, 32*f*
  OpenMP parallelization, 216
  Puma, 25, 26*f*, 30, 37
  sequential implementation, 215
  SPARC T-series, 32, 32*f*, 33
  Steamroller, 25, 26*f*, 31, 37, 37*f*
Chunking, 10
Clang block syntax, 136, 137, 138
Coalesced memory accesses, 218, 219*f*, 220*f*
Coalescing technique, 196
Coarse-grained buffer SVM, 159, 159*t*, 262, 262*t*,
  263
CodeXL
  AMD
    main modes, operation, 231
    Microsoft Visual Studio plug-in, 232
    stand-alone application, 232
  debugging
    API-level, 244
    heterogeneous environment, 243
    high-level overview, 243, 243*f*
    OpenCL compute kernels, 244, 245
  KernelAnalyzer
    Analysis view, 242, 242*f*
    offline compiler and analysis tool, 238
    session explorer, analysis mode, 239, 240*f*
    statistics and ISA views, 239, 241*f*
  profiling
    Application Timeline Trace/GPU performance,
      232
    CPU performance, 237
    GPU kernel performance counters,
      236, 237*f*
    Host API Trace View, 235, 235*f*
    OpenCL application trace, 233, 234*f*
    profiler mode, 232
    session explorer, 233, 233*f*

    summary pages, 236
Command barriers, 113
Command markers, 113
Command queues, 47, 279, 280, 297
Concurrent and parallel programs, 7, 8*f*
Constant memory, 61, 93, 175, 225
CPU. *See* Central processing unit (CPU)

D

Data race, 166, 166*f*
Data sharing and synchronization, 11
Debugging
  CodeXL (*see* CodeXL, debugging)
  printf function, 246
Device-side command-queues
  advantages, 133
  creation specifications, 135
  fork-join parallelism, 132, 133*f*
  kernel enqueuing
    block syntax, 136, 137, 138
    dynamic memory allocation, 139
    event dependencies, 141
    NDRange parameter, 134
  nested parallelism, 132, 133, 133*f*
Device-side enqueuing, 49, 133
  block syntax, 136, 137, 138
  dynamic local memory allocation, 139
  event dependencies, 141
  flag operation, 134
  NDRange parameter, 134
Device-side memory model
  constant memory, 175
  generic address space, 178
  global memory
    buffers, 168
    image objects (*see* Image objects)
    pipes, 173
  local memory, 175
  memory ordering and scope
    acquire, 182
    acquire-release, 182
    atomic operations, 183
    fences, 185
    relaxed, 181
    release, 182
    sequential, 182
    unit/multiple devices, 183
    work-group, 183
    work-item, 182
  memory spaces, 163, 164*f*
  private memory, 178
  synchronization
    atomic operations, 166

barrier function, 165
    hierarchy of consistency, 164
Divide-and-conquer methods, 2
Document classification, 213

E

Execution model
    command-queues, 47
    context, 45
    definition, 42
    device-side enqueuing, 49
    events, 48

F

Feature generation algorithm, 213, 214f
Feature histogram
    OpenMP parallelization, 216
    sequential implementation, 215
Fences, 185
Fine-grained buffer SVM, 159t, 160, 262, 262t
Fine-grained parallelism, 10
Fine-grained system SVM, 159t, 161, 262
First in first out (FIFO). *See* Pipes

G

Global memory, 60, 168, 201, 203f,
        204f, 205f
    access pattern, 204
    buffers, 168
    byte selection, 204, 204f
    image objects (*see* Image objects)
    vs. local memory, 209
    memory bandwidth, 202
    nonconsecutive element access, 202, 203f
    off-chip memory, 204, 205f
    performance, 202
    pipes, 173
    utilization, 201, 202
Graphics processing units (GPUs), 3, 16, 77
    AMD Radeon R9 290X architecture, 34, 35f
    AMD Radeon HD 6970 GPU architecture, 25,
        27f
    AMD Radeon HD 7970, 62, 62f, 223, 225, 227
    handheld, 33
    kernel performance counters, 236, 237f
    NVIDIA GeForce GTX 780 architecture,
        34, 36f

H

Hardware-controlled multithreading, 196
Hardware trade-offs
    APUs, 27

cache hierarchies, 28
CPUs, 16
    frequency and limitations, 17
GPU, 16
    memory systems, 28
    multicore architectures, 25, 26f, 27f
    SIMD, 21, 21f
    SoCs, 26, 27
    superscalar execution, 18, 18f
    thread parallelism
        SMT, 22, 23, 23f, 24f
        temporal multithreading, 24, 25f
    vector processing, 21, 21f
    VLIW, 19, 20f
Haskell OpenCL (HOpenCL)
    advantage and disadvantage, 293, 294
    execution environment, 295
        buffers, 297
        command queues, 297
        contexts, 296
        kernels, 298
        program object, 298
        vector addition, 298
    module structure, 294
    platform and devices, 296
    reference counting, 295
Heterogeneous computing
    concurrent and parallel systems, 7, 8f
    GPU, 3
    message-passing communication, 9
    OpenCL, 12
    parallel computing (*see* Parallel
        computing/parallelism)
    parallelism and concurrency, 3
    threads and shared memory, 8
Histogram
    computation, 75, 76
    CPU, 77
    GPUs, 77
    host program, 80
    kernel, 78, 79
    local histogram, 77
    256-bit image, 75, 76f
Histogram builder, 214
    coalesced memory accesses, 218, 219f
    GPU performance, 227, 227t, 228t
    moving cluster centroids to constant memory,
        225
    moving SURF features to local memory, 223
    naive GPU implementation, 217
    OpenMP parallelization, 216
    sequential implementation, 215
    vectorizing computation, 221

Host-side memory model
  allocation options
    accelerated processing units, 156
    data migration, 154
    explicit data transfer, 149, 151*f*, 152
    flags and host_ptr, 149
    flag parameter, 155, 157
    global memory, 149
    mapping, 156, 158*f*
    runtime concept, 149, 150*f*
    shared-memory system, 155
    synchronous execution, 153
    unmapping, 157, 158*f*
    zero-copy data, 155
  buffers, 144
  images, 144, 145
  pipes, 147

I

Image classification
  BoW model, 213
  feature generation algorithm, 213, 214*f*
  histogram builder, 214
    coalesced memory accesses, 218, 219*f*
    GPU performance, 227, 227*t*, 228*t*
    moving cluster centroids to constant
      memory, 225
    moving SURF features to local
      memory, 223
    naive GPU implementation, 217
    OpenMP parallelization, 216
    sequential implementation, 215
    vectorizing computation, 221
  image clustering, 214
Image clustering, 214
Image convolution algorithm
  blurring filter, 91, 92*f*
  C++ API, 95
  embossing filter, 91, 92*f*
  host API signature, 94
  host program, 96
  Image2D and ImageFormat constructors, 95
  image memory objects, 93
  input and output images, 95
  OpenCL kernel, 93
  serial implementation, 91
  visual representation, 91, 91*f*
Image objects
  device-side memory model
    coordinates, 169, 170
    filtering modes, 171
    samplerless read functions, 171
    sampler object, 170

  Z-order mapping, 172, 172*f*
  host-side memory model, 144, 145
Image rotation, 83, 83*f*
  C pseudocode, 84
  host program, 87
  image objects, 86
  image sampler, 85
  implementation, 84
  pixel-based addressing, 85
  remainder work-groups, 86

K

KernelAnalyzer
  Analysis view, 242, 242*f*
  benefits, 238
  offline compiler and analysis tool, 238
  session explorer, analysis mode, 239, 240*f*
  statistics and ISA views, 239, 241*f*
Kernel execution model
  barrier operation, 125
  broadcast functions, 129
  built-in kernels, 132
  C function, 121
  native kernels, 130, 131*f*
  NDRange parameter, 121
  parallel primitive function, 129
  predicate evaluation function, 128
  SIMD execution, 122
  synchronization, 124, 125
Kernel programming model
  compilation and argument handling, 53, 54*f*
  definition, 42
  execution, 55
  vector addition
    algorithm, 50, 50*f*
    NDRange, 52, 52*f*
    work-item, 51, 53

L

LDS. *See* Local data shares (LDS)
Level 2 (L2) cache system, 31, 195
Local data shares (LDS), 194, 195, 200,
      209*f*, 210*f*
Local memory, 61
  AMD FX-8350 CPU, 191, 192*f*
  software-managed cache
    benefits, 206
    cache support, 205
    eight-bank LDS, 209, 209*f*
    kernel parameterization, 210
    padding addition, bank conflicts removal, 209,
      210*f*

programmer-controlled scratchpad memory, 205
single work-group prefix sum, 206, 207
16-element array, data flow, 207, 208*f*

M

Memory checking, 245
Memory model
    address spaces, 62
    vs. AMD Radeon HD 7970 GPU, 62, 62*f*
    data transfer commands, 59
    definition, 42
    memory objects
        buffers, 57
        images, 57
        pipes, 58
    memory regions, 60
        constant memory, 61
        global memory, 60
        local memory, 61
        private memory, 61
Message-passing communication, 9
Message Passing Interface (MPI), 9
Morton-order mapping, 172, 172*f*
MPI. *See* Message Passing Interface (MPI)
Multiple command-queues, 118
    OpenCL layout, 118
    parallel execution, 120
    pipelined execution, 119, 119*f*

N

Natural language processing, 213
Nbody application, 234*f*, 235, 235*f*
Nested parallelism, 132, 133, 133*f*
node-webcl module, 286, 287

O

OpenCL. *See* Open Computing Language (OpenCL)
OpenCL application trace
    Application Timeline View, 234, 234*f*
    application trace profile file, 233
    high-level structure, 234
OpenCL kernel
    binary, 238
    debugging
        breakpoints, 245, 246*f*
        Multi-Watch window, 245, 247*f*
    performance evaluation, 239
OpenCL mapping
    AMD FX-8350 CPU
        AMD Piledriver architecture, 191
        barrier operations, 189

C code compilation and execution, 187
fine-grained synchronization, 188
high-level design, 187, 188*f*
local memory, 191, 192*f*
runtime, thread creation, 188
work-group execution, x86 architecture, 189, 190*f*
work-groups scheduling, 188, 189*f*
work-item stack data storage, 190
AMD Radeon R9 290X GPU
    control flow management, 197
    hardware threads, 192
    high-level diagram, 193, 193*f*
    ISA divergent execution, 198, 199
    queuing mechanism, 194
    resource allocation, 200
    SCC register, 199
    SIMD unit, 196, 197*f*
    threading and memory system, 194
    three-dimensional graphics, 192, 193
    unit microarchitecture, 196, 197*f*
    wavefront scheduling, 193, 194
global memory
    access pattern, 204
    byte selection, 204, 204*f*
    vs. local memory, 209
    memory bandwidth, 202
    nonconsecutive element access, 202, 203*f*
    off-chip memory, 204, 205*f*
    performance, 202
    return data, 202, 203*f*
    utilization, 201, 202
local memory, software-managed cache
    benefits, 206
    cache support, 205
    eight-bank LDS, 209, 209*f*
    vs. global memory, 209
    hardware utilization, 210
    kernel parameterization, 210
    padding addition, bank conflicts removal, 209, 210*f*
    programmer-controlled scratchpad memory, 205
    single work-group prefix sum, 206, 207
    16-element array, data flow, 207, 208*f*
Open Computing Language (OpenCL)
    features, 75, 76*t*
    heterogeneous computing, 1, 2, 12
    reporting compilation errors, 107
    runtime APIs
        copying input data, 65
        copying output data, 66

Open Computing Language (OpenCL) *(Continued)*
  creating and compiling program, 65
  creating buffer, 64
  creating command-queue per device, 64
  creating context, 64
  discovering platform and devices, 63
  kernel execution, 65
  kernel extraction, 65
  processing steps, 63
  releasing resources, 66
  vector addition, 66
OpenMP parallelization, 216
Out-of-order command-queues,
    116, 279

P

Packets, 58, 99, 147
Parallel computing/parallelism
  chunking, 10
  and concurrent programs, 7, 8*f*
  data sharing and synchronization, 11
  fine-grained parallelism, 10
  multiplying elements of array, 4, 4*f*
  reduction, 5, 6*f*
  shared virtual memory, 11
  SIMD, 10, 11
  task-level parallelism, 5, 6*f*
  task parallelism, 5, 5*f*
Parallel primitive functions, 129
PCI Express bus, 195*f*, 196
Performance improvement, 225, 229
Pipes, 58, 147, 173
Platform model
  abstract architecture, 44
  API, 43
  CLInfo program, 45, 46*f*
  compute units, 43, 43*f*
  definition, 42
Predicate evaluation functions, 128
Private memory, 61, 178
Producer-consumer kernels
  create pipe, 101, 102
  host program, 102
  kernel implementations, 100
  pipes, 99, 99*f*, 100
Profiling
  CodeXL *(see* CodeXL, profiling)
  command states, 230*t*, 231
  developer tools, commands tracking,
    229
  event synchronization, 231
PyOpenCL, 291

Q

Queuing model
  barriers and markers, 113
  blocking memory operations, 111
  callback functions, 114
  events and commands, 112, 114
  for multiple devices *(see* Multiple
    command-queues)
  out-of-order queues, 116
  synchronization points, 111
  user events, 115

R

Relaxed consistency model, 121, 148, 180, 181
Remainder work-groups, 53, 86, 123
Reservation identifiers, 174
Resource allocation, 200
Runtime and execution model
  kernel model
    barrier operation, 125
    broadcast functions, 129
    built-in kernels, 132
    C function, 121
    native kernels, 130, 131*f*
    NDRange parameter, 121
    parallel primitive function, 129
    predicate evaluation function, 128
    SIMD execution, 122
    synchronization, 124, 125
  queuing model
    barriers and markers, 113
    blocking memory operations, 111
    callback functions, 114
    events and commands, 112, 114
    for multiple devices *(see* Multiple
      command-queues)
    nested parallelism *(see* Device-side
      command-queues)
    out-of-order queues, 116
    synchronization points, 111
    user events, 115

S

Scatter-gather methods, 2
Sequential consistency model, 181, 182
Shared virtual memory (SVM)
  address space, 261
  coarse-grained buffer, 159, 159*t*, 262, 262*t*
  fine-grained buffer, 159*t*, 160, 262, 262*t*
  fine-grained system, 159*t*, 161, 262
SIMD. *See* Single instruction multiple data (SIMD)
Simultaneous multithreading (SMT), 22, 23*f*, 31

Single instruction multiple data (SIMD)
 AMD Radeon HD 6970 GPU, 25, 27*f*
 AMD Radeon R9 290X, 34, 35*f*, 196
 NVIDIA GeForce GTX 780, 34, 36*f*
 vs. SPMD model, 11
 vector processing, 21, 21*f*
Single program, multiple data (SPMD) model, 11,
 13
SMT. *See* Simultaneous multithreading (SMT)
SoC. *See* Systems-on-chip (SoC)
SPMD model. *See* Single program, multiple data
 (SPMD) model
Standard Portable Intermediate Representation
 (SPIR), 254, 260, 261*f*
SVM. *See* Shared virtual memory (SVM)
Systems-on-chip (SoC), 26, 37

T

Temporal multithreading, 24, 25*f*
Thread parallelism
 SMT, 22, 23, 23*f*, 24*f*
 temporal multithreading, 24, 25*f*
Transpose, 219, 220*f*, 227, 227*t*

V

Vector addition
 C API, 66
 CUDA C API, 71
 C++ wrapper, 69

POSIX threads, 51
 serial C implementation, 50
Vectorizing computation, 221
Very long instruction word (VLIW), 19, 20*f*, 21,
 27*f*, 31

W

WebCL
 applications
  image processing and ray tracing produce,
   282
  kernel code, 285
  texture usage, argument, 284
  two textured triangles, 283, 284*f*
 implementations, 288
 interoperability, WebGL, 282
 programming
  command queues, 279, 280
  object-oriented nature, JavaScript, 273
  objects, 274, 275, 275*f*
  various numerical types, 276, 277*t*
  WebCL image, 276
  WebGL texture, 283
 server, 286
 specification, 288
 synchronization, 281

Z

Z-order mapping, 172, 172*f*

Printed in the United States
By Bookmasters